PRIVACY MATTERS

OrangeBooks Publication

1st Floor, Rajhans Arcade, Mall Road, Kohka, Bhilai, Chhattisgarh 490020

Website:**www.orangebooks.in**

© Copyright, 2023, Author

All rights reserved. No part of this book may be reproduced, stored in a retrieval system, or transmitted, in any form by any means, electronic, mechanical, magnetic, optical, chemical, manual, photocopying, recording or otherwise, without the prior written consent of its writer.

First Edition, 2023

Privacy Matters

EDITORS

RUCHI RAMESH
BHUMIKA SHARMA
PRITI CHAUDHARI

OrangeBooks Publication
www.orangebooks.in

Contents

Foreward ix
Preface xii
List of Contributors xv
Introduction xx

PART I
Conceptualizing Privacy

1. An Examination of Origin of Privacy and its Theories 2
   Pankaj Dwivedi and Ananya Sharma

2. A Review of Complicated Concept of Right to Privacy: With Reference to Significant Theories 13
   Mawuleabenam Aku Adjahoe and Harriet Debrah Otchere

3. Personal Data in Focus: A Comprehensive Overview of its Varied Facets 23
   Yogesh Sharma and Vidhi Maheshwari

4. Digital Dignity Model: Lessons for Big Tech Giants 35
   Bhupendra Gautam, Ramesh Verma and Vikrant Chauhan

PART II
Legalities of Privacy

5. Efficacy of Right of Privacy in the Digital Ecosystem in Indian Context: With Emphasis on WhatsApp's Updated Privacy Policy 48
   Abha Tiwari

6. Human Rights Perspective of Personal Data Privacy 59
   Anurita Yadav and Harish Kumar Verma

7. A Comparative Study of India's Personal Data Protection Bill, 2018 and United Kingdom Data Protection Act, 2018   68
   Anjali Raghav, Sanskriti Mishra and Richa Raghav

8. Rights of Victims: A Study with Special Reference to Right to Data Protection   76
   Vijay Chaudhary and Poonam

9. Constitutional Aspect of Personal Data Protection Bill, 2019   87
   Avinash Krishna Goswami and Komal Vig

10. Habeas Data: Remedial Procedure for Personal Data Protection   101
    Saquib Ahmed, Bhupinder Singh and Rishikesh Singh Faujdar

11. Article 21 vis-à-vis Personal Data Protection   115
    Renu Rajpoot and Ravi Kant Gupta

12. Right to be Forgotten as Data Protection   127
    Apeksha Rai

13. Securing Financial Trust: A Deep Dive into Credit Information Protection Laws in India   141
    Saif Rahman, Aditya Kumar and Vikrant

14. Information Technology Act 2000: A Look at Data Protection in Practice   153
    Junaid Ul Islam, Muskan Sharma and Piyush Agarwal

15. Analysis of Data Protection Bill, 2019 post Covid: Focus on Legislative Relevance and Judicial Intervention   165
    Aditi Srivastava, Ritu Gautam and Shikha Yadav

16. Safeguarding of Right to Privacy under the Notion of Substantive Due Process of Law in India   176
    Nisha Praveen

17. Right to Privacy and Data Protection as Human Right 190
    Dewa Safi and Yatika Gupta

18. A Study of Personal Data Protection Bill, 2019: With Emphasis on Data Localisation 202
    Sanchita Ray

19. Right to Privacy: An Appraisal of Legal Framework in Bangladesh 214
    Naeem Ahsan Talha and Samiul Azim

20. Navigating the Data Protection Landscape Laws in Africa 227
    Md. Owais Saifi and Muaz Khan

21. Challenges and Issues in Privacy of Student Education Record in the U.S.A. 235
    Ankita Sharma, Salman Khan and Towseef Ahmad Dar

PART-III
Privacy as a Social Issue

22. Intimacy and Boundaries: Exploring Privacy Dynamics in Sexual Relationships 252
    Vijay Kumar Pandey and Mumtaz Zabeen Khan

23. An Overview of Data Theft and Data Breach vis-à-vis Students and Faculty 263
    Siddhant Sharma, Saurabh Kishor and Ahmad Aman Kazmi

24. Privacy Issues in Fertility and Period Tracking Applications: Impact of Dobbs vs. Jackson Women's Health Organisation 275
    Riya Shukla

25. Rights of Non-Human Animals: A Study with Special Reference to Overlooked Right of Privacy of Non-Human Animals 295
    Arrat Banday and Arwa Rafie

26. Headlines versus Humanity Balancing: Fame and Privacy   311
   Shalini Kashmeria and Om Prakash Jha

27. Identity Protection : A Study of Sexual Violence Survivors   324
   Neha Negar Alam, Ritika Shukla and Sonakshi Bandhu

28. Rights of Dead Persons: A Study with Focus on Privacy Rights   336
   Vivek Kumar Shukla and Arun

29. Inclusivity and Privacy: Privacy Rights of Homosexuals, Transgenders and LGBTQ+   349
   Shubham Verma, Smriti Chauhan and Adarsh Chauhan

30. Right of Privacy of Accused and Victims in the Criminal Justice System: Evolving Trends   364
   Shubham Mishra, Manisha Garg and Rishu Sangal

Bibliography   *375*

MADHUSUDAN LAW UNIVERSITY

(State University Established under The Odisha Universities Act, 1989)
Station Road, Cuttack, Odisha - 753 003
Phone No. : 0671-2955177 (O)
Email : vc@mlu.ac.in / Website : www.mlu.ac.in

Professor (Dr.) KAMAL JEET SINGH
Vice-Chancellor

Ref No. ....
Date ....

Foreward

"The quest for privacy is not restricted to man alone, but arises in the biological and social processes of all life."

- Alan F. Westin, Privacy and Freedom (1970)

The understanding of the challenging concept of privacy is shaped by social, cultural, political, psychological and philosophical dimensions. The present Book is an excellent reference for reflecting upon these dimensions with a special focus on the legal dimension of privacy.

Privacy is invaded by uncovering one's hidden world, by surveillance, and by the disclosure of concealed information. An overlap of privacy and, data protection has occurred in the society. Information technologies are at the forefront of accelerating change in society. What is new today is the breadth of technological change, the rate and global reach of these changes, and the scales of their impact. We are living in a world of broadly available technologies, apparently random data collection and extensive surveillance.

These developments are a major obstacle to how we feel and approach privacy, even if they may make it more comfortable for us. No reasonable human would like his personal life to be publicly shared unless mandated or forced up. It applies to each of us and our lives. We value the right of privacy more the moment our privacy gets under surveillance.

We should be working harder to understand the intrinsic value of our data rather than fighting a battle against technological intrusions. With action now, we can keep a space for us to be ourselves and stay alone in the future.

The jurisprudence of the right to privacy has evolved owing to efforts of judges like Justice A. K. Sikri, Justice A. M. Khanwilkar, and the like. Justice K. 8. Puttaswamy case in 2017 cemented the place of the right to privacy as a fundamental right, this case also laid down the need for the implementation of a new law relating to data privacy, expanded the scope of privacy in personal spaces. and discussed privacy as an intrinsic value.

The future of the right of privacy is in danger by the growth of promising developments such as sense-enhanced searches, smart dust devices, etc. There is an urgent need of ensuring that the social costs of the means employed to enhance security do not outweigh the benefits. Law is often challenged by countless advances in technology.

Online privacy faces manifold threats in the digital world ranging from biometrics, CCTV surveillance, RFID systems, smart identity cards and so on. A simultaneous concern is the explosion of private data due to the growth of social networking sites, blogs and the alike. The character of the threats to individual privacy has been influenced by the manner in which information is collected, exchanged and used. We also need to remember that our failure to safeguard privacy would jeopardize associated freedoms such as freedom of expression, freedom of assembly, freedom to access information and finally the stability of constitutional democracies. The governments must give support for genuine Privacy Enhancing Technologies and meaningful Privacy Impact Assessments.

We must not forget that a life without privacy is inconceivable. The Chapter by Mawuleabenam Aku Adjahoe and Harriet Debrah Otchere has highlighted the functions of privacy. There is a requisite that decisional privacy is understood and adopted by all of us, the sooner, the safer. This Book serves as a foundation to understand the significance of the right of privacy, especially in the Indian context. The Chapters of the Book spread over the constitutional dimensions of the right to privacy, rights of privacy in specific contexts and the draft Data Protection law in India. The Book also includes a comparative view of data protection law and what India can learn from other Jurisdictions. The Book will be helpful to understand the social and easpects of the right of privacy. The Book is a must read to understand the intricacies of the right to privacy and the emerging personal data protection law.

[Prof.(Dr.) Kamal Jeet Singh]

Preface

Over the past two centuries, society has witnessed tremendous transformation regarding the concept and nature of the right to privacy. United Nations has been a crucial actor in recognizing and promoting privacy as a fundamental human right. The efforts encompass legal instruments, resolutions, and initiatives aimed at safeguarding individual privacy in the wake of technological advancements and evolving challenges. Without the international recognition of the right to privacy, the rights enjoyed less significance at the national level. General Data Protection Regulation (GDPR) indeed reverberated beyond the borders of the European Union, creating a "domino effect" by influencing data protection laws and practices worldwide.

New technologies have interacted with legal system so as to guide evolving standards of privacy, telecommunications, and criminal law. The Indian Contract Act, 1872, the Specific Relief Act, 1963, the Indian Penal Code, 1860, the Public Financial Institutions Act, 1983 and the Consumer Protection Act, 1986 played a significant role in protecting the paper-based transactions. The Indian Telegraph Act, 1885, before 2000 was perhaps the only law dealing with protection of communication via telegraph. Sections 23, 24, 26 and 30 of the Indian Telegraph Act, 1885 ensure protection to the communications. Chapter IX of the Indian Evidence Act, 1872 deals with privileged communications and provides protection to such communication. Sections 126-129 provide barrister, attorney, pleader or vakil, etc. exemption from disclosure in a Court of law of any communication between them and clients.

Both Indian Contract Act, 1872 and Specific Relief Act, 1963 provide for compensation in case of breach of contract. They deal with contracts in general, including contracts dealing with personal data. The Indian Post Office Act, 1898 provides the legal framework for the functioning of postal services in India during the British colonial period. It ensured the secrecy and privacy of letters and postal communications. It prohibited the opening, detaining, delaying, or detouring of any postal article by unauthorized persons. It also specifies penalties for offenses related to violating the secrecy of postal articles. Unauthorized opening or tampering with postal articles is a punishable offense. It further provides for compensation in case of loss, delay, or damage to postal articles. If a postal article was lost, delayed, or damaged during transit, the sender or recipient was eligible for compensation. There are some exemptions and immunities to the postal department and its employees, specifying circumstances where they would not be held liable.

Further, the Mental Health Act, 1987, Section 126 of the Medical Termination of Pregnancy Regulations, 2003 cover the duty of the medical professionals and legal professionals to maintain protection of data exchanged with them. Under Section 5, the Official Secrets Act, 1923; the Official Secrets Act, 1923 of the Census Act, 1948; Rule 11 of Central Civil Services (Conduct) Rules, 1964; Rule 9 of All India Services (Conduct) Rules, 1968; Proviso to Section 17 (1) of the Registration of Births and Deaths Act, 1969; and Sections 4, 8,10 of the Public Records Act, 1993, variety of official information and public records enjoy protection.

This Book is more explicit than some others on how the concept of privacy is looked upon and definitely covers multi-pronged approach towards the privacy right. Through the thought-provoking narratives, this Book aims to illuminate the complexities of privacy, discovering its delicate balance with security, freedom, and technology. It is an exploration of our modern age, where digital footprints trace our every move, and where the concept of privacy is both a shield and a battleground. The Book is divided into Five Parts.

International professionals and scholars have collaborated with Indian academicians and students in the Book. Information Technology Experts have complimented the knowledge of legal academicians, students and research scholars. Such alliances can catalyze the sort of transformational change we need in our society. It is difficult to point out any particular Chapter as the Core of the Book. The culmination of multitude of dimensions of privacy makes the Book unique and purposeful. The contributors have made sincere attempts to present suggestions to safeguard the right of privacy in the technological age by adopting technical advancements, amending laws and creating awareness. It is hoped that more discussions on the right of privacy would flow as an outcome of the book. The anticipation is that this book will allow students and scholars to develop comparative perspectives, in the most accessible and contextualized way possible. The Book can be referred by scholars, judges, lawyers, policymakers and others who seek to understand the history, attributes and legal dimensions of privacy. The value of the book lies in its integration of a very diverse set of perspectives to provide a roadmap and stimulus for future more focused and in-depth inquiries.

We are grateful to Prof. (Dr.) Kamal Jeet Singh, Vice-Chancellor, Madhusudan Law University, Cuttack for his introductory remarks for the Book. His good wishes are highly appreciated. The editors like to express deep appreciation for Sr. Ravinder Singh Bhangu, Punjabi University Patiala for designing cover page of the book and also all the contributors of this book to bring this academic endeavour to fruition.

Ruchi Ramesh
Bhumika Sharma
Priti Chaudhari

List of Contributors

Dr. Pankaj Dwivedi, Associate Professor, Department of Law (ABVSLS), Chhatrapati Shahu Ji Maharaj University, Kanpur, U.P., India.

Ms. Ananya Sharma, B.B.A.L.L.B. (Hons.) Student, SSOL, Sharda University, Greater Noida, U.P., India.

Ms. Mawuleabenam Aku Adjahoe, B.A.L.L.B. (Hons.) Student, SSOL, Sharda University, Greater Noida, U.P., India.

Mr. Harriet Debrah Otchere, Ph.D. Research Scholar, University of Cape Coast, Cape Coast, Ghana.

(CS) Dr. Yogesh Sharma, Deputy Registrar, Sardar Patel University, Mandi, H.P., India.

Ms. Vidhi Maheshwari, B.B.A.L.L.B. (Hons.) Student, SSOL, Sharda University, Greater Noida, U.P., India.

Dr. Bhupendra Gautam, Associate Professor, SSOL, Sharda University, Greater Noida, U.P., India.

Dr. Ramesh Verma, Assistant Professor, Department of Law, Himachal Pradesh University, Shimla, H.P., India.

Mr. Vikrant Chauhan, Advocate, District and Sessions Court, Solan, H.P., India.

Ms. Abha Tiwari, Head (Legal) and Data Protection Officer, Renault India Pvt. Ltd., Chennai, Tamil Nadu, India & CIPP/E , CIPM, FIP.

Ms. Anurita Yadav, Ph.D. Research Scholar, SSOL, Sharda University, Greater Noida, U.P., India.

Dr. Harish Kumar Verma, Dean, ICFAI Law School, The ICFAI University, Jaipur, Rajasthan, India.

Ms. Anjali Raghav, Ph.D. Research Scholar, SSOL, Sharda University, Greater Noida, U.P., India.

Dr. Sanskrit Mishra, Assistant Professor, SSOL, Sharda University, Greater Noida, U.P., India.

Ms. Richa Raghav, B.A.L.L.B. (Hons.) Student, SSOL, Sharda University, Greater Noida, U.P., India.

Dr. Vijay Chaudhary, Assitant Professor, University Institute of Legal Studies, Himachal Pradesh University, Shimla, H.P., India.

Ms. Poonam, Ph.D. Research Scholar, Himachal Pradesh University, Shimla, H.P., India.

Dr. Avinash K. Goswami, Assistant Professor, SSOL, Sharda University, Greater Noida, U.P., India.

(Prof.) Dr. Komal Vig, Dean, SSOL, Sharda University, Greater Noida, U.P., India.

Mr. Saquib Ahmed, Ph.D. Research Scholar, SSOL, Sharda University, Greater Noida, U.P., India.

Dr. Bhupinder Singh, Professor, SSOL, Sharda University, Greater Noida, India.

Dr. Rishikesh Singh Faujdar, Assistant Professor, Department of Law, Nagaland University, Nagaland, India.

Ms. Renu Rajpoot, Ph.D. Research Scholar, Faculty of Juridical Sciences. Rama University, Kanpur, U.P. India.

Dr. Ravi Kant Gupta, Associate Professor, Juridical Sciences, Rama University, Kanpur, U.P. India

Ms. Apeksha Rai, Advocate, Supreme Court of India, Arbitrator for Prasar Bharti, Govt. of India, New Delhi, India.

Mr. Saif Rahman, B.A.L.L.B.(Hons.) Student, SSOL, Sharda University, Greater Noida, U.P., India.

Mr. Aditya Kumar, VKYC Conc Reviewer, Standard Chartered Bank, Gurugram, Haryana, India.

Dr. Vikrant, Human Resource Business Partner, IDE Technologies India Pvt. Ltd., Noida, U.P., India.

Mr. Junaid Ul Islam, B.A.L.L.B.(Hons.) Student, SSOL, Sharda University, Greater Noida, U.P. India.

Ms. Muskan Sharma, B.A.L.L.B. (Hons.) Student, S.S.O.L. Sharda University Greater Noida, U.P., India.

Mr. Piyush Agarwal, B.B.A.L.L.B. (Hons.) Student, S.S.O.L., Sharda University Greater Noida, U.P. India.

Ms. Aditi Srivastava, Ph.D. Research Scholar, S.S.O.L., Sharda University, Greater Noida, U.P. India.

Dr. Ritu Gautam, Assistant Professor, S.S.O.L., Sharda University Greater Noida, U.P. India.

Ms. Shikha Yadav, Assistant Professor, Asian Law College, Noida, U.P. India.

Ms. Nisha Praveen, Ph.D. Research Scholar, Department of Law, Aligarh Muslim University, Aligarh, U.P. India.

Ms. Dewa Safi, M.A. International Relations, School of International Legal Studies Jawaharlal Nehru University, New Delhi, India.

Ms. Yatika Gupta, Ph.D. Research Scholar, SSOL, Sharda University, Greater Noida, U.P., India.

Dr. Sanchita Ray, Assistant Professor (Political Science), SSOL, Sharda University, Greater Noida, U.P., India.

Mr. Naeem Ahsan Talha, Research Assistant, Bangladesh Institute of Labour Studies, Dhaka, Bangladesh.

Mr. Samiul Azim, Apprentice Lawyer, Dhaka Bar Association, Dhaka, Bangladesh.

Mr. Md. Owais Saifi, B.A.L.L.B. (Hons.) Student, SSOL, Sharda University, Greater Noida, U.P., India.

Mr. Muaz Khan, JEE Aspirant, New Delhi, India.

Ms. Ankita Sharma, B.B.A.L.L.B. (Hons.) Student, SSOL, Sharda University, Greater Noida, U.P., India.

Mr. Salman Khan, Advocate, Supreme Court of India, New Delhi, India.

Mr. Towseef Ahmad Dar, Advocate on Record, Supreme Court of India, New Delhi, India and Ph.D. Research Scholar, SSOL, Sharda University, Greater Noida, U.P., India.

Mr. Vijay Kumar Pandey, Ph.D. Research Scholar, Dr. Bhimrao Ambedkar University, Agra, U.P., India.

Dr. Mumtaz Zabeen Khan, Assistant Professor, Rayat College of Law, (Affiliated to Panjab University), Railmajra, (SBS Nagar), Punjab, India.

Mr. Siddhant Sharma, Managing Associate, Inttl Advocare, Noida, U.P., India.

Dr. Saurabh Kishor, Assistant Professor, SSOL, Sharda University, Greater Noida, U.P., India.

Mr. Ahmad Aman Kazmi, B.A.L.L.B. (Hons.) Student, SSOL, Sharda University, Greater Noida, U.P., India.

Ms. Riya Shukla, B.A.L.L.B. (Hons.) Student, SSOL, Sharda University, Greater Noida, U.P., India.

Ms. Arrat Banday, B.A.L.L.B. (Hons.) Student, SSOL, Sharda University, Greater Noida, U.P., India.

Ms. Arwa Rafie, Student, Department of Political Science, Jamia Milia Islamia, New Delhi, India.

Dr. Shalini Kashmeria, Assistant Professor, Department of Law, Himachal Pradesh University, Shimla, H.P., India and Assistant

Director, Centre for Canadian Studies, Himachal Pradesh University, Shimla, Himachal Pradesh, India.

Mr. Om Prakash Jha, Advocate, Gujarat High Court, Ahmedabad, Gujarat, India.

Ms. Neha Nagar Alam, Ph.D. Research Scholar, Department of Social Work, Jamia Millia Islamia, New Delhi, India.

Dr. Ritika Shukla, Assistant Professor, SSHSS, Sharda University, Greater Noida, U.P., India.

Ms. Sonakshi Bandhu, Ph.D. Research Scholar, Department of Law, Himachal Pradesh University, Shimla, H.P., India.

Mr. Vivek Kumar Shukla, Ph.D. Research Scholar, Law Department, BSA College, Mathura (Affiliated to Dr. Bhimrao Ambedkar University), Agra, U.P., India.

Mr. Arun, Ph.D. Research Scholar, Law Department, BSA College, Mathura (Affiliated to Dr. Bhimrao Ambedkar University), Agra, U.P., India.

Mr. Shubham Verma, Advocate, Allahabad High Court, Prayagraj, U.P., India.

Ms. Smriti Chauhan, Assistant Professor, SSOL, Sharda University, Greater Noida, U.P., India.

Mr. Adarsh Chauhan, B.A.L.L.B. (Hons.) Student, SSOL, Sharda University, Greater Noida, U.P., India.

Mr. Shubham Mishra, Assistant Professor, Department of Law, Bharti Vidyapeeth, deemed to be University, New Delhi, India.

Ms. Manisha Garg, Assistant Legal Officer, Bureau of Investigation, Punjab Police, Punjab, India.

Mr. Rishu Sangal, Senior Executive Officer, Sharda University, Greater Noida, U.P., India.

Introduction

In modern context, privacy is commonly seen as the right of individuals' to control information about themselves. The recent changes has brought privacy to the center stage as the advances in information and communication technologies (ICTs) and wide adoption have exponentially increased the amount of personal information being collected by various agencies. Broadly, the promises of big data and 'data driven decision-making' have raised wider concerns for the future. In the mid 1980s, Mason (1986) suggested that the advent of increased use of information technologies or the information age would lead to four major concerns about the use of information- privacy, accuracy, property and accessibility. His prediction proved to be accurate for all areas especially privacy. The information communication technologies (ICTs) have enabled collection of processing of vast amount of personal data such as criminal records, shopping behaviour, medical history and driving records this has increased the public concern about the individuals' privacy.

Based on the acknowledgement that the technological development in relation to digital age has lead to substantial privacy risks. Privacy and data protection are inherently interconnected. Individuals, in their capacities as citizens, customers, and consumers, must have the tools and means to exercise their right to privacy and shield themselves and their data from misuse. Equally important is the clarity of responsibilities for those handling data, ensuring that they implement measures to safeguard personal data, reduce infringements on the right to privacy, and are held accountable when they do not meet these obligations. This is especially critical in the context of personal data. Personal data, as elaborated upon below, is information processed by automated means or stored in a structured filing system that pertains to an individual. Data protection revolves around preserving our fundamental right to privacy by regulating the handling of personal data: it grants individuals rights over their data and establishes systems of accountability and distinct duties for those overseeing or engaging in data processing.

The concern about privacy is concern about conditions of life and it is so in the law as it is elsewhere The predicament seems the sort for which we might invoke Prof. H.L.A Hart's observation that 'In law as elsewhere, we can know and yet not understand'. With the Supreme Court's decision in the Gridwold vs. Connecticut, the scope of the legal protection of privacy has achieved new significance. It is contended that there is a conceptual muddle surrounding the legal right of privacy and that development of a legally protected interest in privacy requires recognition of the particular condition of human life that is sought to be protected.

To safeguarding privacy in the digital era is crucial for effective and sound democratic governance. Despite growing global awareness of data protection and privacy rights, there is still a deficiency in the legal and institutional frameworks, procedures, and infrastructure needed to ensure data and privacy rights are upheld. The vast amount of data being generated and the swift advancement of technology, including advanced profiling, tracking methods, and artificial intelligence, have rendered some existing data protection laws obsolete and inadequate for addressing the current state of data processing. These frameworks do not adequately encompass the novel possibilities for data processing that have arisen with the evolution of technologies integrated into governance systems and business models. Furthermore, the escalating use of personal data and the emergence of new data processing technologies emphasize the increasing importance of establishing a robust data protection framework.

While many states have implemented some form of privacy protection, these frameworks often prove inadequate and lag behind the evolving uses of data and the challenges they present. It is imperative that data protection laws are updated to address emerging issues effectively.

Over time, the landscape of these issues has expanded, and new challenges have arisen. The prevailing narratives we challenge have evolved, and new stakeholders, both supportive and opposing, have come into our sphere of influence.

The governments worldwide are undergoing significant policy and infrastructure changes with the goal of fostering economic opportunities, attracting international investments, ensuring societal security, and fortifying their institutions. The governments are continuously introducing new policies that require more data from individuals, marking a profound shift in the relationship between individuals and the state as data accumulates. Industry also plays a pivotal role by endorsing these concepts, supporting the sale of such systems, providing tools and services, and potentially controlling data. This all leads to what we refer to as data-intensive systems. These systems process data about people, generate additional data about individuals, and rely on data to make decisions concerning them.

With data-intensive systems, governments and industries frequently identify new prospects for surveillance, revenue generation, and control, often lacking sufficient safeguards. The strongest push for these changes is observed in emerging economies, where legal and technical protections are weakest, decision-making processes lack transparency, the rule of law is limited, and the responsibilities of the private sector are unclear. Innovations in policy and technology are largely unchecked and unregulated. This situation will profoundly impact privacy, reshape the dynamics of power, introduce new possibilities for oppression, exacerbate existing inequalities, discrimination, and exclusion, and potentially give rise to novel forms of these issues.

Furthermore, there are systemic structural challenges. Public consultation, transparency in resource allocation, and oversight or audits of these systems' functioning are frequently lacking. Governments are increasingly relying on the industry to implement systems and operate software, while the industry depends on governments to grant access to data. This blurs the distinction between government and industry, amalgamating their respective responsibilities and duties. Our devices and infrastructure are being designed with a primary focus on exploiting data. Increasingly, individuals find it challenging to retain control over how data about their lives is shared and processed.

Consequently, both industry and government are gathering our data without restraint. Their goal is to create a data-driven world that empowers them to collect our data, identify patterns and similarities, generate intelligence, and make decisions that impact our lives and futures.

We are ill-prepared for the future that is already taking shape. Our legal frameworks are not yet equipped to address these emerging risks. Our technologies are vulnerable and prone to data leaks. As a result, our own security is compromised.

This book offers a holistic view of privacy extending its boundaries to individual, social and legal aspects. It explores privacy by mapping out different legal and conceptual approaches to privacy protection in the context of datafication. It provides an essential staring point to explore the entwinement of technological, ethical and regulation dynamics. A review of the researches and work demonstrate that even today the privacy and its implications are largely unaddressed. The book gives a clarion call to maintain minimum level of privacy and create a robust system with standard framework.

PART I
Conceptualizing Privacy

1

An Examination of Origin of Privacy and its Theories

Pankaj Dwivedi and Ananya Sharma

Abstract

Different theories provide different frameworks for understanding privacy and its role in society, and they continue to influence discussions about privacy and data protection in various fields, including law, ethics, and technology. Today, data is a resource that is more important than ever before for all organizations we can imagine. Data may now be collected widely, successfully, and cost-effectively thanks to contemporary advances and patterns including sensor systems, IoT, online computing, and data analytics. Data confidentiality and safety, however, are crucial if data are to be utilized to their maximum potential. We are currently confronting novel, challenging data security and privacy concerns even though data security and privacy have been the subject of extensive research during the last three decades. A few of these difficulties result from the requirement to balance privacy with the use of data for safety in applications including security for the homeland, combating terrorism, and nutrition and health security, as well as from growing concerns about confidentiality around the use of data. The widespread use of new data gathering and processing devices, such those used in IoT systems, increases the data attack surface, which leads to other difficulties.

Keywords - *Informational privacy, data protection, theory, evolution, ancient.*

Introduction

All people have the right to privacy just by virtue of being alive. Physical integrity, individual freedom, the right to free speech, and the freedom to move or think are also included. Thus, privacy encompasses more than just the physical body and includes integrity, individual autonomy, data, voice, consent, objections, movements, thoughts, and reputation. As a result, it is a relationship that is neutral and free from interference, unwelcome intrusion, or invasion of personal space between an individual, a group, and an individual. All contemporary societies agree that maintaining one's privacy is crucial, and they do it not only for ethical considerations but also for legal ones.

Legally speaking, the right to privacy is a very new idea. Its origins can be traced back to a legal journal essay written in December 1890 by Samuel Warren and Louis Brandeis. According to Roscoe Pound, this piece nothing less than adds a chapter to our law. Ironically, Warren and Brandeis were the ones to create an absolute definition of the right to privacy in 1890. When Warren and Brandeis first discussed the right to privacy, they said that it was an accepted rule of law that guaranteed protections for anyone's "inviolate personality". To put it simply, Warren and Brandeis believed that everyone has the right to maintain their mental validity by exerting authority over material that both reflects and influences their personalities. They classified the individual's right to privacy under the more comprehensive heading of their right to solitude. The right to privacy is a subset of the even more universal right to enjoyment of life, which is in turn a subset of the individual's fundamental entitlement to life.

The 5th Amendment to the United States Constitution states that "No person shall be... deprived of life, liberty, or property, without due process of law... ". The right to life is one of the well-known triangles of fundamental, innate, private liberties. Warren and Brandeis deliberately separated the right to privacy from the right to liberty and from the right to property, in contrast to recent decisions by the U.S. highest court. Warren and Brandeis contended that while the right to liberty "secures extensive civil privileges," privacy is not one of them. They contrasted the right to privacy's focus on spiritual concerns with the right to property, which included a person's interests in material things, "every form of possession-intangible as well as tangible."

Origin of Privacy in Ancient Civilizations

Different ancient civilizations had different levels and types of privacy, depending on things like culture, social structure, technology, and legal systems. The concepts of privacy, property rights, and confidentiality existed in ancient civilizations like Mesopotamia, Ancient Egypt, Ancient Greece, and the Roman Empire. Although the idea of privacy in the past may not have been the same as what we understand today, there were undoubtedly fundamental ideas that paved the way for modern ideas of privacy and individual rights.

Sumerian and Babylonian communities, as well as Mesopotamian societies (c. 350-300 BC), had laws defending private property and family rights. However, there was no formal definition of privacy as we know it today. Ancient Egyptians treasured their dwellings and personal privacy (c. 3100-332 BC). People enjoyed a sense of ownership over and security for their things since houses contained private spaces. Ancient Greeks placed a strong emphasis on domestic privacy, particularly at Athens (c. 8th century-146 BC). However, there was considerably less separation between private and public affairs in the polis (city-state), where civic engagement, notably conversations and arguments, was greatly appreciated.

Romans used the term "domus" to refer to the privacy of the house and family throughout the Roman Empire (c. 753 BC-476 AD). However, this privacy was more concerned with family and domestic matters than it was with the protection of private facts or information. It began to clearly manifest in the modern age, particularly during the Enlightenment in the 17th and 18th centuries, as we now know it. The basis for contemporary privacy laws and values were laid during this time by concepts of individual rights, autonomy, and personal independence.

The Roman idea of domus was essential to the privacy movement. It depicted the house and the neighbourhood where family life took place. The family lived in and operated out of the domus, which was a private area. It was regarded as a private haven for family members. The Romans understood the value of keeping private and public lives separate. Despite the high significance placed on public life, particularly for males interested in commerce, law, or politics, the home was seen as a private haven where family concerns were handled. Roman homes frequently separated private and public regions in their floor plans and privacy arrangements. In addition to numerous private apartments (cubicula) for family members, they frequently contained a central courtyard, which served as a semi-public area for greeting visitors. Additionally, there were inner courtyards and gardens that offered a calm and private atmosphere. The law protected the ownership and management rights of private property held by individuals. In Roman culture, especially among the upper classes, ladies frequently had a private space to themselves within the house, such as the gynaeceum. This gave them the freedom to conduct private affairs out of sight of unrelated guys.

Public baths, or thermoe, were an essential component of Roman civilization. Even though these were public locations, Romans cherished their privacy while bathing and set aside particular sections for seclusion and gender segregation. Romans respected privacy in correspondence and employed wax or seals to guarantee the secrecy and reliability of their letters and documents.

While times past civilizations enjoyed aspects related to private space, ownership of property, and a certain level of confidentiality within the family or home, the concept of privacy as a fundamental human right protecting personal information and autonomy in the digital age is something that started to take shape more clearly in the modern era, especially during the Enlightenment.

Theories of Privacy

The emergence of privacy rights can be attributed to a combination of historical, philosophical, technological, and societal factors. Over time, as societies evolved, individuals recognized the need for protections to maintain their personal autonomy, dignity, and control over their personal information. Privacy is a complex and multifaceted concept that has been the subject of various theories and approaches in different disciplines, including philosophy, law, sociology, and information technology.

Control Theory of Privacy

The control theory of privacy is a social psychological theory proposed by Irwin Altman and Dalmas Taylor in 1973. The theory suggests that individuals have control over their personal information and decide how much information they want to disclose or keep private. According to the control theory, privacy is the state of being able to control the level of information shared about oneself with others. The theory emphasizes the importance of autonomy, which means individuals have the right to choose what information to share with others and what information to withhold. The theory identifies several factors that influence an individual's privacy preferences, including individual differences in personality, culture, social norms, and environmental factors. For example, people with introverted personalities tend to value their privacy more than outgoing individuals. The control theory of privacy suggests that individuals are motivated to maintain a certain level of privacy, and they become uncomfortable when that level is violated. The theory also highlights the importance of providing individuals with control and choice over their personal information, such as giving them the ability to opt-in or opt-out of data sharing or providing transparent privacy policies. Overall, the control theory of privacy provides a framework for understanding why individuals value their privacy, the factors that influence privacy preferences, and the ways in which privacy can be preserved.

The Informational Privacy Theory

It emphasizes the importance of controlling personal information and its use in modern society. According to this theory, privacy is the ability of an individual to control or restrict the collection, use, and dissemination of his or her personal information. It includes the right to know what information is being collected, who is collecting it, and for what purpose it is being collected. Westin identifies four key elements of informational privacy. Privacy as autonomy or control over personal information, Privacy as limited access to personal information, Privacy as secrecy or confidentiality of personal information and Privacy as information quality or accuracy of personal information. He argues that individuals have a reasonable expectation of privacy, and any invasion of that privacy should only occur with their consent or under narrow and well-defined circumstances. The Informational Privacy Theory has influenced privacy laws and regulations worldwide and has been used as a basis for developing privacy policies and practices by individuals, corporations, and governments. As the digital economy continues to grow, the Informational Privacy Theory remains relevant in addressing new privacy challenges, such as data breaches, online tracking, and surveillance.

The Contextual Integrity Theory of Privacy

The contextual integrity theory emphasizes the importance of social contexts and norms, and the Privacy as Restricted Communication theory emphasizes the role of privacy in facilitating intimate communication. The Contextual Integrity Theory of Privacy emphasizes the role of context and social norms in shaping privacy expectations. According to this theory, privacy expectations are context-specific and depend on the norms and expectations of various social contexts, such as family, workplace, and online communities. Nissenbaum argues that privacy is not simply about control over personal information, but also about more abstract values like trust, respect, and autonomy within social contexts. Privacy expectations may vary depending on the context, and it is important to consider the social norms and expectations of each context in addressing privacy concerns. The Contextual Integrity Theory of Privacy has also influenced privacy laws and policies, emphasizing the importance of understanding the specific contexts in which personal information is collected, used, and shared. This theory highlights the importance of considering the social norms and values of diverse communities and cultures and recognizing that privacy expectations are not necessarily universal or fixed.

Confidentiality Theory

The Privacy as Confidentiality theory focuses on protecting personal information from unwanted disclosure. emphasizes the importance of protecting personal information from unwanted disclosure and maintaining confidentiality. According to this theory, privacy is not merely the control over personal information but also the secrecy of certain kinds of personal information deemed private by an individual. Gavison identified four main components of privacy as confidentiality: Secrecy is the ability to keep certain personal information confidential. Control is the ability to control the dissemination of personal information. Limited access: the ability to limit access to personal information. Respect for privacy: the social value of respecting an individual's desire for privacy Gavison also argued that privacy should be balanced against other competing values, such as national security, free expression, and public interest, and should be subject to reasonable limitations. Overall, the Privacy as Confidentiality theory argues for a right to privacy as a means of preserving the autonomy and dignity of the individual and has been influential in shaping legal and policy discussions around data protection, confidentiality and personal privacy.

Limited Access Theory

Privacy as Limited Access theory emphasizes controlling access to personal information. expands on the concept of privacy as control over personal information by emphasizing the importance of limiting access to personal information. According to this theory, privacy is the ability to restrict access to personal information, even if an individual has no desire to control or share that information. Schoeman argues that privacy is important because it enables individuals to create a space for themselves separate from the public sphere, where they can be themselves without fear of judgment or scrutiny. The Privacy as Limited Access theory emphasizes the importance of consent and situational context in determining privacy expectations. Schoeman distinguishes between four types of privacy: physical privacy, informational privacy, decisional privacy, and associational privacy. These different types of privacy all relate to the idea that individuals have a right to control access to certain aspects of their lives. The Privacy as Limited Access theory has been influential in shaping privacy laws and regulations that govern the collection, use, and dissemination of personal information. It highlights the importance of protecting individual rights to privacy and has been used in legal and policy discussions around issues such as data protection, surveillance, and government access to personal information.

Restricted Communication Theory

Privacy is the ability to control access to oneself in order to maintain certain types of relationships. Fried argues that privacy is important because it enables individuals to form intimate relationships with others, and that the right to privacy is based on a desire for a certain type of social interaction. Fried distinguishes between two different types of privacy: decisional privacy and informational privacy. Decisional privacy concerns an individual's right to make important decisions about their own life without interference from others. Informational privacy concerns an individual's right to control access to personal information about themselves. Privacy as Restricted Communication Theory has been influential in shaping legal and policy discussions around issues such as data protection, surveillance, and government access to personal information. It emphasizes the importance of protecting individual rights to privacy in order to enable individuals to form intimate relationships and maintain autonomy over their own lives.

Privacy as a Boundary Management Process

This theory views privacy as a process of managing boundaries between oneself and others. Individuals decide when and how to open or close their boundaries, adjusting their level of openness based on the situation and relationship. Ira Rezak, Alan Westin, Sandra Petronio have contributed to the understanding of privacy as a boundary management process.

Privacy Paradox Theory

The privacy paradox refers to the observed discrepancy between individuals' expressed concerns about privacy and their actual behaviors regarding personal information sharing. This theory explores the factors influencing this discrepancy, such as perceived benefits, trust, and convenience. Alessandro Acquisti, lorrie faith cranor, Joseph Turow,etc. have contributed to the understanding and exploration of the Privacy Paradox, acknowledging the intricate interplay of psychological, social, and contextual factors that influence how individuals perceive and act upon privacy concerns in the digital age.

Protection Motivation Theory

Protection motivation theory addresses individuals' responses to perceived threats to their privacy. It explores the different factors that influence their motivation to protect their personal information, viz. perceived vulnerability, efficacy of protective measures, Perceived Self-Efficacy, Perceived Vulnerability and perceived rewards. PMT was initially proposed by Ronald W. Rogers in 1975 and has been adapted and extended by various researchers since then.

Theory of Planned Behavior (TPB)

This theory posits that an individual's intention to disclose personal information is influenced by their attitudes, subjective norms, and perceived behavioral control. These factors affect their decisions regarding privacy-related actions. It was originally developed by Icek Ajzen and has been widely used in various domains to predict and explain behaviors, including those related to privacy.

Miscellaneous Theories

Informational Self-Determination Theory proposed by privacy scholar Gustav Radbruch, emphasizes the right of individuals to control how their personal information is collected, processed, and shared. Instrumental Value Theory argues that privacy is important because it helps to foster and protect other important values, such as intimacy, autonomy, and trust. Solitude Theory proposed by Anthony Giddens, argues that privacy is important because it allows individuals to withdraw from the demands of society and engage in self-reflection.

Conclusions

The simple idea that we are individuals first frequently takes a back seat to being a part of society. Every person needs a private area for whatever activity they choose to engage in (if it is lawful, of course). As a result, the State grants everyone the freedom to enjoy those private moments. According to Clinton Rossiter, privacy could be a unique form of reasonable independence that can be viewed as a test of securing autonomy in at least some intimate and spiritual matters. The most unique experience a person can have been this sense of independence. There, people live in complete freedom. Frequently, this is a right against the earth rather than the State.

The psychology of privacy is a field that explores how individuals perceive, value, and behave regarding their personal information and boundaries. Several theories and models help explain the psychological aspects of privacy. Different theories provide different philosophical perspectives on privacy and address various aspects of privacy. While the control theory emphasizes individual agency and autonomy over personal information, the informational privacy theory highlights the importance of limiting the collection, use, and dissemination of personal information. On the other hand, the Privacy as Confidentiality theory focuses on protecting personal information from unwanted disclosure, and the Privacy as Limited Access theory emphasizes controlling access to personal information. The contextual integrity theory emphasizes the importance of social contexts and norms, and the Privacy as Restricted Communication theory emphasizes the role of privacy in facilitating intimate communication. Overall, these theories provide different frameworks for understanding privacy and its role in society, and they continue to influence discussions about privacy and data protection in various fields, including law, ethics, and technology. Understanding and navigating privacy in contemporary society often requires an interdisciplinary approach that considers legal, ethical, social, technological, and psychological dimensions.

References

1. https://medium.com/the-ferenstein-wire/the-birth-and-death-of-privacy-3-000-years-of-history-in-50-images-614c26059e.
2. https://brewminate.com/our-sense-of-privacy-from-the-ancient-world-to-modern-technology/.
3. https://edri.org/our-work/evolution-concept-privacy/#:~:text=What%20John%20Adams%20deemed%20unacceptable,to%20%E2%80%9Cbeing%20let%20alone%E2%80%9D.
4. https://theconversation.com/your-sense-of-privacy-evolved-over-millennia-that-puts-you-at-risk-today-but-could-improve-technology-tomorrow-175474.
5. https://plato.stanford.edu/entries/privacy/#:~:text=Privacy%20allows%20one%20the%20freedom,with%20respect%20and%20self%20respect.
6. Hugl, Ulrike, "Approaching the value of Privacy: Review of theoretical privacy concepts and aspects of privacy management" (2010). AMCIS 2010 Proceedings. 248.
7. Samuel D. Warren and Louis D. Brandeis, The Right to Privacy, Harvard Law Review, Vol. 4, No. 5. (Dec. 15, 1890), pp. 193-220.
8. https://www.vox.com/ad/21136449/privacy-data-technology.
9. https://medium.com/@venkatakrishna.jonnalagadda/the-value-of-protecting-privacy-and-information-technology-e6818732afa3.
10. https://www.forbes.com/sites/forbestechcouncil/2020/03/04/the-unique-values-placed-on-privacy/?sh=4177bdbb2d9a.

2

A Review of Complicated Concept of Right to Privacy: With Reference to Significant Theories

Mawuleabenam Aku Adjahoe and Harriet Debrah Otchere

Abstract

Various legal encyclopedias have delved into the definition of 'privacy.' Deriving from the Latin words "privatus" and "privo," which relate to deprivation, privacy essentially denotes an individual's intent to safeguard their life from unwanted intrusions or examinations. Black's Law Dictionary explicitly defines the 'right of privacy' as an individual's entitlement "to be free from undue publicity," and it broadly encompasses various fundamental rights, including liberty, which primarily serve as protections against government intrusions. The right to privacy is a fundamental human right recognized in numerous legal traditions and international human rights documents. It encompasses the presumption that individuals should have an area of autonomous development, interaction, and liberty, free from unwarranted state intervention and excessive external intrusion. This right protects individuals' personal and familial information, their homes, and their communications. With advancements in technology, the right to privacy has become even more crucial, leading to greater emphasis on data protection, digital privacy, and protection from surveillance. However, like all rights, the right to privacy is not absolute and can be limited for legitimate reasons, including national security and public safety. Various fields such as sociology, psychology, law, and philosophy have explored the concept of privacy. While the idea of privacy may seem straightforward, defining it precisely remains a challenge.

Keywords - *Privacy, public safety, human right, data protection, fundamental rights.*

Introduction

The right to privacy is a fundamental tenet of human rights. Since the dawn of human civilization, privacy has been integral to our existence. Early legal systems, such as those in medieval Anglo-Saxon and German tribal societies, offered protections for a freeman's property, along with compensation for any damages or insults to it. People inherently want to be shielded from unwanted intrusions, hoping their spaces, belongings, bodies, and personal data remain undisturbed. This innate human longing encompasses protections over physical spaces, belongings, and personal data. However, the scope and interpretation of privacy can vary across societies due to factors like location, culture, and religion. Studies from the late 20th century highlight a growing public concern for privacy, a trend that continues to escalate. Efforts to internationally recognize the right to privacy gained momentum after World War II. During this period, the European Union spearheaded the acknowledgment of privacy rights, with several member states implementing related laws. In the previous century, the scope of privacy was more restricted, such as preventing unauthorized entry into someone's home, forbidding wiretapping, and prohibiting the reading of personal letters. Konvitz notes that privacy rights were referenced in some of America's earliest legal codes, philosophical texts, and traditions. Yet, the modern interpretation of privacy, particularly its status as a fundamental human right, has been significantly influenced by technological advancements, especially computers and the internet, in the latter part of the 20th century. Ragland mentions that the early understanding of 'privacy' in American courts was ambiguous, wavering between being viewed as a personal or property right. Westin, meanwhile, chronicles the evolution of privacy in America, framing it in the context of technological progress.

Simon Chesterman outlined the evolution of 'privacy development' in three distinct phases. In the late 19th century, the foundational idea of privacy was established in the USA as the right to 'be let alone.' This arose in response to sensationalist journalism, the advent of the camera, and evolving perceptions about the appropriate role of the mass media. During the latter half of the 20th century, with the rise in computerized information, there was a notable increase in the government and other entities accessing data. As the 21st century began, the proliferation of social networks and mobile devices led to a massive influx of information circulation. This prompted a shift towards emphasizing the right to protect personal data rather than solely focusing on the right to privacy.

Diverse Theories

The entire theory of privacy varies across societies. This variation is reflected in the diverse definitions provided by experts from different cultural backgrounds, legal traditions, and academic disciplines. The multitude of definitions underscores the lack of a single universally accepted definition of privacy. Shils commented, "The concept of privacy is nebulous and challenging to pin down precisely." As a sociologist, Shils described privacy as a "zero-relationship" between individuals or between groups and individuals. Essentially, we discuss a person's or a group's privacy in relation to other individuals. Privacy concerns emerge when an individual's or group's solitude is potentially violated. Shils introduced the idea of "shared privacy", where someone willingly reveals information to others as opposed to involuntary information disclosure. Nonetheless, privacy isn't an absolute concept; its preservation doesn't hinder communication among individuals or groups. Post believes that privacy is a complex value with contrasting characteristics and varied meanings, leading him to question its effective addressal. As such, privacy remains an elusive concept to define, being simultaneously encompassing and elusive.

Moore posits that 'Privacy' is a nuanced concept that's challenging to precisely define. He describes it as either a state of being or a moral expectation that others abstain from specific actions. His approach to understanding privacy centers on the idea of an individual's right to remain inaccessible or maintain discretion over their information. Moore's interpretation of privacy as a condition or right is more descriptive than prescriptive. In simpler terms, privacy allows individuals to control access to themselves and their data. Kalven emphasizes that privacy is paramount in any refined society. Bygrave echoes this sentiment, suggesting that the human yearning for privacy stems from societal influences. He builds upon Moore's viewpoint, arguing that the societal demand for privacy arises in intricate societies that can discern between private and public realms. According to Bygrave, elements like culture, religion, and philosophy, combined with technology and organizational structures, are foundational to understanding privacy. Bloustein offers a comprehensive perspective, positioning privacy as a "general theory" that harmonizes various legal trajectories. He underscores the political, psychological, and societal facets of privacy, introducing the concept of "individual privacy". In his eyes, the primary focus of privacy is an individual's right to avoid unwarranted and excessive exposure. Furthermore, Bloustein asserts that the prevailing privacy laws aim to uphold individuality, freedom, and dignity, penalizing any breaches thereof. Gross perceives privacy as a condition where access to information about individuals is limited. Jourard, from a psychological perspective, views privacy as an individual's inclination to hide specific details from others. The rights to identity and privacy are often seen as intertwined, both being facets of overarching personality rights. They encapsulate the inherent respect and honor due to every individual, stemming from the principles of dignity and self-determination. Interestingly, the right to privacy is intricately linked with freedom of expression, with both rights reinforcing each other. Parker posits that any definition of privacy should adhere to three main criteria: it must align with the data it describes, be simple, and be easily interpretable by legal professionals and the judiciary. Post analyzed three contrasting perspectives on privacy mentioned in the Prologue to The Unwanted Gaze: associating privacy with knowledge generation, linking it to dignity, and tying it to freedom. Post contends that while the first view shouldn't be deemed a matter of privacy, the second provides insight into privacy if it draws attention to social structures. He believes the third perspective, relating privacy to freedom, is the most potent as it justifies constraints on governmental policies and rules.

Alan Furman Westin's View on Privacy

According to Jeffrey, following Louis Brandeis, Alan Furman Westin stands out as a pivotal figure in privacy research. His acclaimed 1967 book, "Privacy and Freedom," along with various articles, laid the groundwork for contemporary privacy laws, notably the Privacy Act of 1974. Westin was instrumental in the

U.S., connecting early concepts of privacy with the rise of new technologies, especially the advent of computers. The insights from leading privacy scholars, namely Professor Allan Westin and David Flaherty, greatly influenced the team crafting the OECD Guidelines between 1978-80. Westin conceptualizes privacy as an individual, group, or institution's prerogative to decide when, how, and to what degree their information is shared with others. Essentially, it's an individual's control over which facets of their personal data can be accessed by others. He further elaborated that it represents a "domain of democratic politics." In his view, privacy is a crucial aspect of life deserving scholarly rigor, proactive defense, and consistent scrutiny from everyone. He emphasized that privacy extends to social collectives and associations, and that there should be a circumscribed, temporary right to government processing.

Westin identified three distinct forms of surveillance. Physical Surveillance entails observing an individual's actions, speech, and whereabouts using unconsented auditory or visual devices. Data Surveillance refers to the processing of individual and group data by collecting, storing, sharing, and integrating it through systems like computers. Physiological Surveillance employs techniques to gather personal data, predominantly health and physiological details, without the individual's knowledge.

Westin contended that various elements like culture, tradition, way of life, religion, economic systems, and political structures influence the facets of privacy. Consequently, considering these factors, each society requires a tailored political framework. In Westin's perspective, the primary purpose of privacy is to empower individuals and groups with the choice of when and how their expressions, thoughts, or actions are exposed to the public. He emphasizes that the essence of privacy is to shield individuals from unwanted exposure, particularly when they haven't provided consent. Essentially, Westin posits that individuals should have the autonomy to determine the extent, timing, and recipients of their personal information sharing.

W.A. Parent's View

W.A. Parent defined privacy as the state where no undocumented personal knowledge about an individual is held by others. He categorized information into 'documented' and 'undocumented'. To him, privacy revolves around the latter. When personal data is made public, such as through news reports of someone's past conviction, it's considered documented personal information. This documented information is purposefully left out of his definition of privacy. Essentially, he believes that privacy exists when others remain unaware of an individual's undocumented personal details, emphasizing the idea of "lacking undocumented personal knowledge about someone."

Privacy, according to Parent, safeguards against unwarranted access to non-public personal knowledge. He believed that while privacy belongs to a set of values, it should be defined distinctly. Parent distinguished between the state of privacy and the right to it, asserting that privacy is the absence of others having any undocumented personal knowledge about someone.

For Parent, personal knowledge encompasses information individuals typically prefer to keep private, sharing perhaps only with close family, trusted friends, or professional colleagues. He intentionally factors in 'given society' and 'given time' to his definition, highlighting that the perception of personal data can shift across societies and eras. Only considering undocumented information, he omits documented details like court proceedings, official records, or news reports but makes exceptions for certain cases, such as non-public medical records.

Parent criticized many scholarly interpretations of privacy, suggesting they're in "hopeless disarray."

He felt that many studies overlooked related values like autonomy and solitude. Parent disagrees with Posners' perspective on secrecy and seclusion as true aspects of privacy, believing it muddies the waters. He also disapproved Warren and Brandeis's "right to be let alone" theory for being too expansive and blending privacy with other similar values. Parent rejected defining privacy as 'control over information,' seeing it as too encompassing. Moore critiques Parent, suggesting that Parent's definition leaves it up to society to determine what's documented and what isn't, viewing this as a merely descriptive, rather than normative, approach to defining privacy.

Development of Privacy Right in 20th Century

In the common law legal systems, particularly in the UK, cases concerning privacy typically revolve around principles like breach of confidence, nuisance, defamation, and trespass. A pertinent legal inquiry emerges: can this conventional method of safeguarding privacy rights address the newly emerging intricate privacy challenges? With the advent of data protection laws and public demand, courts have been inclined to acknowledge a novel tort related to privacy.

Historically, the Pavesich case marked the USA's inaugural recognition of a common law privacy right. The momentum to recognize privacy rights gained traction with the UK's Human Rights Act 1998, which mandates courts to consider the European Convention for the Protection of Human Rights and Fundamental Freedoms (ECHR).

In 1932, Kacedan advocated for the recognition of privacy rights as a common law right. Citing the New York Civil Rights experience, he asserted that sole reliance on legislation is insufficient to fully protect privacy rights, given the myriad of scenarios it encompasses. He emphasized that legislative rules can be rigid, while court judgments offer flexibility.

Posner dissected the torts of privacy under Common Law. He believes that while the Common Law's tort of privacy was inspired by Warren and Brandeis's paper, the law has diverged significantly from their original proposal. According to Posner, privacy torts primarily address private infringements rather than governmental ones.

Richards and Solove suggested approaches to tackle privacy challenges via tort law. Tort law must evolve to reflect modern understandings of privacy, striking a balance between the purely public and private realms. It should consider the societal contexts in which personal data is shared and broaden the tort of breach of confidence. Tort law requires a more nuanced understanding of the harms involved. Courts should better comprehend the interplay between privacy tort remedies and free speech. They further observed that modern courts often juxtapose free speech with privacy, a sentiment influenced by Prosser.

Indian Law Perspective

The Indian Constitution stands as the nation's supreme law, acting as the ultimate authority. It's evident that our Constitution is an evolving and adaptable text, morphing in response to societal and environmental changes. Within its myriad of fundamental rights, the right to privacy has a distinct importance and is safeguarded under Article 21. This Article explicitly proclaims that no individual should be stripped of their life or personal freedom. The inherent connection between privacy and a person's life and liberty underscores its inclusion in the fundamental rights assured by Article 21.

Historically, the discussion around the foundational right to privacy in India can be tracked back to a sequence of verdicts from the Supreme Court. The legitimacy of a search and seizure operation executed by authorities was called into question, particularly as it pertained to the Dalmia Group of Delhi. While challenging the operation's legality through a writ petition, the Group posited that their privacy and fundamental rights, as inscribed under Articles 19(1)(f) and 20(3) of the Constitution, were infringed. After extensive analysis by an Eight-Judge Constitutional Bench of the Supreme Court, it was determined that search and seizure procedures, when conducted in adherence to legal frameworks, do not infringe upon personal privacy or fundamental rights. The court's ruling underscored that, unlike the Fourth Amendment of the US Constitution, the Indian Constitution does not explicitly list the right to privacy as a foundational right.

The argument was that these provisions contravened citizens' rights under Articles 19(1) (d) and 21 of the Constitution. In its judgment, the Court highlighted that unauthorized police intrusions into personal privacy were at odds with the democratic ethos of "ordered liberty." However, the court's majority opined that the

Indian Constitution doesn't specifically guarantee the right to privacy.

Justice Subba Rao advocated for recognizing the right to privacy within the term "personal liberty" as stipulated in Article 21. He articulated that beyond merely protecting an individual's freedom of movement, it also encapsulates the right to safeguard personal space. Though the Indian Constitution doesn't expressly label the right to privacy as a fundamental one, it remains an intrinsic element of personal liberty, a value cherished by all democracies.

Section 5 of the Indian Telegraph Act empowers both Central and State Governments to record phone conversations, given specific conditions. The Supreme Court asserted that such surveillance is a stark infringement on the right to privacy and can only be employed in extraordinary situations. They delineated clear guidelines for the use of the said section, including regular reviews and oversight to ensure compliance with constitutional rights.

The crux of the Supreme Court's verdict underscored that phone tapping is a profound breach of an individual's privacy rights, as enshrined in Article 21. While certain Acts, like the Indian Telegraph Act, 1885 and the Information Technology Act, 2000, provide the government with surveillance powers, their application must always adhere to constitutional mandates.

Conclusions

Privacy encompasses various rights, such as the right to solitude and control over one's personal information (data protection). A study of privacy concepts suggests that it represents an individual's zone where they prefer to remain inaccessible to others. This includes rights like solitude and control over personal data. Despite its innate nature in humans, diverse interpretations of its essence and concept have been put forward. Westin is possibly best known for his canonical book "Privacy and Freedom" from 1967, where he is considered to be the first person to have laid the foundation for the field of privacy law.

References

1. Konvitz, M. R. (1966). Privacy and the law: A philosophical prelude. Law and Contemporary Problems, 31(2), at 272.
2. Chesterman, S. (2012). Who Killed Privacy? Straits Times, 26.
3. Bygrave, L. A. (2010). Privacy and data protection in an international perspective. Scandinavian Studies in Law, 56, at 175.
4. Jeffrey Rosen, Professor of law at George Washington University and legal affairs editor of the New Republic.
5. Westin, A. F. (1967). Privacy and Freedom, New York: H: Wolff.
6. Kirby, M. (2011). The history, achievement and future of the 1980 OECD guidelines on privacy. International Data Privacy Law, 1(1)
7. Westin, A. F. (1966). Science, Privacy, and Freedom: Issues and Proposals for the 1970's.
8. Parent, W. A. (1983). Privacy, morality, and the law. Philosophy & Public Affairs, 12(4).
9. Kacedan, B. W. (1932). The Right of Privacy. Boston University Law Review, 12
10. Posner, R. A. (1978). Right of privacy, the. Ga. L. Rev., 12(3).
11. http://faculty.washington.edu/moore2/DP.pdf.
12. Georgia Supreme Court in Pavesich v. New England Life Ins. Co., 1905.
13. Richard A. Posner, "The Right of Privacy," 12 Georgia Law Review 393 (1977).

3

Personal Data in Focus: A Comprehensive Overview of its Varied Facets

Yogesh Sharma and Vidhi Maheshwari

Abstract

Information-based theft, identity fraud, and other types of harm are all made possible by identity-relevant information, which is analogous to guns and ammunition in information societies. Information can simultaneously be used for society's benefit. Data collecting can occur prior to, during, or following a commercial transaction, and the customer may be aware of it or not. Information should be used in a way that increases its value, such as through cooperation, remixing, and validation. Misrepresentation, misidentification, and dilution are examples of destructive applications that make the knowledge less valuable. Regulation of Personal Data varies from jurisdiction to jurisdiction. Effective handling and safeguarding of personal information is vital for fostering trust, honoring privacy rights, and adhering to ethical norms. People possess the entitlement to understand the utilization of their data and retain authority over its usage. Conversely, organizations bear the obligation of treating personal data with care, ensuring its security, and complying with relevant laws and rules. Given the continued prominence of personal data in our digital era, it is imperative for individuals, enterprises, and policymakers to remain updated about the shifting privacy and data protection landscape. This knowledge is essential to guarantee the ethical and conscientious utilization of personal data. Thus, the present paper aims to explore how personal data may be protected globally. The paper seeks to throw a light upon the approaches and framework for data protection.

Keywords *- Framework, International, Data, Security, Information.*

Introduction

Personal data refers to any information that relates to an identified or identifiable individual. It encompasses a broad range of data that can be used to identify, locate, or contact a specific person. Personal data is at the core of privacy and data protection concerns, as it contains sensitive information about individuals' identities, characteristics, behaviors, and interactions. Personal data can include various types of information, such as names, addresses, phone numbers, email addresses, social security numbers, financial details, medical records, employment information, and online identifiers. It extends to both offline and online contexts, encompassing data collected through interactions with organizations, websites, applications, devices, or other sources.

The handling of personal data is subject to legal and regulatory frameworks, which vary across jurisdictions. These frameworks aim to protect individuals' privacy and establish guidelines for organizations collecting, processing, and storing personal data. They typically require organizations to obtain informed consent for data collection, ensure data security, provide individuals with control over their data, and limit the use of personal data to lawful purposes. The advent of advanced technologies, such as artificial intelligence, big data analytics, and the Internet of Things, has further emphasized the importance of personal data. As data-driven practices become more prevalent, there is a growing need to strike a balance between utilizing personal data for innovation and ensuring individuals' rights and protections. Proper management and protection of personal data are essential to maintaining trust, respecting privacy rights, and upholding ethical standards. Individuals have the right to know how their data is being used and to have control over its use. Organizations, on the other hand, have a responsibility to handle personal data responsibly, securely, and in compliance with applicable laws and regulations. As personal data continues to play a significant role in our digital society, it is crucial for individuals, organizations, and policymakers to stay informed about the evolving landscape of privacy and data protection to ensure the responsible and ethical use of personal data.

Importance of Personal Data in Governance

Personal data plays a crucial role in governance, particularly in the context of data-driven decision-making and policy formulation. Some key reasons why personal data is important in governance include -

Evidence-based Decision Making

Personal data provides valuable insights and evidence that can inform policy decisions and governance processes. By analyzing aggregated and anonymized personal data, policymakers can gain a deeper understanding of societal trends, challenges, and needs, which can help in formulating effective policies and strategies.

Targeted Policy Interventions

Personal data enables policymakers to identify specific segments of the population that may require targeted policy interventions. By analyzing demographic, socio-economic, and behavioral data, governments can design policies and programs that address the specific needs and circumstances of different groups, leading to more efficient and effective governance.

Monitoring and Evaluation

Personal data allows for the monitoring and evaluation of government initiatives and programs. By collecting and analyzing relevant data, governments can assess the impact and effectiveness of their policies, identify areas for improvement, and make evidence-based adjustments to their governance approaches.

Public Service Delivery

Personal data can facilitate the delivery of public services. For example, by collecting and analyzing citizen data, governments can personalize and streamline the provision of services such as healthcare, education, social welfare, and transportation, ensuring that resources are allocated efficiently and effectively.

Identifying Fraud and Corruption

Personal data can be utilized to detect and prevent fraud and corruption within the governance framework. By analyzing data patterns and conducting risk assessments, governments can identify irregularities and anomalies, enabling them to take necessary actions to mitigate risks and ensure transparency and accountability.

Participatory Governance

Personal data can enable increased citizen participation in governance processes. By leveraging technology and data, governments can gather feedback, opinions, and preferences from citizens, fostering a more inclusive and participatory decision-making environment.

Emergency Management and Public Safety

Personal data can play a critical role in emergency management and ensuring public safety. By utilizing real-time data and analytics, governments can respond effectively to crises, allocate resources efficiently, and implement preventive measures to protect citizens.

While personal data holds significant potential for governance, it is essential to prioritize privacy, data protection, and ethical considerations. Governments must establish robust frameworks and regulations to ensure the responsible collection, storage, and use of personal data, safeguarding individuals' rights and maintaining public trust. Overall, personal data, when appropriately collected and analyzed, can enhance governance processes, improve policy outcomes, and contribute to more responsive and citizen-centric governance.

Personal Data: Concept, Definition and Classification

Facts and social definition, decision-making, and gathering procedures are used to produce data. They connect to the reason they were built, serve those interests, and are characterized by those interests. They can only be comprehended in the framework of society in which they were created, and what constitutes data will vary depending on the setting. Data has always been utilized for a reason; they're intended to serve a particular purpose, and this interest is what determines how they are defined, chosen, and collected as well as what will be accomplished in conjunction with them. The main idea is that information cannot be adequately understood apart from the social settings in which it was created and the purposes it was intended to further.

Meaning and Definition of Personal Data

Personal information encompasses any information, messages, or views that are related to a specific person and that person would reasonably be expected to regard as particular or confidential and desire not to disclose or possibly prevent from being collected, used, or circulated. Facts aren't restricted to linguistic material; they also include photographs, DNA and biological data, biometric information (such as the ability to recognise a person's fingers, confront, or eye), and an ever-growing variety of details concerning an individual. Despite being completely harmless alone, an element of knowledge can become a factor really secret as soon as it is paired with an additional resource of similarly harmless material. Anything collected isn't personally identifiable by themselves, in any circumstance. Health record, statement from a bank, or graphic account revelation are all harmless unless they are attributed to a specific person; it only happens whenever the identities of the individuals is known that the material becomes private. Culture-related in addition to changeable norms determine the character of communication. Information can be viewed as extremely personal in one view and not at all confidential in a different one with privacy not being a property of the material itself. Personal information- It can be identified as the beliefs that comprise information items and their combinations that uniquely identify specific persons.

Test to Ascertain Personal Data

The test to ascertain whether a particular data is of personal nature or not is whether - it may be linked to an individual, thereby revealing his identity. The concept of personal data has descriptive and normative aspects. Consequently, any description of "personal information" has to relate about each of the aforementioned aspects, i.e., the accuracy of the data and the user's acceptable standards for how it will be utilized. Certain facts regarding and in relation to persons may not be connected to certain persons. Non-personal knowledge is what is usually related to data of this kind. This comprises statistics as well as condensed intimate information when a person's identification is ambiguous or where the connection with that subject has become severed. In some situations, the data has been anonymous or masked to the point where it is impossible to infer the true identity of the person using the material that is still available. Normally, data that is not personally identifiable is not protected by regulations governing privacy since it is incapable of being used to identify a specific person.

Classification of Personal Data

Table below identifies the sensitive information as it is specifically specified in the Council of Europe Convention of 1981, the UN Guidelines of 1990, and the EU Data Protection Directive of 1995. Furthermore, it demonstrates that the three instruments' three shared data sets include racial origin, political views, religious and philosophical ideas, and sexual behaviour. Contrarily, criminal convictions were only covered by the Council of Europe Convention of 1981; colour was only covered by the UN Guidelines of 1990; and health and union membership were covered by two of them.

Table-1: Sensitive Data under Primary International Instruments

Sr. No.	Council of Europe Convention 1981,	UN Guidelines, 1990	EU Data Protection Directive, 1995
1.	Racial origin	Racial or Ethnic origin	Racial or ethnic origin
2.	Political opinions	Political opinions	Political opinions
3.	Religious or other beliefs	Religious/philosophical/other beliefs	Religious and philosophical beliefs
4.	Sexual life data /Sex life	Sex life	Sex life
5.	Health data	-	Health
6.		Membership of an association and Membership of a trade union	Trade-union membership
7.	-	Colour	-
8.	Criminal convictions	-	-

Compiled by the Researchers. It may be noted that OECD Guidelines do not define sensitive data.

Sensitive Data as a Special Category of Protected Data

Sensitive data requires stricter security measures because they are inherently more vulnerable compared to other data. Highly classified information was first mentioned in the Union's Council of

Europe Convention on Personal Data of 1981. The term "sensitive data" refers to private information that reveals biological source, thoughts on politics, religious beliefs, labor organization affiliation, including the collection and use of medical or sex-related data. Due to its extremely sensitive nature, personal data has been classified as sensitive data. Swiss Federal Data Protection Act, 1992 protects Personality profiles under Article 12. Personality assessments constitute assemblages of details which enable an analysis of somebody's core attributes (for instance, staff records frequently fit into this category). The many expressions used "revealing," "referring to," "relating to," "as to," and "on "appear to be fairly similar but might have significance, particularly when it comes to situations where some sensitive information may be inadvertently "revealed."

Sensitivity reasoning appears to suggest the fact that all relevant data ought to be bound by an equal level of constraint. Awareness checklists have to be written in a manner which clearly conveys its merely illustrative nature. Hence a result, their constituent parts can continually be enhanced or changed. Contextualized Perspective to Sensitive Data, once embraced by nations like Austria and Germany, posits that individual data constitutes problematic in accordance with the circumstances surrounding it. It is a general classification. The goal behind the collection and use of personally identifiable information, or because its treatment is meant to expose sensitive data, is taken into account by the context-based method of handling sensitive data. Numerous provincial and federal organizations have endorsed it. Any information therefore needs to be evaluated with considering the circumstance which governs how it is used. That particular passions between the controllers and the prospective subjects of the personal information, the reason why information are gathered, the terms and circumstances that apply when the information are processed, and any potential negative impacts upon the individuals involved are the various variables that, when taken in tandem, enable the variety of purposes and impact about the handling can be distinguished, and consequently decide the level of the vulnerability of the procedure. Merely a purpose-based strategy is currently prominent and popular.

Personal Identifiable Information (Data)

A key element in data security legislation, personally identifiable information (data), calls for an extensive definition in the context of contemporary data analysis and behavioral advertising technology. The accessibility of numerous knowledge about individuals makes it easier to transform non-personally known data into a single one, and technologies has begun to pose a significant threat towards the non-Personally Identifiable Information half that the split. To prevent including almost all information, the scope must be understood.

The framework plots data along an arc which starts at the juncture where there is no danger of recognition and concludes at that point where people have been recognized. The PII 2.0 paradigm offers the potential existence of collecting data regarding a determined, recognizable, or non-identifiable individual. A specific individual is considered recognized when their true nature has been proven; someone can be recognized once there is a non-extreme likelihood that they will one day be recognized. Such data has an elevated to medium risk of proof of identity, whereas non-identifiable material provides a far lower risk. All the principles of Fair Data Practices should typically be followed for referencing an identifiable individual in material. Regarding recognizable facts, the three main Ethical Knowledge Practices are privacy and security, openness, and knowledge reliability.

Information may be linked to a person in three different ways: by bearing a relation to their authorship, by bearing a relation to their description, or by bearing a relation to their instrumental mapping.

Categorization of Data Subjects: Primary and Secondary Data Subjects

The existing data protection law supports the concept because certain data may only include identifiable as that of an identifiable individual or a "primary" information user. Persons besides the principal recipients of information are not covered by the law's tailored safeguards for data. Alongside the development of technology, the main information exposed is being granted rights such as availability, autonomy, the ability to refuse to the utilization of their data for promotional purposes, plus the ability to avoid being bound by entirely computerized decisions. The main data user is the person to whom the knowledge is related. Information should be regarded as the private data of everybody if it may be related in an applicable manner with more people to one "described or recognizable" subject. As a result, any individuals to whomever the information might inadvertently pertain constitute the supplementary controllers. Authentication must be greater than an unlikely event if information must fulfill the legal criterion of "identifiability."

Vistas around Information Dissemination and Consequential Effects

The evildoers who could carry out these deeds include hackers, zealots, or disgruntled insiders, to further particular agendas; thieves, for their own revenue, etc.; terrorists or other malign organizations, to further its reason; business organizations, for spying on industry or to cause disruption to rivals; consequently, governments, to covert operations as well as revenue generation, or as a weapon of war.

The destructive use of information depends upon who the information user is and what are his goals in using the information. It shows that destructive use of information is not restricted to either a particular class of destruction or to a particular class of users. Government, commercial enterprises, friends, family etc. are also involved in destructive use in addition to the usually pinpointed category of criminals, news media, employers etc.

Data Abuse Pyramid

The knowledge corruption triangle serves as a visual representation for the different variables that contribute to knowledge misuse. The peak of the tower represents "misuse" of our personally identifiable information, which is whenever knowledge has been utilized for theft, fraud, or other illegal acts. Leaks, which occur whenever organizations inappropriately disclose or grant permission to obtain information about individuals, are next, and "insecurity," it refers to the overall insufficient safety given our personally identifiable information by those organizations that store it, is last, are at the bottom of the list. The legislation has to move its emphasis from the highest level of the system's abuse structure, which is misconduct, to the next levels, which include leakage and vulnerability.

Mandatory Volunteerism

As a way to demonstrate one's identity, giving over one's data and allowing oneself to have one's actions electronically followed and documented is more accepted. People are occasionally compelled to provide particulars in order to use internet services. Users frequently accept permission forms without studying them because they must move forward, granting assent on its own, disobeying confidentiality laws or demands by scrolling onto or confirming it before doing so. The state's coercive authority, which may compel people to operate as stipulated by law, limits the ability of a person to negotiate the limits of data confidentiality and exert some degree of autonomy in the setting of the general population sector.

Information Balance Approach

The idea of data privacy might be weighed versus the requirement for unrestricted exchange of data amid an economy that prospers. Conflicts of trust or adaptable information utilization are required to achieve balance. Contemporary economies cannot run properly without the transfer of private information, which is frequently advantageous to customers (data subjects), organizations (data holders), and other parties (data brokers). The quicker recourse to financing and coverage, customization, and personalization that result from activities using sensitive information benefits clients. Since it's important for clients and data users to get comfortable sharing knowledge while worrying about how it may be misused, confidence needs to be built between them and those organizations engaged in the gathering, processing, etc. of sensitive data. Some of the elements that might aid in building trust include autonomous government, business standards of behavior, and self-control on the part of organizations. People' preferences about what is disclosed to them have to be respected as opposed to having their information used in an indiscriminate manner.

Conclusions

Personal data includes information about an individual's identity, contact information, biographical information, financial and employment information, health and medical history, online identifiers, biometric data, location data, social and demographic information, and genetic information. These elements describe the many dimensions of a person's personal information taken as a whole. To ensure privacy and data protection, it is essential to comprehend and manage personal data. To protect people's rights and interests in connection to their personal data, laws and regulations have been put in place. Organizations that gather, handle, or retain personal data must abide by these rules and take the necessary precautions to protect the data and respect the privacy of persons.

Given the variety of uses for which personal data may be put to use, it is crucial for both individuals and organizations to understand the data they gather, how it is put to use, and the objectives for which it is processed. Maintaining trust and upholding people's rights to privacy and data protection requires transparency, informed consent, and appropriate data processing procedures. It is crucial to maintain vigilance in protecting personal data and adjusting privacy rules to deal with changing difficulties as technology develops and new data sources appear. Protecting personal information helps to uphold trust, create responsible data practices, and ensure the ethical and secure use of data in the digital age. It also supports people's right to privacy.

References

1. Sharon Booth, "What are 'Personal Data'?" A study conducted for the UK Information Commissioner (The University of Sheffield, 2004).
2. Raymond Wacks, Privacy- A Very Short Introduction, (Oxford University, New York, 2010).
3. James Waldo, Herbert S. Lin and Lynette I. Millett (eds.) Engaging Privacy and Information Technology in a Digital Age (National Academic Press, Wahington, 2007).

4. Council of Europe Convention deals with sensitive data.
5. Data Protection Directive 95/46/EC.
6. Federal Data Protection Act, 1992.
7. Douwe Korff, "EC Study On Implementation of Data Protection Directive- Comparative Summary of national laws" (University of Essex - Human Rights Centre, Cambridge September 2002) available at www.garanteprivacy.it/garante/document?ID=455584 (accessed on 03 July,2023).
8. Paul M. Schwartz and Daniel J. Solove , "The PII Problem: Privacy and a New Concept of Personally Identifiable Information", 86 New York University Law Review 1814 (2011).
9. Mark J Taylor, "Data Protection: Too Personal to protect?", 3(1) SCRIPT-ed ,71 (March 2006).
10. Richard O. Hundley and Robert H. Anderson, "Emerging Challenge: Security and Safety in Cyberspace" , In Athena's Camp: Preparing for Conflict in the Information Age, (RAND, Cambridge ,1997).
11. Daniel J. Solove "The New Vulnerability: Data Security and Personal Information" 113 Anupam Chander, Margaret Jane Radin and Lauren Gellman (eds.) Securing Privacy in the Internet Age (Stanford University Press, 2008).
12. Gary T. Marx, "Soft Surveillance: The Growth of Mandatory Volunteerism in Collecting Personal Information- "Hey Buddy Can You Spare a DNA?" Dissent, Winter 2005.
13. Fred H Cate, "The Privacy Problem: A broader view of information privacy and the costs and consequences of protecting it" 18 (First Amendment Centre, Washington,2003)
14. Marty Abrams, "The Economic Benefits of Balanced Information Use", CEI Staff (ed.) The Future of Financial Privacy: Private choices versus political rules (Competitive Enterprise Institute, Washington, 2000).

4

Digital Dignity Model: Lessons for Big Tech Giants

Bhupendra Gautam, Ramesh Verma and Vikrant Chauhan

Abstract

Technology companies operate at a faster pace than governments and often exist in domains where they possess a substantial informational edge over regulators. Big Tech frequently defends its data practices by asserting that they don't take users' data without consent. Instead, they frame it as a mutual exchange where users willingly provide their data in exchange for "free services". Big Tech have intruded into our personal lives, and once they gain access, they tend to remain entrenched indefinitely. Consequently, despite the growing awareness of the importance of data dignity, major tech corporations continue to track activities, collect data about people, and market these insights without constraints. Companies spanning various industries, especially Big Tech giants like Facebook and Google, persistently monitor and surveil customers for their own advantage, while the customers often remain unaware or resigned to this reality. While the immediate effects on each individual may seem minor, the larger repercussions on society as a whole are significant and far-reaching. The true value of users' data far exceeds its current market valuation. Big tech companies are reaping massive profits by monetizing user data without adequately compensating individuals for their valuable contributions. Users should refer to the latest privacy policies and updates from these companies for the most current and accurate information regarding privacy measures. Regulating competition in the digital economy doesn't necessitate an entirely new set of principles. Focusing enforcement efforts on how major technology corporations exploit data to undermine competition and bolster their market dominance will go a long way.

Keywords - *Technology, Company, data, user, regulator.*

Introduction

The world is on an accelerating trajectory in data production, and the value of data is expected to grow rapidly too. Companies that are already proficient in collecting and effectively managing data are well-positioned to continue gathering additional data in the future and capitalize on this valuable asset. The expertise in data management, analytics, and monetization will be a crucial advantage. Various sectors like data services and hardware companies, encompassing those involved in structuring unstructured data, AI development, AI-as-a-Service (AIaaS), AI hardware, and quantum computing, are anticipated to reap substantial benefits from the growing emphasis on data. As businesses aim to accelerate their investments in data to keep pace with the fast-paced digitalization of the world, these entities will play a pivotal role in shaping the future landscape of data-driven innovations and technologies.

Unchecked, data markets operate akin to a functional autocracy. There is no other market globally allowed to operate with such minimal oversight and such imbalanced terms, heavily favoring an oligopoly. Big Tech Giants, referring to major technology companies such as Google, Facebook (Meta), Amazon, Apple and Microsoft have faced increasing scrutiny regarding privacy concerns. Privacy maximization in the context of these tech giants involves implementing measures to protect users' personal data and ensure transparency and control over how that data is collected, stored, and utilized.

Governments are continuously lagging behind, striving to comprehend and address evolving digital technologies and services, only to witness the emergence of new, previously unimaginable ones. Presently, there is minimal regulation to govern these activities or enforce accountability upon the tech behemoths. Their extensive global presence enables them to strategically manage their corporate identities, locations, and operations in a manner that circumvents the existing limited laws and restrictions.

Dark Side of the Business of Tech Companies

Online platforms that depend on targeted advertising as a key revenue source actively strive to accumulate extensive personal information about their users. Over an extended period, technology companies have operated with minimal constraints, allowing them to collect, utilize, and distribute user data without significant limitations or oversight. The Security.org team, which included Gabe Turner, a former attorney for the New York State Department of Financial Services, conducted a thorough review of the privacy policies of major tech giants such as Facebook, Twitter, Amazon, Apple, and Google in 2023. This evaluation aimed to uncover the extent and nature of data collection and usage by these prominent tech companies. When it comes to extensive data logging, Google takes the lead, which aligns with their core business model deeply rooted in data. On the other hand, Apple stands out as the top company prioritizing privacy, retaining only essential data to maintain your account.

Twitter and Facebook, while storing more data than necessary, have varying degrees of data retention. Facebook tends to hold a substantial amount of data, largely consisting of user-inputted information. Amazon falls below Apple in the privacy rankings, likely attributed to their lesser reliance on advertising revenue compared to Google, Facebook, and Twitter. From the start, corporations claimed they had privacy-focused policies, empowering individuals to decide for themselves. Facebook, during its inception, specifically highlighted a priority on privacy, setting itself apart from MySpace. However, this commitment was not upheld. For instance, in 2016, Facebook allowed Cambridge Analytica to harvest privacy data from over 87 million users without violating any of its own policies. Facebook was not the sole offender; countless companies collect our data stealthily and without our consent.

Digital advertising has revolutionized the way companies market products, ranging from high-end fashion to everyday groceries, by allowing them to connect with potential customers. However, it has also introduced a novel avenue for political campaigns, political action committees, and private citizens with specific agendas to reach and influence voters. Unlike political ads aired on television or radio, which are heavily regulated and require detailed disclosures, online political advertisements operate with relatively lax constraints. This regulatory gap has enabled malicious actors to exploit online platforms, tailoring content to each voter's ideological inclinations and preconceived notions. The lack of substantial oversight over ads on online platforms exacerbates this issue.

Users often benefit from the free accessibility of numerous tech platforms, yet they unknowingly surrender their personal information with limited comprehension of the extent, type, or utilization of the data retained by tech companies. Additionally, they possess limited capabilities to halt the ongoing collection of their data. This lack of transparency and control does not just affect individual users, it extends to the broader political systems and processes. When major tech companies mishandle user data and create vulnerabilities, it opens the door for individuals or groups seeking to exploit social and political divisions, posing a significant risk to society.

Innovative tech companies have undeniably facilitated novel avenues for individuals to establish meaningful connections. However, the rise of online platforms has simultaneously given rise to a substantial forum for malicious actors to share and proliferate violent and extremist material, fake news, and disinformation. Rather than proactively regulating their platforms, tech companies have predominantly relied on users to report inappropriate content. Nevertheless, in recent times, online platforms have started to take measures to mitigate the dissemination of harmful content, recognizing their responsibility to conduct closer monitoring of the content hosted on their platforms.

Big Tech often argues that they are not taking people's data; rather, they engage in a kind of exchange where we provide our data in return for "free services" such as social media, email, and photo sharing, which enhance our lives by making them more convenient and enjoyable.

Central to these enforcement measures is a growing global agreement that data represents an overlooked yet significant source of market influence within the technology sector. This realization prompted the Canadian House of Commons' Standing Committee on Access to Information, Privacy, and Ethics to propose a shift in competition enforcement strategies within the tech industry. They advocate moving away from approaches primarily focused on pricing and instead emphasize evaluating the value of data involved in mergers between companies. Recognizing the potential of data collection to diminish competition, the committee has further advocated for the implementation of principles concerning data portability and system interoperability.

The traditional "consumer welfare standard" centered primarily on low prices has proven inadequate in addressing market concentration in the tech sector. Dominant technology companies have managed to evade thorough scrutiny by providing their services either for free or at minimal costs, effectively sidestepping the traditional evaluation of consumer welfare based solely on pricing. They tend to align with their main source of revenue and give precedence to the concerns of advertisers over those of users.

Data Dignity and Mediators of Individual Data

Unlike physical assets, data is a quasi-infinite and non-linearly expanding asset. The world currently generates over 2.5 quintillion bytes of data daily, a figure expected to grow at an accelerating rate with the increasing number of people and devices connected to the internet. Not all data holds equal value. Information such as customer details, product status, company sales, and social media engagements can vary in their importance. Various factors, including quality, accuracy, timeliness, and scale, can further influence the assessment of data's value.

Data Dignity

Data dignity, a concept introduced by Jaron Lanier and Glen Weyl, advocates for compensating users for the use of their data. This innovative idea transforms data into a form of property owned by the user, and companies would need to provide compensation to users for monetizing their data. While this approach would challenge the prevalent freemium model, where users often endure ads to access services for free, it ensures a more equitable arrangement where users are fairly rewarded for the value of their data. Data Dignity strives to reshape the relationship between individuals and their data, advocating for greater control, fairness, and ethical treatment in the digital age.

Approaches to Data Valuation

Three common approaches can be applied to data valuation that are used for valuing other types of assets as well - Market-based, Cost-based, and Cash flow-based.

Market Based Approach

This perspective aligns equates social media users (Monthly Active Users - MAUs) with data. Users not only provide personal information but also generate and distribute digital content while consuming advertisements. In the context of many social media platforms, users serve as both the data-producing product and the consumer, enabling the data to hold value (e.g., through targeted ad delivery). Thus, considering users as a form of data is a suitable approach for analyzing social media platforms.

The effectiveness of a company in capitalizing on each user directly impacts the value of the data associated with each user. The more proficient a company is at monetizing user interactions, preferences, and behaviors, the more valuable their data becomes. Additionally, growth expectations significantly influence a company's overall valuation. Forecasts of future user acquisition, engagement, and enhanced monetization capabilities play a crucial role in determining a company's perceived value and potential. Balancing current monetization strategies with promising avenues for future growth is fundamental in assessing a company's worth in the market.

Cost Based Approach

Assessing the cost of data collection, storage, and analysis provides a different approach to determining the value of data. Data is considered to have at least a minimum valuation, which should exceed the total cost of acquiring, storing, and analyzing it. If the value derived from the data is less than the cost of ownership, it may not be worth collecting or retaining. This approach ensures that data collection and storage efforts are justified by the value and insights gained from that data, promoting efficiency and cost-effectiveness in data management.

Estimating data storage costs can indeed vary based on negotiations with storage providers or a company's decision to build and maintain its data centers. Moreover, predicting the exact amount of data that will be stored and for how long is challenging due to evolving data usage patterns and technology advancements.

Another significant limitation is that the cost-based method only establishes a baseline value for data, considering the current expenses associated with it. It does not account for the potential future benefits, insights, or revenue that can be derived from the data. Future value, innovations, or unforeseen opportunities linked to the data are not factored in, making this approach inherently limited in assessing the comprehensive value of data.

Cash Flow Based Approach

A cash flow-based analysis offers a valuable perspective in assessing the worth of data. Analyzing the cash flow generated from existing data and projecting its growth provides insights into the potential value that data holds for a company. Moreover, recognizing that data often exhibits increasing returns to scale is crucial. As a company accumulates more data, it can enhance its value exponentially by uncovering patterns, insights, and opportunities that wouldn't be discernible with a smaller dataset. Linking free cash flow to data value is a sound approach, allowing for a more comprehensive understanding of how data contributes to a company's financial performance and overall valuation. This integrated assessment considers both the current cash flow generated from data and the future growth potential, enabling a more holistic evaluation of data's worth.

The network effect plays a significant role in data-rich companies. The more data these companies collect, the better they can refine and enhance their products or services. This, in turn, attracts more users, who generate even more data, creating a positive feedback loop. The accumulation of complementary information adds substantial value to the platform and contributes to its dominant position in industries like social media, search, and e-commerce. In a cash flow-based analysis for such companies, it's vital to not only consider the current value of data but also anticipate how this value might grow as the platform continues to amass more diverse and extensive data. Recognizing the potential for exponential growth in data value through this accumulation of complementary information is essential for a comprehensive and accurate valuation of these data-centric businesses.

Urge for Mediators of Individual Data

Mediators of Individual Data (MIDs) are a union-like organization.to undertake various essential roles on behalf of its members that are presently absent within the digital economy. In the data dignity model, Mediators of Individual Data (MIDs) play a crucial role by acting as representatives for individuals, seeking compensation from companies based on the data accessed. However, this model retains a centralized approach to data access, where individuals consent to and utilize services provided by big tech companies. These companies remain the initial recipients and processors of the data. Data unions, MIDs and similar entities can function as protective mechanisms on behalf of users.

Data rights mediators would employ legal and technical experts to comprehensively study how companies utilize user data, aiming to represent the best interests of their constituents. Rather than requiring individuals to decipher technically and legally intricate Terms of Service contracts, a well-equipped mediator would assess the terms on behalf of users. They would conduct periodic audits of technology platforms and data consumers, scrutinizing their data usage.

One potential concern is the conflict of interest, as companies have a financial incentive to withhold or manipulate information regarding the accurate details of data usage from the MIDs. This dynamic poses a challenge to achieving a truly transparent and fair compensation process. Striking a balance between user privacy, consent, compensation, and accurate data assessment remains a key aspect to address in implementing the data dignity model effectively. The conflict between governments and major tech platforms regarding user data underscores the importance of deliberating on the necessity of an intermediary or advocate who can effectively champion the concerns of individuals generating this data.

Challenges in Extracting Value from Data

It is uncertain how MIDs would interpret the relative worth of processed data. For example, a healthcare company utilizing personal health data for consultations and a wearable device company extracting and transmitting a user's health profile from the same data present contrasting value assessments. MIDs would encounter difficulties in advocating for individuals, given that the monetary value of data hinges on numerous factors such as data sensitivity, purpose, scale, and associated risks, resulting in complex permutations and combinations. MIDs would also need to analyze how the monetary value of data might fluctuate based on an individual's position within the social hierarchy.

The data dignity model endeavors to address a pivotal concern within the current data economy. Nevertheless, it introduces its own inherent shortcomings. The primary issue could lie in the concept of assigning a monetary value to users' personal data, potentially encouraging tech companies to maximize their utilization of accessed data. It's not solely about quantifying the economic worth of personal datasets, as assumed by the data dignity model, but also about the broader mechanics of accessing, processing, and transferring data without legitimate and proportionate justifications or interests.

The world needs a multidisciplinary community of technologists and experts to design standards for privacy protection across technological stacks. At the core of the framework is respect for a concept called Data Dignity.

Conclusions

Users and customers' personal data online is in the hands of Big Tech corporations, not under their control, and even the governments show reluctance in taking action. More and more tech experts are promoting the concept of "data dignity," emphasizing our right to have greater influence over the usage of the personal information. Commerce achieves fairness only when both parties understand the value of the goods or services involved. Big Tech has deliberately and systematically made it difficult for users to discern the true terms of this trade. Privacy, a valuable asset, is being monetized not by us, the data owners, but by those who exploit it. As citizens, people lack control over the monetary worth that they are generating.

By conceptualizing data as a form of property, individuals would receive compensation for their data, and they would also be obliged to compensate others for the use of their data in services. This approach aims to enhance transparency and narrow the divide between tech industry giants and individual users.

Collectively, users, tech companies and the governments have the power to establish a framework for an ethical internet, integrating inherent privacy standards. It is within our hands to reclaim the original vision of the internet and enable upcoming generations to have faith that they can engage, collaborate, and thrive in a digital realm while safeguarding their privacy. Globally, legislators are initiating efforts to advocate for public disclosure rules aiming to impose fresh mandates on online platforms. These regulations would mandate platforms to maintain comprehensive records of all online political advertisements. Additionally, they would require platforms to inform users about the sponsors of the political advertisements they are presented with, enhancing transparency in the political advertising sphere.

A growing perspective suggests that the digital era might not necessitate a complete overhaul of competition law objectives. Instead, it calls for a reevaluation of how enforcers apply current principles. Programmatic and technological solutions for privacy are attainable when businesses take the initiative to develop them, citizens advocate for their implementation, and the government establishes the necessary frameworks that emphasize their importance. In an upcoming piece focused on progressing towards Data Dignity, these aspects will be further explored and elaborated upon. Promoting digital dignity involves ensuring that individuals are treated respectfully, fairly, and ethically in the digital realm. Large tech giants can play a significant role in upholding digital dignity by implementing various strategies and initiatives.

References

1. https://mondo.com/insights/tech-giants-rank-protecting-privacy/.
2. https://www.eff.org/press/releases/att-verizon-other-telco-providers-lag-behind-tech-industry-protecting-users.
3. https://www.security.org/resources/data-tech-companies-have/.
4. https://iapp.org/resources/article/big-techs-shift-to-privacy-2/.
5. https://fortune.com/2022/01/28/big-tech-data-privacy-ethicaltech/.
6. https://www.forbes.com/sites/forbestechcouncil/2022/02/16/what-does-big-tech-actually-do-with-your-data/?sh=5d8fc8a2515f.
7. https://www.justsecurity.org/72439/dont-blame-privacy-for-big-techs-monopoly-on-information/.
8. https://fortune.com/2022/02/28/data-privacy-regulation-consumer-demands-big-tech/.
9. https://www.ikigailaw.com/article/150/why-should-tech-companies-care-about-human-rights.
10. https://www.fordigitaldignity.com/.
11. https://www.un.org/techenvoy/sites/www.un.org.techenvoy/files/230203_Alliance_for_Universal_Digital_Rights.pdf.
12. https://www.brookings.edu/articles/big-tech-threats-making-sense-of-the-backlash-against-online-platforms/.
13. https://timesofindia.indiatimes.com/readersblog/techlawbites/data-dignity-revolutionary-but-impractical-41022/.
14. https://onezero.medium.com/getting-cash-for-our-data-could-actually-make-things-worse-3793c52ec7e5.
15. https://www.xische.com/all-articles/2019/7/01/the-bold-idea-behind-data-dignity.
16. https://rm.coe.int/beyond-data-ownership/1680a1321d.
17. https://www.cigionline.org/articles/should-tech-firms-pay-people-their-data/.

18. https://gpai.ai/projects/data-governance/data-justice-in-practice-a-guide-for-impacted-communities.pdf.
19. https://www.undp.org/sites/g/files/zskgke326/files/2023-04/UNDP%20Drafting%20Data%20Protection%20Legislation%20March%202023.pdf.
20. https://www.zbw.eu/econis-archiv/bitstream/11159/435399/1/EBP078174910_0.pdf.
21. https://www.newyorker.com/science/annals-of-artificial-intelligence/there-is-no-ai.
22. https://www.zdnet.com/article/microsofts-new-data-dignity-team-could-help-users-control-their-personal-data/.
23. https://www.mybff.com/discover/data-dignity-in-web3-your-personal-data-is-more-important-than-you-think.
24. https://blog.datadividendproject.com/this-week-in-data-101-whats-a-mid/.
25. https://www.newyorker.com/science/annals-of-artificial-intelligence/there-is-no-ai.
26. https://www.expressvpn.com/blog/what-is-big-tech/.
27. https://projects.itforchange.net/state-of-big-tech/state-of-big-tech-capitalism-in-the-age-of-intellectual-monopoly/.
28. https://projects.itforchange.net/state-of-big-tech/rigging-the-rules-how-big-tech-uses-stealth-trade-agreements-to-undermine-and-prevent-digitalization-in-public-interest-and-how-we-can-stop-them/.
29. https://pop-umbrella.s3.amazonaws.com/uploads/83f0b3b9-516e-49d7-8753-8c668d4f8c95_2020__ASIA_DIG_REPORT__1_.pdf.
30. https://www.ineteconomics.org/perspectives/blog/big-tech-not-only-market-but-also-knowledge-and-information-gatekeepers.
31. https://www.nasdaq.com/articles/the-value-of-data-in-a-digital-world.

PART II
Legalities of Privacy

5

Efficacy of Right of Privacy in the Digital Ecosystem in Indian Context: With Emphasis on WhatsApp's Updated Privacy Policy

Abha Tiwari

Abstract

In India, the Right to Privacy is acknowledged as a fundamental right. This fundamental right extends to the digital sphere, where individuals participate in a vast digital ecosystem consisting of diverse platforms, applications, and services. Within this ecosystem, personal data is constantly generated, collected, and processed, serving purposes such as personalized experiences, targeted advertisements, and service enhancements. A pivotal event in this digital landscape was WhatsApp's privacy policy update in January 2021, which stirred significant apprehensions among users. The update essentially altered data sharing practices between WhatsApp and its parent company, Facebook. Users voiced concerns about the increased sharing of specific data, such as phone numbers and transaction information, with Facebook. The consent provided for this data sharing was perceived by some as inadequately informed and, in essence, a prerequisite for using the service, potentially contradicting the principles of genuine consent. Furthermore, users expressed fears that the policy infringed upon their privacy and encroached upon their right to control their personal information. As a response, both the judiciary and Competition of India took action against Meta. It is essential to implement clear regulations and informed consent mechanisms to guarantee that individuals maintain control over their personal data and that technology companies remain accountable for their data processing practices, adhering to privacy laws and fundamental principles.

Keywords - *Competition Commission of India, balance, privacy, WhatsApp, Constitution.*

Concept of Digital Ecosystem

Digital ecosystem refers to a network of interconnected IT resources that operate collectively. This network includes suppliers, customers, trading partners, applications, third-party data service providers, and their respective technologies. The pivotal factor for the ecosystem's success lies in its interoperability. Commonly spearheaded by market share leaders, digital ecosystems draw inspiration from the keiretsu model and rapidly drive transformations across various sectors like consumer goods, automotive, and healthcare. By integrating business-to-business (B2B) practices, enterprise applications, and data, organizations can effectively manage both existing and emerging technologies, automate processes, and sustain business growth.

Allowing an ecosystem to grow organically and without management can be detrimental to a business. Therefore, when constructing an ecosystem, it's vital to meticulously identify and regulate all dependencies. Crafting a digital ecosystem map is a crucial step in establishing a robust ecosystem. This visual representation details all digital tools and platforms employed within the organization, illustrating processes, data transfer mechanisms, and automation levels. Effectively mapping the ecosystem involves documenting systems that are presently unconnected or unable to exchange data, alongside identifying system users and responsible maintenance personnel.

Digital Ecosystem Management (DEM) has emerged as a novel discipline in response to the digital transformation and the integration of digital ecosystems within businesses. DEM primarily focuses on leveraging the ecosystem's potential to foster business growth by tapping into collective creativity and utilizing all available resources.

Examples of Digital Ecosystem in Daily Lives

Illustrations of digital ecosystems can be seen in contemporary banking applications, where a seamless integration of services like expense management, digital wallets, online banking, and digital passbooks occurs within a single platform. For instance, Danske Bank, a Danish firm, innovatively integrated customer data with housing market listings to provide potential homebuyers with comprehensive information, including tax estimations, realtors' catalogs, and trustworthy financial advice.

Similarly, the healthcare sector has witnessed substantial benefits from digital ecosystems. These ecosystems encompass every aspect of a patient's journey, from scheduling appointments and storing test results to recording prescriptions and sending appointment reminders. Digital healthcare ecosystems play a vital role in enabling healthcare organizations to maintain compliance with industry and government requirements, such as the Health Information Exchange (HIE), the Health Insurance Portability and Accountability Act (HIPAA), and the Health Information Technology for Economic and Clinical Health Act (HITECH).

Moreover, the automotive industry is progressively embracing digital ecosystems. Previously, automotive manufacturers would form alliances with original equipment manufacturers or establish contractual relationships with numerous suppliers for obtaining necessary parts. However, contemporary auto companies now utilize a diverse ecosystem comprising over thirty partners from various industries and countries to manufacture technologically advanced cars that are autonomous, electric, and seamlessly connected to company's digital platform.

Developments with Regard to Whatsapp Privacy Policy in India

On 14th October 2022, the Honble Supreme Court of India, dismissed the appeal filed by Meta-Whatsapp against the CCI probe into their Privacy policy. This tug of war started back in 2021, when Whatsapp rolled out its 'take it or leave it" privacy policy. The CCI had initiated a suo mottu case under Section 26(1) of the Completion Act by directing the Director-General, CCI (DG) to conduct an investigation in order to examine the potential abuse of dominance exercised by both Whatsapp-Meta platforms under Section 4 of the Act. Interalia the plea taken by Whatsapp before the High Court was that the users had opted voluntarily and hence were bound by the terms of Service, in any event those who did not wish to share their information were free to delete their accounts The Ministry of

Electronics and Information Technology (MeitY) is in the process of promulgating the Personal Data Protection Bill and that these tech platforms would be answerable to the provisions as stipulated therein.

After careful consideration of the arguments of CCI, the Bench concluded that "WhatsApp is the most widely used app for instant messaging in India. A communication network/platform gets more valuable as more users join it, thereby benefiting from network effects. The OTT messaging platforms not being interoperable, communication between two users is enabled only when both are registered on the same network. Thus, the value of a messaging apps platform increases for users with an increasing number of their friends and acquaintances joining the network. In India, the network effects have indubitably set in for WhatsApp, which undergird its position of strength and limit its substitutability with other functionally similar apps/platforms. This, in turn, causes a strong lock-in effect for users, switching to another platform for whom gets difficult and meaningless until all or most of their social contacts also switch to the same other platform. Users wishing to switch would have to convince their contacts to switch and these contacts would have to persuade their other contacts to switch. Thus, while it may be technically feasible to switch, the pronounced network effects of WhatsApp significantly circumscribe the usefulness of the same. The network effects have been reflected when despite increase in downloads of the competing apps like Signal and Telegram, user base of WhatsApp apparently did not suffer any significant loss. Further, Whatsapp also happens to be the second largest player in terms of market share in the relevant market of instant messaging and thus the next sizeable alternative available to users is Facebook Messenger, which too is a Facebook Group company. Thus, the conduct' of WhatsApp/ Facebook under consideration merits detailed scrutiny".

The Bench further noted that "the users are not likely to expect their personal data to be shared with third parties ordinarily except for the limited purpose of providing or improving WhatsApp's service. However, it appears from the wordings of the policy that the data sharing scheme is also intended to, inter alia, 'customise', 'personalise' and 'market' the offerings of other Facebook

Companies." In addition to these two pleas, the tech platforms had also taken the plea that they are separate and distinct legal entities. In this regard, the Court found merit in the submission and reiterated that it was one of the key issues with the 2021 Policy whereby there was a propensity to share the data of its users with Facebook Inc., the parent company of WhatsApp. Solely for the reason that the policies itself do not emanate out of Facebook Inc., Whatsapp cannot hide behind the fact that it is the direct and immediate beneficiary of the data sharing mechanism envisaged by the policies needless to mention that policy itself uses the words that the data sharing scheme is also intended to, inter alia, 'customise', 'personalise' and 'market' the offerings of other Facebook Companies Subsequently the Hon'ble Justice Yashwant Varma dismissed the plea of Facebook India Online Services Private Limited's petition challenging the probe initiated by Competition Commission of India (CCI) against it in connection with the national regulator's investigation into WhatsApp's privacy policy of 2021 observing that there has to be some end to "luxury to ligate".

The crux of the matter is that Facebook India had approached the Court arguing that it has nothing to do with WhatsApp's privacy policy, despite which CCI has clubbed it with Facebook Inc. and WhatsApp. Meanwhile, the Hon'ble SC while dismissing the appeal stated that "The Competition Commission of India (CCI) is an independent authority to consider any violation of the provision of the Competition Act 2002. When having prima facie opined that it is a case of violation of 2002 Act and thereafter when the proceedings are initiated by the CCI, it cannot be said that the initiation of the proceedings of the CCI are wholly without jurisdiction. The precedent of the Supreme Court has held that the proceedings before the CCI are required to completed be at the earliest. In view of the above, the CCI cannot be restrained from proceeding further with the enquiry/investigation for the alleged violation of the Competition Act. All the contentions available to the parties are kept open. Any observation made by the High Court be considered as tentative/prima facie".

This once again resonates the need for amendments as reported by the Parliamentary Standing Committee on commerce in its 172nd Report in reference with Promotion and Regulation of E-Commerce in India that the presence of an overarching regulatory body that glues together different Ministries/Departments and Authorities that presently regulate e-commerce will strengthen the regulatory regime and bridge the existing gaps in enforcement. Also that a Digital Market Division within the CCI be created as an expert division specifically tasked with regulation of the digital markets with participation from all the existing regulators concerned with e-commerce such as Department for Promotion of Industry and Internal Trade, Ministry of Consumer Affairs, Food and Public Distribution, Ministry of Electronics and Information Technology, Reserve Bank of India, etc. It is pertinent to mention that while on one hand the country continues to be caught in the web of complex global data privacy regulations impacting the economic hemisphere, on the other is trying to strike a balance between start-up ecosystem and need for regulation.

Movement towards Informational Monopoly

The Digital 2022: India Report indicates that there were 658.0 million internet users in India in January 2022. India's internet penetration rate stood at 47.0 percent of the total population at the start of 2022. This further indicates that internet users in India increased by 34 million (+5.4 percent) between 2021 and 2022. At the start of 2020, over 50 percent of India's population was actively using social networks and it is forecasted that by 2025, this penetration would be dive in to 67 percent of the country's population. Needless to mention these are the side effects of witnessing the flourishing telecommunication industry, providing cheap mobile data, blazing the trail of digital communication for the average Indian.

The pertinent question remains- What does this mean for a marketeer? Long shot, the golden opportunity to capitalise the market comprising of the consumers and advertiser. That means slice, dice, profile and target the consumer base monetising the personal data in lieu of the 'free' access to search engines, social networking, video streaming sites etc. The data centered business models of few tech giants such as Facebook (Meta), Google, Amazon, Uber etc., operate in such a manner that they are almost at the tipping edge of "informational monopoly" as they control multi-faced networks. The innovation triggered by digitalisation have generated substantial consumer benefits across the spectrum, simply by creating better accessibility, convenience along with variety at high velocity and low costs. Nevertheless, on the flip side there are severe impact with respect to competition in terms of market structure, conduct of firms, consolidations etc. Each of these practices had/has the potential to impair the competition intensity, growing concentration of market power and rising costs. Abuse of dominance stems from the economic insights wherein a firm is able to unilaterally influence the behaviour of the market in a permanent manner unlike a transient mode. This can be attributed to various causes such as high entry barriers, IP protection and/or regulations. The non-price characteristic of the digital market adds on to the complexity of the multi-faced dynamics of these platforms, considering the need to identify the relevant market where such influence or power is likely to have an impact. Therefore, in such zero price market, the pertinent question is -should such contraction of market be allowed to happen which is most likely to result in abuse of market power by disadvantaging consumer's privacy.

In order to examine this, we have to understand two major questions: What is the degree of protection accorded by the "Right of Privacy" to the data subjects? How effectively is the data subject able to exercise this 'Right of Privacy' or 'right to informational self-determination' in the context of the evolving digital ecosystem.

Degree of Protection of Right of Privacy of Data Subject

The whole context of GDPR essentially can be summarised to say that it is a 'right based regime' wherein a data subject should be able to exercise control and make informed decisions with respect to their personal data. In a study published to visualise the length of the fine print, for 14 popular apps threw up quite interesting fun facts. The shortest terms of the service are at least a few thousand words long. Microsoft service agreement does cover entire suite of product but it takes over an hour to read a bit less time than it would take to read Shakespeare's Macbeth. In all fairness it seems that about 97% of the population between the age group of 18-34, signs up without reading them.

Consent to allow usage of personal data, informed decisions? Any Thoughts! Big Data at the interface deploying Artificial Intelligence The 3V definition of Big Data- Variety, Volume & Velocity power big data that in turn shoots up patterns, trends, behaviours, choices, preferences that are otherwise are not comprehensible for the human capabilities. The proven, demonstrated bias or black box effect cast by deployment of AI and corresponding information asymmetry at the user end, dramatically reduces the possibilities of the paper tiger rights such as-right to access, right to be forgotten, etc. to be exercised. So technically there is a paradox. The balance between the objectives of the controller, armed with highly sophisticated tools versus of the rights of data subjects to be exercised, girded in fine prints running in few thousand words, absolutely stands no match. It may be argued that big data works with anonymised data and that it is not feasible to identify individuals from such data and so the data privacy regulations do not apply. This is again flawed, the reason being that this anonymised data is derived from such aggregated data that may not link an individual but surely relates back to a group classified based on certain opaque parameters. It is highly likely that there can be irreparable discrimination, denial and consequences on individuals, without them ever understanding the same. In the non-binding opinion issued by Advocate General Rantos, in the matter concerning the appeal filed by Meta Platforms against the decision the Higher Regional Court of Düsseldorfa competition authority may, in exercising its powers, take account of the compatibility of a commercial practice with the General Data Protection Regulation. This opinion though non-binding could be the beginning of integrated approach by the enforcement authorities in dealing with or formulating strategies to approach such matters.

Right to Informational Self-Determination

Coming to the second question - How effectively is the data subject able to exercise this 'Right of Privacy' or 'right to informational self-determination' in the context of the evolving digital ecosystem?

Let us examine the few provisions of GDPR Article 17(2) provides that "Where the controller has made the personal data public and is obliged pursuant to paragraph 1 to erase the personal data, the controller, taking account of available technology and the cost of implementation, shall take reasonable steps, including technical measures, to inform controllers which are processing the personal data that the data subject has requested the erasure by such controllers of any links to, or copy or replication of, those personal data." This squarely means that while there is a positive obligation on the Controller to take necessary steps in order to ensure that the data so shared with other Controllers is erased in accordance with the request of the data subject, nevertheless there is not a corresponding mechanism to ensure that this is exercised. It was further dependent on the fact that if such processing is identified at a later date, it may invite consequences, notwithstanding the processing that may continue till then.

Article 19 further reaffirms that "The controller shall communicate any rectification or erasure of personal data or restriction of processing carried out in accordance with Article 16, Article 17(1) and Article 18 to each recipient to whom the personal data have been disclosed, unless this proves impossible or involves disproportionate effort. The controller shall inform the data subject about those recipients if the data subject requests it." This provision again requires that appropriate information be provided tosuch other Parties who may have access to the information and may be processing it for various purposes, however in terms of accountability and/or compliance there are no additional provisions other than to rely on corresponding provision on unauthorised/ illegal processing. Therefore, in the given context, as the tech giants continue to scale newer heights acquiring and processing data in the central scheme of things, this empowerment per se may not bring about the balance that is sought to be achieved. There is a need to bring about appropriate interface that could redress the accumulation and dissemination of data at such massive scale.

References

1. Digital 2022: Report on India , February 2022, available at:
2. https://datareportal.com/reports/digital-2022-india.
3. https://tech.hindustantimes.com/tech/news/unacceptable-whatsapp-privacy-breach-on-google-pixel-7-pro-android-bug-controversy-explained-71683791425595.html#:~:text=An%20alleged%20privacy%20breach%20on,the%20owner's%20permission%20or%20knowledge.
4. https://inc42.com/features/why-industry-and-privacy-experts-are-worried-about-whatsapps-new-privacy-policy/.
5. https://www.devdiscourse.com/article/technology/1685916-whatsapp-privacy-policy-the-controversy-so-for-alarming-the-need-of-data-protection-law-in-india.
6. https://www.financialexpress.com/life/technology-whatsapp-puts-take-it-or-leave-it-privacy-policy-on-hold-in-india-timeline-of-events-surrounding-the-controversial-update-2287589/.
7. https://www.forbes.com/sites/aayushipratap/2021/06/15/whatsapps-fight-with-the-indian-government-over-its-data-privacy-rules-may-have-global-reverberations/?sh=512c1fc35a7a.
8. https://thehackernews.com/2021/01/whatsapp-delays-controversial-data.html.
9. https://www.theverge.com/2021/1/12/22226792/whatsapp-privacy-policy-response-signal-telegram-controversy-clarification.
10. https://www.thequint.com/tech-and-auto/whatsapps-policy-could-lead-to-stalking-of-its-users-cci-to-hc.
11. https://privacydesk.in/publications/articles/whatsapp-privacy-policy-the-controversy-so-for-alarming-the-need-of-data-protection-law-in-india/.
12. https://weeklyvoice.com/cci-directs-probe-agaist-whatsapp-over-privacy-policy-update/.
13. https://www.mobileworldlive.com/asia/asia-news/whatsapp-takes-more-heat-in-india/.

14. Karmanya Singh Sareen vs. Union of India, SLP (C) 804/2017.
15. Re: Updated Terms of Service and Privacy Policy for WhatsApp Users, (Competition Commission of India, 2021).
16. https://indianexpress.com/article/india/supreme-court-whatsapp-data-sharing-policy-plea-hearing-date-8179765/.
17. https://www.nytimes.com/2021/05/25/technology/whatsapp-india-lawsuit.html.
18. https://www.whatsapp.com/legal/privacy-policy.
19. https://www.whatsapp.com/privacy.
20. https://www.internetmatters.org/parental-controls/social-media/whatsapp/.
21. https://www.consumerreports.org/electronics/privacy/how-to-use-whatsapp-privacy-settings-a5254545737/.
22. https://www.digitaltrends.com/mobile/is-now-the-time-to-dump-whatsapp/.
23. https://nordvpn.com/blog/is-whatsapp-safe/.
24. https://www.theverge.com/2021/1/12/22226792/whatsapp-privacy-policy-response-signal-telegram-controversy-clarification.
25. https://www.leapxpert.com/whatsapps-privacy-policy-update-clears-the-way-for-new-features/.
26. https://theprobe.in/stories/the-whatsapp-privacy-policy-saga-indias-data-protection-regime-and-you/.
27. https://www.scobserver.in/cases/karmanya-singh-sareen-union-of-india-whatsapp-facebook-privacy-case-background/.
28. https://internetfreedom.in/explainer-whatsapp-privacy-policy-changes-2021/.

6

Human Rights Perspective of Personal Data Privacy

Anurita Yadav and Harish Kumar Verma

Abstract

In the age of Information Technology, the law on Data Protection will outline the ways through which the citizen's data or the way our personal information would be handled. As data is essentially our personal information, it directly affects our privacy. Data is frequently referred to as new fuel and plays a decisive role in the digital economy. It can easily let anyone understand a person's behavior. For example, targeted advertisement using our previous searches. Implementation of a new law ensuring personal data protection would change the nature and course of cyber security breaches and the whole path to our data protection. It calls for a change in the role of authorities, service providers, and the owner of personal data. Along with the right to privacy and the right to be forgotten as a fundamental right; the consequences of a personal data breach and its violation would attract penal consequences under the data protection law. In the absence of the Personal Data Protection Act, one of the significant breaches into the use of personal data goes unnoticed as with law it must be reported within a stipulated time. Also, what kind of data is collected and for what purpose remains unclear. This paper highlights the meaning, and changing nature of personal data protection, evolving nature of the digital economy, and the legal framework to protect the basic human right of privacy without which life with dignity would not be possible. Further, the paper would try to look into the challenges of data privacy and potent solutions in the field of Personal Data Protection in our country by emphasizing the role of the existing legal framework and its effective implementation in the digital economy.

***Keywords** - Privacy, Data, Protection, Digital Economy, Personal, Surveillance, India.*

Introduction

The term data derives its origin from Latin; data is the plural of the Latin word 'datum'. In a specific sense, data denotes measurements, and information taken out through a survey, census, or questionnaire, whereas in the generic sense, it represents thoughts, observations, and information of the people at large. There are varied types of data; in science, data ranges from data concerning the mode of generation, data concerning location factor, data concerning time factor, and data concerning the term of expression or mode of representation. In social sciences data ranges from data with reference to continuity, data with reference to the scale of measurement, data with reference to origin, and data with reference to the number of characteristics. Data in law connotes recorded information; all kinds of technical information or material developed, obtained, modified, stored, used, shared, etc. As data is essentially our personal information, it directly impacts our privacy. Personal data means any information relating to an identified or identifiable natural person ('data subject'). In the age of information technology, the law on Data Protection sketches the ways through which the citizen's data or the way our personal information can be controlled.

In the current scenario, India lacks specific legislation to govern and regulate the area of data privacy or protection of data. So far, the Contract Act, 1872 along with the Information Technology Act, 2000, and the Information Technology (Reasonable Security Practices and Procedures and Sensitive Personal Data or Information) Rules, 2011 are dealing with the area of data privacy. The shared and obtained information becomes a matter of grave concern in a society where rule of law prevails and people have a guaranteed fundamental right to privacy as an inherent part of the right to life, i.e., Article 21 and read with freedom of speech and expression Article 19(1) (a) which is subject to the reasonable restrictions stated under Article 19(2) of the Indian Constitution. However, there is a dire need for a specific statute to govern and regulate the ambit of protection of data and data privacy in India.

Human Rights Perspective of Data Privacy in the Digital Economy

The concept of Human rights is predicated on the idea that we all are human beings. Human rights are the basic rights inherently present in very human being; they are indivisible, inalienable, and universal in nature. Human rights are possessed by all humans under them being born as human beings. One of the basic human rights is the right to life with dignity and along with this fundamental right. The Courts have further interpreted the right to privacy also as a part of the right to life.

Privacy is not a gift rather it is a pre-condition to act as an autonomous individual which enables individuals to exercise their rights. Privacy enables an individual to act in an independent fashion which allows the individual to strive to act the way they want to. The concept of privacy is often understood as a right to be left alone which is not to be infringed upon. The understanding of privacy has gone through varied degrees of change and has evolved alongside the evolution of human history. Right to privacy in terms of all the information, an individual chooses to share. In the global information-driven society, the right to privacy to be protected is a Constitutional value, then it is required to be protected both online and offline. It talks about a space where individuals have the independence to exercise their rights autonomously.

However, in the digital age of modernization, the right to privacy is to be exercised and protected cautiously under the regulation of law. In the digital world, there is a multitude of challenges posed against liberty and the right to privacy. The right to life and liberty and the concept of privacy is interpreted as an absolute basic right. Privacy denotes a core area that is inviolable and overarching interference by any state or non-state actor will lead to a violation of this human right. The right to privacy is to be protected and legally regulated both online and offline. It is imperative to have specific statutory provisions underlining the role and liability of the user of the digital space while taking into consideration the dire need to protect the personal space of every individual as a basic human right to privacy both online and offline. The main issue with today's digital society is that technology categorizes people into abstract categories as user communities. This phenomenon undermines that people are complex; it is pertinent for the protection and implementation of human rights to recognize the complexity of humanism. One of the major recurring problems is that complexity of humans is ignored whenever human rights are ignored. Human rights have a cultural shift that is to be taken into consideration. Therefore, it is essential that the means and purpose of processing personal data is to be categorized into different groups and to appreciate the complexity of humanism. So, the different perspective is to be taken into account.

India as a signatory of international instruments like the International Covenant on Civil and Political Rights (ICCPR), 1966 has to ensure the protection of the right to privacy which calls for data privacy also in the digital era. Any kind of arbitrary interference can lead to the violation of the right to privacy comprising the right to privacy of personal life, family, home, honor, and reputation.

The main aspect which is covered via the rules is that it covers only sensitive data like passwords, sexual orientation, physical, mental, or psychological health conditions, biometric records, and information related to finance like bank details, medical records, etc. "Rule 4 requires a body corporate to provide a privacy policy on their website, which is easily accessible, provides for the type and purpose of personal, personal information, which is sensitive in nature collected and used, reasonable security practices and procedures." Privacy is of different types; home (spatial sphere) enables the individual to protect from illegitimate invasions of our physical and psychological cohesion; decisional privacy enables an individual the freedom to make decisions regarding their family and personal lives; informational privacy enables the collection and dissemination of data. If the data is about the individual, it contains personal elements and hence it requires protection.

Justice Chandrachud in Puttaswamy's case was of the view that "We are in an information age. With the growth and development of technology, more information is now easily available. The information explosion has manifold advantages but also some disadvantages. The access to information, which an individual may not want to give, needs the protection of privacy. Data protection is a major requirement for informational privacy. Data protection as a human right is important. We have big data which is composed of lots of complex information; new information is created by creating new data patterns; information about already exists but data is not about who I am being, it is about who I am like, what kind of data pattern I correspond to. How can we protect people from this kind of decision? Individuals cannot protect their data. We need some trusted foundation, and mechanisms, we need safeguards that correspond to dynamic data. Social media data change over time. How data is changing over time has to be regulated in order to protect personal data privacy.

Issues and Challenges

Personal Data Protection Bill becomes more important as anyone collecting our information regardless of their intention becomes crucial and requires our permission. Data is frequently referred to as new fuel and plays a decisive role in the digital economy. It can easily make anyone understand a person's behaviour. For example, targeted advertisement using our previous searches. Implementation of a new law ensuring personal data protection would change the nature and course of cyber security breaches and the whole path to our data protection. It calls for a change in the role of authorities, service providers, and the owner of personal data. Along with the right to privacy and the right to be forgotten as a fundamental right; the consequences of a personal data breach and its violation would attract penal consequences under the data protection law. In the absence of the Personal Data Protection Act, one of the significant breaches into the use of personal data goes unnoticed as with law it must be reported within a stipulated time.

What kind of data is collected and for what purpose remains unclear. No one is asked for consent and is not even told for what purpose data is being used. Government or authorities in the absence of any data protection law can work out any exemptions against the right to privacy in the name of exceptional circumstances, which simply might lead to large-scale challenges. Such exemptions would easily lead to greater surveillance, further leading to a violation of the very fundamental human right to privacy.

Cyberspace allows easy access. The ability to move freely online leads to an excess of exploitation and misuse of data that is available online. How these online platforms are to be used; rethinking has to be done. The failure comes from the myopic vision of the platform and its impact and to be taken into accounts the implication of the same. Any law relating to Personal Data Protection will regulate both how the government or any governmental agency and non-state actors (private organizations) in India and abroad shall process the personal data of the individuals. Also, when the data is to be used and how it will process or used either with the consent of the individual or in case of emergency the consent of the state is to be obtained. However, in the absence of any concrete legal mechanism, it is difficult not just to regulate and protect personal data. In the current scenario, it is the Information Technology Act, of 2000 protects from data breaches happening through the computer.

In the absence of any comprehensive laws governing personal data protection, there is a gross violation of the right to privacy which underpins the right to dignity along with freedom of speech and expression also to the breach of the human rights of individuals in the digital era as it would lead to the violation of the right to privacy; privacy a human right recognized by the United Nations Declaration on Human Rights, the International Covenant on Civil and Political Rights and in various other international and regional instruments. In this situation, any personal data/information can be easily misused or used in any political, social, commercial, religious, or economic at the hands of state or non-state actors in any manner.

One of the major issues of personal data privacy is that individuals are completely oblivious about the fact that how the information provided by them would be used or misused. They have no control over it once it is out there in the system in the absence of any legal mechanism its proper and systematic regulation becomes difficult and fixing accountability and liability becomes a challenge in the lack of law enforcement mechanisms concerning personal data privacy. There is an absence of informed consent and violation of the right to be deleted happens rampantly. In the absence of any legal definition of data privacy it becomes a herculean task for the state to regulate both personal and social behaviour of the individual online and offline in the context of protecting personal data privacy as both sharing and using information must be performed responsibly. The lack of a comprehensive legal framework poses a lot of challenges in a democratic country like India, where a large growing population is using digital space on regular basis for professional or personal work.

Conclusions and Suggestions

In terms of Personal Data Protection, the road ahead becomes a challenging point as the existing legal provisions concerning Personal Data Protection laws in our country are ambiguous.

The question of personal data or personal information becomes even more crucial in the absence of any concrete legislation. With the changing pattern of business, transaction, availing or providing services; it has now become pertinent in the digital age to use online mechanisms for the fulfilment of daily chores; whether it is hiring a service to pay Bills, everything requires the use of the online platform. Usage of online platforms makes it necessary for the customer to register themselves on the portal or the platform in question for which dissemination of private information becomes necessary; ranging from name and other private details to phone numbers to location everything is being shared. All in the lack of any stringent and concrete legislation dealing with the mechanism of data collection, its storage and utilization becomes a challenge as a misuse of all this confidential information can easily happen, and fixing responsibility and accountability is the biggest issue.

To make the legal framework effective, the researchers present some solutions -

i) Content moderation is required by ensuring that the public platforms are not exploited, and this can be ensured with the help of regulation through a statutory mechanism.

ii) There is a requirement for an increase in data literacy; people should be educated. Awareness must be created as a society. Data protection laws are to be used as laws enabling individuals to become more aware and responsible in terms of understanding their role along with responsibility towards society and to themselves.

iii) People must participate and understand the need for data privacy responsibly. The mechanism of data disaggregation must be dealt with in an organized manner. Self-identification and transparency are key elements in ensuring privacy which is a fundamental right of every individual.

iv) Accountability is the core element in protecting privacy which is an inherent part of the right to life with dignity. It is possible with the implementation of the codified specific law on data privacy or law governing the protection of data. With the proper systematic regulation of digital space, it would be possible to ensure the personal data privacy for the protection of the basic human right called right to privacy.

References

1. Yao-Huai, L., 2005. Privacy and data privacy issues in contemporary China. Ethics and Information Technology, 7, pp.7-15.
2. Bygrave, L.A., 1998. Data protection pursuant to the right to privacy in human rights treaties. International Journal of Law and Information Technology, 6(3), pp.247-284.
3. Bygrave, L.A., 2014. Data privacy law: an international perspective.
4. Chen, J., 2016. Asian Data Privacy Laws: Trade and Human Rights Perspectives.
5. D.Y. Chandrachud J. at para 457, Puttaswamy v. UOI (2017) 10 SCC 1.
6. Delgado-Santos, P., Stragapede, G., Tolosana, R., Guest, R., Deravi, F. and Vera-Rodriguez, R., 2022. A survey of privacy vulnerabilities of mobile device sensors. ACM Computing Surveys (CSUR), 54(11s), pp.1-30.
7. Greenleaf, G., 2012. The influence of European data privacy standards outside Europe: implications for globalization of

Convention 108. International Data Privacy Law, 2(2), pp.68-92.
8. Greenleaf, G., 2017. 2014-2017 Update to Graham Greenleaf; s Asian Data Privacy Laws-Trade and Human Rights Perspectives. UNSW Law Research Paper, (17-47).
9. Horvitz, E. and Mulligan, D., 2015. Data, privacy, and the greater good. Science, 349(6245), pp.253-255.
10. Information Technology (Reasonable Security Practices and Procedures and Sensitive Personal Data or Information) Rules, 2011.
11. Jain, P., Gyanchandani, M. and Khare, N., 2016. Big data privacy: a technological perspective and review. Journal of Big Data, 3, pp.1-25.
12. Kirby, M., 2017. Graham Greenleaf, Asian Data Privacy Laws: Trade and Human Rights Perspectives.
13. Makulilo, A.B., 2015. Asian Data Privacy Laws, Trade and Human Rights Perspective, by graham greenleaf.

7

A Comparative Study of India's Personal Data Protection Bill, 2018 and United Kingdom Data Protection Act, 2018

Anjali Raghav, Sanskriti Mishra and Richa Raghav

Abstract

The major drawback of digital technology came in the 21st century that is people are more inspired to work online but we often forget that older people, adults, and children are unaware of the cons of cyberspace. In a new era of digitalization, the concept of privacy emerges as a basic need of people at a global level. In 2018, the European Union formulated General Data Protection Regulation, 2018. The purpose is to ensure the right to privacy and personal data protection and security of data. This step of the European Union is a milestone in ensuring the protection of human rights globally. Digitalization has resulted in the violation of the right to privacy which violates Article 21 i.e. Right to life and Personal liberty concerning personal data protection and security of data in the Indian context. This research paper aims to present a comparative study of the United Kingdom Data Protection Act, 2018 which is in line with the European Union General Data Protection Regulation, 2018 and the recently proposed Bill - Personal Data Protection Bill, 2018 in India. The research paper seeks to find out the legislative intention and policy Framework in the United Kingdom and India in light of Personal Data Protection.

Keywords - *Data Protection, Digitalization, Human Rights, Right to Privacy, Constitution.*

Introduction

One of the core human rights is the right to the protection of personal information. Protecting privacy. Personal data protection aims to Protect privacy and ensure fundamental rights and freedoms when collecting, utilizing, and processing personal data. Starting from the 20th Century, India moved towards the LPG Reforms of 1991 (Liberalization, Privatization, Globalization Reforms). This policy aims to reform and improve GDP (Gross Domestic Product). For better implementation of the same, India started moving towards digitalization and a cashless economy to encounter some major issues like corruption, and black money and try to improve the quality of life of the people of India. Information technology will be used more and more to collect personal data, which could have both positive and harmful effects on individuals. Hence, this arises a major issue concerning the Right to privacy. Informational self-determination is now seen as a fundamental component of the rule of law.

The relevance acquired by the data has risen to previously unheard-of levels in the last several decades as a result of a strongly digitalized world and an increasingly digital India. The majority of cyber security attacks in India in recent years have been motivated by the desire to steal data. Due to the absence of strict data protection laws in India that could provide adequate protection to the citizens' sensitive and personal data in the recent past, numerous instances of data breaches, including the hacking of social media accounts, theft of credit and debit card details, and other privacy breaches, go unreported.

The Tribune Newspaper made the shocking assertion in an investigation published in 2018 that the complete Aadhaar Database, which contains the personally identifiable information of over 1.3 Billion Indians, could be accessed by paying a pitiful sum of 500 INR. To highlight the gaps in our data protection framework, this research paper was undertaken to examine the current Bill concerning personal data protection legislation in India while contrasting it with the UK's Data Protection Regulation Act, 2018. India has more than 500 million online users, and that number is rising.

It is currently the largest market in the digital economy, growing at a rate of more than 8% annually. As India's digital economy experiences an unparalleled boom, it may soon prove to be exceedingly difficult to deal with the problems brought on by a large number of digital transactions.

There will be a full implementation of the General Data Protection Regulation (GDPR). Although it is the most comprehensive set of laws on the subject to date, this data privacy law is by no means the first and is not expected to be the last.

The UK Data Protection Act, 2018, aims to update the requirements of the 1998 Act by considering how the data protection landscape is evolving. The Act also aims to modify the United Kingdom's legal system to adopt the GDPR. Given that the UK has left the EU, the GDPR will no longer apply to it, and for purposes of the law, it will be regarded as a third nation. The constraints it wants to impose on the breadth and depth of the right to privacy are the most important component of India's future data protection law.

Since the legislation is still in its infancy, it must take some time for the courts to develop a clear strategy for determining how far the right to privacy can be applied. The Puttaswamy ruling will undoubtedly launch a regime that will significantly protect the data privacy of Billions of Indians. It would be incorrect to assume that Puttaswamy marks the completion of the effort to protect citizens' data privacy. At this point, our main concerns are what the Puttaswamy ruling means, how it was justified, and how it would affect India's impending data privacy law.

Rights to Privacy

Informational self-determination is now seen as a fundamental component of the rule of law. The idea of data protection has changed from being a state to a mechanism to prevent improper implications with personally identifiable information and a key component of the social structure that views the right to informational self-determination as a necessary component of any society under the rule of law is the identifiable information of the citizens.

The rule of law prevails only when there was a prevalence of reasonableness and non-arbitrariness in society. Nowadays, personal privacy would be considered to be a vital part of Article 21 of the Constitution. Article 21 of the Constitution ensures the right to privacy this would also include the protection of personal data in cyberspace. The notion of the fact that data protection regulations have advanced to the point of being regarded as fundamental rights comes from the recognition of the right to privacy. In a similar vein, the Supreme Court of India ordered the Central government to create a data protection code only after identifying the right to privacy as an integral component of the right to life and liberty protected by Article 21 of the Indian Constitution.

Data Protection Policies of the European Union and the United Nations

Human dignity plays a vital role and defines as an unalienable fundamental right in the European Union. In this aspect of dignity, privacy, or the right to a private existence, the ability to be independent, in charge of the information about oneself, and the ability to be left alone is crucial. In addition to being a fundamental human right, privacy also has societal importance. Almost every nation in the world acknowledges privacy in some form, whether it is in its constitution or other laws. In addition, data protection is not yet recognized as a universal human right. The European Charter of Fundamental Rights, Article 8 of the European Convention of Human Rights, and Article 12 of the Universal Declaration of Human Rights all recognize the right to privacy and private life under Article 7. These are well-recognized rights by the international institutions which play a major role in formulating new laws.

Legal Regime Under the United Kingdom Data Protection Act, 2018 and India's Data Protection Bill, 2018

The United Kingdom has a national law governing personal data protection. Due to the existence of state-level laws in the U.S. and the U.K., it is simpler to establish liability in these countries. India's judiciary has widely discussed the concept of privacy, which was the ultimate source of helping people's mindset concerning the conceptions of data privacy. However, India's scenario differs greatly from that of the aforementioned nations. The Personal Data Protection Bill was ultimately introduced in Parliament by the Indian government on December 11, 2019, following more than two years of contentious debate. Ravi Shankar Prasad, India's Ministry of Information Technology, assigned this crucial legislation to a joint parliamentary committee for examination rather than pushing for its swift passage. The law will be discussed in the Indian Parliament in 2020 when the committee delivers its report on it, with the governing party very expected to secure a sizable majority in both legislatures. This rule has significant ramifications for nearly every company attempting to do business in India as India works to establish a complete data policy framework. Due to its size, GDP, and a large number of new people using the internet, India has a special ability to influence worldwide online businesses and global policies.

The discussion surrounding data protection in India culminated during the K.S. Puttaswamy v. Union of India (2017) "right to privacy" lawsuit procedures. In a groundbreaking ruling, a nine-judge panel of the Supreme Court of India upheld the right to privacy as a basic freedom. To create India's data protection policy throughout the lawsuit, the Indian government assembled a team of experts. Additionally, the Bill contains criteria that were absent from the original proposal, such as a strengthened right to erasure, obligations related to "anonymous data," and particular specifications for "social media mediators." There may be more chances for public input if the data protection authority ("DPA") is given a new need for policymaking. However, the major challenges behind the personal data protection Bill were many claims that in the cyber world, it doesn't matter where the data is physically located because the secret key might still be hidden from governmental agencies. The terms "national security" or "legitimate purposes" are ambiguous and arbitrary, which could result in the state meddling in citizens' personal affairs. Technology monoliths such as Facebook and Google oppose it and have questioned the protectionism of the data localization policy because of concern that it would spread to other nations. Social media corporations, industry professionals, and even ministers rejected it, claiming that now it had too many flaws to be efficient and profitable for customers and companies.

Later on, changes Personal Data Protection Bill, 2019, was thoroughly examined by the Joint Parliamentary Committee were made in order to create a complete legal structure for the digital ecosystem after this too many amendments were proposed. A thorough legislative framework is being developed in light of the Joint Parliamentary Committee's report. So, it is suggested that you withdraw. That is why this Bill was withdrawn due to these reasons the above-said Bill was withdrawn.

On the other hand, before the United Kingdom's Data Protection Act, 2018 was passed in May 2018, the United Kingdom had a statute governing data protection called the Data Protection Act of 1998 (DPA 1998), which was passed on March 1, 2000. Operations of the company are impacted by the Privacy and Electronic Communications Regulations (PECR) 2003, and digital advertising regulations have undergone changes. It includes the processing of location and traffic data, as well as the use of cookies and other comparable techniques, as per assignment help UK authorities. To replace the current ePrivacy Directive, the European Commission has proposed a draught regulation on privacy and electronic communications (Raul, 2018). The Data Protection Act of 2018 is an upgrade to the Data Protection Act of 1998 which places more focus on corporate responsibility and privacy. In contrast to the Data Protection Act of 1998, the latter modification also operates in tandem with the GDPR.

Major revisions from the Data Protection Act (1998) to the Data Protection Act include the following (2018) Exemptions from the right to be erased under the Data Protection Act are being controlled in accordance with the GDPR. May 25, 2018, Regulations that had been put into effect would be implemented for the EU Members and would still be in full force in the United Kingdom.

The Queen reaffirmed in her 2017 speech that the UK would continue to be an EU member state and that the Laws would go into effect, with the government expecting to put up legislation to carry them out. After the Brexit period, a measure is anticipated to be passed. The proposed Data Protection Bill's Regulation's implementation requirements are the subject of the law. The UK government planned to amend the data protection laws based on the Regulations when the New Data Protection Bill draught was due to be published in 2017.

Conclusions

Data is a valuable resource in the digital age that should be regulated by sovereign nations. If we talk about India there a moment for a robust data protection regime has come in this atmosphere. The Personal Data Protection Bill, 2018 keeps in mind the user's privacy while emphasizing user rights. It would be necessary to create a privacy commission in order to enforce these rights. The proposed legislation intends to make it possible to process personal data while acknowledging people's rights and "the necessity to process personal data for authorized purposes." It proposes a Data Protection Board to monitor compliance and apply fines, with the maximum fine claimed to not exceed five billion rupees and permits cross-border data exchanges with "certain notified nations and territories." The Data Protection Act of 1998 was the primary legislation governing the use and protection of personal data in the United Kingdom before the General Data Protection Regulation (GDPR) came into effect in 2018. To align with the European Union's General Data Protection Regulation, U.K. passed the Data Protection Act, 2018. It outlines principles that organizations must follow when processing personal data, including principles related to lawful processing, purpose limitation, data minimization, accuracy, storage limitation, integrity and confidentiality, and accountability.

References

1. Jason Asbury, Maria McClelland, Kris Torgerson, India Vincent & Jennifer Boling, Law and Business Technology: Cyber Security & Data Privacy Update, 20 Transactions: TENN. J. BUS. L. 1065, 1067-71 (2019).
2. Rs 500, 10 minutes, and you have access to Billion Aadhaar detailshttps://www.tribuneindia.com/news/archive/nation/rs-500-10-minutes-and-you-have-access-to-Billion-aadhaar-details-523361 (Accessed 25/10/2022).
3. Orla Lynskey, Deconstructing Data Protection: The Added-Value of a Right to Data Protection in the EU Legal Order, 63 INT'L & COMP. L.Q. 569, 577-81 (2014).
4. KS Puttaswamy v. Union of India, 2017 SCC OnLine SC 996.
5. Constitution of India, 1950.
6. UK's Data Protection Regulation Act, 2018.
7. General Data Protection Regulation, https://gdpr.eu/what-is-gdpr/.
8. https://edps.europa.eu/data-protection/data-protection/legislation/history-general-data-protection-regulation_en.
9. https://www.tandfonline.com/doi/full/10.1080/13600834.2019.1573501.
10. https://www.hrw.org/news/2018/06/06/eu-general-data-protection-regulation.
11. https://www.digitalguardian.com/blog/what-gdpr-general-data-protection-regulation-understanding-and-complying-gdpr-data-protection"complying-gdpr-data-protection.
12. https://eucrim.eu/news/new-data-protection-framework-eu-institutions/.
13. https://iapp.org/resources/topics/eu-gdpr/.

8

Rights of Victims: A Study with Special Reference to Right to Data Protection

Vijay Chaudhary and Poonam

Abstract

Right to information, right to participation in legal proceedings, including attending court hearings, right to protection and safety, right to have their safety and privacy considered throughout the legal process, right to compensation and restitution, right to Victim Impact Statement, right to be informed of offender's Status, etc. are some of the rights of victims. Data protection in the context of victim data is a critical aspect of safeguarding the privacy, security, and rights of individuals who have experienced various forms of victimization, including crimes, accidents, or other traumatic events. The rights of victims and data protection are crucial aspects of contemporary legal system that aims to safeguard individuals' interest and ensure justice. The intersection between these two domains explores the importance of data protection in the context of victim's rights and the challenges and potential solution that arise. Victims of crimes and abuse have the right to fair treatment, support throughout the legal process. However, in the digital age the collection, processing, and storage of vast amount of personal data pose challenges to protecting victims' privacy, dignity, and overall wellbeing. There is a need to balance the collection and use of personal data for investigation, focusing with the fundamental rights of victims including their right to privacy and protection from secondary victimization. It highlights the potential risk of data breaches, unauthorized access and the revictimization of individuals due to mishandling of their sensitive information.

Keywords - *Victims, Rights, Privacy, Data Protection, Crimes.*

Introduction

Just as certain persons are thought to have a high probability in indulging into criminal behavior, so also some others may have a great likelihood of being victimized. The Preamble of Indian Constitution is a fundamental document which secures all its citizens the justice whether it is social, economic, or political. All the citizens of India are entitled to have equal rights and equal justice, so the victims are. The Indian criminal justice system has much focus on the offender, sentencing and corrections. The discipline remains miniscule on research focusing on the victim, psychological and emotional harm, compensation, rights, and patterns of behavior of victims. In the existing system of criminal justice administration, the approach to address a victim is such that once a victim always a victim and it is very difficult to establish a victimless society. As the number of laws in in an increasing trend, so is the trend in the number of crimes and consequently the number of victims is also increasing proportionally. People prefer to commit crime for their individual gains and goals at the cost of victimizing other people. Of late, there has been a change in the attitude of not only the state, but also the people and society at large for providing protection and compensation to the victims keeping in view the gravity of loss caused to them due to the criminal act of the offender.

Concept and Meaning of Victim

The concept of victim is not new. It has its roots in many ancient languages that covered a great distance from north-western Europe to the Southern. The term victim in general parlance refers to all those who experience injury, loss, or hardship due to any cause and one of such causes may be crime.

Meaning of Victim

The definition of a victim is a person who has had something bad happen to him. An example of a victim is a person who was killed or robbed or otherwise had a crime committed against him. An example of a victim is a person who was cheated out of money by a scam.

Webster's New World College Dictionary

"One who is harmed or killed by another: a victim of a mugging, a living creature slain and offered as a sacrifice during a religious rite, one who is harmed by or made to suffer from an act circumstance, agency, or condition: victim of war, a person who suffers injury, loss, or death because of a voluntary undertaking: you are a victim of your own schemes, a person who is tricked, swindled, or taken advantage of the victim of a cruel hoax."

Oxford Dictionary

"A person harmed, injured, or killed because of a crime, accident or other event or action: victims of domestic violence earthquake victims, a person who is tricked or duped: the victim of a hoax, a person who has come to feel helpless and passive in the face of misfortune or ill-treatment, a living creature killed as a religious sacrifice, sacrificial victims, for the ritual festival."

U.N. Declaration of Basic Principles of Justice for Victims of Crime and Abuse of Power, 1985

"Victims" means persons who, individually or collectively, have suffered harm, including physical or mental injury, emotional suffering, economic loss, or substantial impairment of their fundamental rights, through acts or omissions that are in violation of criminal laws operative within Member States, including those laws proscribing criminal abuse of power."

"A person may be considered a victim, under this Declaration, regardless of whether the perpetrator is identified, apprehended, prosecuted, or convicted and regardless of the familial relationship between the perpetrator and the victim. The term "victim" also includes, where appropriate, the immediate family or dependants of the direct victim and persons who have suffered harm in intervening to assist victims in distress or to prevent victimization."

Origin and Development of Concept of Victim

The origin of concept of victim or victimology as a part of criminology may be traced back to 1940s when founders of this branch of knowledge notably Mendelson, Von hentig initially tended to use the term. The concept of victim or victimization has changed its ancient roots to its modern definition. The field of study that analyses victim is known as victimology and it has evolved as well. victimology examines several factors including victim attitude and conduct their relationship with offenders and societies treatment of them.

The father of victimology is two German criminologists Hans-Von-hentig and Benjamin Mendelson. They studied the behaviour characteristics and vulnerability of crime victims. A shift in the definition and study of victims came with the women's movement of the 1970's and 80s. Those in the women's movement worked to provide care for victims of rape and domestic violence, creating Rape Crisis centres and other form of support and advocacy. As a result of victimology studies in 1970s and beyond and social movements such as feminism, today there are many different support groups and organizations dedicated to helping victims' families and friends of missing persons, parents of murdered children and mothers. Against drink and driving are just a few of the groups that provide counsel and support to victims and their families. Even the terminology has changed as many victims now prefer to call themselves "survivors".

Categorization of Victim

Mendel Sohl studied victims since their contribution to crimes and classify them into various categories. Completely innocent victim for example children person in sleep, Victims with minor guilt and victims of ignorance such as pregnant women, Voluntary victims such as the one who commits suicide or are killed by euthanasia, victims who are more guilty than the offender such as persons who provoke others to commit suicide and Criminal types of victims who commit offences against others and get guilt or hurt by others in self-defence.

Victims of Sexual Offences

Victim privacy and personal integrity gets violated that in term causes physical and psychological harm and for many its effect is a long term one, impairing the capacity for personal relationship, altering their behaviour and values and generates endless fear. Victims who report for sexual offences suffers at each stage after reporting the police, during investigation, during medical examination of victim of rape or at the trial. The witness of victim also suffers harassment, humiliation, financial loss, loss of time. All these resulting in mental pain and suffering to the victim. Though constitution of India provides for equal justice and free legal Aid under Article 39-A but in practice criminal justice system does not adequately compensate the victim of rape for pain, suffering and loss of earning. In the end, even the offender is punished, victim does not gain anything as there is no scheme to rehabilitate and treat that victim.

Victims of Motor Accident Cases

Victims of accident are those who sustain bodily injury, causes either permanent or temporary disability or the legal representative of deceased who dies because of accident case. It may arise because of use of motor vehicle, railway train, aircraft, a ship, or wide operating machine in a factory. The victims of accident have the right to claim compensation under statute. There is no such right of other victim though compensation has been awarded in few cases by a discretion of Courts.

Victims of Social Offences

Social offences include crime of atrocities committed based on caste and hatred. On Commission of atrocity the victim suffers not only bodily or mental pain but also eminent feeling of insecurity which is not present in the victim of any other crime. Even after recovery of bodily injury he continue suffers mental pain. During rest of his life his physical strength is deteriorated making him unfit in his profession and occupation which also affects the economic condition of victim. This results into deterioration physical, mental, educational, social, economic, and sociological status of victim. Victim suffers direct financial losses, and he must spend lots of money on treatment besides his wealth is wasted in litigation. Commission of atrocity affects adversely on the education progress not only of the victim but also of his family members.

Victims of Abuse of Power

Victims of abuse of powers includes those persons who are either victims of illegal detention or police atrocities custodial violence of like. Every individual has inalienable right to life and personal liberty that has guaranteed by Article 21 therefore this Article became a support of poor against government lawlessness. The Supreme Court has attempted to fill lacuna in the field of compensation for police accesses by using its power under Article 32 of Indian Constitution. Article 22 of Constitution of India protects every individual from illegal detention.

Crimes' Victim

Victims mean the person or persons who have suffered financial, social, psychological, or physical harm because of an offence, and includes, in the case of any homicide, an appropriate member of the immediate family of any such person. Therefore, the term 'crime victim' generally refers to any person, group, or entity who has suffered injury or loss due to illegal activity. The harm can be physical, psychological, or economic." The legal definition of victim' typically includes a person who has suffered direct, or threatened, physical, emotional, or pecuniary harm because of the commission of a crime; or in the case of a victim being an institutional entity, any of the same harms by an individual or authorized representative of another entity. Group harms are normally covered under civil and constitutional law, with hate crime' being an emerging criminal law development, although criminal law tends to treat all cases as individualized.

Rights of Victims

The rights of victims vary by country and legal system, but there are common principles and standards that generally apply to victims of crimes. Victims of rights fall under different categories.

General Rights of Victims

Right to be treated with self-respect, right to notification, right to be present, right to be heard, right to rational protection from terrorization and injury, right to restitution, right to information, right to compensation especially for crimes of violent nature, right to speedy proceedings and rights to privacy are the general rights of victims. Victims may have the right to receive compensation for losses and expenses incurred as a result of the crime. This can include medical expenses, property damage, and lost wages. They also have the right to receive restitution from the offender. In some legal systems, victims have the right to participate in restorative justice processes, which focus on repairing the harm caused by the crime and promoting healing and reconciliation.

Rights of Victims under Indian Constitution

Our Constitution of India is the supreme law of the land and the mother of all existing laws. The Indian Constitution includes some provisions for victim's rights, their protection, and respects the idea of victim compensation. Article 14 and Article 21 inculcates some vital fundamental rights that are to be read with Directive Principles of State Polices Mentioned in Articles 39A, 41, 46, and 51C. As per Article 39A the state offers free legal assistance and guarantees for promoting justice on the grounds of equal opportunity. Article 41 of the Indian Constitution is relevant to the concept of victimology in a very broad manner as it commands inter alia so that the state might start making provision to secure public support in cases of incapacitation and in cases of unjustifiable want. If one empathetically interprets and imagines creatively one can discover the early stages of constitutional victimology. Moreover, Article 21 assures against unfair deprivation of life and liberty by compelling the state to compensate victims of criminal violence.

Rights of Victims under Indian Penal Code

The Indian Penal Code is applicable to all Indian citizens who commit crimes within the Indian Territory. It is a list of offences and its punishment. The Code describes offence as an act or omission punishable by law. One of the major advantages to victims protection was received by the Criminal Law Amendment Act, 2013 since, for the first time, it had introduced a number of new crimes for protection of women against acid attacks, sexual harassment, voyeurism and stalking and it also widened the scope of definition of rape in IPC.

The two significant remedies of criminal justice system are compensation and restitution which now, have become civil remedies during the modern period. This invited the attention of various jurists to analyze the problems of victims from a different perspective to improve their position and bring them on equivalence with the accused.

Rights of Victims under Cr.PC.

The victim is represented by the Public Prosecutor who is appointed by the state. A proviso has been added to Section 24(8) which allows the victim to choose an advocate of his choice for assisting the public prosecutor according to the amendment of 2008. However the Code identifies few rights that favor the victims, but they are not as operative as those of rights of accused. For example, the code grants a right to victim to choose his own private lawyer, but the authority given to that lawyer is limited to appointing where he can only submit the written arguments after the evidence is recorded and only after the court permits.

Rights of Victims and Data Protection

One of the most important aspects of privacy is the right to be forgotten. In India, this right is not well protected. In fact, there are a few cases where people have had their personal information published online, even after they have asked to remove it. This can have a negative impact on their reputation and their ability to find work. Another issue that is impacting privacy is data collection. The right to privacy and data protection has emerged as a key issue in the digital era. Recent trends show that the right to privacy is being increasingly recognized as a fundamental right. The right to data protection includes the right to be free from unauthorized access, use, or disclosure of one's personal information. The right to data protection also includes the right to be informed about the collection, use, and disclosure or non-disclosure of one's personal information that also includes the information related to victim and his family. This is especially true in the context of the digital world, where individuals have a greater degree of control over their personal information. There are many instances where the identity and personal data related to victim especially rape victims and victims of atrocities have been published and disseminated despite of prohibition of disclosure of identity and data related to those victims under various statutes. Victims and witnesses, but also suspects of crimes have the right to have their data duly protected in the context of a criminal investigation or a law enforcement action.

Police and criminal justice authorities will apply the principles of data protection by design and data protection by default at the beginning of any process to do with personal data, for example when developing new databases. Those responsible for processing personal data will be held more accountable for their work.

For example, authorities must appoint data protection officers to take care of personal data protection within their organisation. They must also ensure the national supervisory authority is notified of serious data breaches as soon as possible. Every citizen must have an equal right of access to their personal data. Even the victims must always have the right to approach the police and criminal justice authorities directly and ask for access to their personal data. If those authorities decide to accept such a request, they must provide the personal data free of charge. The authorities may also decide to limit the right of access when they want to prevent hindering an ongoing investigation or to protect national security or the rights and freedoms of others. Such limitations must be in line with the necessity and proportionality requirements of statute.

Access to victim details must be restricted to authorized personnel only, such as law enforcement, legal professionals, healthcare providers, and support service staff. Implement strict access controls to prevent unauthorized access. Clear policies for the retention and deletion of victim data must be in place, ensuring that data is kept only for as long as necessary and securely deleted when no longer needed. Whenever possible, anonymize or pseudonymize victim data to reduce the risk of identifying individuals. This can enhance privacy while still allowing for analysis and research. Training to staff handling victim data on data protection principles, privacy laws, and best practices must be conducted.

Conclusions

The right to privacy for victims of crimes is a fundamental aspect of ensuring their well-being, safety, and dignity throughout legal processes and beyond. This right is recognized and protected in various legal systems and international human rights standards. Protecting the privacy of victims of motor accidents is of paramount importance to ensure their well-being, dignity, and mental and emotional recovery. The right to privacy and data protection in the digital era is a complex and sensitive issue. There are several important considerations to consider when designing and implementing policies and procedures related to these rights. First and foremost, it is important to ensure that any data collection and processing activities are carried out in a transparent and fair manner. Individuals should be able to understand why their data is being collected and how it will be used. Second, it is important to ensure that any data that is collected is properly protected. This means that data should be kept confidential and only used for the purposes for which it was collected. Finally, it is important to ensure that individuals have the right to access their data and to change it. Balancing the need for transparency and information sharing with the imperative to protect the privacy and well-being of motor accident victims is crucial in promoting a just and supportive environment for individuals affected by such incidents. Legal and ethical frameworks should be continually evaluated and updated to address evolving challenges related to privacy in the context of motor accidents.

References

1. Anil Trehan, Penology and Victimology (Shreeram Law House, Chandigarh) 2011.
2. UN Declaration of Basic Principles of justice for victims of crime and abuse of Power, 1985, available at: https://www.ohchr.org/en/instruments-mechanisms/instruments/declaration-basic-principles-justice-victims-crime-and-abuse.
3. N.V. Paranjape, Criminology Penology and Victimology (Central Law Publications, Allahabad) 2011.
4. Ahmad Siddique, Criminology, Penology and Victimology 315 (EBC Publishing Pvt. Ltd. Lucknow) 2021.
5. Constitution of India, 1950.
6. The Motor Vehicle Act, 1988.
7. Krishna Pal Malik, Penology, Victimology and Correctional Administration in India, (Allahabad Law Agency, Faridabad) 2011.
8. S.S. Srivastava, Criminology, Penology and Victimology (Central Law Agency, Allahabad) 2017.
9. Indian Penal Code, 1860.
10. The Criminal Law (Amendment) Act, 2013.

9

Constitutional Aspect of Personal Data Protection Bill, 2019

Avinash Krishna Goswami and Komal Vig

Abstract

The Personal Data Protection Bill, 2019 was introduced in the Lok Sabha on 11th December 2019 and submitted to the Joint Parliamentary Committee of both Houses of Parliament for study and recommendation on 12 December 2019. This law mentions both personal and non-personal data and categorizes itself as a fundamental foundation for preserving the privacy of data in both digital and non-digital formats. This measure was aimed to defend the individual's basic right to privacy, as provided by Article 21 of the Indian Constitution. Following the Supreme Court's ruling in Justice K.S. Puttaswamy v. Union of India, the right to privacy has been recognised as a fundamental right. This law defines a framework applicable to the processing, storage, and transfer of any type of personal data in various economic, academic, industrial, and societal sectors. This law also includes measures concerning Non-Personal Data. On this measure, the joint parliamentary committee has made recommendations and prepared a report that identifies many discrepancies from the 2019 draught law. On 16th December, 2021, the committee chaired by Sh. P.P. Chaudhary submitted a report suggesting modifications and suggestions. The goal of the researchers is to examine the proposed legislation and the report on it by the joint parliamentary committee in light of the constitution's vision for Personal Data Protection. On 3rd August 2022, the measure was dropped after the house passed a resolution declaring that they will present a completely new law tackling this issue.

Keywords - *Personal Data, Bill, Privacy, India, Constitution.*

Introduction

Privacy is the condition of being alone without external interference. It protects an individual's personal information from being in the public domain by constructing a wall and regulating the borders, shielding them from uninvited interference and allowing them to regulate their own life. Article 12 of the Universal Declaration of Human Rights Act of 1948 reads, "No one shall be subjected to arbitrary interference with his privacy, family, home, or communication, nor will his honor or reputation be attacked." Article 21 of the Indian Constitution recognizes the Right to Privacy as one of the Fundamental Rights vested in the inhabitants of India.

Evolution of Right to Privacy

The declaration of the Right to Privacy as a Fundamental Right has a history, as it was not a part of Article 21 of the Indian Constitution from its creation. It fought for almost 63 years before becoming a member of it. Privacy was first examined in the case of MP. Sharma v. Satish Chandra, in which the court rejected the idea of Right to Privacy on the grounds that it was not included in the Constitution. In Kharak Singh v. State of U.P., the Supreme Court of India declared, "In this case, the Right to Privacy was claimed to challenge the police monitoring of the accused." The court in this case also rejected the claim about the Right to Privacy, finding that it is not included in the Indian Constitution. However, Subba Rao J.'s dissenting opinion supported the principle of Right to Privacy." The court in Gobind v. State of Madhya Pradesh considered the idea of Right to Privacy as a component of the Right to Personal Liberty but did not recognize it as a fundamental right. Even in R. Rajagopal v. State of Tamil Nadu, the court acknowledged the Right to Privacy as a constitutional position, but it was not yet recognized as a Fundamental Right. In State of Maharashtra v. Madhukar Narayan Madikar, the Supreme Court upheld a prostitute's right to privacy, ruling that "even a lady of questionable morality is entitled to her private, and no one may intrude it at will." In the wake of the Maneka Gandhi v. Union of India case, the scope of Article 21 of the Indian Constitution has been broadened to include additional rights that are integral to the Right to life and personal liberty. In the case of Justice K.S. Puttasawamy (Retd.) v. Union of India, the 9-

judge bench of the Hon'ble Supreme Court ruled unanimously: "Right to Privacy as a Fundamental Right under Article 21 of the Constitution of India." The Court has also ordered the creation of a mechanism to regulate the privacy of the people, so as not to violate Article 21 of the Indian Constitution.

Right to be forgotten is the right to have personally identifiable information erased from the internet, search databases, websites, and other public platforms. This right was first acknowledged by the European Union in 2014, when the European Court of Justice ruled in the case of Google Spain vs. Mario Costeja Gonzalez that European data protection law gives individuals the right to request that search engines such as Google remove certain results for queries relating to their name. When selecting what to delist, search engines must consider if the content in question is "inaccurate, insufficient, irrelevant, or excessive," as well as whether the public has an interest in the information continuing in search results.

A search engine is a website that searches, recognizes, gathers, and organizes content in a database according to Keywords or characters input by the user; it is especially useful for identifying websites on the World Wide Web. These search engines may include sensitive, personal, outdated, or irrelevant information, making the right to be forgotten a fundamental component of the right to privacy. The court ruled that search engines are subject to the European Union's data protection directive because the data found, indexed, and stored by search engines and made available to their users include information relating to identified or identifiable natural persons and would constitute "personal data" under Article 2(a) of Directive. The right to be forgotten plays a crucial role when the directive's terms are violated. The regulation specifies that the controller of such data or the operator of search engines is responsible for ensuring compliance with Article 6(1). This decision recognised the right to be forgotten, allowing individuals to request that search engines remove or delete unnecessary or outdated personal data.

Status of Right to Forgotten in India

In India, the "Right to be Forgotten" is a developing basic right that, via numerous court pronouncements, is seen as an inherent aspect of the right to life and personal liberty (Article 21). Although there is no official mechanism to control this right in India as there is in the United Kingdom, the judicial judgement has expressed a clear position about the preservation of this right and instructed the Parliament to establish laws governing the Right to be Forgotten. Right to Privacy encompasses not /only the protection of physical privacy, but also the protection of digital privacy that may directly impact the dignity of the individual.

Judicial Outlook

In Sredharan T vs. State of Kerala, the Kerala High Court acknowledged "Right to be Forgotten" as a component of the Right to Privacy. The Petitioner filed a Writ Petition requesting that the court remove the name and personal information of the rape victim from the search database in order to protect her identity. "The court held in favor of the petitioners, recognizing the 'Right to be forgotten,' and issued an interim order directing the search engine to remove the petitioner's name from orders posted on its website until further orders are issued."

In Sri Vasunathan vs. Registrar General, the High Court of Karnataka acknowledged the "Right to be Forgotten in sensitive matters involving women in general and very sensitive instances including rape or harming her modesty and reputation". J. Reddy noted, "This is in accordance with the trend in western nations of the "Right to be forgotten" in sensitive instances involving women in general and very sensitive cases including rape or hurting the modesty and reputation of the individual in question."

In the case V. vs. High Court of Karnataka, the Court ruled in favor of the petitioner. "The court determined that "this would be consistent with the trend in western countries, where the "Right to be forgotten" is routinely applied in sensitive cases involving women in general, as well as particularly sensitive cases involving rape or harming the modesty and reputation of the individual involved."

In Sudhanshu Rout vs. State of Odisha, the Orissa High Court "addressed the right to be forgotten as a remedy for victims of sexually explicit videos/pictures often shared on social media, a venue where rejected lovers intimidate and abuse women."

In the case of Justice KS Puttaswamy vs. Union of India, the Supreme Court of India emphasized that "the acknowledgment of Right to be Forgotten does not entail that all elements of a person's previous life have to be erased, since some may have societal ramifications." If we were to recognize a comparable right, he would no longer want his personal data to be processed or retained and should be allowed to have it removed from the system if it is no longer essential, relevant, or accurate and serves no legitimate purpose."

In this case, Jorawer Singh Mundy @ Jorawar Singh Mundy vs. Union of India and others, the Delhi High Court stated, "there may be irreparable harm inflicted to Mundy's social life and professional prospects notwithstanding his acquittal in the 2013 case." Therefore, Google was told to delete the judgement from its search engine and Indian Kanoon was instructed to block the judgement." A temporary measure of protection was granted to him.

Additionally, the Supreme Court has placed restrictions on this privilege. Such as in the context of the right to freedom of expression and information, the execution of a public duty for the public good, the existence of a legal obligation, or the discovery of historical, scientific, and statistical data. This right conflicts with several other rights, such as Article 19 of the Indian Constitution, poses a threat to journalism, and imposes unjustified restrictions on the Right to Information, among others. Therefore, there is a need for a system that clarifies the Right to be Forgotten and a regulatory body for such rights. This is the impetus for the 2019 Personal Data Protection Bill, which aims to prevent the vulnerability of an individual's personal data.

Report of the B.N. Srikrishna Committee

After the case of Justice KS Puttaswamy vs. Union of India, the court ordered Parliament to establish a regulatory framework to manage the violation of privacy of the person and a regulatory system to oversee Privacy rights in the digital age. As a result, in August 2017, the BN Srikrishna Committee, chaired by Justice B.N. Srikrishna, was established to explore issues related to data protection and provide a regulatory system to penalize data breaches. On July 27, 2018, the Expert Committee presented its findings and Bill draught to the Ministry of Electronics and Information Technology.

The study includes a section on the definition of personal data, as it is essential to clarify what constitutes personal information. It specifies that data from which an individual may be directly or indirectly identified or identifiable are considered personal data. The Committee endeavored to distinguish between the protection of personal and sensitive personal data, since the handling of sensitive personal data might result in more harm to the individual. Sensitive data relates to private matters for which there is a greater expectation of privacy (e.g., caste, religion, and sexual orientation of the individual).

When we discuss consent-based processing, it is one of the first concerns that arise. Consequently, the committee declared that consent must be regarded as a prerequisite for the processing of personal data. Permission in this context does not imply simple consent, but rather free and informed consent, and the data protection rules must adequately safeguard the interests of vulnerable populations such as children. Regarding sensitive personal data, there should be specific consent. In addition, the committee concluded that it is impractical to get consent in all situations, hence there should be a distinct system for processing data without consent. It has divided it into four distinct categories: where it is necessary for the state to carry out its welfare functions; in conformity with the law and court orders; in order to preserve an individual's life; and in other restricted circumstances.

The Committee has also suggested the establishment of an institution that will investigate any violations of the data protection regime and can take measures in response to such violations. All of these responsibilities will be handled by the data trustee, who is accountable for such administration. The committee has also proposed revisions to other laws, including as the Information

Technology Act of 2000 and the Aadhaar Act of 2016, in order to strengthen data protection regulations. The committee has also considered the fiduciary connection between the individual's interests about his personal data and the data service provider having access to it. Therefore, the service provider of these data is required to treat the personal information of individuals fairly.

Personal Data Protection Bill, 2019

The Personal Data Protection Act of 2019 aims to respect the rights of data owners while building a firm foundation for privacy protection. In addition, the measure implements "digitally enabled consent," which ensures that consent is supplied in real time and that the data owner always has the ability to revoke information. Following the KS Puttaswamy case, which declared the Right to Privacy to be a Fundamental Right, a committee led by Justice Sri Krishna was created to draught the Personal Data Protection Bill, 2019. The privacy framework was made available for feedback from the general public, privacy experts, and academics in order to address the shortcomings of the 2018 draught and make it more dynamic and suited to the requirements of the quickly expanding digital world. These contributions finally contributed to the Personal Data Protection Act of 2019

The Personal Data Protection Bill 2019 was a comprehensive proposal for data protection legislation proposed in December 2019 to the Lok Sabha. The Act attempted to protect individuals' right to data privacy. In addition, it sought to establish a relationship of trust between the data principle, the owner of personal data, and the data fiduciary, the entity responsible for choosing how and why personal data will be treated.

The Personal Data Protection Bill, 2019 will regulate how data trustees handle the personal data of data principals. Data stewards would be subject to obligations and required to treat personal information in accordance with legal requirements and other non-consensual grounds. The rights of data principals would include access, deletion, and portability. It has an exemption clause that allows the federal government to exclude any agency from the law's application. It required the establishment of a Data Protection Authority to execute the law. It stipulates both penalties and incentives. The Data Protection Bill of 2021 incorporates revisions to the Personal Data Protection Bill of 2019 proposed by the JPC.

Report of the Joint Parliamentary Committee

The report of the Joint Parliamentary Committee proposes 81 modifications and 12 suggestions to the Bill in order to close the present gaps. The Data Protection Act of 2021 amends the scope and objectives of the Personal Data Protection Act of 2019. It is intended to restrict the scope of the proposed legislation to digital data, as stated in the Long Title and Preamble, which promotes protecting "digital privacy" rather than "privacy" as the Personal Data Protection Bill of 2019 recommends. Second, it is proposed to replace "personal data" with "data" in the title of the Personal Data Protection Bill, 2019. As a result, the proposed draught suggests Data Protection Bill 2021 rather than "Personal" Data Protection Bill 2021 for the title of the new law. It stresses the effort to include non-personal data in the new framework. The part on the legislation's material scope now suggests that it applies to "the processing of non-personal data, including anonymized data." The Joint Parliamentary Committee proposes that a framework for non-personal data be included in the same act when the non-personal data rules become official. Third, the draught legislation now includes the phrase "state interest and security." State security is an essential objective, but it must be ensured that it does not result in wide, indiscriminate data processing that undermines privacy and leads to monitoring. Among the most important recommendations are:

Consent for Processing Personal Data

The 2019 PDP Bill contains a provision mandating consent for the processing of personal data. The DP Bill 2021 stipulates that the provision of goods or services cannot be "denied on the basis of the exercise of choice." This clause related to the notion of free consent and strengthens the position of data subjects. The data subject cannot be refused a service if they refuse to agree to the processing of their personal data.

Regarding Right to Forget or Erasure

Under the Right to be Forgotten, the committee acknowledged the necessity to protect an individual's privacy; yet there may be cases in which such erasure is not possible due to legal obligations. As a consequence, it was suggested that the DPA evolve in accordance with global best practices and formulate legislation that ensure data principals' rights may be exercised. In contrast, data stewards may fulfil these responsibilities most efficiently. It must also take the government's interests into consideration.

Regarding Protection of Children's Data

The committee proposed getting a child's permission again under the Majority Act when he reaches the age of majority, which is 18 years old. However, the services will continue unless the individual withdraws consent or opts out. In addition, a Significant Data Fiduciary has been introduced under Article 26(1)(g), as a fiduciary that works exclusively with children's data must register with the DPA. Under clause 16, the committee also deleted the concept of a Guardian Data Fiduciary since it was deemed unnecessary.

On Social Media Intermediaries

The committee observed that the majority of social media intermediarie serve as internet-based mediators and communication platforms. As a consequence, the committee proposed adopting the term "social media platform" instead of "social media intermediary" since it is more appropriate. As a result, it recommended inserting a provision that defines a social media platform as "a platform that primarily or exclusively facilitates online interaction between two or more users and enables them to generate, publish, distribute, disseminate, or access anything using its services."

Personal Data Protection Bill and Article 21 of the Indian Constitution

Article 21, which is regarded the most organic and progressive provision in the Constitution of India, is the heart and spirit of the document. This is the only article that discusses the Right to Life and Personal Liberty, as well as other rights that are inextricably linked to these two rights. Maneka Gandhi v. Union of India was a landmark decision that resulted in a wider reading of Article 21. Right to Privacy as a fundamental right was codified in Article 21 alongside the rights to life and personal liberty.

Personal Data Protection Bill was drafted to preserve the Right to Privacy. Currently, the number of Internet users in India is growing exponentially. Consequently, there is a growing demand for a regulatory structure to safeguard data privacy. Although 81 amendments and 12 suggestions have been offered by the Joint Parliamentary Committee as a result of the Bill's privacy-infringing gap.

General Data Protection Regulation and Indian Laws

In today's world, when every task is performed digitally, data protection has become one of the most important issues on the planet. The European Union recently enacted one of the strictest privacy regulations in the world, known as GDPR (General Data Protection Regulation), which went into effect on May 25, 2018, establishing a high security standard and imposing severe fines for violations.

The Personal Data Bill, 2019, which was presented to the Lok Sabha on December 11, 2019 was heavily impacted by the General Data Protection Regulation. The primary objective of the Bill was to address the rising concern about data privacy and data protection, to penalize those who engage in fraudulent operations in the digital economy, and to prevent them from invading the privacy of individuals.

There are a number of differences between Indian and European data privacy laws, despite the fact that they share significant commonalities. JPC has advised that terms such as data fiduciary, data processor, and data principles are comparable to GDPR's controller, processor, and data subjects, and the definition of data fiduciary has been expanded to align with GDPR's. Even the implementation transition term for the PDPB is being maintained at two years, comparable to the GDPR. The JPC has advised that data processing be conducted in a fair and transparent way that ensures transparency and privacy; hence, the GDPR also incorporates the idea of informed permission. Clause 16 of the Personal Data

Protection Bill 2019 discusses the processing of Personal and sensitive Personal data of children, and the GDPR says the same thing; the only variation is in the wording, since they both refer to personal data of children. The GDPR has a paragraph about the Right to Erasure, while the PDPB makes specific reference to the Right to be Forgotten. If we consider the limitation time, the GDPR specifies that a breach of personal data must be reported to the authorities within 72 hours. The JPC has a similar term, and there are several other parallels that demonstrate the GDPR's influence on the Personal Data Protection Bill, 2019.

The Personal Data Protection Bill of 2019 has its own stances, which distinguish it from the GDPR of the European Union. In comparison to GDPR, the Personal Data Protection law has a broader and more expansive reach. As the central government has exempted such data processors from the scope of PDPB in the context of outsourced services, i.e., when the processor is contracted by a person or organization located outside of India, or when the processing relates to a person located outside of India, GDPR does not have a comparable concept. The PDPB permits the government to obtain non-personal data for a defined purpose, but the GDPR does not control anonymized data in this manner. If the same phrase appears in two regulations, then they differ. GDPR discusses the preservation of data as long as it is anonymized and no longer individually identifiable, but PDPB contains no such idea and expressly stipulates that data should be deleted permanently after the purpose has been met. In the GDPR, the right arises only when the data is gathered or processed on the basis of a contract or permission, but in the PDPB, the right extends regardless of the legal basis. The protection afforded to children is present in all jurisdictions, but there is a variation with regard to the age element, since GDPR defines a kid as someone under the age of 16 while PDPB specifies 18 years. PDPB places a greater focus on legal principles than GDPR. The timeframe for data access is limited to 30 days, although the PDPB specifies a different timeframe. The adjudicating officer is the authority responsible for determining the Right to be Forgotten, whereas under GDPR, the controller is responsible.

Analysis of Emerging Legal Position

According to the Joint Parliamentary Committee's study, it is difficult to categorise data as personal or non-personal. Therefore, one of the report's primary concerns is the scope or unambiguous definition of personal and non-personal data. This is why the committee has proposed renaming the law from the Personal Data Protection Bill to the Data Protection Bill; this is a sufficient justification because not all data may be classified as personal. In addition, the measure itself permits the government to access certain data based on necessity. There are significant parallels between the GDPR and the proposed legislation, including the consent provision and the clause about the transition time. There are additional differences regarding the penalty clause and the restriction on data transmission beyond India.

After the Bill was presented to the Lok Sabha on December 11, 2019, it was forwarded to the Joint Parliamentary Committee for additional review. The committee presented 81 revisions and 12 recommendations to the draught measure, leading to its withdrawal on August 3, 2022. This measure will be replaced with a new comprehensive framework and modern digital privacy legislation. Any act that is enacted must be in accordance with Part III of the Constitution of India; therefore, the new Bill data protection laws that is to be drafted must comply with this principle and be drafted in such a way that it meets every criterion and encompasses every aspect that led to the protection of Privacy rights that are guaranteed to every citizen of India.

With the exception of the Information Technology Act of 2000, which does not specifically address privacy violations, there is currently no particular legislation that regulates privacy breaches. Article 21 of the Indian Constitution recognizes the Right to Privacy as a fundamental right, while Articles 32 and 226 of the Indian Constitution allow for its violation to be contested. The Constitution of India is the guiding principle, and all laws are drafted in accordance with it; hence, it serves as a defender of the rights of people and individuals.

Conclusions

A primary priority of the legislation is preventing the abuse of personal information of a huge number of populations. This number is predicted to reach 900 billion by 2050 in India. Currently, 600 billion Indians utilize the internet. Consequently, there is a strong need to develop a legal framework that would help in protecting the data privacy of persons and penalize offenders. Because the Bill included various loopholes that needed to be closed in order to establish effective regulation, it was abandoned. Different suggestion led to the withdrawal of the same. This statute will replace with a new comprehensive framework and modern digital privacy legislation. As Bruce Schnier correctly stated, "Privacy is an intrinsic human right and a prerequisite for upholding the dignity and respect of the human situation."

References

1. Indian Constitutional Law, M.P.Jain 6th edition, Lexis Nexis Butterworths Wadhwa Nagpur.

2. Google Spain SL, Google Inc. v. Agencia Espa ̃nola de Protecci ́on de Datos (AEPD), Mario Costeja Gonz ́alez, 2014 ECLI:EU:C:2014:317

3. Name Redacted v. The Registrar General, 2017 SCC OnLineKar 424.

4. Sredharan T v. State Of Kerala,Civil Writ Petition No. 9478 of 2016

5. Justice K.S Puttaswamy v Union of India, (2017) 10 SCC 1, AIR 2017 SC 4161.

6. https://www.thehindu.com/news/national/over-50-indians-are-active-internet-users-now-base-to-reach-900-million-by-2025-report/article66809522.ece.

7. https://www.statista.com/statistics/255146/number-of-internet-users-in-india/.

8. https://www.iamai.in/sites/default/files/research/Internet%20in%20India%202022_Print%20version.pdf.

9. https://prsindia.org/files/bills_acts/bills_parliament/2019/Summary-JPC%20Report_PDP%20Bill,%202019.pdf.

10. https://gdpr-info.eu/.

11. Maneka Gandhi v. Union of India, AIR 1978 SC 597.

10

Habeas Data: Remedial Procedure for Personal Data Protection

Saquib Ahmed, Bhupinder Singh and Rishikesh Singh Faujdar

Abstract

In the modern world where the collection of data and storage of data on online platforms are rising, it has become important to the individual to protect their data. Data privacy is crucial because people need to feel confident that their personal information will be treated carefully if they are going to engage in online activity. Data privacy refers to a person's right to decide for themselves when, how, and to what extent their personal information is shared with or conveyed to others. Privacy is a genus and data protection are species. The right to privacy is protected by data protection legislation in many jurisdictions since it is regarded as a fundamental right. An action which is a kind of writ known as a "habcas data" is one that is taken before the courts to allow the protection of a person's identity, privacy, honour, and freedom of information. Under Indian law, the writ of habeas data is not recognized in any way. A writ of habeas data is an extremely helpful instrument for defending a person's right to privacy and would be very beneficial for citizens to possess. Since India has a comprehensive Right to Information Act, 2005 and certain aspects of the habeas data are accessible under it.

Keywords - *Privacy, Constitution, Data Protection, Habeas Data, India.*

Introduction

In the modern world, where the collection of data and storage of data on online platforms are rising, it has become important to the individual to protect their data. Personal data privacy is a critical problem across the world. Every country now experiences issues with data security and infringements on the privacy of individuals. In terms of instances of violations of personal data rights, India is also making progress. Governments have a duty to protect citizens' rights to privacy and to keep data users' and service providers' personal information private. There have been several judicial decisions in which courts have dealt with the right to privacy and issues associated with it. In addition to judicial creativity declaring right to privacy as a part of Article 21 of the Indian Constitution, there have been numerous indirect general laws in context of right to privacy and data protection in India. International Standards, Guidelines and Privacy Codes are also recognizing right to privacy. However, the Government of India has been slow in responding to enact a specific law to protect personal data of individuals. Still an enactment of an omnibus piece of law on data protection seems a distant dream in a country which has been a strong supporter and signatory of plethora of International human rights instruments. In absence of the explicit personal data protection law, an inclusion of the habeas data writ in Indian Constitution seems to be a viable solution in area of data security issue.

Meaning and Concept of Habeas Data

The habeas data writ means 'you should have the data'. It is a constitutional right to protect, personal lawsuit filed in court, to protect the image, privacy, honour, information self-determination and freedom of information of a person. Habeas data has been described as 'a procedure designed to safeguard individual's freedom from abuse in the information age'. This writ is available to citizens as a mechanism to assure control over sensible personal data. It is designed to stop the abuse of sensible personal data of the individual which will be harmful to him. This writ is available as a constitutional right in some of the countries and jurisdictions of the World that afford protection in case of violation of right to be informed, right to be forgotten, right to access to data and right to object to personal data etc. Though, the writ varies country to country, but it is intended to protect the privacy, honour and freedom of information of an individual.

The history and origin of the habeas data writ can be traced to certain European legal mechanism that protected privacy of the individual. The Council of Europe 108th Convention on Data Protection, 1981 has been the predecessor of the habeas data right. In general, the Habeas data writ can be brought up by any citizen against any register to find out what information is held about his or her person. Aggrieved person whose data has been processed can request the correction, updating or even for the destruction of the personal data held by data users.

Status of Habeas Data at the International Level

At international level, there are countries and jurisdictions in which habeas data writ or right has been adequately recognised in statutes and constitutions. In various countries, the Habeas Data writ is used to protect personal data violation incidents.

Brazil

Brazil has been the first country in which habeas data writ was used and recognised as a major safeguard to protect personal data rights of the individual. It was the first Latin American country to adopt the writ of habeas data in 1988 and was strengthened by its national Congress in 1997. The Constitution of the Federative Republic of Brazil, 1988 has specified the habeas data action to cure the right to correction and access to the personal data of the data subjects. Brazilian Constitution however does not offer any remedy in case if the data users fail to update or destroy the data of the data subjects after use. Under the Brazilian Constitution the habeas data action can be presented before several authorities. For example, Supreme Federal court is empowered to initiate legal proceeding in case of habeas data writ against the acts of the President of the Republic, Directing Boards of the Chamber of Deputies and the Federal Senate, Federal Audit Court, Attorney General of the Republic and the Supreme Federal court itself. It indicates that power of the highest court of the Brazil to entertain writ is extensive and it covers varieties of authorities whom against writ can be initiated.

Paraguay

The Constitution of Paraguay, 1992 has a provision for the habeas data writ. The scope of the writ is wider under Paraguay Constitution as compared with the Brazilian Constitution. Under the Constitution of Paraguay, 1992, the competent authority or court can secure updating, rectification or destruction of entries made in official or private registries of a public nature if they are wrong or if they are illegitimately affecting rights of the data subjects. The habeas data action can be initiated under these circumstances. Under the Brazilian Constitution, there was no provision for updating and destruction or removal of data after use. But both these rights of data subjects are protected under Paraguay Constitution in addition to right to access to information and know how the information is being used and for what purpose.

Argentina

The Argentine Republic Constitution 1853 (amended in 1994) has a provision for the writ of *ampro*. The word habeas data is not specifically mentioned under the constitution because the Argentinean government had merged several individual constitutional complaints under the name of *ampro*. However, irrespective going into the controversy of nomenclature of the writ under Argentine Republic Constitution, it is crystal clear from the reading of Section 43 of the Argentina Constitution that personal data protection can be secured through prompt and summary proceeding regarding constitutional guarantees, provided there is no other legal remedy. Bare reading of the Section 43 of the Argentinean Constitution makes it clear that most of the rights of the data subjects like right to obtain information about personal data, their purpose, right to rectification and the right to suppression of false data have been covered and redressed by the competent courts.

However, besides the rights protected under Paraguay and Brazilian Constitutions, the Argentinean Constitution has also included right of confidentiality of data and prohibition to broadcast or transmit incorrect or false information by press.

Colombia

There is no explicit provision as such on-habeas data in Colombian Constitution; however, the courts in Colombia through various judgements have implanted and made habeas data a fundamental part of the Colombian Constitutional system. The Colombian Constitution has provisions relating to privacy and data of the individuals within it. The Constitution of Colombia, 1991 defended the right to know, access, update and rectify personal data of the individuals. The obligations have been imposed on the data banks of the public and private entities to process personal data in a fair manner.

Peru

New Peruvian Constitution 1993 amended in 2021 has created and provided the habeas data within its framework. Under the Constitution, the writ of habeas data operates in case of an act or omission. The writ lies against any authority, official or person that violates or threatens the rights of individuals. Under the Constitution, individuals have a right to request information and right not to provide information affecting personal and family privacy. Thus, the writ has been a significant constitutional protection under Peruvian constitution. In addition to the above countries and jurisdictions, the idea of habeas data action is also debated and found reflection within the legal system and Constitutions of the Costa Rica and Philippines.

Sketch of the Proposed Writ of the Habeas Data in India

The violation of fundamental and statutory rights should not go unaddressed. However, data rights of individuals are frequently violated and in absence of statutory mechanism, rights remain unaddressed most of the time. So, the habeas data writ can be incorporated in Indian Constitution by amending it. The researchers seem the inclusion of the writ of the habeas data as a viable solution to address the data rights and privacy issues. Certain questions are likely to arise into mind such as: Against whom the writ would be maintainable or enforceable? What would be its nature and scope? On what grounds it would be granted? What would be the benefits of the inclusion of the new writ in Indian Constitution and last but not the least, what would be the extraterritorial application of the writ? To answer this questions and to demonstrate how the writ might be useful to protect individuals' data rights, the researchers have drawn a sketch of the habeas data writ in this Part of the paper.

Nature, Scope and Maintainability

Under the India legal system, jurisdiction to issue 'prerogative writs' has been given to the Supreme Court and to the High Courts of Judicature of all Indian states. Part III of Indian Constitution deals with enforcement of fundamental rights. Article 32 empowers the Supreme Court and Article 226 to the High Court. So, the writ of the habeas data would also be included in Part III as fundamental right. The Supreme Court of India under art 32 and High Court of each state under Article 226 would be competent courts to issue the writ of habeas data.

Further, the writ of habeas data like other writs given in the Constitution would be maintainable against the State. The term 'State' as defined in Article 12 includes Central and State governments, local authorities, government departments and other instrumentalities. The term 'other instrumentalities' have been defined liberally by the Indian judiciary to include statutory and non-statutory corporation.

For the purpose of writ of habeas data writ, data controller, data processors either in government sector or private sector would fall within the ambit of the term state under Article 12. The PDP Bill, 2019 defines data fiduciary as entity or individual who decides the means and purpose of processing personal data. The Bill governs the processing of personal data by government, Indian companies and foreign companies dealing with personal data of individuals in India. If we look at the definition of the term state under Article 12, it becomes clear that government and companies in India would be held liable for violation of individuals' data rights. So far as the foreign companies are concerned, if their head offices are located outside India but there any sub offices are operational in India and dealing with processing of data, they even would come within the definition of the state and hence accountable for violation of individuals' data rights.

Moreover, Indian judiciary by expanding the term 'other authority' under Article 12 can bring various data users and controllers' having some connection with personal data of the data subjects within the meaning of the term state and therefore individuals' data rights would be enforceable against such authorities. Thus, the outline of the writ of the habeas data drawn above could be effective to provide remedy in case data subjects' rights like right to be informed, right to rectification, right to withdraw consent, right to access to data and right to erase are violated.

Need and Benefits of Inclusion

After discussing the outline of the habeas data action, it becomes crystal clear that it could be an effective constitutional remedy to deal with data rights of the people in India. The researchers now would like to point out the justifications to include the writ as constitutional remedy in Indian Constitution.

The procedure to file the habeas data writ is simple as no detailed obligation of facts and evidence are involved in writs. Procedure under Articles 32 and 226 is summary and no procedural formalities are required. Even letters, emails and postcards were treated as writ petitions. For example, in a case telegram was treated by Indian court as petition. It indicates, that even in violation of right to privacy letter, postcard and e-mail can be treated as writ petition and the court would not insist on the observance of procedural technicalities. The writ of the habeas data like other constitutional writs could be entertained in the form of simple letters written and affidavits. In case of other petitions, lower court can appoint commissions to verify the veracity of facts produced before it, follow all procedural technicalities and record the evidence. But these all formalities are normally not applied in writ petitions.

Indian higher judiciary is guardian of all fundamental rights of the individuals obviously including rights of the data subjects. The Apex Court or High Courts can take *Suo motu* cognizance of the cases of violation of rights of the individuals. So, if data rights are violated of data users, the Apex Court and High Court need not wait for the writ petition to be filled. These courts may take Suo moto notice of the violation of fundamental rights of individuals. Exercise of *Suo motu* jurisdiction by courts is useful especially in case of blatant violation of law affecting the public at large. The courts while exercising *Suo motu* jurisdiction will issue notices etc. to the respondents at their own.

Enforcement of Rights by the Highest Court of the Country

The action can be implemented within existing judicial structures in India i.e., the Supreme Court under Article 32 and before the High Courts under Article 226. Having separate judicial structures to redress the grievances of the data subjects, there is no need to create special government agencies. Habeas data assurance is receiving a full constitutional strength in most of the countries in which it is being included in their respective legal system. In civil system of law, this the highest level of protection possible, and faster procedures and better courts usually accompany it. Many studies have already spoken high for the effectiveness of the habeas data writ.

The writ of habeas data if incorporated in Indian Constitution would mean that the relief in case of data breaches would be available within the highest law of the land. If specific data protection law came into being within coming years even, then the habeas data provision should be kept retained as its retaining would complements the specific data protection law. Also, enforcement of fundamental right of privacy and personal data rights of individuals can be better protected via constitution rather than under any statute.

Stale claims are not maintainable in courts. They are imperfect right which cannot be enforced. No period of limitation has been prescribed for the filing of the writ petition. Inordinate delay in filing petition to enforce ordinary statutory rights may not be entertained but the Supreme Court has excused inordinate delay in filing writ petition to enforce fundamental rights. The Supreme Court in the case of *Narmada Bacho Andolan vs. Union of India* entertained delayed writ petition on the grounds that the issue of the violation of fundamental rights were involved in the case. While the court in this case refused to deal with claims asserted by the petitioners on the ground of laches but in case of enforcing fundamental rights of dam outsees plea of laches was not rejected.

Conclusions and Suggestions

The foregoing discussion makes it amply clear that the existing indirect laws, rules and regulations on privacy right and protection of personal data are ineffective and flawed. The judicial efforts in evolving fundamental right to privacy and protection of personal data seem effective but it is not a permanent solution.

The GDPR, 2018 applicable and followed in European member countries is the best regulation on personal data protection from which several other Latin American countries have taken lessons. The GDPR, 2018 affords protection to rights of data subjects. Several rights like right to access to data, right to correction, right to erasure, right to withdraw consent and right to be informed have been basic rights provided to data subjects under the GDPR. The enactment of PDP Bill in India could not take shape of law till date which is a serious concern. The PDP Bill has several notable provisions which are in line with best data protection practices followed globally but the problem is that if this law is approved even then data protection will remain a significant issue as most of the laws in India remain in moribund like situation in absence of their proper implementation after enactment.

The complicity and procedural technicalities usually seen in the Indian courts in enforcing ordinary rights is a major hurdle in hundred percent implementation of the PDP law. Under such circumstances, the researchers have proposed to add a writ of the habeas data in Indian constitution so that procedural and other legal technicalities normally experienced in enforcing rights of the individuals can be subsided and rights of data subjects can be addressed via habeas data action filed in the highest court of the country. The habeas data writ would be useful to promptly address the rights of the data subjects because all writ petitions are based on summary procedure and judges can also exercise Suo moto jurisdictions in favor of citizens. There would be no time limit pressure to entertain the writ petition and courts in the past have allowed writ petitions that have been filed after inordinate delay.

It is true that no legal system is free from defects so the habeas data action may be hampered if judges would not be techno savvy and burdened to dispose of backlog of cases. Few recommendations given below may be useful to strengthen the statutory mechanism on personal data protection in India. Also, recommendations have been given below to make writ of the habeas data more effective on its inclusion in Indian constitution.

Individuals' data rights are required to be protected under every circumstance. Governments have to ponder over how to protect data rights of the data subjects. This part of the paper offers some recommendations for the law and policy makers in India.

i) The PDP Bill is pending before JPC. This Bill would be the first specific law on personal data protection. Therefore, it is recommended to give final approval to this Bill as soon as possible after making some in this Bill as per the best data protection practices prevalent in EU countries.

ii) Under PDP Bill, it is mandatory to take consent of individuals before processing their data but too many exceptions have also been provided to do so. Thus, the Bill ends up diluting power of the Bill. It is therefore recommended to reduce exceptions to take consent and in substantial number of cases, the data fiduciaries should have duty to take consent of individuals to process their personal data.

iii) Clause 9 of the PDP Bill imposes obligation on the data fiduciary to delete the data after use, but procedure and system to delete data is not clearly specified. It is thus recommended that a proper procedure is required to be notified to data Principal how and when personal data must be deleted.

iv) Under the draft Bill neither the data fiduciary nor the Data Protection Authority shall have any duty to inform the data subject about the breach of his or her personal data. However, the data protection authority can publish breach on their website, but data breach notified on website may go unnoticed therefore it is recommended to fix clear responsibility of the data fiduciary to inform data principal about breach of personal data. Also, publication of data breach on website may further exposes the data principal to immense number of leaks of his personal data and thereby its abuse. Hence this practice should be prohibited.

v) A voluminous personal and sensitive data crosses Indian borders for the purpose of processing, storage, and use. The Data Bill does not provide a strong enforcement mechanism to prevent it. It is therefore recommended that DPA should appoint a team of separate data handling experts in the Bill who can filter what data may or may not be allowed to be transferred cross border.

vi) Under the Draft Bill, sensitive and personal data related to information such as religion, or to matters of national security is accessible to the government. No doubt, this arrangement has been given in the Bill to protect national interest but in the name of national interest open ended access can lead to misuse of the personal data of the data principal. Therefor in this context, it is recommended to clearly define the terms like national interest, national security and sensitive data within the Bill.

vii) The GDPR of EU has the best data protection practices. But some of the rights which are stipulated within GDPR are not available in DP Bill. Therefore, it is recommended to bring DP Bill in line with best data protection practices prevalent in the GDPR, 2018.

viii) It is recommended to amend Indian Constitution to include writ of habeas data in Indian Constitution under Article 32 and Article 226.

ix) It is recommended to appoint more judges in higher judiciary so that the writ of habeas data may be decided promptly. The backlog of variety of other cases before high judiciary may hamper disposal of the writ of habeas data so appointing more judges would resolve all problems.

x) Judges are the professional who may not be well acquainted with data processing technicalities and problems. This can also hinder effective use of the writ to address data rights in India. In this context, it is recommended that special techno savvy staff can be appointed in Supreme Court and High Court who can assist court in understanding the data security related issues. Further, judges should be trained and made aware time to time about data security technical issues.

References

1. M.P. Sharma and Ors. vs. Satish Chandra, District Magistrate, Delhi, 1954 SCR 1077.
2. Kharak Singh vs. U. P, AIR 1963 SC 1295, (1964)1 SCR 334.
3. Govind vs. Sate of M.P (1975)2 SCC 148.
4. R. Rajagopal and Anr. vs. State of Tamil Nadu (1994)6 SCC 632.
5. People's Union for Civil Liberties vs. Union of India, (1997)1 SCC 301.
6. Selvi vs. State of Karnataka, AIR 2010 SC 1974.
7. K.S Puttaswamy vs. Union of India, (2015)8 SCC 735.
8. The Contract Act, 1872.
9. Indian Penal Code, 1860.
10. The Indian Copyright Act, 1957.
11. The Information Technology Act, 2000.
12. Information Technology (Reasonable Security Practices and Procedures and Sensitive Personal Data or Information) Rules, 2011.
13. The Credit Information Companies Regulation Act, 2015.
14. Universal Declaration of Human Rights, 1948.
15. International Covenant on Civil and Political Rights, 1966.
16. Convention on the Rights of the Child, 1989.
17. International Convention on the Protection of all Migrant Workes.
18. European Convention for the Protection of Human Rights and Fundamental Freedoms.
19. American Convention on the Human Rights.
20. African Charters on the Rights and Welfare of the Child.
21. U.N Special Rapporteur on the Right to Privacy.

22. Marcin Rojszczak, "Does Global Scope Guarantee Effectiveness? Searching for a New Legal Standard for Privacy Protection in Cyberspace" Information *and Communications Technology Law 22-24(*2020).

23. Kristian P. Humble, "International Law, Surveillance and the Protection of Privacy", The International Journal of Human Rights,: Available at https://doi.org/10.1080/13642987.2020.1763315.

24. OECD Guidelines on the Protection of Privacy and Trans Border Flows of Personal Data 1980.

25. Kamlesh Bajaj, "Promoting Data Protection Standards through Contract: The Case of the Data Security Council of India", Review *of Policy Research* (2012).

26. Canadian Model Code for the Protection of Personal Information, 1995, Cloud Security Alliance Model Code.

27. Kristian P. Humble, "International law, Surveillance and the Protection of Privacy," *The International Journal of Human Rights* (2020) available at: https://doi.org/10.1080/13642987.2020.1763315.

28. Falcon, Enrique, "Habeas Data: Conceptoy Procedimiento (1996) Editorial Abeledo Perrot, Buenos Aires.

29. A. Charles "Recent Development in Latin America and Asia are Driven by Local Interests and Technology". *Privacy and American Business* (1998). Available online at: http://Hudson.idt.net/pad/global.html.

30. Marc-Tizoc Gonzalez, "Habeas Data: Comparative Constitutional Interventions from Latin America against Neoliberal States of Insecurity and Surveillance "90 *Chicago-Kent Law Review* 641-68(2015).

31. Chintakrindi Venkateswarlu vs. Head Constable 6th Town Police, 1997 CriLJ 3319.

11

Article 21 vis-à-vis Personal Data Protection

Renu Rajpoot and Ravi Kant Gupta

Abstract

Privacy is a fundamental human right enshrined in many international treaties. It is important for the protection of human dignity and is one of the important pillars of a democratic country. It supports the rights of self and others. Privacy is a right that all human beings enjoy by virtue of their existence. It also extends to physical integrity, individual autonomy, free speech, and freedom to move, or think. This means that privacy is not only about the body, but extends to integrity, personal autonomy, data, speech, consent, objections, movements, thoughts, and reputation. Therefore, it is a neutral relationship between an individual, group, and an individual who is not subject to interference or unwanted invasion or invasion of personal freedom. All modern societies recognize that privacy is essential and recognize it not only for humanitarian reasons but also from a legal point of view. With the advancement of social networking sites and technology, the right to privacy being given the status of a fundamental right becomes extremely difficult. However, on the other side, the right to privacy of a person includes their right to seclude information that is of personal nature. The Privacy Bill, 2011 protects the citizens from identity theft, including criminal identity theft and financial identity theft. The Data Protection Authority of India is to monitor development in computer technology and data processing. The authority also has the power to investigate any data breach and issue orders to ensure security interests. The Bill establishes that an interception not adhering to the guidelines thereof may lead to imprisonment or a fine. In addition to this, the authority is to receive recommendations and give representation to the public on any matter pertaining to data protection.

Keywords - *Article 21, Fundamental right, Data, Privacy, Constitution.*

Introduction

Privacy is associated with personal autonomy. It arises from the idea that some laws are natural or exist in man. 'Natural rights' are known as 'inalienable rights' because they are inseparable from the characteristics of Human. The human basis in life cannot exist without the reality of nature. In 1690, John Locke argued in the "Second Government Act" that people's lives, freedoms and property were necessary by law, a special area of protection.

The 'Right to Privacy' is an important guaranteed right and recognized with the upheld by the Supreme Court of India in 2017. The right to privacy is also considered a human right in accordance with Article 12 of the Universal Declaration of Human Rights. Privacy is an ideology and main aim of this, to create an outside influence in the society. William Blackstone (in 1765), spoke of "natural liberty" in the British Constitution. According to him, the immutable laws of nature give people rights. All the rights are divided into the 'right to personal security', 'the right to personal freedom' and the 'right to property'. The right to personal security refers to the enjoyment of this right without interfering with the life, weapons, body, health, and reputation of individuals.

Privacy in Indian Context

In India, the 'Right to privacy' is not only a 'Human Right' but also known as a 'fundamental right' and is protected by the Article 21 of the Constitution of India. Most recent recognition of this right was in 2017 by Apex Court in the verdict of the Justice K.S. Putaswamy. As a result, the right to privacy is recognized as a fundamental right within reasonable limits, to the extent necessary for the protection of the public and national interests.

'Natural rights' are not only granted by the state but also by the almighty God. They are important to people because they are people. They are equal among people, regardless of class or class, gender, or orientation. Life and personal liberty are inalienable rights. These rights are honorably separated from human life. Individual's dignity, human equality with equity and the pursuit of freedom are the pillars of the Indian Constitution.

Therefore, secrecy must first be exercised in order to fulfill one of the guarantees in Part III. Thus, when the right holder asserts the right to privacy before the Constitutional Court, the right to privacy is not only in Article 21, but also in Article III. It may also appear in other forms recognized in the chapter. In the current context, Sections 19(1), 20(3), 25, 28 and 29 are valid and effective rights through the exercise of the right to privacy.

In this context, the Apex Court of India said that individuals have the 'right to privacy' including personal information, correspondence, and other private matters. It was also decided that the state should ensure that the privacy of its citizens is protected from direct interference. Apart from the recognition of the right to privacy in Indian law, there are many other laws that protect the privacy of people. This includes Information Technology Act 2000, Indian Penal Code, 1860 and Right to Information Act, 2005. As part of its efforts to protect the 'privacy of citizens', the government of India has also issued the Personal Data Protection Act 2019, which aims to regulate the collection of data. storage and processing of personal data by businesses. The aim and objective of this law is to protect the personal information of individuals and to enforce their privacy rights. In 2016, the government also announced the Aadhaar Law to provide each citizen with a unique identification number and keep their data secure and private.

Privacy and Article 21

The 'fundamental right' known as the right of privacy in India covers at least the following three aspects: Liberty, Aim, Validity. Article 21 deals with the privacy of individuals too. When the state violates a person's bodily rights, such as the right to freedom of movement; Personal information affects the mind, not the person's body, thus confirming that a person can control its publication. personal information. Therefore, unauthorized use of data may constitute a crime; private choice that preserves people's freedom of personal choice. In ADM's Jabalpur case, the court judges concluded that Article 21 is the only place that protects all the rights to life and liberty of the person, and once abolished these rights will be completely abolished. According to the various landmark verdict of the Supreme Court of India, Article 21 of part III of the Indian

Constitution. 'Right to privacy' under Articles 21 is a fundamental right of Indian citizens.

Courts have specifically recognized three criteria that must be met for an Article 21. The Court accepted a liberal interpretation of fundamental rights in response to the challenges posed by the evolving digital age. It advocates the preservation of personal identity and privacy and the extension of personal freedom into the digital realm. The Supreme Court decision of 6th September, 2018 allowed homosexuality in India and legalized homosexuality among consenting adults. With this resolution, India, the world's largest democracy, joins the United States, Canada, South Africa, the European Union and the United Kingdom in recognizing this important right.

Privacy Concerns in India

Online privacy is a concern due to the ubiquity of social media and messaging apps. Because these platforms collect personal information and share it with many third parties, there are concerns about the protection and misuse of personal information. The lack of consensus on the collection and processing of personal data by different organizations such as government, private sector and service providers is another major problem in India.

People are often unaware of where and how their personal information is collected and used by others. Data protection has become a major issue in India as more and more countries use technology. Aadhaar, financial information, medical information etc. Important personal information, including personal information, has been leaked and stolen many times. The Privacy Act, 2019 was introduced to address some of these issues and regulate the collection, storage and processing of personal information.

India has raised privacy concerns regarding the use of surveillance tools such as facial recognition and biometrics.

The Indian government is accused of using this technology to track and monitor large numbers of citizens. The lack of appropriate legislation regulating the use of this technology has raised concerns. The absence of a legal framework is another problem in terms of protecting the privacy of individuals and controlling the use of personal information. While the Privacy Act, 2019 aims to address some of these concerns, it has yet to become law.

Government's Privacy Policy

The Government of India has implemented a number of measures to protect the privacy of its citizens. The boundaries that people form with others in society are not only physical but also informational. Different relationships have different boundaries. Privacy helps prevent awkward situations in the community and reduce social anxiety. Most of the information about individuals can fall under the phrase "not relevant to you".

For information obtained voluntarily, a breach of confidential information and confidentiality may be considered a breach of trust. This is especially true in relationships where honest disclosure of information is required, such as doctors and lawyers. Individuals have the right to control their privacy when submitting their personal information to various sites and services. But it is important that people understand the purpose of the data and be able to organize and organize it. Freedom in democracy means freedom and control over human lives, which is impossible if important decisions are kept confidential with-out our knowledge or participations.

Everyone should have the right to control his life and the image he presents to the entire world, and to control his commercial use. It also means that a person can be empowered by the law to prevent unauthorized use of his image, name and various other aspects of his life and personality for commercial purposes. Just because someone allows someone, to enter their house/property does not mean that other people can enter the house/property. Do not harm or interfere with the rights of others, in this age of social and cultural practices, this applies to the use of technology as much as to the body, especially in a country like ours that prides itself on its diversity. Important One of the fundamental human rights is protected and recognized as a fundamental right by states and non-states.

The sanctity of 'privacy' lies in its relationship with respect: it allows people to live meaningful lives while preserving the deepest aspects of humanity. Although the legal expectation of privacy differs between social and private spaces and private and public spaces, it is most important to note that privacy is not lost or destroyed by someone's presence in the public space. Moreover, privacy itself is a prerequisite for respect. Additionally, privacy issues arise when the state tries to get into the bodies and minds of citizens.

The 'right to privacy' is part of 'human dignity'. The 'sanctity of privacy' lies in its, relationship with respect. Secrecy protects the deepest part of humanity from unnecessary interference, thus making life meaningful. It is about privacy, personal freedom and the right of every person to make important decisions that affect life.

Privacy rights and disclosures work. At the normative level, privacy supports the timeless importance of the security of life, freedom, and liberty accordingly. At the 'descriptive level', privacy presupposes a set of rights and interests that underlie decisions about freedom. Privacy at its core includes the protection of personal privacy, family life, marriage, childbearing, family, and the sanctity of sex. Confidentiality also means the right not to interfere.

Privacy protects personal freedom and recognizes people's ability to control important aspects of their lives. Personal preference in determining the lifestyle is in the nature of the individual. Privacy preserves heterogeneity and acknowledges the diversity of our culture. While the legal expectation of privacy differs between social and private spaces, and between private and public spaces, it is important to note that privacy is not lost or destroyed simply because someone is in the public space. Privacy is linked to people as it is an important part of human dignity. Improper disclosure of personal information is one of the privacy violations. The document addresses the traditional rivalry between the 'freedom of expression' and honor with respect for personal privacy. Both are very important rights. Neither is more important than the other. The importance of freedom of expression is often nicely emphasized, but the importance of privacy is not.

It is also the basis on the modern democratic nation/state. An appropriate level of privacy is essential for human health and development. Boundaries over the state's prying eyes on public life are the essence of freedom. Tracking data is the subject of intense debate across the region in the area of privacy, for example personal data based on appearance and clothing choice. Interception of government phones and obtaining personal information over the Internet are other areas of privacy. Current usage stems from the Indian Association's attempt the collection of the biometric/ digital data of all residents in the country.

Few are some areas of special interest. Examples above illustrate some of the nature and rights of privacy. It is unbelievable that anyone in the country would allow the dignitaries of the state to arbitrarily confiscate their homes and properties or to have soldiers in them without permission. I don't think anyone wants the government to tell them what to eat, how to dress, or who to associate with in the personal, economic, social, or political life. Article 19(1)(c) guarantees citizens' freedom of social and political association.

Personal Connection is Still a Mystery

Our age is the information age. The age-old "knowledge is power" as implications for ubiquitous knowledge. Technology has made life more interconnected. As people spend, more and more time virtual/online every day, the Internet has become ubiquitous. People connect with others and use the internet based of communication tool. The Internet is used to do business and buy goods and services. People visit the Web to search for information, send emails, use chat services, and download videos. Online shopping has become an alternative to a day trip to the neighborhood store.

Online banking is redefining the relationship between banker and customer. Online business created a new platform for job security. Updated online music radio. Online books have opened the doors of a new world for book lovers. Travel agencies have been transformed by web portals offering everything from restaurants to lounges, airline tickets to theaters, tickets to concerts, music and more.

These are some of the reasons why people access the internet every day. However, every transaction a user makes and every website he visits takes place electronically, usually without his knowledge. These electronic devices contain useful information that can provide information about the user type and preferences. Together, they reveal the essence of personality: diet, speech, health, hobbies, sexual orientation, friendship, clothing and belonging, politics. Collectively, information provides a picture of what is important and what is unimportant, what needs to be made public, and what is best kept.

Data mining techniques and 'knowledge discovery/searching' can be combined to originate or create truth about people. Metadata and Internet of things have the power to reshape human life in ways that have yet to be fully realized. This leads to the creation of new information about the person, as Christina, Manioc is points out in her enlightening article; something he doesn't have. "This raises big questions for the courts.

When Supreme Court Ruled Against the Right to Privacy

In the past, the Supreme Court of India has pronounced to limit or limit the 'right to privacy' in cases related to homeland security, rule of law and public interest.

In A.K. Gopalan v. State (1950), Supreme Court ruled that 'right to life' and the guarantee of personal liberty under the Article 21 of the Indian Constitution do not cover the 'right to privacy'. It declared that the protection of private life does not include a narrow definition of personal freedom. In the decision of, Justice K.S. Puttaswamy (retd.) v. Union of India (2017), Supreme Court overturned the decision and recognized the right to privacy as a fundamental right protected by the Indian Constitution.

In Kharak Singh v. State of U. P., Supreme Court of India has ruled that laws that allow police to visit "known persons" or people who may be in the homes of known persons are illegal. Kharak Singh often wakes up from his slumber when the police arrive at his house at different times. These visits violated the applicant's right to life, which the court said was limited only by law and not by administrative authorities such as the Uttar Pradesh Police. The petitioner claimed that tracking the criminal repeatedly violated of the 'right to privacy', but the court rejected this claim because the

Constitution of India does not recognize this right. This rule is important.

Supreme Court Decision Affirming Privacy

In a landmark decision of Puttaswamy, The Supreme Court of India recognized the 'right to privacy' as a fundamental right enshrined in the Indian Constitution. Puttaswamy. The Court said that the right to life and the protection of 'personal liberty', which are included in Article 21 of the Constitution of India, prioritize the right to privacy. Courts have also recognized the importance of privacy as a prerequisite for 'protection of human dignity and freedom', as well as the enjoyment of other fundamental rights. The protection of the right to privacy in India has been heavily influenced by this decision, which is hailed as an important step towards the protection of human freedoms.

Exceptions to Privacy in India

India has many laws and regulations that protect people's privacy rights. However, this right has some limitations. According to the Indian Penal Code, 1860 privacy rights may be restricted if necessary to protect India's nation and justice, national security, relations with other nations, public order or morals, or certain conditions. To criticize, defame or incite violence. The Supreme Court of India has argued that the right to privacy is absolute and can be limited to protect public health and national security. The Courts have ruled that in some cases, the right to privacy can be restricted to prevent crime if necessary. The right to privacy may also be restricted by government surveillance, interception of electronic communications or the collection of biometric data. The government may also restrict privacy rights in dealing with foreign individuals or groups, or where information is important to national security.

Individuals may also waive their privacy rights in the context of contracts or agreements with third parties. For example, an individual may agree to provide personal information to a company in order to obtain services or enter into a contract.

Conclusions and Suggestions

Present world witnessed that privacy is limited by the 'power of government' as well as private organizations. Impact of the digital age has led to an influx of 'information's' on the internet. People will 'forget' but the 'internet' will never forget.

The idea of "violation of privacy" is not an early "interference in the business of others" thought process. Things are not that simple. Any effort to remove the file from the web/Internet does not completely remove it. The footprints are still there. So, in the digital world, protection is the norm and forget the struggle.

Technology makes some things almost permanent, making it difficult to get rid of past mistakes and start a new life. People are not 'statical', they changed and evolve throughout their lives.

They are constantly evolving. They made a mistake. But they have the right to rebuild themselves, change and correct mistakes. Being, privacy that nurtures this ability and unleashes the negative things you have done in the past. May they not suffer from childhood mistakes and injustices throughout their lives. Children's privacy needs to be protected not only in the virtual world, but also in the real world. States may have legitimate reasons to collect and store information outside of national security. In the welfare state, the government implements programs that benefit the poor and disadvantaged in society. It is important for the country to ensure that scared public resources are not wasted because resources are diverted to those who are not worthy as buyers. The allocation of resources for 'human development' comes with 'legitimate concerns' that their use should not be directed towards inequality.

Data mining aims to ensure that resources are appropriately allocated to legitimate beneficiaries as necessary for governments to continue collecting real data. However, information collected by the government should be used for the legitimate purpose of the government and not used for unrelated purposes without permission. Ensure, that the 'legitimate concerns' of the 'State/Nations' are well protected while maintaining privacy. Crime prevention, investigation and income protection are legitimate aims.

India needs a way forward to strengthen enforcement and protection of privacy rights.

i) The Government of India has enacted the 'Personal Data Protection Act, 2019' to regulates the collections, storage, processing and transfer of personal data. The law must be strong to protect the public's 'right to privacy' and to provide adequate protection against the misuse of personal information.

ii) Indian citizens should be more aware of their privacy rights. The government should run public awareness campaigns to educate people about their right to privacy and how to protect them.

iii) India needs a law to protect the right to privacy. The Indian government should pass a law defining privacy and provide mechanisms to enforce it. The law should include penalties for privacy violations.

iv) The law is very important for the protection of privacy rights in India. Courts should be vigilant in protecting the public's right to privacy and apply the law that protects the individual.

v) Technology greatly simplifies the impact of privacy. The government has a responsibility to ensure that public and private organizations use technology that respects the public's right to privacy.

vi) India should work with other countries to protect the privacy of citizens as it is a global issue.

vii) India should participate in international discussions and seek to set global standards for self-defense.

References

1. ADM's Jabalpur v. Shivakant Shukla, AIR 1976 SC 1207.
2. S.V Joga Rao, Computer Contracts and Information Technology Law (2nd Ed. 2005).
3. Haelan Laboratories Inc v. Topps Gum Inc, 202 F.2d 866 (2d Cir. 1953).
4. Michael L. Rustad, SannaKulevska, "Reconceptualizing the right to be forgotten to enable transatlantic data flow", (20315) 28 Hary JL and Tech 349.
5. La Forest J. in R. v. Dyment fR. v. Dyment, 1988 SCC Online Can SC 86: (1988) 2 SCR 417].
6. A.K. Gopalan v. State, AIR 1950 SC 27.
7. Kharak Singh v. State of U. P., 1964 SCR (1) 332.
8. Justice K.S. Puttaswamy v. Union of India, (2017) 10 SCC 1. https://aptitude8.com/blog/data-mining-what-it-is-and-how-to-report-the-results.
9. Indian Penal Code, 1860.
10. Constitution of India, 1950.

12

Right to be Forgotten as Data Protection

Apeksha Rai

Abstract

The Costeja case (Google Spain case) underscored the affirmation that the "right to be forgotten" constitutes a fundamental human right, as evidenced by the ruling of the European Court of Justice against Google. Consequently, the European Union adopted the idea of the "Right to be forgotten". A person has the right to request that certain search results relating to their name be removed from search engines like Google. This right is based on European data protection legislation. Before determining whether to delete material, search engines must evaluate the information's accuracy, sufficiency, relevance, and appropriateness. They must also consider the public interest in keeping the content accessible in search results. A "right to erasure" similar to the one recognized by the European Court of Justice in earlier legislation is introduced in Article 17 of the General Data Protection Regulation (GDPR), which the European Union implemented in 2018. Similar legislation has also been approved by several nations outside of the E.U. As an illustration, in July 2015, Russia passed a law allowing its residents to ask for the removal of a link from Russian search results if it violates Russian law or includes false or outdated information. Serbia and Turkey have each established their own versions of the right to be forgotten.

Keywords *- GDPR, European Court of Justice, Citizens, Union, Privacy.*

Introduction

In the modern era, social media has taken a firm grip on our lives. A person's online presence is often considered synonymous with their existence. The digital world has increasingly become the arbiter of one's credibility in today's society. The quick advancement of web correspondence innovation has given us phenomenal admittance to different parts of individuals' lives, enveloping both positive and negative features. Subsequently, our protection is continuously reducing, prompting incessant openness of individual matters to the open arena. While we may enjoy gossip and information about others that we find online, we should put ourselves in their shoes. Just imagine if the most embarrassing moment of your life became widely known worldwide simply by conducting a search. It would undoubtedly be a dreadful experience for you and your family.

Personal information has surpassed the boundaries of official records and government records in the modern day, when social media websites like Facebook, Twitter, and Google dominate. Nowadays, people are easily found online, and their personal information is accessible. It is really concerning that online personal information accessibility has undergone such a significant transformation in both nature and breadth. It is worth noting that appearing in a Google search does not require one to be exceptionally accomplished or have committed a criminal offense.

Background

Regarding the constitutional right to be forgotten and how it applies to internet platforms, a lawsuit in Argentina was effectively resolved. A first court ruling was won by renowned Argentine musician Virginia Da Cunha in 2009, requiring Google and Yahoo to remove online search results that connected her to prostitution or pornography. However, the appeals court reversed this decision in 2010, and towards the end of 2014, the Argentine Supreme Court decided in favor of the websites.

The Court of Justice of the European Union (CJEU) evaluated the right to be forgotten in 2014, which was a significant development. It's crucial to remember that the idea of forgetting has a historical background that goes back further than this particular time period. Before the CJEU's decision, legal arguments over this topic had already started and were still going strong today.

The EU Data Protection Directive already in place included the right to be forgotten, which was recognized by the CJEU in 2014. This meant that, in accordance with the law, people might ask for the removal of material from the internet that had grown out of date. In this situation, Google was seen as a data regulator in charge of upholding individuals' right to control their own data.

By setting a precedent for the EU's authority to execute judgements against American companies, even though those companies' servers were situated outside of Europe, such in California, the decision generated controversy. Google claimed that the EU data security norm did not apply since it did not handle data in Spain, where the issue was first brought. Instead, Google maintained a sales office there. Google has had more than 2.5 million requests to erase data from Europe since the decision. While some contend that the data is in the public interest and shouldn't be deleted, the organisation claims to have cooperated with about 43% of these requests.

Although New York State temporarily proposed legislation recognising this right and mandating web directories to erase erroneous, irrelevant, insufficient, or inappropriate information about persons, there is no legal right to be forgotten in the United States. The Act forbade the removal of data pertaining to crimes that have already been adjudicated, topics of considerable current public interest, or justifiable concerns like cruelty.

In the U.K., preliminary hearings for Google's first "right to be forgotten" lawsuits were held in 2018. In these cases, fund managers tried to have their convictions overturned in accordance with an English law intended to help criminals get back on their feet.

Since around 2014, Google and France have been involved in legal disputes on the reach of the right to be forgotten. The CJEU is presently hearing the case, and France is threatening to have all of the world's web directories remove whatever material it doesn't get its way. There are worries that someone from outside of Europe may use their IP address to obtain the right. Despite Google's attempts to restrict its growth, the right to be forgotten was eventually made available to all European users on Google's European domains. The right to be forgotten in Europe is anticipated to improve greatly as a result of the General Data Protection Regulation (GDPR). The Right to Erasure is outlined in Article 17 of the GDPR and enables anyone to ask for the immediate deletion of their personal data by a regulatory body.

In India, the Personal Data Protection Bill of 2019 (PDP Bill) addresses the Right to be Forgotten. The Right to be Forgotten has not yet received formal approval, nevertheless. Nevertheless, the Supreme Court found the right to privacy to be a basic right, integral to the right to life and personal freedom under Article 21 of the Constitution, in the case of Justice K.S. Puttaswamy (Retd) v. Union of India in 2018. Any cutting-edge framework created for the preservation and administration of legal data should take into account rights like the Right to be Forgotten in light of the execution of the core e-courts project in Phase III. A quick Google search may reveal a lot of information about a person, thus jeopardizing their reputation and dignity, which are guaranteed by Article 21 of the Indian Constitution. As technology develops and information gets more digitalized. In accordance with international law on this matter, many high courts have specifically recognized the right to be forgotten in their rulings.

Definition of Right to Be Forgotten

Individuals have the ability to request the removal of their publicly available data from many sources, including internet platforms, search engines, libraries, blogs, and other public venues, under the right to be forgotten. This option is applicable when the disputed personal data is no longer essential or relevant. Through the General Data Protection Regulation (GDPR), the European Union has acknowledged and established this right as a legal entitlement, and several courts in the EU and England have upheld it.

Who can be Forgotten and Why?

There is currently no specific law in India that establishes the right to be forgotten. The Personal Data Protection Bill of 2019 recognizes the existence of this right, nonetheless. Any entity has the right to limit or safeguard the ongoing publication of their personal data under specific conditions, according to Section 20 of the Bill. These conditions include: When the intent behind data collection is no longer essential or relevant, when the person has revoked their permission for the use of the data and while the PDP Bill or any other relevant law was broken while the data was gathered. The adjudicating officer named in the Bill must issue an order in order for this clause to be enforceable. Before making such an order, the officer must take into account a number of considerations, including the delicate nature of the personal information, the amount of access and availability that is sought to be restricted or avoided, as well as the scope of the disclosure, an individual's standing within society, the significance of the personal data to the public and the information release's type and the person's activity.

Comparative Analysis Between the European Union and India

To safeguard the personal information of persons in the European Union (EU), a set of legally enforceable laws known as the General Data Protection Regulation (GDPR) was developed. Without regard to whether they expressly target EU citizens as possible clients, all websites that get traffic from Europe must comply with the GDPR. Therefore, every website that draws users from Europe must comply with the GDPR.

Section 17 of this regulatory framework contains information on the right to be forgotten. It is crucial to understand that this right only pertains to data that is already in existence at the time a request is made and excludes any data that may be created in the future. It is also critical to know that the right to be forgotten is conditional and only applies in certain situations.

Comparison with Indian Bill

As mentioned earlier, the right to be forgotten is acknowledged in Section 20 of the **Personal Data Protection Bill**. Additionally, there are several supplementary provisions that support the core principles of this right. The "right to correction and erasure," which interacts with the "right to be forgotten," is addressed in clause 18. It includes the removal of personal data that is no longer required for processing and evaluation as well as the correction of erroneous or deceptive personal data. The data trustee is required to notify the people and organizations with whom the information was shared whenever such modifications or erasures are made.

A data trustee is prohibited under clause 9 from keeping a person's personal information longer than it was required to, unless the person gives their consent willingly or it's required by law. Additionally, data trustees must periodically evaluate whether keeping personal data on file is necessary. Clause 36(b) states that the right to limit the disclosure of personal data does not apply where the information is needed to uphold a legitimate authority or claim, defend against accusations, seek legal counsel, or for similar reasons.

Comparison with the U.S.A.

Various nations worldwide have shown diverse responses to the Right to be Forgotten concept. The European Union stands out for its notable advancements in this area, implementing several measures to enhance its provisions. One significant milestone was the introduction of the General Data Protection Regulation (GDPR) in April 2016, which superseded the 1995 Data Protection Directive. The Data Protection Directive, established by the European Union in 1995, governed the treatment of personal data within the EU and holds significant importance in EU privacy and human rights legislation.

Article 17 of the GDPR grants individuals the right to seek the deletion of their personal data in different scenarios. These include cases where the data processing does not comply with Article 6(1) regarding lawfulness, situations where the individual's interests and fundamental rights outweigh the data controller's interests, and instances where the protection of personal data is deemed essential. The legislation specifies the specific conditions that enable individuals to exercise their right to have their data erased.

In the 2010 case of Google Spain SL v. Agencia Espaola Protección de Datos, the European Court of Justice ordered Google to remove from its search results any data that was judged "inadequate, irrelevant, or no longer relevant" upon a citizen's request. This important judgement was crucial in maintaining EU data privacy norms and laws, most notably the GDPR. This judgement, sometimes referred to as the "right to be forgotten," is now largely accepted by the general public.

Individuals, such as Gonzalez, have the option to request the removal of information related to them from Google search results. Gonzalez made a request in 2009 to have a newspaper article from 1998 removed when his name was searched. Initially, his request was denied, but he then approached Google directly to have the article removed. Google provides a form on its official website where users can exercise their right to be forgotten by submitting the necessary information for deletion from the search engine's results.

Google can be subject to legal ramifications if it contests a judgement issued by a data protection body. The European Union has given Google the go-ahead to handle removal requests from EU citizens on all of its international domains. The request form requires people to provide their country of residence, personal information, a list of URLs that need to be deleted along with a brief justification for each and supporting legal documentation.

The United States has implemented a comprehensive framework of regulations aimed at safeguarding its populace. In the state of New York, temporary legislation known as Bill A05323 was introduced. Additionally, representatives Tony Avella and David Weprin put forth a proposal in March 2017 that would empower individuals to seek the elimination of information deemed "inaccurate," "irrelevant," "inadequate," or "excessive" if it is determined to be "no longer material to public discussion or discourse" and causing harm.

Prominent cases with substantial consequences encompass Melvin v. Reid (1931) and Sidis v. FR Publishing Corp. (1940). The court concluded that "every person who lives a life possesses the right to privacy, entailing protection from unjustified assaults on their character, social position, or reputation." In the instance of William James Sidis, a former child prodigy desiring a tranquil and unobtrusive adulthood, his intentions were disrupted by an article published in The New Yorker.

In this ruling, the Court demonstrated that there are limitations to one's control over their own life and the information surrounding them, recognizing the cultural value of scattered facts and the inability to disregard one's general reputation at will. Despite these significant advancements, the possibility of government regulations or long-standing accommodations for an individual solution remains uncertain. The right to be forgotten is relatively weak in the United States, as it conflicts with the First Amendment to the U.S. Constitution, which safeguards freedom of speech and expression. Consequently, it is argued that this right may likely result in another form of restriction. The European Court of Justice's ruling in Google Spain SL v. Agencia Espaola de Protección de Datos, 2010, serves as the primary foundation for the Bill.

Analysis of Right to be Forgotten

The freedom to be forgotten can provide important security assurance and be essential in fostering autonomy and independence. Online personal data and digital profiles are highly controllable by both people and non-state entities.

Importance

Granting individuals, the ability to take control of their own information empowers them and allows for greater agency over their own identities. In most cases, personal information found on the internet holds little relevance to public interest matters and holds greater intrinsic value to the individual than to society as a whole. This distinction has been taken into account in the ongoing legal and administrative advances in this field, which distinguish between what is important to a person, what attracts attention, and what furthers the common good.

Criticism

The possible effects of an "overly broad right to be forgotten," which may result in internet censorship and the rewriting of historical records, have been questioned. It is appropriate in some circumstances for people not to always be defined by their history. The Google Spain case helped to clarify this issue by highlighting the significance of key factors such the type and applicability of the information, the public's interest, and the effect on the data subject's public life. It attempted to establish a reasonable balance between internet users' interests and data subject rights.

Google received several requests after the Google Spain verdict, and its 2017 Transparency Report gave details on how it processed these requests and examples of the results. Some responses indicated that URLs were not delisted due to the individual's previous status as a public figure, while others mentioned delisting URLs based on factors such as disengagement from political life or being a minor at the time. Article 19 emphasized the importance of protecting children's rights and the potential negative impact of restricting their ability to move forward and develop a healthy self-awareness by highlighting negative aspects of their past.

The right to be overlooked unquestionably has benefits, but it also has certain hazards, notably in connection to entitlement hunting and possible ramifications for free expression. Online platforms might end up making all decisions about the right to be forgotten without the requisite administrative safeguards in place, acting as the judge, jury, and enforcement. Giving private organizations so broad jurisdiction involves inherent hazards, particularly when it comes to balancing competing rights, which is generally handled by courts. The vague limitations placed on websites have drawn criticism from the Electronic Frontier Foundation because they might lead to internet control.

For and Against the Right

Choosing to exercise the Right to be forgotten does not imply withdrawing from society. Its foundation is the idea that, so long as personal preferences do not negatively impact others, society ought to accept them. The right to be forgotten has its origins in both the right to privacy guaranteed by Article 21 and the right to dignity guaranteed by Article 14.

Key Questions Relating to The Right to Forget

When dealing with private persons, such as the media or news sites, the Right to be Forgotten is typically relevant. This calls into question whether basic rights, which are generally upheld by the state, may also be used to protect private citizens.

Protection versus Data

The presence of conflicting rights, such as the right to freedom of speech or other publication privileges, determines whether the right to be forgotten is applicable in a particular circumstance. For instance, a person could want to remove links to material about their criminal history to make it more difficult for others to discover specific news articles while looking for their name online. This creates a conflict between Article 19's provision for media freedom of speech and Article 21's protection of an individual's basic right to privacy.

The issue to be Forgotten has been the subject of conflicting and odd decisions by several high courts in India since there is no explicit data protection statute that addresses this issue. While frequently ignoring the more profound philosophical issues involved, Indian courts have variously recognized and refused the applicability of the Right to be Forgotten.

Perspectives from the judiciary on the right to be forgotten

American citizen Jorawer Singh Mundy attempted to appeal the Delhi High Court's ruling in a case involving the Narcotic Drugs and Psychotropic Substances Act, 1985 (NDPS Act), in which he was found not guilty of any of the allegations, in the case of Jorawer Singh Mundy v. Union of India (2021). He claimed that the judgment's internet accessibility was damaging his reputation. The Delhi High Court ruled that under the right to be forgotten, anyone can request that details about themselves be deleted from particular web records, making it impossible for search engines to find them. It was further noted that this right allowed people to forget about the past and go on with their lives.

The Karnataka High Court supported the Right to be Forgotten while acknowledging that this is consistent with practices in Western nations where equivalent laws are in place in the case of Name Redacted v. The Registrar General (2017). The court emphasized the necessity to protect the right to be forgotten in delicate situations, such assault cases or situations that have a big impact on a person's image and dignity.

The Madras High Court declared in the case of Karthick Theodore v. Madras High Court (2021) that an accused person has the right to have their name removed from judgements or decrees, particularly those that are in the public domain and are findable online. The court emphasized that it must safeguard people's rights to their reputations and to their privacy until the legislature passes the Data Protection Act. It further noted that if the Data Protection Regime is authorized, it must contain a fair process for dealing with requests to remove the identities of those who have been charged with crimes but acquitted.

Common Doubts on Right to be Forgotten

In Spain, how is Google doing? The Google Spain case concerns a request to have references to private information deleted from Google's database by a Spanish individual. In its judgement from last May, the Court of Justice of the European Union did not go so far as to demand that the data be deleted or removed. To preserve people's rights to data privacy, it did, however, develop a set of guidelines for web search engines.

What requirements are made specifically of online scarch engines? The Court anticipates that search engines like Google will remove a person's name from certain search queries when personal information is judged "irrelevant," "inadequate," or "excessive" in connection to the purpose for which it was processed and gathered.

Exist any exclusions? Yes, the right to be forgotten does not apply in all cases. The right accepts that search results shouldn't be changed when personal information about public figures, such as well-known people, elected officials, or people in the media, is involved since the general public has a genuine interest in obtaining this material.

Is there a website where you may choose to be forgotten? Yes, the right to be forgotten acts as a crucial protection against harmful material that is intentionally or unintentionally spread online that is unjustified, incorrect, inflammatory, libelous, or otherwise damaging.

Conclusions

Article 21 of the Constitution safeguards the Right to privacy as an inherent aspect of the Right to life and personal liberty, and it is also encompassed within the guarantees provided by Part III of the Constitution. The Supreme Court and the Parliament must both conduct thorough analyses of the right to be forgotten and create a framework that successfully strikes a balance between the conflicting demands of privacy and freedom of expression. It is crucial not to leave data uncontrolled given its considerable importance in the digital age. India must thus create a strong data protection regime that effectively handles this issue. Latest occurrences have highlighted the urgent need for the implementation of this Bill. Protecting individuals against advanced-level risks is crucial, and establishing clear conditions with predictable outcomes can help avoid conflicts between fundamental rights.

The Madras High Court claims that judicial decisions are exempt from the Right to be forgotten. The Right to Be Forgotten is still in its infancy in India.

Suggestions

Various suggestions must be taken into account in order to execute this right in India effectively.

i) Implementing a robust data protection policy would greatly contribute to ensuring this right for everyone. It is possible to use the right to be forgotten to improve peoples' security.

ii) Online search engines and major digital platforms can modify their criteria and determine the deletion of specific information by disassociating it. Large firms like Google have kept certain information even after being challenged in the Kerala High Court, demonstrating that this method of protecting the right may be problematic.

iii) Despite the rejection of the PDP Bill, several courts have recognized and incorporated in their judgments, the Delhi and Karnataka High Courts have recognized and respected the Right to be forgotten, while also considering international legal principles. However, there is still significant progress to be made in developing a well-defined approach that adequately protects both the right to personal data and the right to freedom of speech and expression. In the interim, individuals have the option to file a complaint to assert their fundamental right to privacy.

iv) By incorporating and systematically implementing the recommendations, India can establish and effectively enforce the Right to be forgotten. It is important to acknowledge the evolution of this right in various jurisdictions. By taking into account these legal developments and principles, India can make significant progress in establishing and safeguarding the Right to be forgotten, ensuring the protection of individuals' privacy rights in the digital era. A constitutional change is required to include the right to be forgotten as a safety measure and to guarantee that Article 19 limits are suitable. The necessity for governmental actions to address the growth of digital platforms, which might have an impact on the right to be forgotten, is on the rise. For instance, while exercising the right to freedom of speech and access to information, certain limitations might be necessary in order to comply with legal obligations, carry out tasks related to the public interest or public health, achieve scientific or empirical research goals, achieve measurable goals, or establish, exercise, or protect legitimate rights.

References

1. Gorge Brock, The Right to Be Forgotten: Privacy and The Media in Digital Age, available at https://reutersinstitute.politics.ox.ac.uk/sites/default/files/research/files/The%2520Right%2520to%2520be%2520Forgotten%2520Extract.pdf.
2. Jorawer Singh Mundy v. Union of India, 2021 SCC OnLine Del 2306.
3. Name Redacted v. The Registrar General, 2017 SCC OnLineKar 424.
4. Karthick Theodore v. Madras High Court, 2021 SCC OnLine Mad. 2755.
5. Constitution of India, 1950.
6. http://docs.manupatra.in/newsline/articles/Upload/E755F76D-D287-430F-B17E-F805666A7D33.%20Case%20Commentary-Right%20to%20be%20Forgotten%20_%20Civil.pdf.
7. Zulfiqar Ahman Khan v. Quintillion Business Media (P) Ltd., 2019 SCC OnLine Del. 8494.
8. Sri Vasunathan v. The Registrar General (Karnataka HC) (2020).
9. Subhranshu Rout Gugul v. State of Odisha, 2020 (Orissa HC), 2020 SCC OnLIne Ori. 878.
10. X v. YouTube (2021).
11. Jorawer Singh Mundy v. Union of India & Ors [Delhi HC, 2021), 2021 SCC OnLine De. 2306.
12. .Lei Geral de Proteção de Dados (Brazil).
13. California Consumer Privacy Act, 2018.

13

Securing Financial Trust: A Deep Dive into Credit Information Protection Laws in India

Saif Rahman, Aditya Kumar and Vikrant

Abstract

The credit information of individual is statutory protected data. The credit information of individual is store, process and provide by the credit companies or credit institution in India. The Reserve Bank of India has established and has given license to four credit rating agencies of India i.e., CIBIL, High Mark, Equifax and Experian. This information is useful for the lenders in making their decisions. Credit bureaus provide this credit information to lending institutions for a fee. They also provide credit information to individuals who wish to know about their own credit history The Reserve Bank of India (RBI) has levied monetary penalties of approximately ₹25 lakh on each of the four credit information companies presently operating within the nation. This also leads us to questions about the safety of the information shared with the credit institutions in India. Is it safe to adopt and promote credit transaction concept in Banking? Whether the information is secured? Whether any statute prescribes punishments for data breach of credit information? What legal mechanism is in force to ensure the protection of such information? Whether the mechanism is strong and efficient to make a check on likewise scams? And so on. There were so many questions left to be answered. Some of them had been answered and some of them questions were left unanswered. In present paper, an attempt has been made to find answer the questions regarding exiting legal framework.

Keywords - *Credit, Confidentiality, Scam, Financial, India, Consumer.*

Introduction

A vital feature of the financial infrastructure is having adequate and high-quality information about counterparties (sharing of credit information). Credit growth boost up by reducing the knowledge gap between lenders and borrowers. A robust credit information sharing system reduces the cost of intermediation. By enabling banks to efficiently target, price, and monitor loans, it stimulates competition in the credit market. Additionally, it lowers credit defaults, which benefits consumers by lowering average interest rates. Unfortunately, India had faced some blunders in its financial system. The recent one financial fraud is faced by the leading public institution. The Punjab National Bank Scam can be entitled as the biggest scam in Indian banking history. In May 2018, this 14000-crore scam has raised questions on the creditability of banking system of India. In the era of digitalization and rapid technological advancement, the exchange and utilization of credit information play a pivotal role in modern economies. The availability and reliability of credit information are indispensable for fostering financial inclusivity, promoting responsible lending practices, and sustaining a stable financial ecosystem. In India, where the financial landscape is witnessing remarkable growth and diversification, the legal framework for the protection of credit information has emerged as a critical component of the financial regulatory framework.

This research paper delves into the multifaceted legal framework governing the protection of credit information in India. The effective functioning of this framework not only affects the financial sector but also has profound implications for individuals, businesses, and the overall economic stability of the nation. The paper will provide an in-depth analysis of the existing legal provisions, their efficacy, and potential areas for improvement in safeguarding credit information.

Fortunately, there are several legislative provisions to ensure the security of different kinds of information. The Official Secrets Act, 1923; The Census Act, 1948; The Registration of Births and Deaths Act, 1969; Public Records Act, 1993 etc. are some of the examples. Section 3, of Public Financial Institutions (Obligation as to Fidelity and Secrecy) Act, 1983 provides that a public financial institution shall not divulge any information relating to, or to the affairs of, its constituents except in circumstances in which it is, in accordance with the law or practice and usage, customary among bankers, necessary or appropriate for the public financial institution to divulge such information. Information Technology Act, 2000 read with its numerous allied rules accord protection to electronic information. Credit Information Companies (Regulation) Act, 2005 provides for regulation of credit information companies and to facilitate efficient distribution of credit. Section 37 empowers the Reserve Bank to make regulations consistent with the provisions of this Act and the rules made thereunder to carry out the purposes of this Act. The Credit Information Companies Regulations, 2006 have been made by Reserve Bank under the said provision. Together, they ensure protection regarding the credit information.

Importance of Credit Information System

The transparent credit information is a fundamental requirement for effective risk management and financial stability. Credit reporting institutions, such as credit bureaus, credit companies and credit institutions support financial stability and credit market efficiency and stability in two ways. First, Credit reporting systems are used by banks and nonbank financial institutions (NBFIs) to evaluate potential borrowers and track the risk profile of current loan portfolios. Second, in order to perform crucial oversight duties and comprehend the interrelated credit risks faced by systemically important borrowers and financial institutions, regulators rely on credit information. These initiatives ultimately help consumers by resulting in reduced interest rates in a competitive loan market. These efforts lower the risk of default and boost the effectiveness of financial intermediation.

Effective credit reporting systems can reduce a number of market failures that are widespread in global financial markets and are more pronounced in less developed economies. The issues of adverse selection and information asymmetry between borrowers and lenders are lessened by the availability of high-quality credit information. Sharing of information might encourage a responsible "credit culture" by discouraging excessive debt and promoting responsible borrowing and repayment. This lowers the risk of default and enhances the distribution of fresh loans.

The ability to develop a credit history and utilise it as "reputational collateral" to acquire formal credit outside of pre-existing lending ties is perhaps credit reporting's most significant benefit. Small businesses and new borrowers who have little access to physical collateral will especially benefit from this. Evidence from the most recent financial crisis implies that creditworthy borrowers who would have otherwise been denied access to institutional credit were saved from doing so thanks to good loans information.

Credit Information

The term "Credit Information" refers to a report on a person's historical payback behaviour provided by the member banks and financial institutions.

When one applies for loan, the lender's decision is strongly driven by your credit information. Therefore, it is crucial for individual to regularly check his/ her credit information to make it accurate and up to date. One's credit worthiness is determined by your credit score and Credit Information.

Section 2 (d) of Credit Information Companies (Regulation) Act, 2005 describes that "credit information" means any information relating to the amounts and the nature of loans or advances amounts outstanding under credit cards and other credit facilities granted or to be granted, by a credit institution to any borrower, the nature of security taken or proposed to be taken by a credit institution from any borrower for credit facilities granted or proposed to be granted to him; the guarantee furnished or any other non-fund based facility granted or proposed to be granted by a credit institution for any of its borrowers; the credit worthiness of any borrower of a credit institution; any other matter which the Reserve Bank may consider necessary for inclusion in the credit information to be collected and maintained by credit information companies, and, specify, by notification, in this behalf.

Credit Information Company and Credit Institution in India

The Credit Information Bureau (India) Ltd. (CIBIL), which has been incorporated in 2000, became operationalized in April 2004. Three further Credit Information Companies (CICs) were founded after the Credit Information Companies (Regulation) Act (CICRA) was passed in 2005. These Credit Institutions are responsible for creating, managing, updating and securing of the credit score of individuals which is requisite for banking institutions (lenders) to take decisions for borrowing.

Legal Definitions of Credit Institutions

Section 2(e) of Credit Information Companies (Regulation) Act, 2005 defines "credit information company" as a company formed and registered under the Companies Act 1956 /the Companies Act 2013 and which has been granted a certificate of registration under Section 5(2).

Section 2(f) of Credit Information Companies (Regulation) Act, 2005 defines "credit institution" as a banking company and it will include – a corresponding new bank, the State Bank of India, a subsidiary bank, a co-operative bank, the National Bank and regional rural bank; a non-banking financial company as defined under Section 45-I (f) of the Reserve Bank of India Act, 1934; a public financial institution referred to in Section 4-A of the Companies Act, 1956; the financial corporation established by a State under Section 3 of the State Financial Corporation Act, 1951; the housing finance institution referred to Section 2(d) of the National Housing Bank Act,1987; the companies engaged in the business of credit cards and other similar cards and companies dealing with the distribution of credit in any other manner;any other institution which the Reserve Bank may specify, from time to time, for the purposes of this clause.

Credit Information Companies Laws 'CIC Laws' in India

In accordance with the Credit Information Companies (Regulation) Act, 2005, ("Act") the Reserve Bank of India and the Government of India have enacted the Credit Information Companies Regulations, 2006 ("Regulations") and the Credit

Information Companies Rules, 2006 ("Rules") issued under the Act, respectively.

(The CIC Act, the Regulations and the Rules are collectively referred to as the "CIC Laws").

We may understand the data protection principles provided under the Credit Information Companies Act read with the Credit Information Companies Regulations, 2006 and with the Credit Information Companies Rules, 2006.

Provisions Under the Credit Information Companies (Regulation) Act, 2005

The Credit Information Companies (Regulation) Act, 2005 is the legislation which was enacted to regulate the functions of credit information companies (CICs) in India and for efficient distribution of credits and to take care the related matters. The provisions related to credit information in the legislation may be discussed as:

Chapter VI - Information Privacy Principles and Furnishing of Credit Information

The provisions related to privacy principles and credit information are embodied in Chapter VI of the Act. The Credit Information Companies and Credit institutions are required to work in accordance with the provisions of the Act. Chapter VI of the Act impose duties to the Credit Information Companies and Credit institutions to secure the information from loss or any unauthorized access as -

Duty to requisite steps to ensure Accuracy and security of credit information under Section 19

Section 19 casts an obligation upon a credit information company or credit institution or specified user, as the case may be, in possession or control of credit information, to take such steps (including security safeguards) as may be prescribed, to ensure that the data relating to the credit information maintained by them is accurate, complete, duly protected against any loss or unauthorised access or use or unauthorized disclosure thereof.

Duty to adopt Privacy principles under Section 20

Every credit information company, credit institution, and specified user shall adopt the following privacy principles in relation to collection, processing, collating, recording, preservation, secrecy, sharing and usage of credit information.

The principles enshrined the rules are as which may be followed by every credit institution for collection of information from its borrowers and clients and by every credit information company, for collection of information from its member credit institutions or credit information companies, for processing, recording, protecting the data relating to credit information furnished by, or obtained from, their member credit institutions or credit information companies, as the case may be and sharing of such data with specified users; which may be adopted by every specified user for processing, recording, preserving and protecting the data relating to credit information furnished, or received, as the case may be, by it; which may be adopted by every credit information company for allowing access to records containing credit information of borrowers and clients and alteration of such records in case of need to do so; the purpose for which the credit information may be used, restriction on such use and disclosure thereof; the extent of obligation to check accuracy of credit information before furnishing of such information to credit information companies or credit institutions or specified users, as the case may be.

Preservation of credit information maintained by every credit information company, credit institution, and specified user as the case may be (including the period for which such information may be maintained, manner of deletion of such information and maintenance of records of credit information; networking of credit information companies, credit institutions and specified users through electronic mode. Any other principles and procedures relating to credit information which the Reserve Bank may consider necessary and appropriate and may be specified by regulations.

Prohibition on Unauthorized access to credit information under Section 22

information company or a credit institution or a specified user unless the access is authorized by this Act or any other law for the time being in force or directed to do so by any court or tribunal and any such access to credit information without such authorization or direction shall be considered as an unauthorized access to credit information.

No person shall have access to credit information in the possession or control of a credit

Chapter VII – Offences and Penalties

Obligations as to fidelity and secrecy under Section 29

This Chapter describes the penalties for offences if done on part of credit information company. Section 26 of the Act empowers a Court imposing any fine under this Act to direct that the whole or any part thereof shall be applied in or towards payment of the costs of the proceedings, or for such purposes as may be directed by the court.

Every credit information company shall observe, except as otherwise required by law, the practices and usages customary among credit information companies and it shall not divulge any information relating to, or to the affairs of, its members or specified users. Every chairperson, director, member, auditor, adviser, officer or other employees of a credit information company shall, before entering upon his duties, make a declaration of fidelity and secrecy in the form, as may be prescribed in this regard.

Instances of Financial Frauds

Financial fraud continues to be a significant concern for economies worldwide, and India is no stranger to this challenge. In recent years, the country has witnessed several high-profile financial fraud cases, each revealing the need for more stringent regulations and heightened vigilance. In this article, we will delve into some of the latest and most notable instances of financial fraud in India, examining the individuals involved, the tactics employed, and the broader implications on the nation's economy and society.

The PMC Bank Scandal (2019) The Punjab and Maharashtra Cooperative (PMC) Bank scandal sent shockwaves through India's banking sector. It was revealed that senior officials of the bank, including the chairman and managing director, had allegedly colluded to underreport non-performing assets and lend money to a real estate firm without following proper procedures. This resulted in thousands of depositors being unable to access their savings, causing widespread distress.

Yes Bank Crisis (2020)

In March 2020, Yes Bank faced a severe financial crisis, largely attributed to its exposure to risky assets and questionable lending practices. The Reserve Bank of India (RBI) intervened by imposing a moratorium on the bank, restricting withdrawals for a period. This incident raised concerns about the vulnerability of India's banking system and the need for more robust risk assessment mechanisms.

The NSE Co-Location Case (2021)

In a case that shook India's financial markets, the National Stock Exchange (NSE) faced allegations of providing unfair access to certain traders through its co-location services. This controversy raised questions about market integrity, regulatory oversight, and the need for transparency in India's stock exchanges.

The Franklin Templeton Mutual Fund Crisis (2020)

The sudden closure of six debt schemes by Franklin Templeton Mutual Fund in April 2020 sent shockwaves through India's mutual fund industry. The move was attributed to liquidity issues arising from significant exposure to illiquid assets. This crisis highlighted the need for stronger risk management practices in the mutual fund sector.

The Rana Kapoor-Yes Bank Money Laundering Case (2021) Rana Kapoor, the founder and former CEO of Yes Bank, faced allegations of money laundering and accepting kickbacks. His arrest by the Enforcement Directorate (ED) brought the focus back to corporate governance and financial irregularities in India's banking sector. These recent instances of financial fraud have had far-reaching consequences for India's economy and society. They have eroded trust in financial institutions, deterred foreign investors, and emphasized the urgency of regulatory reforms and ethical corporate governance.

Conclusions and Suggestions

The legal framework for the protection of credit information in India represents a critical component of the nation's financial ecosystem, serving as a cornerstone for economic growth, financial inclusion, and consumer protection. As explored in this paper, the framework has evolved significantly over the years, driven by the need to adapt to changing financial landscapes and growing concerns around data privacy.

India's Credit Information Companies (Regulation) Act, 2005, along with the regulatory oversight provided by the Reserve Bank of India, has established a solid foundation for the responsible collection, maintenance, and dissemination of credit data. These regulations have not only facilitated greater access to credit but have also introduced stringent measures for data security and privacy.

The legal framework is not without its challenges. Striking the right balance between data security and the free flow of credit information remains an ongoing concern. The issue of consent and individual rights in the context of credit data poses a complex challenge that requires careful consideration. Furthermore, as technology continues to advance, the impact of innovations like artificial intelligence and blockchain on credit information introduces both opportunities and risks that demand regulatory attention.

The forthcoming Personal Data Protection Bill, when enacted, has the potential to bring comprehensive data protection under one umbrella, including credit information. Its provisions will shape the future landscape of data privacy and security in India, affecting not only how credit data is handled but also how individuals' rights over their data are respected. Beginning from 2005, we have travelled more than 20 years in credit reporting. Data shows that we have made a good improvement in credit information mechanism in recent years, still there is some space for improvements.

In response to these challenges, Indian authorities have intensified their efforts to strengthen financial regulations, enhance transparency, and improve risk management practices. Additionally, the establishment of specialized agencies like the Financial Frauds Investigation Agency (FFIA) underscores the commitment to investigating and prosecuting financial fraud cases effectively.

i) The infrastructure for sharing credit information should be strengthened.

ii) The coverage of the credit information business must be expanded.

iii) The reporting formats must be standardised among Credit Information Companies.

iv) The classification of accounts and their nomenclature based on payment history must be rationalized.

v) The content of credit information reports must be standardized.

vi) The best practices for Credit Information Companies and credit institutions must be established.

References

1. https://www.business-standard.com/about/what-is-pnb-scam.
2. https://www.thehindu.com/news/national/pnb-nirav-modi-case-chronology-of-events/article33932484.ece.
3. Public Financial Institutions (Obligation as to Fidelity and Secrecy) Act, 1983.
4. Credit Information Companies (Regulation) Act, 2005.
5. The Credit Information Companies Regulations, 2006.
6. Press Information Bureau, Government of India, Ministry of Commerce & Industry available at https://pib.gov.in/Pressreleaseshare.aspx?PRID=1551403.
7. The World Bank – Doing Business Archive, available at https://archive.doingbusiness.org/en/rankings?incomeGroup=lower-middle-income.
8. https://www.thehindubusinessline.com/money-and-banking/rbi-imposes-monetary-penalty-on-all-four-credit-info-firms/article67012533.ece.
9. https://bfsi.economictimes.indiatimes.com/news/banking/top-bank-frauds-that-grabbed-headlines-in-fy22/90545177.
10. https://www2.deloitte.com/in/en/pages/finance/articles/deloitte-india-banking-fraud-survey.html.
11. Banking Regulation Act, 1949.

14

Information Technology Act 2000: A Look at Data Protection in Practice

Junaid Ul Islam, Muskan Sharma and Piyush Agarwal

Abstract

Information management, use, and dissemination activities, methods, and principles are collectively referred to as information practice. It includes a broad range of procedures and techniques that businesses and individuals use to manage information efficiently, securely, and morally. The Information Technology Act, 2000, usually referred to as the I.T. Act, is a significant piece of Indian law that covers a number of topics related to electronic commerce, digital signatures, cybersecurity, and the legal foundation for electronic records and communications. In India's digital ecosystem, the Information Technology Act, 2000, plays a critical role in policing electronic transactions, fostering e-governance, and tackling cybercrimes and data protection. Raw facts, observations, or information are referred to as data, and they are often presented as numbers, text, symbols, or multimedia components. Data can be gathered, processed, and analyzed to reveal important insights, aid in decision-making, or disseminate knowledge. It is an essential idea in computer science, statistics, and information technology and forms the cornerstone for knowledge creation and task facilitation. It offers a legal framework that controls different facets of the online world and the digital economy. Organizations are required under Section 43A to use reasonable security procedures to safeguard sensitive personal data, and data breaches are subject to fines. The rules are expanded by Section 72A to include breaches of personal data committed in violation of written contracts.

Keywords *- Information Practice, Electronic Commerce, Digital Signatures, Cybersecurity, Information management.*

Information Technology: What is It?

Information Technology (IT) is the practice of retrieving information using computers or other electronic devices. So many facets of our daily life are supported by information technology, including our workforce, business operations, and individual information access. It has an enormous effect on all aspects of our daily life, including information storage, retrieval, access, and manipulation. Everyone, from large corporations to small solo operations and local businesses, uses information technology. It is used by multinational corporations to manage data and innovate their procedures. Flea market vendors use credit card readers on their smartphones to take payments, while street entertainers advertise their Venmo name to solicit donations. Information technology is used when you keep track of the Christmas gifts purchased using a spreadsheet.

Information Technology Act, 2000: Aims and Objectives

"The Information Technology Act, 2000, also referred as the IT Act 2000, the Indian law that was passed to enable e-commerce in India and to offer legal legitimacy for electronic transactions. The Act was approved by the Indian Parliament on May 9 and went into effect on October 17 of that same year. The Information Technology Act of 2000's primary objectives and provisions include:

Legal Recognition of Electronic Records

The Act gives legal respect to digital signatures and electronic records, equating them to paper documents.

Legal acceptance of digital records

Digital signatures and electronic records are given legal status by the Act, making them comparable to their paper-based equivalents. Compared to their paper equivalents.

Safety of electronic transactions

Digital signatures and electronic authentication are two ways that can be used to safeguard electronic transactions. The Act establishes the legal guidelines for their use.

Electronic governance

It encourages the use of digital tools for governing and doing public business, such as the submission of paperwork electronically.

Cybercrimes and penalties

The Act contains clauses that address several cybercrimes, including hacking, data breaches, and the dissemination of malicious software. Also included are the punishments for such actions.

Privacy and data protection

The Act has rules for safeguarding personal data and information. It creates a framework for handling sensitive personal data and protecting data.

Establishment of Certifying Authorities (CAs)

The Act outlines the procedures for recognizing Certifying Authorities, which oversee creating digital certificates that serve as proof of identification for people and organizations participating in electronic transactions.

Cyber Appellate Tribunal

The Act creates a Cyber Appellate Tribunal to hear appeals against judgments rendered by Adjudicating Officers in accordance with the Act.

Exemptions from liability

Under some conditions, intermediaries, such as internet service providers (ISPs) and online platforms, are excused from legal responsibility for user-posted information.

The IT Act 2000 has been amended several times to keep up with evolving technology and to address emerging cyber threats.

One of the significant amendments was the Information Technology (Amendment) Act, 2008, which introduced changes to enhance cybersecurity and introduced new provisions related to data protection".

What is Data?

The data is the collection information stored in electronic devices in various formats. The various formats of data are pictures, videos, documents, graphs, music etc. There are various types of Data:

Qualitative data

It is a type of data which describes the quality of anything or any person.

Quantitative data

It is a type of data which gives information about the quantity or the numerical information about something.

Structured Data

Data that is structured is well-organized and adheres to a set format or structure. Databases, spreadsheets, and clearly defined data models are frequently where you can get structured data. Examples include numbers, dates, addresses, and categorical information like employee IDs or product names.

Unstructured Data

Unstructured data is harder to examine using conventional techniques because it lacks a set format or organization. It consists of written text documents, pictures, moving pictures, social media postings, emails, and audio files. Unstructured data frequently takes the form of natural language writing.

According to the **Information Technology Act, 2000**. Section 2(o) provides a definition of the word "**data**" which states that "**data**" means a representation of information, knowledge, facts, concepts or instructions which are being prepared or have been prepared in a formalized manner, and is intended to be processed, is being processed or has been processed in a computer system or computer network, and may be in any form (including computer printouts magnetic or optical storage media, punched cards, punched tapes) or stored internally in the memory of the computer.

Data Protection and Provisions under Information Technology Act

Data protection, also known as data security, is a set of processes and strategies which help us safeguard the data stored in an electronic device. Data protection restricts access to the information or data stored in the electronic device.

Any organization that gathers, handles, or maintains sensitive data must have a data protection strategy in place. An effective approach can lessen the effects of a breach or disaster and assist in preventing data loss, theft, or corruption.

The main motive of data protection is to protect the information and make it available under any conditions.

In India, the data protection is regulated under **Information Technology Act 2000**.There are various provisions, which are mentioned in the act, regulated the data protection.

Section 43A- Compensation for Failure to Protect Data

"**Section 43A** covers compensation for not being able to protect the data. This section states that Where a body corporate, possessing, dealing or handling any sensitive personal data or information in a computer resource which it owns, controls or operates, is negligent in implementing and maintaining reasonable security practices and procedures and thereby causes wrongful loss or wrongful gain to any person, such body corporate shall be liable to pay damages by way of compensation to the person so affected.

Explanation. - For the purposes of this section,-

i) Body corporate means any company and includes a firm, sole proprietorship or other association of individuals engaged in commercial or professional activities.

ii) Reasonable security practices and procedures means security practices and procedures designed to protect such information from unauthorised access, damage, use, modification, disclosure or impairment, as may be specified in an agreement between the parties or as may be specified in any law for the time being in force and in the absence of such agreement or any law, such reasonable security practices and procedures, as may be prescribed by the Central Government in consultation with such professional bodies or associations as it may deem fit;

iii) Sensitive personal data or information means such personal information as may be prescribed by the Central Government in consultation with such professional bodies or associations as it may deem fit."

In compliance with Section 43A of the Act, the Central Government also unveiled the Information Technology (Reasonable Security Practices and Procedures and Sensitive Personal Data or Information) Rules, 2011 (the "SPDI Rules") in 2011.

The term Sensitive Personal Data or Information (or "SPDI") was correctly introduced and defined in these Rules, and it is defined as including personal information about any person connected to -

Password, financial details (such as bank account, credit card or debit card information, or specifics of other payment methods), Biometric information problems related to physical, physiological, and mental health, medical history, and sexual orientation.

Section 3 of the SPDI Rules also applies to information that is given to a body corporate for processing or storage as part of a service or pursuant to a legal contract. However, nothing that is made publicly available, in the public domain, released in accordance with the Right to Information Act of 2005, or disclosed in accordance with any other currently in effect law shall be regarded as sensitive personal data or information.

It is important to recognize that the words sensitive personal data or information refer to two distinct concepts: sensitive personal data and sensitive personal information. Any information pertaining to a natural person that, directly or indirectly, when combined with additional information currently available or anticipated to be available with a body corporate, can identify that person is considered Personal Information (PI) under the terms of these Rules.

Pune Citibank Mphasis Call Center Fraud Case

"In 2005, fraudulent online transfers of $3,50,000 from the Citibank accounts of four US customers to a few phony accounts took place. Under the pretense that they would be a helping hand to those clients struggling with challenging circumstances, the staff won the customer's trust and stole their PINs. Instead of breaking through firewalls or decrypting encrypted software, they found weaknesses in the MphasiS system. The court noted that the defendants in this case are former MphasiS contact center employees. Every time an employee enters or exits, they are examined.

The staff members must have committed the figures to memory as a result. The funds were sent through a SWIFT, or Society for Worldwide Interbank Financial Telecommunication, service. Unauthorized access to the victims' electronic accounts was used to commit the crime. As a result, this case is considered a cyber-crime. The IT Act is sufficiently wide to cover these aspects of criminal behavior, and any IPC offense involving the use of electronic documents can be treated on a same footing with offenses involving written materials.

The court determined that Section 43(a) of the IT Act, 2000 is applicable since performing transactions involves illegal access of a certain type.

Similar situations arise all throughout the world, but when they do so in India, it raises major concerns that cannot be disregarded. After reviewing this case, it can be said that there are still a lot of unexplored and unprotected areas of cyber law. Companies should be required to conduct a thorough background check before hiring call center executives, and they should tighten their security measures. The security of the clients' money is their responsibility".

Background checks should not be disregarded when hiring staff, even though they cannot completely prevent the potential of undesirable entering and violating security. National ID cards and a database that lists criminals' names and criminal histories are also available. Additionally, clients need to be warned not to fall for these traps. Additionally, banks must implement strong security measures. The security of the clients' money is their responsibility.

This fraud case made it clear that business cultures and ethics need to be reviewed. It is necessary to have a certain type of corporate culture where long-term success and the value of the people working for a firm are prioritized over short-term greed.

Section 72 - Penalty for Breach of confidentiality and privacy

"Save as otherwise provided in this Act or any other law for the time being in force, if any person who, in pursuance of any of the powers conferred under this Act, rules or regulations made thereunder, has secured access to any electronic record, book, register, correspondence, information, document or other material without the consent of the person concerned discloses such electronic record, book, register, correspondence, information, document or other material to any other person shall be punished with imprisonment for a term which may extend to two years, or with fine which may extend to one lakh rupees, or with both".

It would not apply to the disclosure of a person's personal information by a website, by his email service provider, etc. This section only applies to people who have access to the aforementioned information due to a power granted under the Information Technology Act and its allied rules, such as a police officer, the Controller, etc.

Section 72A - Punishment for disclosure of information in breach of lawful contract

"Save as otherwise provided in this Act or any other law for the time being in force, any person including an intermediary who, while providing services under the terms of lawful contract, has secured access to any material containing personal information about another person, with the intent to cause or knowing that he is likely to cause wrongful loss or wrongful gain discloses, without the consent of the person concerned, or in breach of a lawful contract, such material to any other person, shall be punished with imprisonment for a term which may extend to three years, or with fine which may extend to five lakh rupees, or with both".

According to this clause, it is unlawful to reveal any information including a person's personal information without that person's consent, in violation of a valid contract, or with the goal or knowledge that doing so will likely result in wrongful gain or unjust loss.

The main distinction between Section 72 and Section 72A is how they can be applied; while Section 72 can only be used against legitimate authorities, Section 72A can be used against anybody who exposes information in violation of a legitimate contract or without the subject's consent. It is noteworthy that illegal disclosure by private individuals carries a heavier penalty than improper disclosure by legitimate authorities.

Section 79 - Exemption from liability of intermediary in certain cases

"Notwithstanding anything contained in any law for the time being in force but subject to the provisions of sub-sections *(2)* and *(3)*, an intermediary shall not be liable for any third-party information, data, or communication link made available or hosted by him. The provisions of sub-section *(1)* shall apply if- the function of the intermediary is limited to providing access to a communication system over which information made available by third parties is transmitted or temporarily stored or hosted; or the intermediary does not initiate the transmission, select the receiver of the transmission, and select or modify the information contained in the transmission; the intermediary observes due diligence while discharging his duties under this Act and also observes such other guidelines as the Central Government may prescribe in this behalf. The provisions of sub-section *(1)* shall not apply if the intermediary has conspired or abetted or aided or induced, whether by threats or promise or otherwise in the commission of the unlawful act; upon receiving actual knowledge, or on being notified by the appropriate Government or its agency that any information, data or communication link residing in or connected to a computer resource controlled by the intermediary is being used to commit the unlawful act, the intermediary fails to expeditiously remove or disable access to that material on that resource without vitiating the evidence in any manner.

Explanation. - For the purposes of this section, the expression third party information means any information dealt with by an intermediary in his capacity as an intermediary".

Christian Louboutin SAS V. Nakul Bajaj and Ors. (2018)

The defendant in this case operated the website www.darvey.com and sold a variety of extravagant items, including designer shoes under the name "Christian Louboutin." The plaintiff, Christian Louboutin SAS, claimed that the defendant's website provides the appearance to its visitors that the defendant and the plaintiff are associated, sponsored, or have in some other manner obtained the plaintiff's consent for the sale of the plaintiff's upmarket goods through the defendant's website. As a result, the plaintiff claimed that its trademark rights had been violated and that the website no longer accurately represented the wealth and high status that the plaintiff possessed in relation to its products. The only matter before the honorable bench related to the defendant's protection under section 79 of the IT Act, 2000. The court essentially used the definition of "intermediary" as stated in section 2(w) of the IT Act of 2000 to decide whether an e-commerce platform is eligible for protection under section 79 of the IT Act of 2008.

The website is simply used to accept orders for such products rather than actually selling them through its online platform, the defendants contended in court, therefore it is merely functioning as an intermediary. It only accepts orders from registered vendors who utilize online booking to offer their goods. Since only these registered merchants' goods are featured on the defendants' platform, they are therefore the only ones who are covered under Section 79 of the Information Technology Act of 2000. The truthfulness of the items they were selling was the main source of disagreement between the two parties.

Since no goods had been sold through that website as of the date of the judgement, the sole question for the court to address was whether the putative defendant was protected under section 79 of the IT Act, 2000.

According to the court's decision, the defendant was not an intermediary qualified for assurance under Section 79 and would be subject to intrusion should it be established that the commodities it was transporting were false. The Court decided that the respondent should not be made aware of the suppliers' subtleties and will not carry any items bearing the mark of the aggrieved party without their agreement in the absence of such confirmation. The Court further ordered the respondent to set up a system whereby, upon receiving notification of any fake item from the offended party, the respondent would check the item's veracity with the dealer and evaluate the evidence to decide whether it necessitated expulsion.

The Court further ordered the middleman to have all meta-labels mentioning the wrong party's check removed and to enforce the warranties and assurances given by the wrong party's vendors.

Google India Pvt. Ltd. v. Visaka Industries (2020)

The fundamental facts of the case were that a person (Appellant) had posted several defamatory writings in a group maintained by Google that were directed at the Respondent and some national leaders. The respondent had given the appellant a warning to take action to remove the aforementioned defamatory content, but the appellant made no such move. In light of this, the High Court issued a ruling in favor of the Respondent while pointing out that the Petitioner was ineligible to make any claims under Section 79 of the IT Act.

Conclusions

The Information Technology Act, 2000's Sections 43A, 72, 72A, and 79 are essential for maintaining the safety and preservation of digital information as well as the smooth operation of online platforms in India. In essence, these parts form a body of law that governs many facets of online responsibility, data protection, and cybersecurity in India. They encourage responsible behavior online, safeguard people's privacy and security, and make sure that middlemen contribute positively to the upkeep of a secure online environment. The correct implementation and enforcement of these rules, which is a constant issue in the quickly developing world of technology and the internet, are necessary for these laws to be effective. To keep the Information Technology Act, 2000, relevant and effective moving forward, constant efforts must be made to update and adapt these provisions to new digital risks and difficulties.

References

1. Information Technology Act, 2000.
2. Available at https://www.comptia.org/content/articles/what-is-information-technology.
3. Information Technology Act, 2000.
4. Christian Louboutin Sas v. Nakul Bajaj, (2018) 253 DLT 728.
5. Google India Private Limited v. Visaka Industries, (2020) 4 SCC 162.
6. https://bnwjournal.com/2020/07/17/pune-citibank-mphasis-call-center-fraud/.
7. Information Technology (Reasonable Security Practices and Procedures and Sensitive Personal Data or Information) Rules, 2011 ('the SPDI Rules').
8. https://www.comptia.org/content/articles/what-is-informationtechnology#:~:text=Information%20technology%20(IT)%20is%20the,much%20of%20our%20daily%20activities.
9. https://www.cyberstates.org/.
10. Information Technology (Amendment) Act, 2008.

15

Analysis of Data Protection Bill, 2019 post Covid: Focus on Legislative Relevance and Judicial Intervention

Aditi Srivastava, Ritu Gautam and Shikha Yadav

Abstract

21st century technological developments have created an indispensable arena for 'Cyber space and its regulations' which is an obligatory notion in any fast-developing country. This exploratory research paper presents a critical analysis of treaties, policies, statutes, emerging new theories of cyberspace jurisprudence, new entitlements accepted, adopted by netizens, challenges that are being faced by all the stakeholders, A stringent framework is needed to limit world's leaning towards gathering, analysing, preserving personal data of both public and private sectors, leading to graver implications. Analysis of interaction of statutes such as effective Penal, Constitutional provisions, Indian's Information Technology Act, 2000, (Intermediary Guidelines and Digital Media Ethics Code) Rules, 2021 envisaged to combating cyber threats, upcoming Personal Data Protection Bill, 2019 will play supportive roles to strengthen Indian Cyber Security Framework, easing the interpreting of existing legislation in the best interest of rule of law giving further scope of study to determine socio legal empowerment in cyberspace as Covid-19 pandemic, reminded us the importance of 'Free and Fair Digital Economy' under the 'Digital Initiative' undertaken by Government of India, flagship of Honourable Prime Minister. Primarily Securing data of individual, corporate and governmental information against theft which is being misused or infringed in cybercrimes against the integrity of State upheld by our sacrosanct judicial framework to protect privacy and rights of citizens.

Keywords - *Big Data, Cyber Space, Digital Rights, Habeas Writs, Privacy.*

Introduction

Anyone may now gather, process, send, and store data from anywhere in the world because to the rapid growth of digital technology and the internet's widespread use. The fast development of technology over few decades have given new legal and ethical problems. Unfortunately, the law has not developed as quickly as technology, leaving considerable gaps in how it addresses numerous problems that occur from using these tools. Data protection has been described as one of the most nebulous legal notions that lacks a concise definition. According to legal experts, the word "data protection" is a blanket term that is used to describe everything related to the processing of personal data. It is undeniable that technology is a two-edged sword, offering the chance to protect one's privacy on the one hand while simultaneously playing a crucial part in privacy invasion on the other. It is essential to examine the existing privacy regulations in India in light of this remark.

Relevance of Free and Fair Digital Economy Post Covid 19

Physical infrastructure such as establishing industries was the main emphasis of various countries in the 20th century since, it encouraged by facilitating trade and raising labour productivity. However, by twenty-first century shifting needs of people and countries have changed their focus to creating the infrastructure necessary to enable the delivery of technology-based services. A broad range of technologies that support service delivery over the Internet are referred to as digital infrastructure. For instance, the COVID-19 epidemic sped up development of digital infrastructure internationally including developing countries e.g., African and Latin American nations as a result of the dramatic rise of dependency on the internet and mobile devices. Due to specific logistical constraints, effectively responding to the scope and complexity of cybersecurity incidents during the COVID-19 crisis proved to be an impossible task. Online users' priority had changed from online safety to maintaining their health and avoiding coronavirus sickness, and as a result, they began to react panic kingly to the efforts used to manage the pandemic. The majority of internet responses that centered on panic and despair ultimately led to social engineering exploitations that benefited cybercriminals.

The Identify, Protect, Detect, Respond, and Recover components of the NIST cybersecurity framework (CSF) provide a simple approach for businesses to meet the additional assault surface and threats brought about in the tremor in cybersecurity caused by COVID-19. The NIST CSF portal provides information about the framework and how many firms implemented the technique to enhance their cybersecurity risk management. We use the CSF model to organize our discussion of the global cybersecurity response. To prove that our cybersecurity reaction to COVID-19 "has a method to the craziness", our narrative features a series of tables that exhibit the CSF method and industry reaction instances.

Figure 1.- NIST cybersecurity framework.

Need for Personal Data Protection Law

India's data protection laws now have several issues because there is no suitable legislative structure. Globally, the number of cybercrimes has significantly increased. Physical borders are neither a barrier nor seem to exist in the theft and sale of stolen data, which occurs all over the world. India, which hosts the majority of the world's outsourced data processing, runs the risk of becoming the centre of all cybercrimes. This is mostly because this is still developing branch with no suitable legislation of criminology. However, strong legislative provisions are the only way to achieve an effective solution. The gathering and processing of data forms the basis of constantly expanding plans of business, supporting the operations of technological entities, and serving as a foundation of competitive advantage. The crucial character that data plays in the electronic ecosystems' competitive dynamics takes prompted substantial discussions regarding the substantive connections between competition policy and data protection legislation as well as pushed these two legal fields closer together. The law of data protection is of particular concern to India due to innumerable factors, the most prominent of them being the extensively vast population of India.

The National Academy of Medicine promoted "learning healthcare system," data updated with reference while providing care. As we transition to a quick learning system to address insurmountable health concerns, it is important to strike balance of patient confidentiality and making data accessible for better health care. Right to Privacy breaches, unethical uses of data are not actively addressed, this balance will be thrown off, which will result in the illicit exploitation of citizens' sensitive information to destroy National's integrity. New federal laws priorities the sharing of personal health data, including that provided using patient digital tools. The U.S. health privacy regulations not revised to understand or address difficulties with the establishing of big technology companies into the healthcare sector, did not cover the data of users obtained by digital applications and gadgets.

Judicial Interventions

Hon. Justice K. S. Puttaswamy (Ret.), Karnataka High Court appealed against the Union Government's decision to make Aadhaar obligatory in Honourable Supreme Court of India. Aadhaar is a repository of biometric data, information of individuals residing in India. In addition, its most accepted forms of identification and verification, it is necessary to comply with numerous government directives and to be eligible for many governmental programmes. Because the government made it essential to register in the Aadhaar's database even connecting these details as KYC with citizens' bank accounts. Justice K. S. Puttaswamy felt aggrieved and used his right to do so under Article 32 of Part III of the Indian Constitution. Many people were of the opinion that the government's requirement of the gathering of biometric data infringed fundamental right to privacy, implied in Article 21, which is concerned with the protection of life and personal liberty.

Honourable Supreme Court remarked that there were rulings of Benches that were at odds with one another in their interpretations of the basic right to privacy. The learned counsel informed the bench that right to privacy, is not specifically protected in the Constitution were made in the cases of *M. P. Sharma versus. Satish Chandra*, District Magistrate, Delhi and *Kharak Singh versus. State of Uttar Pradesh*. While the petitioners pointed out that both of the aforementioned rulings were made in the context of *A K Gopalan versus. State of Madras* essentially established that every component of constitution's fundamental rights, which grants unique level of protection. An eleven-judge panel concluded that it constituted bad law. In *Rustom Cavasji Cooper versus. Union of India Bench* and *Maneka Gandhi versus. Union of India*, it was clearly stated that the majority view of *Kharak Singh (Supra)* got overruled. The Hon'ble Three-Judge Bench further examined the situation in light of these arguments and noted that some judgments, including *Gobind versus. State of Madhya Pradesh*, *R Rajagopal versus. State of Tamil Nadu*, and *People's Union for Civil Liberties versus. Union of India* have held that the right to privacy is protected by the Constitution. However, benches with lesser strength than those in *M P Sharma* and *Kharak Singh* made these decisions. Because of the significance of this judgement, the learned three-judge Bench requested a legal ruling on the following issue: Is the right to privacy protected by the Indian Constitution?

So, as to be listed in front of a strong bench. The matter was subsequently registered before Chief Justice of India and Constitution bench, who felt that a nine-judge bench would be suitable to decide it. The right to privacy was subsequently upheld after a nine-judge bench ruled in its favour, concluding, among other things, that "the right to privacy is protected as an intrinsic part of the right to life and personal liberty under Article 21 and as a part of the freedoms guaranteed by Part III of the Constitution." This landmark decision solidified the position of privacy as basic right that serves as the foundation for all upcoming data protection or processing laws. In that ruling on August 24, 2017, the Honourable

Justice D.Y. Chandrachud stated that fundamental right of Article 21 includes right to privacy both being not absolute.

International Framework for Protection of Data of Citizens

Big data is all about strategically and methodically gathered for purposes other than those for which they were initially gathered. Processing, analysing, and evaluating data may be necessary in order to offer personalised services. For instance, unique adverts may be shown to internet users based on the shopping habits of people in a certain location. Monetary dealings, soundness, medicinal handling, remote consumption, specialized activity, route tracking, internet use, electronic card and smartphone use, video or communication monitoring are all possible uses for the process of combining and revaluing this data.

Big data undoubtedly has numerous scientific advantages, but that does not lessen the substantial danger associated with its management. These data can be manipulated, but the use of artificial intelligence-based automotive information further limits the need for human intervention can be faulty and liable to be misused. This suggests that the right to object and other significant rights acknowledged by the sophisticated data protection rules are rendered invalid. Thus, a new challenge to the data protection system around the world has developed from the processing and interpretation of massive volumes of data. The GDPR is aware of the upcoming difficulties with protection of data especially big data. However, a number of significant problems pertaining to the right and the remedies have emerged as a result of the absence of human action.

The GDPR's viewpoint appears to be supported in part by the Indian law. Federal data privacy laws in the US have generally taken a much more liberal approach to data protection than the GDPR in the EU. The protection of online expression and data privacy may be related to a fundamentally different understanding of human rights, as evident by this. Comparatively, many of its peers in the European Union and U.S.A generally see less of the government's role in the safeguarding of online data and information. India is a significant actor in the world of internet regulation. The Indian government has made significant progress toward its goal of being a global leader in democratic data regulation as its commitment to later ratify Budapest Convention. Indian action at the UN General Assembly and elsewhere on internet problems is at high levels and observers have given the country high marks for its capacity to influence global policy.

Regardless of processing of data has any effect on that person's privacy, the right to the protection of their personal data is guaranteed to them each time that processing occurs. Although such processing may violate a person's right to privacy, even in situations when such processing has no influence on that right, a person's right to data protection is nonetheless relevant. The European Court of Justice has interpreted the term "privacy" in a very broad sense, and there are situations in which the mere collection of a person's personal information is considered to have the potential to violate that person's right to privacy as being disclosed to a third party without consent.

Initiative of Legislature to Protect the Data of Citizens

In India, the case of *Justice K.S. Puttaswamy (Retd.) v. Union of India and Ors* ("Privacy Judgment") led to the realisation of the urgent need for data privacy framework. On this basis, the ministry of electronics and information technology established a committee in July 2017 that was composed of ten experts and was headed by B.N. Srikrishna, a former justice of the Supreme Court. The ten-member committee's report on the government-revised data protection law was turned in on July 27, 2018. The Personal Data Protection Bill, 2019 ("PDP Bill") revised version of the 2018 Draft Bill, was then introduced before the Indian Parliament on December 11. The B N Sri Krishna Committee had provided the groundwork for a new age in which a complete code on the data protection regime in India would be established.

A Committee of privacy experts headed by Justice AP Shah was constituted by the Indian government in January 2012 with the mission of reviewing privacy best practises around the world and recommending a framework for legislation in India. The Shah

Committee report's newly released recommendations, which are extremely thorough and comprehensive, will serve as the model for India's privacy legislation. These suggestions can close the huge legal vacuum in India's data protection and privacy framework because all definitional and linguistic errors in preceding Bills have been fixed.

Rectifying the earlier draft of new Digital Personal Data Protection Bill, 2022 (published on Friday, November 18) is more data centric. The Bill is revised to include stronger penalties for non-compliance bearing no relation to the turnover of the breaching company. With provision to start-up compliance standards, to loosened regulations specifically on international data flows, which may provide relief for the major internet corporations. The two potentially serious red flags: universal exemption to government agencies from more onerous requirements and dilution proposed Data Protection Board, which shall oversee the provisions of the proposed legislation. According, Ministry of Electronics and IT (MeitY), the new draft is the delicate balance, which comparatively takes into account other countries' approaches but, adhering the Supreme Court's decision on privacy as it being a basic right subject to reasonable limitations.

Conclusions

As information technology has advanced, data protection has become a crucial by product response towards protection and fair sharing. In India, the Information Technology Act of 2000 regulates data protection (hereinafter, the Act). The definition of "data" is which means any representation of facts, information, knowledge, concepts, or instructions prepared in a formalised manner, intended to be processed or being processed in system or computer network, including optical storage media, computer printouts, magnetic punched cards/tapes stored internally as memory of the computer. Certain provisions in the Act cover the protection of such data and privacy. Data protection regulations have been thought to be necessary recently to meet a variety of purposes. The situation of data protection law in relation to some of the needs is analyzed in the paragraphs that follow.

Customers from abroad and domestic consumers alike have recently expressed concern about the country's data protection and privacy laws as being insufficient. A few incidents have called into question the data protection and privacy standards in India, embarrassing the outsourcing sector. The state of protection in India was a major discussion topic in 2017 and 2018. The government challenged the existence of privacy as a basic right in front of the Supreme Court. According to critics and promoters of privacy differed from Indian culture's perceptions. All attempts to draught a separate piece of legislation for data protection failed. In its most recent ruling on Aadhaar, the Supreme Court addressed how personal data is protected in India. The complete legal obligation as a right of data protection may only be achieved by refraining from interfering with others' rights and violating their privacy. A general approach to data protection might be provided by the institutional status of data protection. The elements of data protection, such as data collecting, processing, storage, security, and access, should operate together in a legal framework to give it particular status as a right. There needs to be universal awareness of the proper fundamental approach to data protection and privacy.

References

1. Vakul Sharma and Seema Sharma, Information Technology Law and Practice, Lexis Nexis, 6th ed., (2019).
2. A K Gopalan v State of Madras, AIR 1950 SC 27 (India).
3. Beatriz Kira, Vikram Sinha, Sharmadha Srinivasan, Regulating digital ecosystems: bridging the gap between competition policy and data protection, Industrial and Corporate Change, Volume 30, Issue 5, October 2021, Pages 1337–1360, https://doi.org/10.1093/icc/dtab053.
4. David Wallace and Mark Visger, Responding to the Call for a Digital Geneva Convention: An Open Letter to Brad Smith and the Technology Community, 6 J.L. and Cyber Warfare 3, 12-13 (2018).
5. European Commission, 'Questions and Answers - Data protection reform' (Press release, 21 December 2015) accessed 13 August 2022.
6. Gobind v State of Madhya Pradesh, (1975) 2 SCC 148 (India).
7. Henfridsson, O., and Bygstad, B. (2013). The generative mechanisms of digital infrastructure evolution. MIS Q 907–931.
8. Justice K S Puttaswamy (Retd.) v Union of India, (2017) 10 SCC 1.
9. Justice Srikrishna Committee Submits Report on Data Protection. Here're Its Top 10 Suggestions, The Economic Times. (July 2020.)
10. Kharak Singh v State of Uttar Pradesh, (1964) 1 SCR 332 (India).
11. Maneka Gandhi v Union of India, (1978) 1 SCC 248 (India).
12. Matthias Berberich, Malgorzata Steiner, Blockchain Technology and the GDPR - How to Reconcile Privacy and Distributed Ledgers, 2 EUR. DATA PROT. L. REV. 422, 431-432 (2016).

13. McGraw, D., Mandl, K.D. Privacy protections to encourage use of health-relevant digital data in a learning health system. npj Digit. Med. 4, 2 (2021) https://doi.org/10.1038/s41746-020-00362-8.
14. M P Sharma v Satish Chandra, District Magistrate, Delhi, (1954) SCR 1077 (India).
15. Noriswadi Ismail and Edwin Lee Yong Cieh, et. at (eds.), Beyond Data Protection 6 (Springer, London, 2013).
16. People's Union for Civil Liberties v Union of India, (1997) 1 SCC 301 (India).
17. R Rajagopal v State of Tamil Nadu, (1994) 6 SCC 632 (India).
18. Rustom Cavasji Cooper v Union of India, (1970) 1 SCC 248 (India).
19. CJEU, Joined cases C-92/09 and C-93/02, Volker und Markus Schecke GbR v. Land Hessen, Opinion of Advocate General Sharpston, 17 June 2010.
20. Sharad Vadehra, Data Protection and the IT Act India, Kan and Krishme, Attorneys of Law, Available at http://www.gala-marketlaw.com/77-gala-gazette/gala-gazette/261-india-data-protection-and-the-it-act-india.
21. Stuart Russel And Peter Norvig, Artificial Intelligence: A Modern Approach, 122-124 (1st Ed. 2009).
22. S Singh, Privacy and Data Protection in India: A Critical Assessment, 53 Journal Of The Indian Law Institute, 104-111(2012).
23. The Indian Express Written by Anil Sasi, Soumyarendra Barik, Edited by Explained Desk, New Delhi, Updated: November 23, 2022, 9:16:55 am.
24. T. Weil and S. Murugesan, "IT Risk and Resilience-Cybersecurity Response to COVID-19," in IT Professional, vol. 22, no. 3, pp. 4-10, 1 May-June 2020, doi: 10.1109/MITP.2020.2988330.

16

Safeguarding of Right to Privacy under the Notion of Substantive Due Process of Law in India

Nisha Praveen

Abstract

The issue of privacy has become a global concern in the era of digitalization, as technological progress continues to redefine the limits of personal information and individual autonomy. This study explores the protection of the right to privacy within the context of substantive due process of law in India. Article 21 of the Indian Constitution provides an assurance of the right to life and personal liberty, which has been repeatedly read by the Supreme Court of India in a broad manner to embrace the right to privacy. The key role of protecting this right is played by the concept of substantive due process, which is grounded in the broader principles of justice and fairness. The study delves into significant legal decisions, like K.S. Puttaswamy v. Union of India, wherein the recognition of privacy as a basic right occurred. Furthermore, it analyses the development of the Court's legal principles in response to present-day issues with data protection, surveillance, and informational privacy. Moreover, the abstract examines the legal endeavors undertaken by the Indian government, particularly the implementation of the Personal Data Protection Bill, with the aim of governing data processing activities and augmenting the safeguarding of individual privacy. Furthermore, it examines the intricate equilibrium between the protection of individual privacy and the considerations of national security in the context of India, emphasizing the necessity for sophisticated legal strategies.

Keywords - *Data Protection, Rights, Privacy, Judiciary, India.*

Introduction

The Indian Constitution incorporates the right to privacy within the framework of the right to life and personal liberty. This right is also recognized by the international convention on Human Rights. The notion of privacy encompasses more than mere seclusion, but also entails the absence of unauthorized intrusions into an individual's personal affairs. Currently, as a result of technological progress, the notion of privacy has garnered increased attention. The fundamental challenge faced in contemporary times is the lack of legislative enactments, laws, or regulations pertaining to privacy.

The establishment of data banks by governmental entities and defense agencies, among others, poses a significant threat to privacy. This concern is compounded by the interception of mail and telephonic conversations, which has sparked substantial issues worldwide. In the contemporary period characterized by the revolution of Information Technology, the concept of privacy has become increasingly intricate. Social media platforms such as Facebook, Twitter, and Google, which maintain their primary servers in several geographical locations, has the ability to obtain confidential data pertaining to numerous individuals globally. If influential organizations such as the North Atlantic Treaty Organization (NATO) were granted access to extensive amounts of information for the purpose of counterterrorism and similar endeavors, what implications would this have for the privacy of individuals?

In the context of globalization, it is argued that individuals are unable to maintain complete privacy due to their tendency to selectively disclose personal information while concealing their deficiencies. This practice can lead to the dissemination of inaccurate information about their talents, potentially impacting future employment prospects and other related outcomes. In this particular environment, there is a pressing need for conducting a comparative analysis of the right to privacy and the progress made in the formulation of legal measures aimed at safeguarding this fundamental right.

The phrase 'Right to be let alone' was initially coined by Justice Cooley in 1888 and then embraced by Louis Brandeis and Samuel Warren in their 1890 publication titled 'The Right to Privacy'. This article highlights the significance of privacy in safeguarding the concept of the 'inviolate individuality'. In the publication titled 'Privacy and Freedom' authored by Professor A.F. Westin in 1970, the concept of privacy is delineated as the inherent inclination of persons towards seclusion, intimacy, anonymity, and reservation. The individual asserts that privacy pertains to the desire of an individual, whether human or legal, to establish boundaries on the degree of intrusion by others into their own sphere, particularly in relation to personal information.

The 1967 Nordic Conference of Jurists on the Right to Privacy addressed the issue of privacy violations and emphasized that when an individual intrudes upon the privacy of another person's family, home, or other personal domains, regardless of whether the intrusion is made public or not, it poses a threat to the individual's dignity and reputation. Consequently, the infringement of privacy encompasses the infringement upon fundamental human rights, such as those pertaining to familial relationships, marital unions, educational pursuits, and personal reputation, among others. A significant global issue is to the insufficiency of legislative measures in safeguarding privacy. In the contemporary context of the Cyber era, it is imperative to provide robust safeguards for privacy rights across all facets of life.

Numerous international conventions, declarations, treaties, and other relevant legal instruments pertaining to the right to privacy merit acknowledgment. According to Article 12 of the Universal Declaration of Human Rights (UDHR), individuals are entitled to protection from any unwarranted intrusion into their family, residence, or other private domains, which includes safeguarding their reputation and dignity. The elimination and protection of such interference shall be ensured through legal measures. Article 17 of the International Covenant on Civil and Political Rights (ICCPR) establishes the prohibition of laws that engage in unauthorized interference with an individual's family, home, or reputation. Likewise, the aforementioned findings pertain to Article 10 of the

International Covenant of Economic, Social, and Cultural Rights of 1966.

In the context of protection of right to privacy and concept of substantive due process, the debate is around the necessity of incorporating a formally acknowledged right to privacy within the rights enumerated in Part III of the Constitution, given the existence of a legal structure that sufficiently safeguards this right. It is important to mention that recognizing a fundamental framework in relation to modification provides insight into the existence of systematic principles that underlie and connect the constitutional laws, beyond the wording of specific clauses. These criteria provide coherence to the Constitution, rendering it a cohesive and integrated entity. Fragments of constitutional law exist, irrespective of whether they are clearly articulated as norms. One illustration of this concept is the principle of reasonableness, which establishes a connection between Articles 14, 19, and 21 of the Constitution. Among them, certain regulations may hold such significance and importance that they can be considered fundamental characteristics or components of the Constitution's 'basic structure', thereby rendering them immune to constitutional modifications. In any event, the differentiation between essential and less fundamental aspects of the Constitution can only be achieved by establishing connections between sections and overarching principles.

Protection of Right to Privacy and the Notion of Substantive Due Process

Dr. B.R. Ambedkar astutely provided a comprehensive analysis of the advantages and disadvantages of opposing perspectives in a neutral and objective manner. There exist divergent perspectives on this matter. One viewpoint posits that it is feasible to depend on the legislative body to refrain from enacting legislation that would infringe upon individuals' fundamental rights. An alternative perspective posits that placing trust in the legislature is unfeasible due to its track record of committing errors and succumbing to influences such as emotional fervor, partisan hostility, and several other causes. Consequently, it is possible for the government to enact legislation that undermines the core principles safeguarding the individual rights of its citizens. Two separate locations were occupied. One proposed approach is to confer upon the court the authority to adjudicate on the decisions made by the legislative body and to question the validity of legislation based on its non-conformity to fundamental principles or sound legal principles.

The second perspective posits that individuals ought to place trust in the legislative body's ability to pass effective and beneficial laws. Drawing definitive findings can be quite difficult. On both sides, there exist potential hazards. The potential presence of party operatives in the legislature cannot be disregarded, as it may result in the erosion of fundamental principles that have an impact on an individual's rights and freedoms. Simultaneously, one cannot disregard the presence of the five or six individuals of the Supreme Court, who engage in the scrutiny of legislative measures formulated by the Legislature. Their evaluation of the legislation's merit or demerit is contingent upon their individual consciences or biases.

The inclusion of Article 22 in the Constitution aimed to protect individuals against arbitrary arrest and imprisonment by incorporating various safeguards, notwithstanding the omission of the phrase 'due process of law' from the initial draught. The absence of a positive form for the term 'due process of law' was a significant consideration leading the Drafting Committee to exclude it, as evidenced by their deliberations. Accepting the opinion that there are implied constraints on the ability to effect change would infuse confusion and ambiguity into the Indian Constitution, contrary to the intentions of the founding fathers who diligently sought to prevent such outcomes.

Due Process and Substantive Due Process of Law

The concept of 'due process' refers to the adherence to established rules and principles in the conduct of legal processes. The concept of 'substantive due process' refers to the legal notion that the Due Process Clauses found in the 5th and 14th Amendments of the United States Constitution necessitate legislation to possess qualities of fairness and reasonableness in its text, while also serving a legitimate governmental aim. The ideals of the rule of law and due process are intrinsically interconnected with the safeguarding of human rights. The effective protection of such rights can be ensured when a citizen has access to the judicial system. In his observation, Justice K. S. Hegde emphasized the paramount significance of individual freedom within a civilized society. The assertion posits that it is a fundamental entitlement inherent to all individuals. According to the provisions of the Constitution, this right is guaranteed. Deprivation of rights can only occur through the proper application of due process of law.

The phrase 'due process of law' has been employed in numerous statutes across diverse contexts in India. The term 'due process of law' or its synonymous counterpart 'law of the land' can be traced back to the early 13th century A. D. The concept of 'due process of law' refers to the exercise of governmental powers in accordance with established legal principles and with appropriate safeguards to protect individual rights, as recommended by commonly accepted principles applicable to the specific case at hand. The phrase 'due process of law' was incorporated into the United States Constitution by the Fifth Amendment, ratified in 1791. This amendment stipulates that "no person shall be deprived of life, liberty or property without due process of law". The aforementioned phrase was employed in the Fourteenth Amendment in the year 1868. The phrase 'due process of law' has been widely regarded as one of the most challenging concepts in the field of law, as it is often difficult to precisely comprehend its meaning. The United States Supreme Court has consistently refrained from providing a comprehensive definition of the term in question, instead favoring a gradual determination of its complete meaning through the process of inclusion and exclusion in the course of its decisions as they arise.

In the context of India, it is important to note that the Indian Constitution does not include a provision similar to the Eighth Amendment. Furthermore, the courts in India do not possess the same level of discretion as the Judges of the Supreme Court of America in applying the test of reasonableness, as permitted by the due process clause. Judicial review stands as a prominent characteristic within the realm of American Constitutional Law. In the United States, the principle of equal protection under the law is founded upon the notion of due process of law. The aforementioned features are not included under the provisions of the Constitution of India. The founding fathers separated abstract judgement from judicial scrutiny. The deliberate withholding or denial of due process as a measure of legal insufficiency was seen. The courts do not take into consideration the wisdom or planning of a particular enactment. The judiciary exhibits a lack of concern regarding the prudence and strategic considerations underlying the constitutional amendments.

Therefore, it can be argued that the Indian Courts lack the authority to declare legislation as ultra vires based on the contention that it breaches the principle of 'due process of law'. The invocation of the standard of due process of law is not applicable under the Constitution of India in relation to the Acts of Parliament or the State Legislature. The invalidity of such an Act cannot be determined solely based on its alleged violation of the due process clause or its perceived ambiguity. The principle of due process was disregarded through the clear limitation of acquired rights and the abandonment of stated theory. The Court, in its application of the doctrine of due process of law, has determined that when the owner of private property is required to bear the expenses of a public improvement that greatly exceed the specific benefits received, it constitutes a taking of private property for public use without adequate compensation, disguised as taxation. The aforementioned idea of due process of law does not apply to India.

Dichotomy Between Right to Privacy and State Welfare

The denial of the right to privacy based on the argument that the State gives welfare benefits to its citizens undermines the comprehensive framework of the constitution. The initial proposal of distinguishing between two sorts of rights, namely justiciable rights and directive rights, was put up by the Sapru Committee in 1945. These rights were deemed vital in shaping the government of the nation. The aforementioned commands possess a significance beyond mere expressions of religious devotion. The framers of the Constitution intended for both the Legislature and the Executive to not only verbally acknowledge these principles, but to also incorporate them as the foundation for all legislative and executive actions undertaken by future governments in governing the country.

The Directive Principles of State Policy must adhere to and operate in a subordinate manner to the Chapter on Fundamental Rights. The court proceeded to determine that the legislative authority of the state cannot be impacted by non-compliance with Directive Principles.

One of the instances, where court has found a contradiction between right to privacy and welfare scheme is that the judiciary engages in the interpretation of constitutional provisions within the context of the prevailing social conditions of the nation. This approach demonstrates a comprehensive understanding and profound recognition of the evolving societal demands, the escalating national needs, the pressing contemporary issues, and the intricate challenges confronting the populace. It acknowledges that the legislature, through its judicious enactment of beneficial laws, endeavors to address these concerns. The preferred approach in the judicial system should be characterized by dynamism rather than static adherence, pragmatism rather than pedantry, and flexibility rather than rigidity. The judiciary, in its role as a vigilant guardian of the fundamental rights bestowed upon the citizens, is tasked with the responsibility of achieving a fair equilibrium between these rights and the wider societal interests. Consequently, in situations where a fundamental right comes into conflict with a broader national interest, the former must be subordinated to the latter.

In accordance with the pronouncement of the Apex Court, articulated by the esteemed Dr. D. Y. Chandrachud, J., it is noted that our Constitution places emphasis on the rights of individuals, ensuring their entitlement to both civil and political rights. Throughout history, there has been a prevailing notion that economic wellbeing is the sole requirement for the impoverished, disregarding their interests in civil and political rights. This perspective has been employed as a means to infringe upon the fundamental human rights of this marginalized population. A well-informed individual should have a willingness to critically evaluate, scrutinize, and express dissent towards the actions and policies of the government. The judiciary has unequivocally dismissed the notion that civil and political rights should be subordinated to socio-economic rights in the context of constitutional litigation. Socioeconomic rights should exclusively serve the intended beneficiaries rather than individuals who do not possess the necessary right. The realization of these benefits can only be achieved under the condition of unrestricted information dissemination. The flourishing of civil and political liberty is contingent upon the presence of governmental policies that are open to scrutiny. The coexistence and reciprocal support of socio-economic, civic, and political rights are imperative, since they cannot be rendered incompatible with one other.

Amartya Sen, a distinguished recipient of the Nobel Prize, examined the responses of various non-democratic regimes in times of severe crises, such as famine, in comparison to the behaviors of democratic societies facing similar situations. An analysis of Sen's work demonstrates that the effectiveness of addressing the problem is hindered by the political safeguard provided by government officials in authoritarian regimes. Amartya Sen observes that the Bengal famine of 1943 served as an illustration of India's democratic deficit, with the constraints imposed on the Indian press and the self-imposed 'silence' of the British-owned media. Political liberties and equitable rights are commonly regarded as integral elements of progress. Amartya Sen used the phrase 'the protective role of democracy' to describe the management of famine situations. He succinctly argues that there exists a subtle resemblance between the conditions of democracy and the prevention of famines. The author posits that despite the devastating impact of famines on global populations, rulers remain unaffected. Monarchs, military commanders, and other high-ranking officials are typically not susceptible to the plight of hunger and are generally unconcerned about the potential political consequences associated with their failure to mitigate famine situations. In contrast, a democratic system would hold the ruling class and political leaders accountable for famines, granting them the authority to take necessary measures in order to prevent such crises.

Privacy as not a Common Law Right

Privacy can be defined as the state of being free from public scrutiny with respect to the intrusion or interference in one's actions or choices. In essence, it might be described as the right to privacy. According to Professor Lawrence Tribe, in order to enhance the prospects of constitutional law, it is necessary to move away from rigid and binary perspectives. Instead, one should consider the social context in which each purportedly protected action and each unauthorized intrusion occur, in relation to the Constitution's principles and framework. This approach acknowledges the influence of various disciplines such as philosophy, sociology, religion, and history, which contribute to our understanding of humanity.

The protection of privacy is encompassed within the fundamental rights to life and liberty guaranteed by Article 21 of the Indian Constitution. Every individual is endowed with the entitlement to safeguard their personal privacy. Justice Dr.D. Y. Chandrachud made an observation that pertains to the idea of privacy, which involves the preservation of a person's private space. This concept is rooted in the principle of human autonomy. The human personality encompasses the capacity for individuals to exercise autonomy in making personal decisions. The central focus pertains to the degree to which individuals might reasonably anticipate privacy. Privacy is an inherent principle that is intrinsically linked to the concept of human dignity. This pertains to a situation in which an individual is not subjected to judgement by others. Privacy has a crucial role in safeguarding an individual's thoughts, beliefs, ideas, and choices from societal pressures that promote conformity. Privacy allows individuals to safeguard their personal lives from being made public.

The analysis of the abrogation or abridgment of basic rights under Chapter III necessitates a comprehensive interpretation, as the restricted reading of the chapter pertaining to fundamental rights is now considered outdated. The interpretation of the Constitution should be conducted in a manner that facilitates the citizens' ability to fully exercise the rights it guarantees. The permissible legislative abridgment of the right of free speech and expression has been established with great precision and strictness. This can be attributed to the recognition that freedom of speech and press are fundamental to all democratic societies. It is understood that without the ability to engage in open political discourse, which is crucial for the effective operation of popular governance, public education cannot thrive. The expansive nature of such freedom may entail the potential for misuse. The framers of the Constitution may have contemplated, alongside Madison who played a prominent role in crafting the First Amendment of the Federal Constitution, that it would be more prudent to allow certain undesirable aspects to flourish rather than risk compromising the strength of those aspects that produce desirable outcomes. For example, the fundamental aspect of personal liberty is the freedom of movement. Therefore, any limitation on the freedom of movement should be considered as a curtailment or denial of personal liberty, depending on the specific nature of the restriction.

Personal liberty encompasses the ability to freely move or change one's location based on individual preference, without being subjected to confinement or limitations, except as prescribed by legal procedures. The rights conferred by the Constitution encompass both positive and negative freedoms. Positive liberty refers to the concept that the State has a responsibility to implement necessary actions in order to safeguard the privacy of individuals. On the other hand, negative liberty serves to shield individuals from unwanted disruptions or intrusions.

According to the observations made by Lordship D. Y. Chandrachud, J., it is important to note that the sheer protection of a right under common law does not imply that said right should be precluded from constitutional acknowledgment. The recognition of the right in the Constitution is based on the draftsmen's perception of its significance and the belief that it necessitated constitutional safeguarding. Once the inclusion of the right to privacy inside the framework of Article 21 is acknowledged, it ceases to be regarded as a mere customary legal right and is no longer susceptible to the ambiguities inherent in statute law, which is subject to examination by the legislative branch.

Conclusions

If the established right to personal liberty is not considered significant, then asserting that the right to privacy exists solely for its own sake and without constitutional protection becomes entirely futile. Justice K. S. Puttaswamy, a former Judge of the High Court of Karnataka, initiated legal proceedings in the Supreme Court on the contentious issue surrounding Aadhar. In the given setting, the Government of India adopted a position and contended that the citizens cannot assert the right to privacy as a basic right. While one newspaper declared the recognition of the 'right to privacy' as a basic right, another newspaper expressed strong skepticism towards the Supreme Court's plea on privacy, dismissing it as baseless. The media has made a premature assessment based on a claim rather than a formal court ruling. The final determination about the acceptance or rejection of the arguments will be made by the court. The three-judge panel of the Apex Court convened and deliberated on the arguments presented by the parties involved. Ultimately, they reached the consensus that there existed a significant level of disagreement.

References

1. Hong Kong, https://www.hkreform.gov.hk/en/index/index.htm.
2. Universal Declaration of Human Rights.
3. United Nations, International Covenant on Civil and Political Rights, 1966.
4. United Nations, https://www.ohchr.org/en/instruments-mechanisms/instruments/international-covenant-civil-and-political-rights.
5. https://www.ohchr.org/en/instruments-mechanisms/instruments/international-covenant-economic-social-and-cultural-rights.
6. Nagaraj v. Union of India, AIR 2007 SC 71.
7. Constituent Assembly Debates, Vol. 7 (13-12-1948);
8. Black's Law Dictionary, 8th Edition.
9. The Right to Privacy: Rights and Liberties under the Law 38 (Bloomsbury Publishing, New York, 2003).
10. Zahira Habibullah Sheikh v. State of Gujarat, AIR 2006 SC 1367.
11. Sudhir Kumar Saha v. Commissioner of Police, Calcutta, AIR 1970 SC 814.
12. Additional District Magistrate, Jabalpur v. Shivakant Shukla, AIR 1976 SC 1207.
13. Thomas Cooley, Constitutional Limitations, Vol. II. P. 74.
14. Additional District Magistrate, Jabalpur, 7(2001) 2 WLR 992 (CA).
15. Jagmohan Singh v. State of U.P., AIR 1973 SC 947: 1973 Cri. LJ 370.
16. Indira Nehru Gandhi v. Raj Narain, AIR 1975 SC 2299.
17. Municipal Committee Amritsar v. State of Punjab AIR 1969 SC 1100.
18. A. K. Gopalan v. State of Madras, AIR 1950 SC 27.

19. Village of Norwood v. Ellen R. Baker, (1898) 43 Law Ed 443.
20. Constituent Assembly Debates, Vol. 7, P. 41; see, D. J. De, *The Constitution of India*, 2nd Edition (2005), P.1367.
21. State of Madras v. Srimathi Champakam Dorairajan, AIR 1951 SC 226: 1951 SCR 525.
22. In Re: The Kerala Education Bill, 1957, AIR 1958 SC 956: 1959 SCR 995.
23. Pathumma v. State of Kerala, AIR 1978 SC 771: (1978) 2 SCC.
24. Justice K. S. Puttaswamy v. Union of India, 2017 (3) KCCR SN 255 (SC).
25. Development as Freedom (Oxford University Press, 2000), p. 178, 179.
26. Jim Bronskill and David Mc Kie, *Your Right to Privacy* xiv (Self-Counsel Press, 2016).
27. R. Rajagopal v. State of Tamil Nadu, AIR 1995 SC 264: (1994) 6 SCC 632: 1994 AIR SCW 4420.
28. I. R. Coelho v. State of Tamil Nadu, AIR 2007 SC 86.
29. District Registrar and Collector, Hyderabad v. Canara Bank, (2005) 1 SCC 496.
30. Near v. Minnesotta, 283 US 607; Romesh Thappar v. State of Madras, AIR 1950 SC 124.
31. A. K. Gopalan v. State of Madras, AIR 1950 SC 27.
32. Sir William Blackstone, *Commentaries on the Laws of England,* 4th Edition, Vol. 1.
33. H. J. Stephen, Commentaries on the Laws of England; Thomas Cooley, *Constitutional Limitations*, 8th Edition, Vol. 1, P. 710.
34. Justice K. S. Puttaswamy v. Union of India, 2017 (3) KCCR SN 255 (SC).
35. Deep Chand v. State of Uttar Pradesh, AIR 1959 SC 648: 1959 Supp (2) SCR 8.

17

Right to Privacy and Data Protection as Human Right

Dewa Safi and Yatika Gupta

Abstract

The right to privacy and data protection is one of the most significant tenets of societal and individual growth of human civilisation in the 21st century. Managing data is frequently a part of building, integrating, or testing computing systems. Sometimes, this data will be personal, and other times, these systems will significantly affect the privacy of those they target (consider data brokers and credit rating services or interact with social networks and search engines, for example. Still, the combination of swiftly evolving digital technologies, growing global utilisation of those technologies, and deadly personal information gathered by many States has resulted in a rapid and significant erosion of privacy rights, particularly rights in one's personal data. In light of these developments, there is an urgent need for clarify the legal status of the right to privacy and data protection under the umbrella protection of the Human rights regime in an international and national sphere.

Keywords - *Privacy, Data Protection, International, Human Rights, Modern.*

Introduction

The right to privacy, often known as data protection, is a multifaceted notion that is now accepted by both the legal system and the general public in modern society. At both the international and national levels, it is one of the most important and fundamental rights mentioned in the human rights regime. The right to privacy signifies the particular rights of an individual to manage the gathering, use, and disclosure of personal information. A few examples of personal information include pursuits, routines, and activities; family and educational records; communications (such as mail and telephone records); and financial and medical records. The existence of erroneous or deceptive digital data about a person that might be swiftly and inexpensively conveyed to an unauthorised third party could potentially cause injury to that person. Although personal data usage is increasing, there are many advantages and potential drawbacks. The fusion of technology has also given rise to new concerns around data protection and privacy rights. Innovative technologies facilitate communication and access to personal data. Data protection and the right to privacy are inherently at odds. The main goal of data protection should be to balance these competing informational interests. However, the privacy rights of people and organisations should not be infringed upon by the security of their data.

The Universal Declaration of Human Rights (UDHR) and the International Covenant on Civil and Political Rights (ICCPR) recognise the right to privacy as a fundamental human right. The global community is currently focusing on tackling both state-sponsored surveillance practices and modern communications firms' spying activities. Although there has been significant progress in this area, the privacy of individuals is still not completely protected. Article 17 of the ICCPR and, most recently, the United Nations Resolution on Privacy in the Digital Age serve as the foundation for the protection provided by the global community and the U.N. The argument over privacy protection centers on what privacy means in the present digital era and how to make monitoring practices compliant with human rights law. On the basis of the effective control test, international law essentially holds governments responsible for their acts (but not always). Nonetheless, there has to be an international legal response to the actions of private communication-based businesses like Facebook as well as the activities of states, frequently known as the Five Eyes states. Activities involving digital surveillance of people's movements without their consent obviously violate Article 17 of the ICCPR.

Significance of Privacy

A fundamental right to privacy serves as the cornerstone on which many other human rights are constructed. Privacy is crucial to autonomy and the preservation of human dignity. In order to protect ourselves from unwarranted intrusion into our life, privacy permits us to set up barriers and regulate boundaries, giving us the ability to decide who we are and how we wish to interact with the world. Establishing limitations to control who has access to our bodies, locations, and objects, as well as our conversations and information, is made easier by privacy. However, it is difficult to conceptualise what privacy and the right to privacy mean. It has been interpreted differently in many contexts. According to Tom Gaiety, "The right to privacy is bound to include the body's inviolability and integrity, as well as the intimacy of personal identity, including marital privacy." Jude Cooley outlined the law of privacy and argued that the phrase "the right to be left alone" is synonymous with the term "privacy." According to Edward Shils, privacy is defined as "zero connection between two or more persons in a manner that there is no relationship or interaction between them, if they so choose" (Edward Shils). Moreover, the law of privacy can be drawn in 1361. The Justices of the Peace Act in England, which allowed for the prosecution of eavesdroppers and peeping toms, can be credited with establishing the first privacy laws as early as 1361. In rejecting a warrant to enter a home and take papers, British Lord Camden wrote in 1765, "We can safely say there is no law in this country to justify the defendants in what they have done; if there were, it would destroy all the comforts of society, as papers are often the most precious property any man can have." in the modern the UDHR which particularly safeguarded territorial and communications privacy, serves as the present privacy standard on a global scale.

According to Article 12 - "No-one should be subjected to arbitrary interference with his privacy, family, home or correspondence, nor to attacks on his honour or reputation. Everyone has the right to the protection of the law against such interferences or attacks".

The right to privacy is expressly mentioned in a number of international human rights agreements. Similar phrase is used in the U.N. Convention on the Protection of the Child, the U.N. Convention on Migrant Workers and the International Covenant on Civil and Political Rights (ICCPR).

On the regional level, these rights are becoming enforceable. The 1950 Convention for the Protection of Human Rights and Fundamental Freedoms, Article 8 states: "(1) Everyone has the right to respect for his private and family life, his home and his correspondence. (2) There shall be no interference by a public authority with the exercise of this right except as in accordance with the law and is necessary in a democratic society in the interests of national security, public safety or the economic well-being of the country, for the prevention of disorder or crime, for the protection of health of morals, or for the protection of the rights and freedoms of others."

Privacy and Data Protection

Privacy and Data Protection laws demand that personal information about people not be automatically made available to others and organizations. Each individual must be able to have meaningful influence over how their data is used. Data protection is a legal measure to stop the misuse of a person's personal information on any medium, including computers. Implementing administrative, technical, or physical barriers is necessary to protect personal information. The protection of data is directly related to privacy. Information about a person, such as his name, address, phone number, occupation, family, and preferences, is frequently accessible at a number of locations, including schools, colleges, banks, directories, surveys, and numerous websites. Such information being given to interested parties may result in privacy invasions like constant marketing calls. The Information Technology (Amendment) Act, 2008 lists the following as the fundamental privacy and data protection principles: defining data; civil and criminal culpability in case of data protection breach; and violation of confidentiality and privacy.

Concept of Data Protection

Data protection is the process of defending sensitive information against loss, tampering, or corruption. As data is created and stored at previously unheard-of rates, the significance of data protection grows. Data protection is the process of defending sensitive information against loss, tampering, or corruption. As data is created and stored at previously unheard-of rates, the significance of data protection grows. according to the section 2(1) o of the Information Technology Amendment Act, 2008 -

"Data means a representation of information, knowledge, facts, concepts or instructions which are being prepared or have been prepared in a formalised manner, and is intended to be processed or is being processed or has been processed in a computer system or computer network, and may be in any form (including computer printouts magnetic or optical storage media, punched cards, punched tapes) or stored internally in the memory of the computer."

Although the term of "data" would be more applicable in the context of cybercrime, the I.T. Act does not include any definitions of personal data.

Law and the Protection of Privacy

The various rulings by the European Court of Human Rights (ECHR) have complied with the guiding principle of Article 17. The ECHR has indicated that "private life is not an exhaustive decision" in its rulings in the cases of Botta vs. Italy, M.K. vs. France, S. and Marper vs. the U.K., and Bensaid vs. the U.K. These rulings have demonstrated the difficulties of defining privacy in its entirety to encompass all nuances that every individual may consider private. The ECHR noted that "protecting personal data is of essential significance to a person's enjoyment of respect for his or her personal data and family life."

The Court of Justice of the European Union (CJEU) rulings on privacy must be considered by the United Nations and the international community. In the case of Schrems v. Data Protection Commissioner, a significant privacy ruling was rendered. The Irish Data Protection Commissioner (IDPC) received a complaint against Facebook that served as the foundation for this investigation. Due to Facebook USA's suspected connection to the PRISM bulk surveillance programme, Schrems contested Facebook's transfer of his data to the United States in his lawsuit. The Safe Harbour agreement for the gathering and transfer of data between the E.U. and the U.S. was declared illegal by the Court of Justice of the European Union (CJEU). According to Schrems' complaint, E.U.

data privacy law prohibits data transfers to non-EU countries unless the entity transferring and holding the data can ensure adequate protection. The Court determined that the Safe Harbour agreement "must be declared invalid" because it did not provide the appropriate protection required by E.U. data protection law. According to the Court, "legislation allowing public authorities to have access to the content of electronic communications on a generalized basis must be regarded as jeopardizing the very basis of the fundamental rights guaranteed by Article 7 of the Charter of Fundamental Rights of the European Union." The Human Rights Committee (HRC) was established in accordance with Article 28 of the ICCPR to look into and oversee how nations are implementing rights, especially those related to privacy. The HRC published a General Comment on Article 17 of the ICCPR, which clarifies terms like "arbitrary interference," "family," "home," and "correspondence" as they are used in European case law. However, it must be emphasised once more that the ICCPR lacks a comprehensive definition of privacy in the digital age and is ambiguous about what is always meant by these "general comments."

Right to Privacy in India

The right to privacy and data protection in India has gained significant attention and importance, particularly in the digital age where data is a valuable commodity and privacy concerns are ever-present. India has made notable strides in recognizing and addressing these issues, primarily through legal frameworks and judicial decisions. The Indian Constitution, adopted in 1950, did not explicitly mention the right to privacy as a fundamental right. Instead, it laid down a framework of fundamental rights that included the right to life and personal liberty the Article 21, which is widely considered to be the cornerstone for the right to privacy.

The recognition of privacy as a fundamental right in the Indian Constitution is significant for several reasons -

Human Dignity and Autonomy

Privacy is integral to human dignity and personal autonomy. It ensures that individuals have the freedom to make choices about their personal lives, relationships, and bodies without unwarranted interference from the state or other entities.

Balancing Rights

Privacy acts as a balancing factor for other fundamental rights. It prevents the state from intruding into the private lives of citizens and curbing their freedoms unjustifiably.

Democracy and Individualism

In a democratic society, the right to privacy safeguards citizens from unwarranted state surveillance and protects them from potential abuses of power. It fosters individualism and personal development.

Technological Advancements

In an era of rapid technological advancements and data proliferation, the right to privacy becomes even more crucial. It protects individuals from unwarranted data collection, surveillance, and breaches of personal information.

Emerging Trends

This Part discusses the emerging trends of right to privacy and data protection in India.

Personal Data Protection Bill, 2019

To address the growing concerns regarding data protection and privacy, India introduced the Personal Data Protection Bill in 2019. The Bill aims to regulate the processing of personal data and establish a framework for the protection of individuals' data rights.

The Bill includes provisions that require certain categories of personal data to be stored and processed only within India. This is seen as a measure to enhance data security and protect the privacy of Indian citizens. Data Processing Restrictions: It establishes restrictions on the processing of personal data, including obtaining consent for data processing, specifying the purpose of data collection, and requiring data fiduciaries (entities processing data) to implement necessary security safeguards. The Bill proposes the creation of a Data Protection Authority of India (DPA) to oversee and enforce data protection regulations, investigate breaches, and promote awareness about data protection. It grants individuals various rights, including the right to access their data, correct inaccuracies, and request the deletion of their data, giving them greater control over their personal information. The Bill outlines conditions under which personal data can be transferred outside of India, emphasizing the importance of protecting data during international transfers.

Aadhaar and Biometric Data

One of the significant debates around data protection and privacy in India revolves around the Aadhaar program. Aadhaar is a unique identification system that uses biometric data such as fingerprints and iris scans to provide a 12-digit identification number to residents. While Aadhaar has been instrumental in facilitating various government services, it has also raised concerns about data security and privacy breaches. In response to these concerns, the Supreme Court of India issued a judgment in 2018, upholding the constitutionality of Aadhaar but imposing restrictions on its use and emphasizing the importance of data protection measures.

India has also taken steps to address data breaches and enhance cybersecurity. The government and regulatory authorities have introduced guidelines and regulations aimed at preventing and responding to data breaches, ensuring that organizations take adequate measures to protect sensitive personal data.

Role of Judiciary for Protection of Privacy

The Indian judiciary played a pivotal role in recognizing privacy as an essential component of personal liberty. Several landmark judgments, including Kharak Singh vs. State of Uttar Pradesh and Gobind vs. State of Madhya Pradesh, acknowledged the implicit presence of privacy within the ambit of Article 21. These judgments established that the state must have a compelling reason to infringe upon an individual's personal liberty, effectively creating a foundation for the right to privacy.

Furthermore, the right to privacy or data protection is not mentioned specifically in the Indian Constitution. The right to privacy has been recognized by the Supreme Court of India as a basic right under Article 21 of the Constitution, which protects the right to life and personal freedom. In the historic case Justice K.S. Puttaswamy (Retd.) and Anr. vs. Union of India (2017) the Aadhaar (Targeted Delivery of Financial and Other Subsidies, Benefits and Services) Act, 2016, was constitutionally challenged on the grounds that it infringed the right to privacy. The Supreme Court of India ruled that the right to privacy is a basic right protected by Article 21 of the Indian Constitution and that the Aadhaar Act's requirement to obtain informed consent before collecting personal information must pass the proportionality test. In State of Karnataka v. Selvi and Others (2010) The admissibility of evidence gathered through narco-analysis and other types of coercive testing was a topic of discussion in this case. Additionally, the Supreme Court ruled that these techniques for gathering evidence violate Articles 20(3) and 21 of the Constitution's protections for an individual's right to privacy and dignity. The most significant milestone in India's privacy journey came in 2017 when a nine-judge bench of the Supreme Court unanimously declared privacy to be a fundamental right under Articles 14, 19, and 21 of the Indian Constitution. This judgment, in the case of Justice K.S. Puttaswamy (Retd.) and Anr. vs. Union of India and Ors., marked a watershed moment for privacy protection in India. It affirmed that privacy was essential to the protection of personal autonomy and human dignity.

Conclusions

Privacy is undeniably a fundamental human right that serves as the bedrock of individual autonomy, dignity, and freedom. Throughout history, societies and legal systems have recognized the intrinsic value of privacy, be it within the confines of one's home, in personal communications, or in the choices one makes about their own body and information. The right to privacy finds its place in international declarations and conventions, national constitutions, and legal systems around the world. It is not a mere luxury but a necessity for the functioning of democratic societies and the protection of human dignity. In the digital age, where information flows rapidly and technology can easily encroach upon our private lives, the significance of the right to privacy has taken on new dimensions. Balancing the legitimate interests of governments and businesses with the protection of individual privacy is a complex challenge.

It is a challenge that must be met head-on to preserve the essence of this fundamental right. Privacy is not just an abstract concept; it affects the way we live, communicate, and relate to the world. It empowers individuals to think freely, to express themselves without fear, and to maintain control over their personal information. In an era where data has become a valuable commodity, protecting privacy is crucial to preventing abuses, safeguarding against discrimination, and ensuring the free exchange of ideas. The ongoing debate and evolution of privacy laws and norms reflect the dynamic nature of this right. It requires constant vigilance, adaptation, and the collective effort of societies, governments, and technology companies to strike a balance between security, convenience, and individual freedoms. In sum, the right to privacy is not just a legal or philosophical concept; it is a cornerstone of human rights that profoundly impacts our daily lives and the society we live in. It is a testament to the value we place on individual autonomy and the acknowledgment that each person's private sphere deserves respect and protection. Upholding and strengthening the right to privacy is not only a legal obligation but also a moral imperative in the modern world.

References

1. UN General Assembly, Universal Declaration of Human Rights, 10 December 1948, 217 A (III), available at: https://www.refworld.org/docid/3ae6b3712c.html [accessed 13 April 2023].

2. UN General Assembly, International Covenant on Civil and Political Rights, 16 December 1966, United Nations, Treaty Series, vol. 999, p. 171, available at: https://www.refworld.org/docid/3ae6b3aa0.html [accessed 13 April2023].

3. United Nations Human Rights Council, Report by the Special Rapporteur on the promotion and protection of the right to freedom and protection of the right to freedom of opinion and expression, 2013, UN Doc., A/HRC/23/40.

4. Human Rights Council, UN Resolution on the Right to Privacy in the Digital Age, 2017, UN Doc., A/HRC/RES/34/7.

5. Nicaragua v United States, ICJ Rep.14, (1986), 115.

6. What is privacy, https://privacyinternational.org/explainer/56/what-privacy.

7. Tom Gaiety, "Right to Privacy" 12 Harvard Civil Rights Civil Liberties Law Review 233.

8. Thomas M Cooley, A Treatise on the Law of Torts 29 (2nd ed. 1888).

9. Edward Shils, "Privacy: Its Constitution and Vicissitudes" 31 Law & Contemp Problems 281 (1966).

10. James Michael, Privacy and Human Rights, UNESCO 1994 p.1.

11. Entick v. Carrington, 1558-1774 All E.R. Rep. 45.

12. Universal Declaration of Human Rights, <http://www.hrweb.org/legal/udhr.html>

13. UNGA Doc A/RES/44/25 (12 December 1989) with Annex, Article 16.

14. A/RES/45/158 25 February 1991, Article 14.
15. Convention for the Protection of Human Rights and Fundamental Freedoms Rome, 4.XI.1950. <http://www.coe.fr/eng/legaltxt/5e.htm>.
16. The News choronic, What we are doing to ensure data protection of Nigerians - Olatunji | (thenews-chronicle.com)
17. Botta v Italy, ECHR, Appl. No 21439/93, (1994).
18. MK v France, ECHR, Appl. No 19522/09, (2013).
19. S and Marper v UK, ECHR, Appl. No 30542/04, (2008).
20. Bensaid v UK, ECHR, Appl. No 44599/98, (2001).
21. Botta v Italy, ECHR, Appl. No 21439/93, (1994).
22. Maximilan Schrems v Data Protection Commissioner, CJEU, C-362/14 (2015).
23. Kharak Singh v. State of U.P and other, 1964 SCR (1) 332.
24. AIR 1975 SC 1378, 1975 CriLJ 1111, (1975) 2 SCC 148, 1975 3 SCR 946
25. Indian Constitution.
26. Justice K.S. Puttaswamy (Retd.) and Anr. v. Union of India, (2017) 10 SCC 1.
27. Selvi and Ors. v. State of Karnataka, (2010) 7 SCC 263.

18

A Study of Personal Data Protection Bill, 2019: With Emphasis on Data Localisation

Sanchita Ray

Abstract

Data localisation simply means restricting the flow of data from one country to another. It means that the personal data of a country's residents should be processed and stored in that country. In India's context, localisation will make it mandatory for companies collecting critical consumer data to store and process it in data centres present within India's borders. Data localization has become a significant policy issue in India very recently. This is primarily due to the perceived economic benefits of processing Indian consumer data, and difficulties accessing personal data for national security and law enforcement purposes. The debate on data localisation is between sovereign interest and business efficiency. Many people believe that localizing Indian consumers' data within India would be more beneficial to the country's economic growth and innovation than allowing data to move freely. While other believe that there are some disadvantages for foreign companies for two reasons. First, as a capital expenditure, these companies would have to pay for data storage and processing capabilities in India. Second, the costs of renting or operating data-related infrastructure would have to be paid on a long-term basis. This article tries to identify the positive and negative consequences of data localisation and also throws light on how states and non-state actors are dealing with data localisation.

Keywords - *Data localization, digitisation, Legislation, Personal Data Protection Bill, European Union.*

Introduction

The importance and use of data in today's technology-driven world is immense. This is understood by both governments and businesses alike. The cross-border data flow has proven to be an important pillar of strength for established as well as growing businesses. The United Nations Conference on Trade and Development in their Digital Economy Report found that businesses using the internet for global trade have a higher survival rate than those who do not. Therefore, it becomes essential for economies, especially growing economies, to protect data during cross-border transfers. Countries mandate data that are created within their borders to remain stored within its territorial boundaries. This process of storing data locally is referred to as data localisation.

Data localization has become a significant policy issue in India in the last decade. This is primarily due to the perceived economic benefits of processing Indian consumer data, and difficulties accessing personal data for national security and law enforcement purposes. India has a variety of different initiatives which have some elements pertaining to or impacting data localization. Early Approaches.

The beginnings of data localization legal approaches in India can be seen to be emerging in a stronger manner in the second decade of the twenty first century. These have been manifested in the Draft National Policy Framework on Electronic Commerce in India, released by the Ministry of Commerce and Industry in July 2018, Proposed amendments to the Drugs and Cosmetics Rules, 1945, released by the Ministry of Health and Family Welfare in August 2018, National Digital Communications Policy, 2018, released by the Department of Telecommunications, Ministry of Communications in May 2018 and approved by the Union Cabinet in September 2018, Reserve Bank of India Notification dated 6 April 2018 entitled "Storage of Payment System Data."

On 6th April 2018, the Reserve Bank of India (RBI) issued a circular mandating provisions ushering in the requirements of data localization in the banking sector in India. The Circular states that "All system providers shall ensure that the entire data relating to payment systems operated by them are stored in a system only in

India. This data should include the full end-to-end transaction details/information collected/carried/processed as part of the message/payment instruction. For the foreign leg of the transaction, if any, the data can also be stored in the foreign country, if required." The primary objective of this policy appears to be to facilitate supervision and monitoring of payment systems in India by the RBI in order to detect suspicious or fraudulent activity. This was India's first foray in the area of data localization. By this notification, The Reserve Bank of India has tended to elaborate the Indian approach on data localization.

In 2019, the Indian government introduced a data protection Bill in the Indian parliament. This Bill proposed the country's first economy-wide data localization framework. That said, more tailored, sector-specific data localization measures have already been implemented in many parts of the Indian economy. For example, the telecommunications sector already requires the local storage and local processing of subscriber information and prohibits the transferring of subscribers' account information overseas. A report produced by the Committee of Experts under the chairmanship of Justice B. N. Sri Krishna provided detailed reasons for proposing the localization of personal data. The same committee then formulated a legislative proposal based on its findings in the form of a 2018 draft known as the Personal Data Protection Bill. The Indian government introduced the 2019 Bill in the Indian Parliament based on this Draft.

Key Features of Personal Data Protection Bill, 2019

The Government of India had introduced the Personal Data Protection Bill 2019 (PDP Bill) in the Lok Sabha on 11 December 2019. Here are some of the key features of the PDP Bill, 2019 -

Categorisation of Data

The Bill categorizes data into three categories-critical, sensitive and general. Sensitive data-financial, health, sexual orientation, biometrics, transgender status, religious or political beliefs and affiliation-can be stored only in India. However, data can be processed outside India with explicit consent. Critical data will be defined by the government from time to time and has to be stored and processed in India. Any data that is non-critical and non-sensitive will be categorized as general data with no restriction on where it is stored or processed. The Bill defines personal data as any data related to an individual,

Data Principal and Data Fiduciary

The Bill introduces the concepts of data principal (the individual to whom the data relates) and data fiduciary (the entity that determines the purpose and means of data processing). Data Fiduciary refers to any person who alone or in conjunction with other persons determines the purpose and means of the processing of Personal Data. Data Principal refers to the individual to whom the personal data relates and where such individual is a child includes the parents or lawful guardian of such a child. Clause 9 of the Draft Bill prescribes that the data fiduciary shall not retain any personal data beyond the period necessary to satisfy the purpose for which it was processed and shall delete the personal data at the end of processing. The personal data may be retained for a longer period only after the data fiduciary gets consent from the data principal.

Consent and Grounds for Processing

The Bill emphasizes obtaining the consent of data principals for processing their personal data. It provides guidelines for valid consent and introduces provisions for processing data without consent in certain circumstances. Clause 12 of the Draft Bill lists out certain cases which provides for processing of personal data without consent. Likewise, recruitment and termination of employment have also been brought under categories of processing personal data. However, if such data meets the criteria of being sensitive data, then such processing cannot be done without prior consent.

Data Localization

The Bill proposes that critical personal data, as notified by the government, must be stored, and processed only within India. Non-critical personal data can be processed outside India but with certain conditions. Critical Personal Data: The PDP Bill empowers the Indian government to categorize certain types of personal data as "critical personal data." The specific categories of critical personal data would be determined by the government in consultation with the Data Protection Authority (DPA).

Storage and Processing within India

Once personal data is classified as critical personal data, the PDP Bill mandates that such data must be processed and stored on servers or data centers located within the territory of India. This provision is intended to ensure that critical personal data remains under the jurisdiction of Indian laws and is subject to Indian data protection regulations. Non-Critical Personal Data-Non-critical personal data, which is not classified as critical by the government, can be stored, and processed outside of India. However, certain conditions and safeguards regarding data protection and privacy may still apply to such data transfers.

Data Protection Authority

The Bill establishes a Data Protection Authority (DPA) as an independent regulatory body responsible for enforcing data protection laws, monitoring, and supervising data fiduciaries, and promoting awareness about data protection. Data Protection Officer (DPO), according to the Bill, each company will have DPO in which work in liaison with Data Protection Authority (DPA).

Cross-Border Data Transfer

The PDP Bill includes provisions for cross-border transfer of personal data. It allows for the transfer of personal data outside of India, including critical personal data, under certain circumstances. These circumstances may include the use of standard contractual clauses, adequacy decisions by the DPA, or specific exemptions provided by the government.

Rights of Data Principals

The Bill grants data principals several rights, including the right to access their personal data, the right to rectify or erase data, the right to data portability, and the right to be forgotten, subject to certain limitations.

Data Breach Notification

The Bill mandates data fiduciaries to report any significant data breaches to the DPA and affected individuals, where such breaches are likely to cause harm.

Penalties and Compensation

The Bill outlines penalties for non-compliance with its provisions, including fines and imprisonment for certain offenses. It also provides for the compensation of individuals who have suffered harm due to data processing activities.

The "Bill" was referred for examination and recommendations to a Joint Committee of both Houses of Parliament (called JPC) on 12 December 2019. The Joint Parliamentary Committee chaired by Member of Parliament Shri P.P. Chaudhary tabled the report on the Bill along with the amended Bill before both Houses of Parliament on the 16th of December 2021. The Committee deliberated for over two years, during which time that Bill underwent substantial changes in scope and nature. A total of 188 amendments have been recommended out of which 91 amendments are of significant nature, while the rest are editing of legal nature in different sections.

Data Localization

One of the key changes in the draft "Bill" proposed by JPC in comparison to the 2019 draft on Data Localization was both the Report and the Bill call for continual storage of sensitive personal data in India and storage and processing of critical personal data only within the territory of India. It also specifies that transfer of critical data outside India be subject to DPA approval in consultation with Government.

Advantages of Data Localization

Data localization refers to the practice of storing and processing data within a specific geographic location. It can be motivated by various factors, such as national laws or regulations, security and privacy concerns, or the desire to keep data closer to users. There are some potential advantages of data localization for India.

Enhanced Data Security

Data localization can improve data security by ensuring that sensitive information remains within India's jurisdiction. By mandating that data be stored locally, the risk of unauthorized access, data breaches, and cyberattacks from foreign entities can be minimized. It allows India to establish stronger regulations and control over the protection of personal and critical data.

Protection of National Interest

Data localization supports India's national interest by safeguarding important data related to national security, defense, and strategic sectors. By keeping such data within the country, India can reduce the potential risks associated with foreign interference or espionage, ensuring critical information is under its jurisdiction and control.

Economic Growth and Job Creation

Data localization can contribute to India's economic growth by fostering the development of local data centers, cloud infrastructure, and technology services. This can lead to the creation of job opportunities in areas such as data management, cybersecurity, data analytics, and software development, supporting the growth of India's digital economy.

Compliance with Local Laws and Regulations

Data localization can help ensure compliance with Indian laws and regulations, including those related to data privacy and protection. It enables the government to enforce stricter control over data handling practices, ensuring that organizations adhere to Indian data protection laws, such as the Personal Data Protection Bill once it becomes law.

Promoting Domestic Innovation

By localizing data, India can encourage domestic innovation and technological advancements. It provides an opportunity for Indian companies to leverage localized data for research and development purposes, creating new products, services, and solutions tailored to the local market needs. This promotes indigenous innovation, reduces dependency on foreign technology, and strengthens India's position in the global digital landscape.

Access to Data for Law Enforcement

Data localization facilitates access to data for law enforcement agencies, enabling them to investigate and prevent crimes more effectively. With data stored locally, it becomes easier for authorities to obtain necessary information for legal proceedings, ensuring that Indian laws can be upheld and enforced efficiently.

It is important to note that while data localization offers certain advantages, it can also have potential drawbacks, such as increased costs for businesses, reduced data sharing for international collaborations, and potential barriers to global digital trade. Balancing these advantages and disadvantages is crucial in formulating an effective data localization policy for India.

Challenges of Data Localization in India

The data generated inside a nation's boundaries be stored, processed, and managed within that nation may be referred as data localization. India, like many other countries, has explored data localization policies. While there may be certain alleged advantages, data localization in India also presents a number of difficulties. Here are some of the challenges associated with data localization in India.

Increased Costs

Implementing data localization measures can result in increased costs for businesses. Setting up local data centers, establishing necessary infrastructure, and ensuring compliance with regulations require significant investments. Small and medium-sized enterprises (SMEs) and startups may face difficulties in bearing these additional costs, potentially hampering their growth and competitiveness. Maintaining multiple local data centers may lead to significant investments in infrastructure and higher costs for global companies.

Impact on Cross-Border Data Flows

Data localization can create barriers to cross-border data flows. It may impede the seamless transfer of data between countries, hindering international trade, global collaborations, and the ability of multinational companies to operate efficiently. This can have implications for various industries, including e-commerce, financial services, and information technology.

Technological Limitations

Building and maintaining robust local infrastructure to support data localization can be challenging, especially in terms of scalability and technological capabilities. The availability of skilled workforce, adequate power supply, and advanced data management technologies are crucial factors for successful data localization. Ensuring the development of these capabilities requires significant investments and efforts. Infrastructure in India for efficient data collection and management is lacking.

Data Access and Innovation

Data localization may restrict access to global datasets necessary for research, innovation, and the development of new products and services. It can limit the ability of businesses, researchers, and startups to leverage diverse datasets for insights, analysis, and technological advancements. Restricted access to international data can hinder innovation and limit the potential for technological breakthroughs.

Compliance Complexity

Data localization can lead to increased compliance complexity. Businesses operating across multiple jurisdictions may face challenges in navigating and complying with diverse data localization regulations. Meeting varying regulatory requirements can be burdensome and time-consuming, particularly for multinational corporations, potentially impacting their operations and efficiency.

International Perception and Trade Implications

Data localization measures can raise concerns among international businesses and trading partners. It may be perceived as protectionist or discriminatory, potentially affecting foreign investment and trade relations. In an increasingly interconnected global economy, trade implications and potential retaliation measures from other countries need to be carefully considered.

Data Fragmentation

Data localization can result in data fragmentation, with different regions or states implementing their own data localization requirements. This fragmentation can create complexities in data management, data sharing, and data integration across different geographical areas within India, potentially hindering the effectiveness of data-driven initiatives and hampering data-driven decision-making processes.

Balancing the advantages and challenges of data localization is crucial for India to develop a comprehensive and sustainable data localization strategy that addresses the country's specific needs while minimizing potential negative impacts.

Conclusions

Data localization in India has been a subject of debate, with both perceived benefits and significant challenges. While proponents argue that data localization can enhance data security, promote data sovereignty, support local businesses, and contribute to India's economic growth but there are also concerns regarding its impact on cross-border businesses, innovation, and data privacy.

Implementing data localization policies must be approached with careful consideration of the potential consequences. Simultaneously striking a balance between protecting data and fostering a conducive environment for innovation and international collaboration becomes essential. The policymakers need to address the challenges related to compliance costs, data security, global data access, and infrastructure while avoiding potential trade implications and legal complexities.

The present situation needs an effective data localization policy which should be crafted through collaboration with stakeholders, including businesses, technology experts, and civil society, to ensure that it aligns with global data trends, respects privacy rights, and supports India's position in the digital economy. Through a thoughtful and pragmatic approach, India can harness the power of data for economic growth while safeguarding the interests of its citizens and businesses in the digital age.

References

1. https://www.thehindu.com/sci-tech/technology/are-data-localisation-requirements-necessary-and-proportionate/article66131957.ece.

2. https://datacatalyst.org/wp-content/uploads/2020/06/Data-Localization-Pavan-Duggal.pdf

3. https://loksabhadocs.nic.in/Refinput/New_Reference_Notes/English/13062022_142456_102120474.pdf.

4. https://loksabhadocs.nic.in/Refinput/New_Reference_Notes/English/23122022_172747_102120411.pdf.

5. https://www.informationpolicycentre.com/uploads/5/7/1/0/57104281/cipl-dsci_report_on_enabling_accountable_data_transfers_from_india_to_the_united_states_under_indias_proposed_pdpb__8_september_2020_.pdf.

6. https://carnegieendowment.org/files/202104 Burman_Sharma_DataLocalization_final.pdf accessed on 23.7.23 at 11.19 am https://datacatalyst.org/wp-content/uploads/2020/06/Data-Localization-Pavan-Duggal.pdf.

7. https://cuts-ccier.org/pdf/data-localisation-indias-double-edged-sword.pdf accessed on 23.7.23 at 11.45am.

8. 8. Maximiliano Facundo Vila Seoane (2021) Data securitisation: the challenges of data sovereignty in India, Third World Quarterly, 42:8, 1733-1750 , https://www.oecd.org/sti/data-localisation-trends-and-challenges-7fbaed62-en.htm.

9. The Great India Data localization puzzle - https://cio.economictimes.indiatimes.com/news/big-data/the-great-india-data-localization-puzzle/89787780.

10. https://www.nipfp.org.in/media/medialibrary/2018/10/WP_2018_242.pdf.

11. https://itif.org/publications/2021/07/19/how-barriers-cross-border-data-flows-are-spreading-globally-what-they-cost/.

12. The "Real Life Harms" of Data Localization Policies- can be accessed at https://www.informationpolicycentre.com/uploads/5/7/1/0/57104281/cipltls_discussion_paper_paper_i_-_the_real_life_harms_of_data_localization_policies.pdf.

13. Information Technology Act, 2000.

14. https://www.meity.gov.in/writereaddata/files/Draft%20Data%20Centre%20Policy%20-%2003112020_v5.5.pdf.

15. https://www.moneycontrol.com/news/business/meity-looks-to-set-up-national-government-cloud-to-store-sensitive-govt-defence-data-locally-9516291.html.

16. https://iapp.org/news/a/meity-considers-easing-data-localization-provisions-in-dpb/.

17. https://icrier.org/others/data-flows-and-data-localisation-an-economic-ana https://telecom.economictimes.indiatimes.com/news/reliance-jio-airtel-paytm-bat-for-personal-data-localisation/96778555.

19

Right to Privacy: An Appraisal of Legal Framework in Bangladesh

Naeem Ahsan Talha and Samiul Azim

Abstract

The Constitution of Bangladesh, although not explicitly articulating the right to privacy, collectively establishes a foundational framework for the protection of individual rights and freedoms, thereby indirectly encompassing privacy rights to a certain extent. This constitutional recognition underscores the government's commitment to upholding the right to privacy as an inherent fundamental right. Concurrently, the Bangladesh government has embarked on a multifaceted journey, marked by the formulation of diverse e-Government strategies and policies, aimed at elevating the efficiency of public service delivery and ensuring the confidentiality and security of data in digital transactions and interactions. In close collaboration with pertinent stakeholders, the government is actively engaged in the development of comprehensive guidelines and frameworks designed to safeguard data protection and privacy across a spectrum of sectors, including but not limited to e-commerce, banking, healthcare, and beyond. This evolving landscape reflects a nuanced interplay between constitutional principles, government initiatives, and collaborative efforts to bolster privacy rights and data protection in Bangladesh's digital age, encapsulating the dynamic fusion of legal, technological, and societal considerations in the pursuit of a more secure and privacy-respecting digital landscape.

Keywords - *Bangladesh, Constitution, Privacy, Rights, Data Protection.*

Introduction

Privacy is a fundamental human right, acknowledged and affirmed in various global declarations and treaties. This right safeguards individual from unwarranted intrusions into their personal lives and data. Article 12 of the Universal Declaration of Human Rights (UDHR) explicitly emphasizes the importance of preventing such intrusions, recognizing privacy as an essential component of human rights. Similarly, Article 17 of the International Covenant on Civil and Political Rights (ICCPR) and Article 16 of the Convention on the Rights of the Child (1989) reinforce the significance of privacy as a fundamental entitlement in the realm of international human rights. In consonance with international human rights principles and constitutional mandates, governments bear the responsibility to protect individuals' data and privacy. Bangladesh, having ratified the International Covenant on Civil and Political Rights (ICCPR) in 2000, took a significant step towards ensuring online safety and data security. This international commitment underscores the country's resolve to protect its citizens' privacy rights.

However, despite these international obligations, Bangladesh has grappled with a host of privacy-related challenges in recent years. These challenges have prompted civil society organizations, legal advocates, and individuals to raise awareness about the importance of privacy rights and to advocate for more robust legal protections. Notable incidents, such as the 2013 cyberattack on the Bangladesh Air Force website, resulting in the exposure of 19 administrator identities, and the 2022 security breach on Facebook, which compromised the data of three million Bangladeshi citizens, have underscored the pressing need for enhanced data security and privacy safeguards.

Moreover, Bangladesh has witnessed widespread misuse of Section 57 of the Information and Communication Technology Act, 2006, which has been a source of concern and controversy across the nation. Additionally, Section 41 of the Digital Security Act, 2018, grants law enforcement agencies the authority to access computer systems and online traffic data without requiring a prior warrant, raising concerns about unchecked government intrusion into citizens' privacy.

Remarkably, in the five decades since Bangladesh's adoption of its constitution, the country has not enacted substantial privacy legislation. Consequently, privacy infringements persist as a common occurrence, affecting individuals from all walks of life. Notably, the media has played a significant role in perpetuating privacy violations by portraying public figures, such as Shamsunnahar Smrity, also known as Pori Moni, and Sabrina Arif Chowdhury, in an unfavorable light and frequently exposing their personal lives. These media intrusions have garnered widespread attention from consumers, both through online and offline channels, and have further underscored the urgency of enacting comprehensive privacy protection measures.

In light of these challenges and the ever-evolving landscape of digital privacy, it is imperative to critically assess the existing legal framework and institutional mechanisms for safeguarding privacy rights in Bangladesh. This scholarly exploration seeks to analyze the current state of privacy rights in the country, identifying the shortcomings and areas in need of reform, and to propose recommendations for the enhancement of privacy protection in Bangladesh. By doing so, this research contributes to the broader global discourse on privacy rights and their significance in the modern digital age.

Constitutional and Legislative Framework vis-à-vis Privacy in Bangladesh

The right to privacy in Bangladesh is a pressing issue in the digital age. There is a lack of explicit recognition and protection of privacy rights in the Constitution of Bangladesh, raising questions about constitutional safeguards. The existing privacy protection regime in Bangladesh is inadequate due to the absence of comprehensive data privacy legislation. Counter-terrorism efforts have also jeopardized the right to privacy, with mass digital surveillance infringing on individual rights. However, limited protection for privacy can be found in Article 43 of the Constitution of Bangladesh, which guarantees the right to privacy of home and correspondence. To address these issues, it is recommended to enact comprehensive data protection legislation and amend the Cyber Security Act, 2015 to ensure the mainstreaming of the right to privacy. Further research is needed to understand the current legal development for privacy in Bangladesh and to inform future policies and strategies.

Constitution of Bangladesh

The Constitution of Bangladesh enshrines the right to privacy as a fundamental and inalienable right. Specifically, Article 43 (b) of the Constitution unequivocally affirms that every citizen possesses the inherent right to privacy, albeit with the important caveat that such a right may be subject to reasonable restrictions imposed by law when the imperatives of public security, public order, or the maintenance of morality necessitate such measures. It states that - Every citizen shall have the right, subject to any reasonable restrictions imposed by law in the interests of the security of the State, public order, public morality or public health – (b) to the privacy of his correspondence and other means of communication.

This constitutional provision stands as a testament to the recognition of the intrinsic importance of privacy within the legal framework of Bangladesh. It reflects both a commitment to international norms and a delicate balance between safeguarding individual privacy and ensuring the broader welfare of society. Moreover, it underscores the dynamic and evolving nature of privacy rights in the face of contemporary challenges, particularly those associated with the rapid advancement of technology and the sharing of personal information.

The constitutional recognition of the right to privacy in Bangladesh, as articulated in Article 43 (b), serves as a cornerstone for the protection of individual privacy rights. It highlights the importance of balancing such rights with legitimate concerns related to public security, public order, and moral values. These scholarly contributions and the constitutional framework are essential components of the ongoing discourse regarding privacy rights in Bangladesh, enriching the understanding of this multifaceted and dynamic aspect of the nation's legal landscape.

Relevant Legal Provisions

Bangladesh Telecommunication Act, 2001; Information and Communication Technology Act, 2006; Digital Security Act, 2018 are some of the legislations relating to data privacy in Bangladesh -

Bangladesh Telecommunication Act, 2001

The Telecommunication Act of 2001 in Bangladesh addresses matters pertaining to privacy in the realm of telecommunications. This legislative framework delineates the provisions concerning the interception of communications and the circumstances under which such interceptions may be authorized. Specifically, Section 67(1)(b) of the Bangladesh Telecommunication Act expressly prohibits any individual from intercepting, utilizing, or revealing any radio communication or telecommunication without obtaining prior consent from either the sender or the intended recipient of the communication. Violating this statutory provision can result in a maximum penalty of three years of incarceration or a fine of up to BDT 300,000, which is approximately equivalent to $2,740, or potentially both sanctions. Additionally, under Section 30(1)(f), the Bangladesh Telecommunication Regulatory Commission is entrusted with the responsibility of ensuring the safeguarding of the privacy of telecommunications.

Information and Communication Technology Act, 2006

The Information and Communication Technology Act of 2006 plays a pivotal role in governing a wide range of digital communication and cybercrime matters within the context of Bangladesh. This comprehensive legislation encompasses various provisions, with a particular focus on deterring unauthorized access to computers, systems, and networks. By doing so, it indirectly serves to safeguard the digital privacy of individuals, ensuring that their online activities and personal information remain protected.

Originating from India's cyber law framework, the Bangladesh Information and Communication Technology Act includes several pertinent sections, notably Sections 54 to 56 and Section 63. These sections address an array of offenses linked to computer access, computer systems, and violations of privacy, thereby reinforcing the legal safeguards in place to protect the privacy of individuals in the digital landscape. These provisions are instrumental in addressing issues related to unauthorized digital intrusion and cybercrimes, underscoring the government's commitment to upholding and maintaining digital privacy in an era marked by advancing technology and evolving security challenges.

Digital Security Act, 2018

The introduction of the Digital Security Act in Bangladesh in 2018 has sparked concerns regarding potential infringements on the rights to privacy and freedom of expression. This legislation was implemented to replace the much-criticized Information and Communication Technology Act, 2006. Its primary objective is to regulate the use of digital platforms and information technology, with a focus on ensuring national security and maintaining public order.

The Digital Security Act encompasses a broad spectrum of offenses related to digital communication, including but not limited to hacking, unauthorized access to computer systems, dissemination of propaganda, cyberbullying, hate speech, and various other cybercrimes. Section 35 of this law introduces the establishment of the Data Protection Office, signalling an effort to address digital privacy concerns. According to Section 35(2), this office will operate under the authority and supervision of the Digital Security Agency, which was established by the Digital Security Act of 2018.

While the Digital Security Act seeks to address cybersecurity and protect against various cyber threats, concerns have arisen regarding its potential impact on privacy and freedom of expression in the digital sphere. Balancing national security and public order with individual privacy and freedom of expression remains a complex and evolving challenge, and the effectiveness of this legal framework in achieving this balance is a subject of ongoing debate and scrutiny in Bangladesh.

Evolving Trends

In December 2020, the government took a significant step by introducing the Digital Security Rules, which mandated organizations to establish assistance centers aimed at facilitating compliance with the provisions outlined in the Digital Security Act of 2018. These regulations specifically address the responsible use of personal data, thereby offering a mechanism for individuals to voice concerns related to privacy infringements and report security issues. This initiative empowers workers to file complaints regarding privacy violations and seek assistance in addressing security-related matters through direct engagement with these assistance centers.

However, concerns have emerged from various quarters, including the Global Data Alliance (GDA), prompting calls for a re-evaluation of certain aspects, particularly within Chapter X of these rules. The GDA advocates for the adoption of their Cross-Border Data Policy Principles as a more suitable policy framework. This approach prioritizes data security and protection while concurrently supporting Bangladesh's economic and technological progress. In accordance with the evolving global policy consensus that underscores secure and reliable data transfers, the GDA's Policy Principles consist of six fundamental tenets.

Amnesty International has expressed concerns about the initial version of the proposed Data Protection Act, which is currently open for public input. According to Amnesty International, this legislation poses a significant threat to privacy rights in Bangladesh. It relies on ambiguous and overly broad clauses, potentially enabling authorities to employ invasive measures, including gaining access to encrypted communications on personal devices, whether physically or remotely. These actions may infringe upon an individual's privacy rights without adequate justification, merely based on the anticipation of possible disruptions to law and order. Additionally, the proposed Act grants authority's immunity from civil, criminal, and other legal actions for any harm caused to individuals during the execution of its provisions. This has raised concerns, given the history of severe human rights violations facilitated by existing laws such as the Digital Security Act. The proposed Data Protection Act appears to align with a pattern in which the government seeks to assert control over various aspects of people's digital lives, which has raised significant apprehension among privacy advocates and human rights organizations.

Judicial Framework for Privacy in Bangladesh

The interpretation of laws and legal principles in Bangladesh is an ongoing and dynamic process, influenced by a variety of factors, including court decisions, legal precedents, statutes, and, most significantly, the Constitution of Bangladesh. The judiciary, particularly the Supreme Court, plays a pivotal role in the process of interpreting and applying the law to specific cases and circumstances.

One of the notable cases that underscore the significance of the right to privacy in Bangladesh is the case of A.K.M. Nasiruddin vs. Government of Bangladesh (2013). In this case, the High Court of Bangladesh delivered a landmark judgment by declaring the sharing of mobile phone users' call records and other personal information without their consent as unconstitutional. This ruling explicitly recognized the right to privacy as a fundamental and constitutionally protected right In a separate case from 2011, involving a woman who discovered a hidden CCTV camera in a beauty parlour, the Bangladesh Human Rights Foundation filed a writ petition. The High Court responded by ordering the removal of all closed-circuit TV cameras from beauty parlours, emphasizing the protection of individual privacy.

Justice Md. Nizamul Huq vs. Government of Bangladesh (2011) revolved around the leaking of a Skype conversation related to the trial of war criminals from the 1971 Liberation War. The leaked conversation raised legitimate concerns about the issues of privacy and confidentiality. In the case of ActionAid Bangladesh vs. The Government of Bangladesh (2010), concerns were raised regarding privacy in the context of using biometric data for a national ID card project. The High Court issued a directive to the government to ensure the protection of privacy and data security.

In the case of The State and Ors. vs. Oli and Ors., (2019), the Supreme Court of Bangladesh made a pivotal ruling affirming the constitutional right to privacy. The Court asserted that every citizen is granted the entitlement to privacy as stipulated in the Constitution. The ruling emphasized the necessity for investigative authorities to adhere to a formalized process when seeking private information and the inadmissibility of using private phone records obtained without following the established procedures as legal evidence.

In a case involving a UNO (Upazila Executive Officer), the Jhenaidah Court upheld an individual's right to privacy and ruled that a public servant cannot seize a citizen's mobile phone to access their private messaging content. The court emphasized the constitutional guarantee of personal privacy and the protection of end-to-end encrypted private messaging. In Aynunnahar Siddiqua and Ors. vs. Government of Bangladesh and Ors., the Supreme Court addressed the collection of personal details by the Dhaka Police and held that it did not violate the right to privacy. The Court concluded that the collection of personal information was carried out in the public interest and that the relevant legal provision was not in violation of the Constitution. In the case of Dr. Shahidul Alam (2019), the Supreme Court affirmed the High Court's directive, which had suspended the investigation of Dr. Shahidul Alam under Section 57 of the Information and Communication and Technology Act, 2006. The case underscored the importance of upholding the right to freedom of expression and protecting individuals from unwarranted legal actions related to online speech. Finally, in the case of Bangladesh v. H.M. Ershad (2001), it was emphasized that police officers and other public functionaries cannot enter a citizen's house, conduct searches, or seize property without lawful authorization. The case underscored the need for restrictions on such actions to be directly linked to specified matters and not excessive, ensuring that the law provides checks against arbitrary or illegal exercises of power.

These cases collectively highlight the evolving landscape of privacy rights and their legal interpretations in Bangladesh, reinforcing the importance of safeguarding individual privacy while maintaining the rule of law.

Conclusions

Privacy-related concerns within the legal framework of Bangladesh are addressed through a multifaceted approach that encompasses constitutional provisions and legislative acts, notably the Digital Security Act of 2018. The Bangladesh

Telecommunication A of 2001 serves as the fundamental legal underpinning for the evolution and oversight of the telecommunications industry in the country, facilitating the expansion of telecommunications services and technologies.

However, the proposed Data Protection Act of 2022, rather than fortifying privacy rights, emerges as a potential encroachment on individual privacy. Furthermore, this proposed legislation exonerates authorities from any accountability in the process of accessing personal data, whether through physical or remote means. Notably, this envisioned law may supersede existing legal instruments, possibly taking precedence over the pivotal Bangladesh Right to Information Act of 2009, a cornerstone for upholding citizens' access to critical information in the contemporary context. These developments underscore the dynamic and often intricate landscape of privacy rights in Bangladesh, necessitating a careful balance between individual privacy and governmental imperatives while continually reinforcing the importance of protecting personal data in the digital age.

References

1. The Constitution of the People's Republic of Bangladesh, 1972.
2. The Bangladesh Telecommunication Act, 2001.
3. Information and Communication Technology Act, 2006. (Bangladesh)
4. Digital Security Act, 2018. (Bangladesh)
5. ActionAid Bangladesh vs. The Government of Bangladesh (2010).
6. A.K.M. Nasiruddin vs. Government of Bangladesh (2013).
7. Justice Md. Nizamul Huq vs. Government of Bangladesh (2011).
8. Aynunnahar Siddiqua and Ors. vs. Government of Bangladesh and Ors., 2017 37 BLD 181.
9. https://www.amnesty.org/en/latest/news/2022/04/bangladesh-new-data-protection-bill-threatens-peoples-right-to-privacy/.

10. https://www.atlanticcouncil.org/in-depth-research-reports/issue-brief/inside-bangladeshs-new-data-protection-laws/.
11. http://www.supremecourt.gov.bd/resources/documents/705451_DeathRef61of2011.pdf.
12. https://www.tbsnews.net/bangladesh/court/jhenaidah-court-upholds-right-privacy-against-dsa-charges-310165.
13. https://carnegieendowment.org/2021/12/09/how-bangladesh-s-digital-security-act-is-creating-culture-of-fear-pub-85951.
14. https://www.thedailystar.net/recovering-covid-reinventing-our-future/fourth-industrial-revolution-and-digital-transformation/news/right-privacy-bangladesh-the-internet-era-chipped.
15. https://www.thedailystar.net/toggle/news/3-million-bangladeshi-fb-users-personal-data-exposed-during-massive-data-leak-fb-2071777.
16. https://www.reuters.com/article/cbusiness-us-cyber-attack-idCAKCN18B0AC-OCABS.
17. https://www.tbsnews.net/bangladesh/court/jhenaidah-court-upholds-right-privacy-against-dsa-charges-310165.
18. https://www.thedailystar.net/recovering-covid-reinventing-our-future/fourth-industrial-revolution-and-digital-transformation/news/democracys-digital-challenge-2961596.
19. https://www.amnestyusa.org/countries/bangladesh/.
20. https://www.ohchr.org/en/press-releases/2023/03/bangladesh-turk-urges-immediate-suspension-digital-security-act-media.
21. https://www.ohchr.org/sites/default/files/documents/countries/bangladesh/OHCHR-Technical-Note-on-review-of-the-Digital-Security-Act-June-2022.pdf.
22. https://www.thedailystar.net/opinion/views/news/why-the-draft-data-protection-act-concerning-3271311.
23. https://www.oecd-ilibrary.org/sites/15c62f9c-en/index.html?itemId=/content/component/15c62f9c-en.
24. https://dig.watch/updates/un-ohchr-releases-2022-right-to-privacy-in-the-digital-age-report.

25. https://www.globalencryption.org/2022/09/global-encryption-coalition-steering-committee-statement-on-the-ohchr-report-on-the-right-to-privacy-in-the-digital-age/.

26. https://www.ohchr.org/en/press-releases/2022/09/spyware-and-surveillance-threats-privacy-and-human-rights-growing-un-report.

27. https://globalfreedomofexpression.columbia.edu/cases/the-case-of-shahidul-alam/

28. https://www.aarcentre.com/ojs3/index.php/jaash/article/view/22/181.

29. https://globaldataalliance.org/wp-content/uploads/2022/09/09072022gdabgdpa.pdf.

30. https://www.bankinfosecurity.asia/bangladesh-to-propose-privacy-law-a-15898.

31. https://www.amnesty.org/en/latest/news/2022/04/bangladesh-new-data-protection-bill-threatens-peoples-right-to-privacy/.

32. Universal Declaration of Human Rights.

33. International Covenant on Civil and Political Rights (ICCPR).

34. Convention on the Rights of the Child.

35. Md., Toriqul, Islam. (2022). An assessment of privacy regime in Bangladesh: a legal analysis. UUM journal of legal studies, 13 doi: 10.32890/uumjls2022.13.2.4

36. Mohsin, Dhali., Sonny, Zulhuda., Suzi, Fadhilah, Ismail. (2021). The digital economy and the quest for privacy protection in Bangladesh: a comparative legal analysis. IIUM Law Journal, 28(2):567-596. doi: 10.31436/IIUMLJ.V28I2.451.

37. Md., Abu, Bakar, Siddique. (2016). "Right to Privacy and Counter-terrorism in the Digital Age: A Critical Appraisal for Bangladesh". IOSR Journal of Humanities and Social Science, 21(07):64-72. doi: 10.9790/0837-2107086472 Md., Abu, Bakar, Siddique. (2016).

38. "Right to Privacy and Counter-terrorism in the Digital Age: A Critical Appraisal for Bangladesh". IOSR Journal of Humanities and Social Science, 21(07):64-72. doi: 10.9790/0837-2107086472.

39. Md., Zahidul, Islam., Asma, Jahan. (2015). Right to privacy: is it a fundamental right in Bangladesh Constitution?. 1(1):1-7.
40. Monowar, Islam. (2022). Legal Development for Privacy and Data Protection in Bangladesh. Global privacy law review, 3 (Issue 4):221-235. doi: 10.54648/gplr2022025.

20

Navigating the Data Protection Landscape Laws in Africa

Md. Owais Saifi and Muaz Khan

Abstract

The security of personal data has become a top priority in our increasingly linked society. Africa is hardly an exception, since the region is undergoing a rapid digital revolution. This Article offers a thorough review of the various African countries' changing data protection laws and policies. We examine the various legislative frameworks controlling data privacy across the continent, ranging from South Africa's strict Protection of Personal Information Act (POPIA) to Nigeria's Nigeria Data Protection Regulation (NDPR) and beyond. We explore the fundamental values and rights protected by important laws via a close assessment of those laws, giving light on the obligations of businesses and organizations to protect personal data. We also talk about the potential and problems that the patchwork of laws presents, emphasizing the necessity of compliance and harmonization in an increasingly international data world.

Keywords - *Africa, Data Protection, Privacy, Information, Business.*

Introduction

Data privacy has become an urgent global problem in a time when information is rapidly digitizing and online activities are becoming more commonplace. Personal information about persons is protected by data protection laws, which are regulatory frameworks that make sure that information is gathered, used, and kept responsibly and securely. These regulations aim to achieve a compromise between enabling the advantages of data-driven technology and safeguarding people's right to privacy. Data protection laws have becoming more popular throughout Africa as countries realize how crucial it is to control how personal data is used. Although the specifics of these laws differ from nation to nation, the fundamental objective to set standards for the legitimate and ethical handling of personal information remains the same.

What is Data Protection and Why is it Important?

The process of managing data to maintain the confidentiality, integrity, and accessibility of sensitive information is known as data protection, sometimes known as data privacy or information privacy. It involves a range of safeguards, policies, and procedures intended to guard against unauthorized access to, disclosure of, change of, or destruction of private or sensitive information. Maintaining privacy, upholding moral standards, and adhering to legal and regulatory obligations ultimately require data protection. It is a country's obligation towards company and there clients to ensure that their data and personal information is protected and kept safe to ensure the privacy of the data.

Data protection's Fundamentals

There are certain essentials of the concept of Data Protection –

Confidentiality

Ensuring that only authorized parties or persons can access data. Access to sensitive information must be restricted, and encryption and access restrictions must be used.

Integrity

Assuring the accuracy and correctness of data. There are safeguards in place to stop unapproved modifications, tampering, or corruption of data, whether deliberate or unintentional.

Access

Ensuring that data is accessible to authorised users when they need it. In order to ensure that data can be recovered in the event of events or failures, backup and disaster recovery procedures must be put into place.

Data minimization

Reducing the risk of data exposure and abuse by gathering and processing strictly the necessary information that is required for the intended purpose.

Security Measures

Putting in place organisational and technological security measures, such firewalls, encryption, access restrictions, and recurring security audits, to guard against hacking or unauthorised access to data.

Compliance

Following to the rules and legislation governing data protection in the country where the data is processed. These regulations frequently specify how data should be managed, including rights provided to data subjects and reporting of data breaches.

Accountability and Transparency

Taking responsibility for data handling procedures and being open and honest about how information is gathered, used, and shared with people.

Best Regime with Data Protection Laws in Africa

This part shall discuss data protection laws in various African countries:

Mauritius

The Data Protection Act 2017 (DPA) came into force on 15 January 2018 and supersedes the earlier 2004 law. And was the best data protection law in Africa for the time being. The Data Protection Authority of Mauritius plays a central role in managing and regulating data protection matters in the country. It is primarily responsible for overseeing and enforcing data protection laws and regulations, as well as handling complaints related to data privacy. The data privacy and protection laws in Mauritius are aligned with international standards.

Morocco

Article 24 of the Constitution of Morocco, 2011 provides that any person has the right to the protection of their private life. In 2009, Morocco enacted Law No 09-08 relating to the protection of individuals with regard to the processing of personal data. Morocco's data protection legislation, known as the "Moroccan Data Protection Act" (Loi 09-08), plays a vital role in preserving individuals' privacy and overseeing the ethical management of personal information. Implemented in 2009, this law brings Morocco in line with global data protection norms and standards.

South Africa

Information regulator have taken steps to implements the 2018 data protection regulations as the per the As of February 26, 2021, Regulation 5 came into effect. on March 1, 2021, Regulation 4 on May 1, 2021, and the Remnant Regulation started on July 1, 2021.

South Africa's data protection law, known as the Protection of Personal Information Act (POPIA), has been in full effect since July 1, 2021. This comprehensive legislation emphasizes informed consent, grants individuals' various data rights, mandates data security measures, and enforces accountability for organizations handling personal data. POPIA also regulates cross-border data transfers and necessitates the reporting of data breaches to the Information Regulator (IR). Compliance with POPIA is crucial for businesses operating in South Africa to safeguard individuals' privacy rights and avoid penalties, highlighting the increasing significance of data protection in the digital age.

The IR is responsible for all of South Africa. It is independent and subject only to the Constitution and the law. The IR must be impartial, carry out his duties, and exercise his powers without fear, favour, or prejudice.

Nigeria

The Data Protection and Privacy Act of Nigeria was signed into law in June 2023 and is one of the most comprehensive data protection laws in Africa. It applies to all organizations that collect, use, or process personal information of Nigerian residents.

The right to privacy is established under Section 37 of the Constitution of the Federal Republic of Nigeria ensuring that their private information and affairs are protected from unauthorized intrusion or interference, this constitutional clause is essential for upholding the privacy rights of Nigerian citizens and residents. Section 37 establishes the legal framework for data protection and privacy-related issues in Nigeria and emphasizes the significance of protecting people's private.

The regulator responsible for regulating the NDPR is the National Information Technology Development Agency (NITDA). The NDPR provides the rights of data subjects, the obligations of data controllers and data processors, and the transfer of data to a foreign territory. Although other laws contain provisions for data protection, the NDPR is the frontrunner in the Nigerian data protection landscape.

Kenya

The Cybersecurity and Data Protection Act of Kenya was enacted on November 25, 2019 and applies to all organizations that collect, use, or process personal information of Kenyan residents.

The legislation defines the rights and responsibilities of data controllers and data subjects, with a focus on the necessity of security precautions and precise data. It also mandates the designation of Data Protection Officers (DPOs) for certain companies and the regulation of data breach notifications. It governs the handling of personal data both inside and internationally transferred. The adoption of this law demonstrates Kenya's commitment to harmonizing its data protection procedures with international norms and ensuring that, in a world that is becoming more and more data-driven, personal information about individuals is handled responsibly and ethically.

Togo

Togo's "Protection of Personal Data" law, issued in the Official Journal in October 2019, regulates the entire lifecycle of personal data, including its collection, processing, transmission, storage, and usage within the nation. This legal framework upholds the principles articulated in Article 28, which protect the fundamental rights of citizens concerning privacy, dignity, and the integrity of their personal image. Moreover, the law institutes the Data Protection Authority, entrusted with the responsibility of supervising and guaranteeing adherence to the legal stipulations governing the handling of personal data.

Ghana

The "Data Protection Act, 2012" (Act 843) is the name of the data protection law in Ghana. This legislation governs how personal data is gathered, used, and handled in Ghana. The rights and obligations of data subjects and data controllers are outlined, together with the principles and regulations regulating data protection and privacy. The regulatory body in charge of upholding the Data Protection Act's requirements and enforcing its enforcement is the Data Protection Commission (DPC). The DPC plays a pivotal role in safeguarding data subjects' rights, monitoring data controllers' activities, and promoting responsible data handling practices in the country.

Draft Data Protection Laws in Africa

This part shall discuss draft laws-

Ethiopia's Data Protection Proclamation of 2023

This draft law is being reviewed by the Ethiopian government. It has been criticized by some privacy advocates for not giving data subjects enough rights.

Nigeria's Cybercrime (Prohibition, Prevention, etc.) Act, 2015

It aims to combat cybercrime and establish legal frameworks for cybersecurity. The country has been working on updating and strengthening its cybersecurity laws.

Kenya

Kenya was in the process of developing comprehensive cybersecurity legislation to address various cyber threats. The proposed laws aim to enhance digital security and protect critical infrastructure.

South Africa

South Africa had the Cybercrimes and Cybersecurity Bill under consideration in Parliament. This Bill sought to address cybercrime and enhance the country's cybersecurity measures.

Conclusions

Africa's data protection environment is complex and constantly changing. As African countries struggle with the difficulties of protecting personal data in the digital era, it is characterised by a varied spectrum of legislative frameworks, ranging from comprehensive to fledgling. Despite the apparent trend towards increasing data protection procedures and conforming to international standards, the following important conclusions may be drawn from this investigation.

The approaches to data protection taken by African countries are very diverse, with some adopting strict legislation and others still in the early phases of regulation. For enterprises that operate across national borders across the continent, this variety may provide difficulties. To enable cross-border data flows and strengthen privacy rights, several African countries are actively working to align with international data protection regulations, such as the EU's GDPR. Due to scarce resources and variable degrees of enforcement commitment, it is still difficult in some areas to effectively implement and enforce data privacy legislation.

There is a rising need for creating capacity in the area, which includes education and awareness efforts to encourage comprehension and adherence to data privacy rules. With the emergence of multinational corporations and digital technologies, it is imperative to harmonise data protection regulations across the continent in order to promote cross-border data flows and guarantee uniform standards. Owing to improved internet access and digital literacy, Africans are becoming more aware of their rights to data privacy. It is a complex challenge to strike the correct balance between preserving data privacy and promoting economic development and innovation, which calls for careful examination of legislative measures. Data protection continues to face difficulties due to the rapid advancement of technology. A critical component of legislative development is preparing for emerging technologies and the consequences they will have for privacy.

Mauritius has the best data protection law after which comes Morocco. Countries like South Africa and Nigeria have significantly laws in last three Years, the rest of African Countries are also fallowing suit but there still some countries like Libya, Sudan Somalia, Liberia and Sierra Leone are some countries which still have no law regarding data protection.

The data protection environment in Africa is dynamic and complicated, marked by both success and difficulties. It urges ongoing cooperation between international partners, corporations, civil society organisations, and governments in order to create and put into place strong data protection regimes that both protect people's rights and foster innovation and economic progress. Addressing these issues is becoming more and more important as Africa's digital footprint grows in order to protect the privacy and data rights of its expanding people.

References

1. Data Protection Act, 2012 (Ghana).
2. Law No. 2019-014 Relating to the Protection of Personal Data (Togo).
3. The Cybersecurity and Data Protection Act, 2019 (Kenya).
4. The Data Protection and Privacy Act, 2023 (Nigeria).
5. Constitution of Federal Republic of Nigeria, 1999.
6. Data Protection Act, 2017 (Mauritius)
7. No. 09-08 relating to the protection of individuals with regard to the processing of personal data, 2009. (Morocco)
8. Protection of Personal Information Act, 2021 (South Africa).
9. Constitution of Morocco, 2011.
10. https://www.appknox.com/blog/data-security-laws-in-africa.
11. https://www.trade.gov/market-intelligence/south-africa-personal-information-act.
12. https://dataprotection.africa/morocco/
13. https://www.trade.gov/market-intelligence/south-africa-personal-information-act.

21

Challenges and Issues in Privacy of Student Education Record in the U.S.A.

Ankita Sharma, Salman Khan and Towseef Ahmad Dar

Abstract

An individual enjoys right to privacy in various capacities such as rights of victims, rights of patients, right of sexual partner, rights of students etc. The Family Educational Rights and Privacy Act (FERPA), one of the nation's strictest laws protecting privacy, protects student education records, which are official and unclosed documents. All documentation that schools or education authorities maintain regarding pupils are considered education records. According to FERPA, often known as the Buckley Amendment, which offers parents and postsecondary students the right to inspect and verify the rights of education records. The following succinctly outlines FERPA's requirements: The statute limits the disclosure of student data, preserves privacy, clarifies what an education record is, and provides parent right to review and appeal. The summary includes a list of additional requirements as well as the Family Policy Compliance Office's contact information. The present paper analyses FERPA in various demesnes.

Keywords - *Confidentiality, Education Records, FERPA, Security, Student Privacy.*

Introduction

People have the right to privacy in a variety of contexts, such as patients, victims, lovers, students, and others. "Privacy is the right of people, groups, or institutions to control how, when, and to what extent, information about them is shared with others.

The Family Educational Rights and Privacy Act (FERPA), one of the nation's strictest privacy protection statutes, protects student education records as official and confidential records. Education records are any documents that schools, or educational organisations keep regarding students, according to FERPA, also referred to as the Buckley Amendment. Parents have the right to check and verify the accuracy of education records, just like postsecondary students do. This and other "privacy" rules in the United States guarantee that data about residents gathered by educational institutions and governmental organizations can be distributed only for certain and legally defined purposes. Since FERPA's passage in 1974, Congress has strengthened privacy protections for educational records through this legislation, defining and elaborating on family rights and the roles of the agencies charged with upholding those rights. It provides eligible students or their parents more control over their academic records.

Without the express agreement of an eligible student or, if the student is a junior, the student's parents, educational institutions are not allowed to disclose "personally identifiable information in education records" (20 U.S.C.S. 1232g(b)). FERPA gives parents (if the student is under 18) and eligible students (those who are 18 or older or attending a postsecondary institution) certain rights with regard to their education information. These rights include the right to inspect and analyze their records, request amendments to inaccurate information, and control the disclosure of their information. FERPA defines education information broadly, encompassing any information that are directly related to a student and maintained by an educational institution or by a party acting on the institution's behalf. This can include academic transcripts, class schedules, disciplinary records, and more. Any student who has turned 18 or is enrolled in a post-high school institution qualifies as an eligible student.

Family Educational Rights and Privacy Act

The U.S. Code (20 USC 1232g), which incorporates all FERPA modifications, contains the legal citation for FERPA. 34 CFR Part 99 of the Federal Register contains the FERPA regulations. Public Law (P.L.) 103-382 contains the FERPA modifications from 1994.

Impact of Privacy in Education

The term "privacy in education" covers a wide range of attitudes, customs, and legal provisions pertaining to students' right to privacy inside the educational system. The concept of privacy expectations, the Family Educational Rights and Privacy Act (FERPA), the Fourth Amendment, and the Health Insurance Portability and Accountability Act of 1996 (HIPAA) are among the ideas that are frequently linked to privacy in education. To safeguard student data (such as academic document and other private information) and the confidentiality of medical history are the two privacy issues in education that cause the most worry. Many academics are currently debating on the opportunity of students' privacy rights, from K–12 to even tertiary school, as well as how to manage student information in a time of instantaneous way in to and dissemination of details.

Privacy Supposition

The expression "expectation of privacy," which is akin to the "right to privacy," expresses how people naturally want to protect their sense of private. The legal definition of privacy as it currently exists in American law does not specifically grant this right to people. People frequently invoke the Fourth Amendment in bench proceedings to protect them against any steps that include unquestionable invasions of their privacy, such as warrant-required searches. But because there are so many subjective factors to take into account, the U.S. Supreme Court has initiated it challenging to define an objective, unbiased definition of "expectation of privacy" over time.

Privacy expectations for students

The privacy of student education document is a crucial aspect of educational institutions and is typically governed by various laws and regulations, with one of the most significant being the Family Educational Rights and Privacy Act (FERPA) in the United States. FERPA, enacted in 1974, is a federal law that protects the privateness of student education records.

Rights of Parents or Eligible Students

Various actions are permitted by parents or qualifying students: examine and analyse the student's academic records that the school keeps. Unless it is out of the question for parents or permitted students to study the original records (for instance, because they reside far away), schools are not needed to disclose copies of records. If you think a school's records are erroneous or deceptive, ask them to be corrected. The parent or qualified student has the opportunity to a speak if the school find not to modify the record. If the school chooses not to update the record following the hearing, the parent or entitled student has the ability to include a declaration explaining their position. Put a stop to the disclosure of personal data and Obtain a copy of the institution's access to educational records policy also allowed.

Any document from a student's education record cannot be released by schools without the parent or eligible student's written consent. Schools at risk of losing federal funds if they do not abide by FERPA. Private and parochial elementary and secondary schools are not covered by FERPA since they typically do not receive funds from any programme run by the US Department of Education. However, private postsecondary institutions frequently do get such financing and are governed by FERPA.

Allowable Disclosures

According to FERPA, schools may disclose details from a student's education record to the following individuals or entities without that student's permission or in these circumstances - School administrators with a genuine interest in education, Officials designated for an audit or appraisal, Pertinent parties in relation to student financial aid, Organizations undertaking specific studies on the school's behalf or for them, Accreditation bodies, in times of emergency involving health and safety, the appropriate officials, in accordance with a juvenile justice system and specific state law, state and local authorities and to abide by a court order or properly issued subpoena.

Privacy Dimensions of FERPA

A federal law known as the Family Educational Rights and Privacy Act (FERPA) gives parents access to their children's educational records, the ability to request that the records be amended, and some control over the disclosure of personally identifiable information from those records.

Family Educational Rights and Privacy Act (FERPA) safeguards privacy

FERPA protects both paper and digital data and is applicable to public schools as well as state or local organizations that administer education programmes and receive federal funding. Most of the states are also having privacy protection statutes that supplement FERPA and further limit the sharing of information from student records. State legislation may augment FERPA, but adherence to it is essential for schools to maintain their eligibility for federal education funding.

According to FERPA, local education authorities and schools must annually inform parents of their rightness. The notification must adequately notify their parents who are disabled or whose native tongue is not English. The FERPA rights yearly notification must state that parents have the right to access and examine records, as well as to request their amendment if they think the records are erroneous. Additionally, parents have the moral to agree to the dissemination of any personally identifiable document contained in the record, unless otherwise permitted.

FERPA ensures that both custodial and noncustodial parents have the same access to student information unless the school has proof that these rights have been revoked by a court order or a state statute. Students become "eligible students" and acquire FERPA-protected rights when they turn eighteen or enroll in a postsecondary educational institution. However, for tax purposes, parents still have access to the student document of any dependent student.

Education Record

Information on a student that is kept in educational institutions in any finding of recording, including handwriting, print, computer media, video or audio tape, film, microfilm, and microfiche, are included in education records. Examples include birthdate, birthplace, addresses of parents and/or guardians, and emergency contact information for parents; Grades, test results, courses taken, extracurricular activities, academic specializations, and formal letters pertaining to a student's standing in school; Records of special education; discipline history ; Medical and health records that the institution generates, acquires, and keeps ; and record of attendance, education, courses done, accolades received, and grade attained, Private information such as student's ID number, social security password, photograph, or other details that would easily enable identification.

Not shared with anybody, private notes taken by teachers and other staff members are not regarded as educational records. Additionally, records developed and kept by the law enforcement division of a school or district do not qualify as educational records.

According to the school system's student records policy, personal document about a student may be made public as part of the education record, which is sometimes referred to as directory information. Every student's name, address, and phone number, as well as other details commonly found in school yearbooks or athletic programmes, may be included in directory information. Other examples include student images, athlete height and weight information, names and photos of participants in several extracurricular activities or prize recipients.

Schools need to publicly inform parents each year of the categories of information deemed to be directory information. Parents have the right to request the removal of any or all of the information on their kid that they do not want made publicly available without their agreement by a certain deadline after being informed of their review rights.

Parent Review and Appeal guaranteed under FERPA

Parents may seek adjustments or corrections if they discover an education record is false or deceptive after reviewing it, and schools and education organizations are required to act quickly upon these requests.

According to an agency's annual notice of policy for exercising the right to edit information, requests must be made in writing. The schools or agencies must evaluate if the request to alter a record is in line with its own evaluation of the information correctness within a reasonable amount of time. A parent must be given the chance for a hearing if their request is rejected. The parent may add an explanation to the clarification of the information if the dispute over the record persists after the hearing. The restrictions of FERPA do not apply to grades and educational choices made by school staff members about students.

Despite the fact that schools are not obligated by federal law to give copies of records to parents, even though parents have the right to access records, this is not always the case. Schools may impose a reasonable price for acquiring data, and they are prohibited from destroying records while an access request is being processed.

Disclosure of Student Records limited by FERPA

When parents have given their previous written approval, when certain legal requirements are met, or when it is otherwise permitted by local agencies' student information policies, local education agencies and schools may distribute information from students' education information. Information kept by third parties in place of schools, such as state and municipal education organizations, middle administrative levels, academics, psychologists, or healthcare professionals employed by or under contract to schools, are subject to the same restrictions on disclosures.

The standards for identifying school authorities enclosed by an agency, including teachers, who have a legitimate educational attentiveness must be specified whether an education agency or a school district has a policy of sharing information. In general, if school authorities need to evaluate a student's academic record in order to perform their official duties, they have a genuine educational interest.

Without the parent's prior permission, teachers and school officials who interact with pupils and the schools to which students applied for admission may also have access to educational information. Additionally, state and local education officials may be given access to student records information in order to conduct audits or review information in accordance with federal requirements. In response to subpoenas or court orders, schools may also reveal information about student records without the parents' permission. Unless the subpoena is issued to enforce a law and specifically states not to contact the parent, a school administrator must make a reasonable effort to inform the parent before complying with the subpoena. In times of emergency, school officials can release data from student information to safeguard the health or safety of the students or others.

Some schools or school systems feel that taking part in research projects or policy reviews is in the best interests of the general pupil. The school or school system must first get the parent's permission before disclosing student records for these uses. The written authorization must be naming the records that will be made available, indicate the rationale behind the records' release and decide which organizations or people will receive the records.

In principle, until the school or agency destroys the education related records, information concerning each request for information access and each disclosure of information from an education record must be kept as part of the record. A documented description of the limitations on the re-release of any information must be provided to outside parties receiving records.

Supplemental FERPA Provision

The Improving America's Schools Act tightened FERPA's privacy protections for children and families in 1994 by amending a number of its provisions. The crucial areas are affected by the amendments. The schooling information of their children kept by state education agencies may be viewed by their parents. For five years, education records cannot be accessed by any other third party who improperly re-releases personally identifiable information of the records. Without the parent's prior authorization, administrators from other educational institutions may receive information regarding the disciplinary measures imposed against kids. Without informing parents, schools may divulge records in response to some subpoenas and judicial orders from law enforcement.

Privacy of Student Education Records

Some key points about the privacy of student education records are discussed in this Part.

Consent

Generally, educational institutions must obtain written consent from the student (or parent, if the student is a minor) before disclosing personally identifiable information (PII) from a student's education records. There are exceptions, such as when disclosure is to school officials with legitimate educational interests, to comply with a subpoena, or in cases of health and safety in urgent situation.

Rights to Review or Amend Records

Students and parents have the right to evaluate and request changes to education information they believe are inaccurate or misleading. If the institution does not comply with the request, there is a formal process for challenging the records.

Directory Information

Schools may disclose certain information considered "directory information" without consent unless the student has requested otherwise. Directory information typically includes a student's name, address, phone number, and other basic information.

Annual Notification

Educational institutions are required to provide an annual notification to students and parents regarding their FERPA rights and the school's policies on education records.

Penalties for Non-Compliance

Institutions that violate FERPA may lose federal funding. Additionally, individuals found guilty of improperly disclosing education records can face fines and imprisonment.

Security and Paternalism: The Morality of Collecting Student Data

For numerous American high school students, their everyday academic routine often commences with the familiar act of opening their laptops and accessing an educational platform. Throughout their day, they invest most of hours crafting essays, honing mathematical skills, communicating with teachers via email, and completing assessments in a digital form. Even at schools that enforce restrictions on in-class phone usage, students often engage in social messaging using school-provided electronic devices that eventually become an extension of their personal belongings. However, what may elude many of them is the fact that both educational institutions and external companies have the extent to gather their personal communications as data, and in certain instances, employ them as potential evidence.

Educational institutions have a genuine concern for safeguarding their students against online badgering and potential self-harm or can cause harm to others. To address these issues, school administrators must monitor software. This software is designed to detect specific keywords in emails, instant messages, or search queries that may indicate bullying (e.g., "gay") or self-harm (e.g., "suicide"). When such keywords are found, notifications are set off, informing law enforcement and, in some situations, school administrators.

For instance, in September 2021, a Minneapolis school district's monitoring software generated more than 1,300 alerts for school administrators, indicating that students had acquired "questionable content." Each alert extracted flagged text from students' messages, emails, or school documents, forwarding it to school administrators for their examination. In other school districts, monitoring software took the step of escalating mentions of suicide to involve the police.

A nationwide survey involving parents of school-aged children revealed that most parents were not in Favor of their child's educational data being shared with law enforcement agencies. Despite growing and widespread concern among parents regarding the sharing of student data and the prevalent use of educational platforms in schools, students and their parents lack viable options for opting out of interactions with companies whose data collection technique and policies pose potential threats to students' privacy.

Apart from the primary objective of safeguarding students, both education researchers and creators of educational software share a keen interest in harnessing the extensive data generated by students to enhance their educational experiences. Educational technology rooted in artificial intelligence (AI) seeks to "adapt to students' individual needs" by utilizing their data to look after their progress and devise tailored learning strategies. Developers of educational software aspire to gain insights into how students engage with their work, with the goal of enhancing future educational offerings at the same time, education researchers aim to leverage student data to gain insights into learning processes and disparities in education.

However, the collection of data is not without its drawbacks. In 2016, the Electronic Frontier Foundation conducted a study of 118 education technology software services and apps that were commonly utilized in schools. The findings were concerning: 78 of these services retained students' data even after they had graduated, and only 48 of them took measures to encrypt personal records about students. Some school districts have instituted requirements for educational software providers to disclose their data collection practices to parents and offer them the option to exclude their child from data collection. However, the survey revealed that only 55 percent of parents had received such disclosures, and 32 percent reported being unable to opt out. This lack of data encryption, transparency, and choice raises serious concerns. Despite the existence of policies aimed at providing transparency and choices, most students and parents remain unaware of what data is being collected and who has access to it.

Similar intrusions into the privacy of adults are commonplace. The delicate balancing act between children's safety and education on the one hand, and protecting their privacy on the other, is complicated by their special ethical status. One perspective on childhood privacy, known as the paternalism view, positions students as minors who require protection and guidance from responsible adults who make decisions on their behalf. Parents and legal guardians can use laws like the Family Educational Privacy Rights Act (FERPA) to shield their child's educational records from external parties. Nevertheless, within this framework, the child has limited privacy when it comes to their parents and teachers. Parents and school administrators have the authority to access their social-emotional learning journals and text messages at any time. The child is essentially considered a "moral patient" -someone deserving of protection but lacking the autonomy to make independent choices without supervision.

From an alternate perspective, the fundamental role of a child is not merely to be shielded but rather to "discover and develop her own identity." This process involves a child's exploration and play, which contribute to the cultivation of her autonomy, agency, and the capacity to make independent choices. When a child is conscious of being monitored during her experiments and understands that her decisions and explorations may be misinterpreted and met with punishment, it hinders her ability to explore freely. Moreover, privacy is vital for a child's development in the context of her relationships with others. Respecting the privacy of children's communications allows them to form authentic friendships, as true friendship relies on a relationship between two individuals that cannot thrive under constant surveillance by a third party.

Respecting the digital privacy of children also plays a crucial role in nurturing trust-based relationships between children and adults, as argued by philosopher Kay Mathiesen. A child's motivation to uphold trust increases when they are trusted, which in turn improves their capacity to behave in a trustworthy manner. In contrast, surveillance actions can erode both the child's trust in the adult and the adult's trust in the child, even in the absence of any wrongdoing being exhibit. Concerns have been raised by researchers that digital surveillance may have detrimental effects, potentially reducing a student's civic engagement and their willingness to seek assistance for mental health concerns. Therefore, according to this viewpoint, parents and school administrations have an obligation to respect the privacy rights of children unless there is a compelling reason to violate them. Continuous, unjustified background surveillance is seen as inappropriate. In summary, upholding children's digital privacy is not only about safeguarding their personal space but also about fostering trust, responsibility, and their overall well-being.

The point of view shares common ground on certain matters. Neither students nor their parents intend to initiate false alarms that could lead to law enforcement involvement, nor do they knowingly consent to educational platforms selling identifiable student data to commercial entities. However, the overarching challenge persists. Determining when to regard children as dependent individuals in need of protection and when to treat them as responsible decision-makers is, as philosopher Tamar Schapiro has contended, the fundamental dilemma of childhood. Waiting for the resolution of adult data privacy issues before addressing children's digital privacy is not a viable option.

Contextual Integrity in Terms of Privacy and Justice

The evaluation of contextual integrity in terms of privacy and justice takes into account the social identities of individuals involved and how they engage with their respective roles. Concerns regarding the privacy of students and their private information that can become more complex when intertwined with existing biases and forms of discrimination, such as those related to socioeconomic class, sexual orientation, race, and immigration status. A report from the Centre for Democracy and Technology (CDT) highlights that students from low-income backgrounds are disproportionately subjected to digital surveillance. This is due to the practice of many schools providing laptops and other devices to low-income students, which inadvertently results in increased monitoring of students' online activities. In certain instances, school authorities have the capability to monitor the applications a student uses and track their browsing history in real-time. Privacy issues were further exacerbated by the introduction of virtual learning during the COVID-19 epidemic as schools greatly increased the circulation of laptops to support online learning.

The privacy of LGBTQ students is compromised by school surveillance software, as demonstrated by an incident in a Minneapolis school district. Similar to Gaggle, this software occasionally detects LGBTQ-specific phrases like "gay" and "lesbian" on the grounds that they might denote bullying. Unintentionally, this resulted in one LGBTQ student's identity being revealed to their parents.

This fear of inadvertent outing may cause LGBTQ students to limit their online interactions. This is especially concerning since queer youth often turn to online communities to connect with peers who share their identities and gain a better understanding of themselves.

Moreover, learning platforms can exacerbate existing systemic racism and bias in school disciplinary actions. Black and Hispanic students have historically faced harsher punishments, such as suspensions, expulsions, or arrests, for similar offenses as White students. AI-based educational software may perpetuate these biases, as they can inherit the biases of the teachers and educators who use them. For instance, a study at the University of Michigan looked at the consequences of using ClassDojo, a behaviour management software for K-8 students. It found that ClassDojo had the potential to reinforce teacher biases, as it appeared to validate teacher stereotypes about which students were likely to be "disrespectful" or "disruptive." Additionally, the research revealed that ClassDojo had adverse psychological effects on student privacy violations also disproportionately affect the students whose documents are not properly recorded. While FERPA prohibits school officials from directly sharing student information, including immigration status, with government agencies like Immigrations and Customs Enforcement (ICE), there are other avenues for ICE to access this data. The "third-party doctrine" suggests that when individuals voluntarily provide their information to third parties like banks, phone companies, or software vendors, they no longer have a "reasonable expectation of privacy." When educational websites or student survey providers sell student data to data brokers, it creates an opportunity for ICE to purchase information about undocumented students. Undocumented pupils might stop attending class as a result of this if they are worried that their family members might be deported if their immigration status is made public.

Conclusions

In conclusion, educational software remains a valuable tool for school systems, allowing them to provide high-quality, personalized instruction and expand access to education. However, the challenges concerning student privacy are likely to persist and potentially worsen. Current federal privacy regulations like FERPA do not hold school districts and educational software providers accountable to government standards for student privacy and data security. Therefore, there is a pressing need for updates to these regulations to address these evolving issues.

However, addressing these concerns may require more than just a simple regulatory update. It's essential to ensure that school administrators and educational software providers prioritize the contextual integrity of information transmission when it comes to student data. Additionally, policies need to shift towards a student-centric perspective on children's rights and privacy, rather than a solely parent-centric approach. This comprehensive approach is crucial to safeguarding the privacy of students in the digital age.

References

1. https://gcncralcounsel.wayne.edu/legal/ferpa#:~:text=The%20Family%20Educational%20Rights%20and,are%20recipients%20of%20federal%20funding.
2. https://nces.ed.gov/pubs97/web/97859.asp.
3. https://www2.ed.gov/policy/gen/guid/fpco/ferpa/index.html.
4. https://thereader.mitpress.mit.edu/privacy-and-paternalism-the-ethics-of-student-data-collection/.
5. Scott-Hayward, C. S. (2015). "Does Privacy Require Secrecy? Societal Expectations of Privacy in the Digital Age". American Journal of Criminal Law. 43 (1): 19–59.
6. "Expectation of Privacy". *LII / Legal Information Institute*. Retrieved 2020-12-13.
7. Davis, A. A. (2001). "Do Children Have Privacy Rights in the Classroom?". Studies in Philosophy & Education. 20 (3): 245–254. doi:10.1023/A:1010306811944. S2CID 142378047.

8. Dinger, D. R. (2001). "Johnny saw my test score, so I'm suing my teacher: Falvo v. Owasso Independent School District, peer grading, and a student's right to privacy under the Family Education Rights and Privacy Act". Journal of Law & Education. 30 (4): 575–626.
9. Elliott, Teressa L. (2014). "Student Privacy Rights--History, Owasso, and FERPA". Journal of Higher Education Theory & Practice. 14 (4): 34–47.
10. Hunt, Stacie (2016). "Data Collection on School-aged Children through Common Core". I/S: A Journal of Law & Policy for the Information Society. 12 (305): 1–23. hdl:1811/80039.
11. Peterson, Dylan (2016). "Edtech and Student Privacy: California Law as a Model" (PDF). Berkeley Technology Law Journal. 31 (2): 961–995. doi:10.15779/Z381G4B. JSTOR 26377778.
12. Amiraullt, Ray J. (2019). "The Next Great Educational Technology Debate: Personal Data, Its Ownership, and Privacy". Quarterly Review of Distance Education. 20 (2): 55–70. ISSN 1528-3518.
13. Stahl, William. "Student Data Privacy, Digital Learning, and Special Education: Challenges at the Intersection of Policy and Practice". Journal of Special Education Leadership. 29 (2): 79–88.

PART-III
Privacy as a Social Issue

22

Intimacy and Boundaries: Exploring Privacy Dynamics in Sexual Relationships

Vijay Kumar Pandey and Mumtaz Zabeen Khan

Abstract

Privacy in sexual relations contribute to the development of a society that respects and upholds the rights of individuals to make informed, consensual decisions about their sexuality and intimate relationships. Various domestic laws in most of the developed and developing countries have recognized the rights of transgender individuals and emphasized the importance of providing equal rights, protection, and recognition to transgender and gender-diverse individuals, contributing to broader sexual freedom and inclusivity. It is important for individuals to be aware of their rights regarding privacy in sexual relations, communicate openly with their partners about their boundaries and expectations, and seek legal assistance if their privacy rights are violated. Additionally, education and awareness about consent, privacy, and healthy relationships are essential to promote a culture of respect and understanding in society. Respecting and upholding the right to privacy within the context of sexual and reproductive health and rights is crucial to promoting autonomy, dignity and well-being. It contributes to a society where individuals can exercise their choices free from fear, coercion, and discrimination.

Keywords - *Privacy, sexual, education, freedom, couple, transgender.*

Introduction

Privacy is a fundamental human right that encompasses a wide range of personal matters, including sexual relations. It involves the right to keep certain aspects of one's life, including intimate relationships, confidential and protected from unwanted intrusion or scrutiny by others. The majority of individuals, spanning all age groups, tend to keep details about their sexual experiences within close-knit circles. Our discussions about our sex lives are typically limited to a relatively small number of people, and our actual sexual histories are shared with even fewer individuals. In contrast, businesses often utilize sexual messaging and real sex videos, etc. as tools to generate profit, adhering to the common saying, "sex sells." However, when it comes to individuals, there's a more cautious and reserved approach in discussing and engaging with matters related to sexuality.

In the context of sexual relations, privacy is crucial to ensure individuals can engage in consensual and intimate interactions without fear of judgment, discrimination, or violation of their personal boundaries. This includes the right to choose who to engage in sexual relations with, when to engage in them, and in what manner. Laws and societal norms vary across different cultures and countries regarding privacy and sexual relations. Generally, laws and social standards aim to protect individuals' right to privacy in their intimate relationships, as long as these relationships are consensual, legal, and respectful of the rights and boundaries of all parties involved.

Indian law generally respects privacy and personal choices, including choices about one's intimate relationships. The right to privacy, as affirmed by the Supreme Court of India in various judgments, provides protection for personal decisions related to relationships, sexuality, and lifestyle choices. However, societal attitudes and cultural norms can sometimes lead to challenges or discrimination based on perceived moral or religious beliefs. It's essential to be aware of and respect the laws and cultural norms of the society in which one lives while also advocating for personal rights and freedoms.

Indian Cultural Perspective on Sexual Relations

Indian cultural perspectives on sexual relations are evolving due to globalization, changing social norms, and generational shifts. While traditional values still hold sway in many parts of the country, there's a noticeable shift towards more open and progressive attitudes, especially among the younger population in urban areas. It's essential to consider this diversity and complexity when understanding the Indian cultural perspective on sexual relations. Understanding and interpreting historical attitudes toward sexual privacy necessitates examining the cultural and societal norms prevailing during different periods.

Kama Sutra and Ancient Texts

The Kama Sutra, an ancient Indian text on love, relationships, and sexuality, is a notable example that discusses sexual relations, consent, and intimacy. While it does not directly address privacy, it provides insights into ancient Indian perspectives on sexual expression and relationships.

Temples and Sculptures

Ancient temples in India often feature intricate sculptures depicting various aspects of life, including sexuality and relationships. These sculptures are seen as artistic expressions rather than invasive intrusions into one's privacy.

Cultural Celebrations and Festivals

India has diverse cultural festivals that may involve expressions of love, fertility, and traditional rituals related to sexuality. These celebrations are public events and are generally viewed within the context of cultural and religious practices.

Historical Royal Courts and Palaces

The lives of kings, queens, and the nobility were often a matter of public record. However, details of their intimate lives were generally kept private and restricted to the inner circles of the royal family.

Components of Right to Privacy in Sexual Relations

The right to privacy is an integral and essential component of sexual and reproductive health and rights (SRHR). It encompasses an individual's ability to make informed decisions regarding their sexual and reproductive life, free from interference, discrimination, and coercion. Privacy is fundamental to protecting one's personal autonomy, dignity, and integrity in matters related to sexual health, family planning, and reproductive choices. The right to privacy intersects with sexual and reproductive health and rights on different grounds.

Confidentiality and Medical Records

The right to privacy ensures that individuals' medical and reproductive health information remains confidential. Health professionals must maintain patient confidentiality, securing medical records and sensitive health data.

Consent and Decision-making

Privacy is closely linked to consent. Individuals have the right to make decisions about their own bodies and reproductive health. This includes the right to consent to or decline medical treatments, contraceptives, abortions, or other interventions without coercion.

Access to Reproductive Healthcare

The right to privacy guarantees individual's access to a range of reproductive healthcare services without judgment or unwanted disclosure of their choices. This includes accessing contraception, family planning advice, fertility treatments, and safe abortion services.

Safe and Private Spaces for Care

Individuals have the right to seek healthcare in safe and private settings. Medical facilities should provide a respectful, non-discriminatory environment that ensures privacy during examinations, consultations, and treatments.

Protection from Coercion and Discrimination

Privacy safeguards individuals from coercion or pressure from others, be it a partner, family member, or society, regarding their sexual and reproductive choices. Discrimination based on sexual orientation, gender identity, or reproductive decisions is a violation of privacy.

Reproductive Choices and Autonomy

Privacy supports an individual's right to make choices regarding family planning, pregnancy, childbirth, and abortion without undue interference. This includes the right to decide when and how many children to have.

Freedom from Surveillance and Stigmatization

The right to privacy protects individuals from unwarranted surveillance, stigmatization, or discrimination based on their sexual activities, reproductive choices, or health conditions.

Education and Information

Privacy is connected to an individual's right to access comprehensive and accurate sexual and reproductive health information. This information should be provided in a confidential and non-judgmental manner.

Judicial Approach on Sexual Relations

The U.S. and Indian Courts have expanded the concept of sexual relations -

Stance of Supreme Court of U.S.

Since the 1960s, the Supreme Court has assessed the constitutionality of various governmental initiatives targeting the regulation of different aspects of sexual behavior. These initiatives encompassed attempts to control contraceptive use, possession or dissemination of obscene materials, and engagement in same-sex intimate activities by individuals. In instances where the Court nullified specific governmental actions in this domain, it frequently leaned on the presence of a privacy right enshrined in the Constitution.

In 1965, the Supreme Court, in Griswold v. Connecticut, initially recognized a protected right of marital privacy when it struck down a state law that banned the use of contraceptives. The law, in the Court's understanding, operated directly on an intimate relation of husband and wife and their physician's role in one aspect of that relation and impermissibly intruded upon the fundamental right of privacy surrounding the marriage relationship. At the time, the Court concluded that this privacy right stemmed not from the Fourteenth Amendment's Due Process Clause, but from the Bill of Rights.

Eisenstadt v. Baird (1972), Building on Griswold, this case extended the right to privacy regarding contraception to unmarried individuals, affirming that the state could not prohibit the distribution of contraceptives to unmarried persons.

Roe v. Wade (1973), U.S. Supreme Court established a woman's legal right to have an abortion under the constitutional right to privacy.

Doe v. Bolton (1973), a U.S. Supreme Court case decided on the same day as Roe v. Wade, clarifying and expanding the right to have an abortion by defining health exceptions.

Miller v. California (1973) A U.S. Supreme Court case that established the Miller test for obscenity, protecting speech and materials that are not considered obscene and therefore enjoy First Amendment protection.

Bowers v. Hardwick (1986) this case, later overturned by Lawrence v. Texas, upheld Georgia's sodomy law criminalizing homosexual acts, highlighting the evolution of the Court's stance on sexual privacy and LGBTQ+ rights.

Lawrence v. Texas (2003) is a U.S. Supreme Court case that struck down a Texas statute criminalizing homosexual sodomy, establishing a right to privacy regarding consensual adult sexual relations.

Obergefell v. Hodges (2015), U.S. Supreme Court legalized same-sex marriage across all fifty states, affirming the right to marry as a fundamental aspect of personal autonomy and privacy.

Gonzales v. Carhart (2007), U.S. Supreme Court upheld the Partial-Birth Abortion Ban Act, limiting certain abortion procedures but without overturning Roe v. Wade or Casey.

These cases represent significant legal milestones related to sexual privacy, reproductive rights, sexual orientation, and freedom of expression. The outcomes of these cases have had a lasting impact on the legal framework surrounding sexual privacy in the United States.

Indian Cases

India has a rich and diverse cultural tapestry shaped by its history, religions, traditions, and social norms, which also influence perspectives on sexual relations. India is a vast and heterogeneous country with numerous subcultures and belief systems, so attitudes towards sexual relations can vary widely.

State of Maharashtra v. Madhkar Narayan Mardikar (1991), this case highlighted the importance of consent in sexual assault cases and established that lack of consent is a crucial element to prove sexual assault.

Sakshi v. Union of India (2004), this case discussed the need for legal reforms to address sexual violence and the importance of consent in intimate relationships.

National Legal Services Authority v. Union of India, (2014), the Supreme Court recognized transgender individuals as a third gender and affirmed their fundamental rights to equality, non-discrimination, and protection of their gender identity. This judgment was a significant step toward ensuring the rights of transgender individuals, including their sexual freedom.

Rajesh Sharma v. State of Uttar Pradesh (2017) Though this case primarily dealt with misuse of Section 498A of the Indian Penal Code (related to cruelty against a married woman), it raised discussions about consensual relationships and the right to choice in marital matters.

Independent Thought v. Union of India (2017) While this case primarily dealt with child marriages and the age of consent, it indirectly emphasizes the importance of consent in sexual relations.

K.S. Puttaswamy (Retd.) & Anr. v. Union of India & Ors. (2017), commonly known as the "Right to Privacy" case, this landmark judgment recognized the right to privacy as a fundamental right encompassed within the right to life and personal liberty under Article 21 of the Indian Constitution. The ruling has broad implications for all aspects of privacy, including sexual privacy.

Navtej Singh Johar & Ors. v. Union of India (2018) involved a historic decision by the Supreme Court of India that decriminalized consensual same-sex relations between adults by partially striking down Section 377 of the Indian Penal Code. The ruling recognized the right to privacy and individual autonomy, affirming the dignity and equality of LGBTQ+ individuals.

In Shafin Jahan v. Asokan K.M. & Others (2018), the Supreme Court upheld the right to choose one's life partner as a fundamental right, reaffirming the right to privacy and personal liberty in relationships and marriages.

These cases demonstrate the role of Indian courts in interpreting and evolving laws to uphold the sexual freedom and rights of individuals, promoting gender equality, dignity, and autonomy in matters related to sexuality and intimate relationships. The legal landscape continues to evolve, and ongoing efforts strive to further protect and advance sexual freedom and rights in India.

European Court

Toonen v. Australia was a case before the United Nations Human Rights Committee. In this case, the Committee found Australia's criminalization of homosexual acts to be a violation of the International Covenant on Civil and Political Rights (ICCPR), reinforcing the global trend towards recognizing and protecting the rights of LGBTQ+ individuals.

In Modinos v. Cyprus (1993), the European Court of Human Rights reiterated its stance, affirming that any law criminalizing consensual homosexual acts violates the right to respect for private life. This underscores a consistent jurisprudential approach to protect the rights and privacy of LGBTQ+ individuals.

Norris v. Ireland, emphasized that the potential offense caused to those who consider homosexuality immoral should not warrant legal penalties when only consenting adults are involved. This reinforces the principle of privacy and the right to engage in private homosexual acts without fear of criminalization.

In Dudgeon v. The United Kingdom (1981), the European Court of Human Rights ruled that criminal laws prohibiting consensual homosexual acts between adults violated the right to respect for private life. The Court emphasized that societal moral objections, without harm to others, should not justify penal sanctions against consenting adults engaged in private homosexual acts.

Conclusions and Suggestions

Safeguarding sexual privacy is fundamental for enabling individuals to exercise sexual autonomy, self-governance, and closeness. Failing to respect sexual privacy may perpetuate the oppression of women and underprivileged communities. This aspect warrants distinct safeguarding, akin to other vital privacy concerns such as health, financial, communications, children's, and intellectual privacy. Ongoing public debates and discussions, both online and offline, are contributing to a more open dialogue about sexual relationships, consent and privacy, challenging stereotypes and promoting a culture of respect and understanding. The younger generation, often well-versed in privacy concerns, has been active in advocating for sexual privacy and rights, utilizing social media and other platforms to share their perspectives and experiences. Individuals have the right to be free from any form of sexual violence, abuse, harassment, or assault. They should be protected by laws and societal norms that condemn and punish such actions. They have the right to be free from any form of sexual violence, abuse, harassment, or assault. They should be protected by laws and societal norms that condemn and punish such actions.

Some suggestions to realise rights in relation to sexual matters are -

i) Providing emotional safety and support to each other ensures a conducive environment for private discussions about sexual matters and the overall well-being of the relationship.

ii) Engaging in sexual activities that both partners consent to and enjoy is essential for maintaining a healthy and enjoyable sexual relationship within marriage.

iii) Recognizing and respecting the diversity of relationships, including various sexual orientations, preferences, and identities, is vital in upholding privacy and inclusivity.

iv) Ensure access to affordable, confidential, and non-judgmental sexual healthcare services, including family planning, contraception, sexual health screenings, and mental health support.

v) Promote empowerment through education and awareness, encouraging individuals to learn about their rights, assertiveness, and the importance of setting boundaries in relationships.

vi) Individuals should have the freedom to choose their partners and types of relationships, be it monogamous, polyamorous, open, or other consensual relationship dynamics.

vii) People should have access to sexual health information, family planning services, contraception, reproductive healthcare and the right to make informed choices regarding their reproductive health and family planning.

References

1. htttps://thewire.in/law/supreme-court-aadhaar-right-to-privacy.
2. https://core.ac.uk/download/pdf/215570758.pdf.
3. https://www.thehindu.com/opinion/op-ed/this-too-is-a-right/article22378799.ece.
4. https://www.brookings.edu/articles/the-need-for-sexual-privacy-laws/.
5. https://www.who.int/teams/sexual-and-reproductive-health-and-research/key-areas-of-work/sexual-health/defining-sexual-health.
6. https://constitution.congress.gov/browse/essay/amdt14-S1-6-3-6/ALDE_00013817/.
7. K.S Puttaswamy Vs Union of India, (2017) 10 SCC 1.
8. Griswold v. Connecticut, 381 U.S. 479, 481–84 (1965).
9. Roe v. Wade, 410 U.S. 113, 152 (1973).
10. Bowers v. Hardwick, 478 U.S. 186, 190–91 (1986).
11. https://iapp.org/news/a/the-fundamental-right-to-privacy-wins-again-consensual-same-sex-relationships-no-longer-a-crime-in-india/.
12. https://www.techpolicy.com/articles/sexual-privacy.
13. https://www.dailycal.org/overexposed-evaporating-privacy-in-our-sex-lives.
14. https://worldsexualhealth.net/wp-content/uploads/2013/08/Declaration-of-Sexual-Rights-2014-plain-text.pdf.

23

An Overview of Data Theft and Data Breach vis-à-vis Students and Faculty

Siddhant Sharma, Saurabh Kishor and Ahmad Aman Kazmi

Abstract

Academic integrity remains a fundamental principle in today's times, emphasizing honesty, originality, and responsible conduct in academic pursuits. It is essential for maintaining the credibility and reliability of the academic community. Despite the evolving technological landscape and the proliferation of digital resources, the core principles of academic integrity remain steadfast. Plagiarism, data fabrication and falsification, inappropriate authorship practices, and failure to comply with ethical guidelines are some of the categories of research misconduct. Data theft regulations can vary significantly depending on the country and jurisdiction in question. Academic integrity is a concern worldwide, and universities and educational institutions take measures to prevent and address such issues. Academia regulates data theft and protection through a combination of legal, ethical, and institutional measures. It's important to note that regulations and practices can vary based on geographic location, specific institutions, and changes over time. It is crucial for individuals in academia to prioritize ethical conduct, honesty, and integrity in their research practices to maintain the credibility of the academic community. Researchers are expected to follow ethical principles such as obtaining informed consent from participants, ensuring anonymity and confidentiality, and using data only for the intended research purpose. The regulatory landscape and best practices are evolving over time.

Keywords - *UGC, academia, theft, data, ethics.*

Introduction

"Ethics is not definable, is not implementable, because it is not conscious; it involves not only our thinking, but also our feeling".

- Valdemar W. Setzer

Data theft regulations can vary significantly depending on the country and jurisdiction in question. Offline data theft refers to the unauthorized access, acquisition, or copying of sensitive information or data from physical sources or devices, without the need for an internet connection. This can include stealing data from devices like computers, smartphones, external hard drives, USB drives, paper documents, and other physical storage media. Offline data theft can have serious consequences for individuals and organizations, as stolen data can be used for identity theft, financial fraud, corporate espionage, and other malicious activities. Online data theft, also known as cyber theft or data breach, refers to the unauthorized access, acquisition, or theft of sensitive information from computer systems, networks, or digital platforms. This stolen data can include personal, financial, or confidential information that can be used for fraudulent or malicious purposes. Online data theft is a significant concern in today's digital age, as it can lead to identity theft, financial loss, reputational damage, and other serious consequences for individuals and organizations.

Open Access

Open access to data in academia has numerous benefits, but it also comes with certain challenges. Sharing certain research data openly might compromise individuals' privacy or reveal sensitive information. Open access data may not always undergo the same rigorous peer review process as traditional publications, leading to potential inaccuracies or poor quality. Properly organizing, documenting, and maintaining open data requires resources and effort, which researchers might not always prioritize. Researchers may be hesitant to share data openly because they might not receive proper recognition or credit for their efforts. Determining who owns the data and how it can be used can become complicated, especially in collaborative projects or when data includes contributions from multiple sources. Instead of restricting access to this data, the creators or owners of the data choose to share it openly with the public. This can be done through various means, including websites, online repositories, or data-sharing platforms.

Open data can be misused or misinterpreted by individuals lacking the necessary expertise, leading to incorrect conclusions. Maintaining open access repositories or platforms requires ongoing resources, which might be challenging to secure in the long term. Different academic disciplines have varying norms and standards for data sharing, making it difficult to establish universal guidelines. In some academic cultures, sharing data openly might not be common or might be met with skepticism. Some research data can be extremely complex, requiring specialized knowledge to interpret and analyze effectively. Efforts to address these issues include creating guidelines for responsible data sharing, promoting transparent data management practices, and developing tools to make data more accessible and understandable to a wider audience.

While the data is freely accessible, it often comes with specific licensing terms. Common open access licenses include Creative Commons licenses, which dictate how the data can be used, shared, and attributed. These licenses can range from very permissive (allowing virtually any use) to more restrictive (requiring attribution and prohibiting commercial use, for example).

Open access data may contain personal or sensitive information. Ensuring the privacy and security of individuals represented in the data is a significant concern. Data anonymization and ethical considerations are important when dealing with such data. Dealing with the challenges of open access and data sharing in the modern world involves finding a balance between promoting transparency and protecting privacy or sensitive information. It's important to establish clear guidelines and standards for data sharing, ensure proper anonymization of sensitive data, and implement secure platforms for sharing information. Collaboration among stakeholders, including researchers, institutions, and policymakers, can help create effective frameworks that promote open access while addressing concerns about data security and privacy.

Instances of Data Breach in India

Data theft instances in academia pose a significant threat to the core principles and progress of the academic community. The erosion of trust, hindrance to research progress, compromised sensitive information, and intellectual property concerns all contribute to academia's diminishing impact. Unfortunately, academia in India is witnessing downfall with the rise of cases of research misconduct in various forms. There have been numerous cases of plagiarism in Indian academia, where researchers have been found to copy content from other sources without proper attribution. Plagiarism undermines the integrity of research and scholarly work.

IIT Kharagpur Data Breach (2019)

A breach at the Indian Institute of Technology (IIT) Kharagpur led to the leak of personal data of thousands of students. The breach involved unauthorized access to the institute's database.

Manipal University Data Breach (2019)

Manipal Academy of Higher Education reported a breach in which personal data of students, staff, and alumni was compromised. The breach involved unauthorized access to their database.

Delhi University Data Breach (2020)

Delhi University's online portal faced a data breach that exposed personal information of students applying for admission. The breach raised concerns about the security of online platforms in Indian universities.

Jawaharlal Nehru University Data Breach (2020)

JNU experienced a data breach where confidential information about faculty members and students was leaked online. The breach highlighted vulnerabilities in the university's information security systems.

Banaras Hindu University Data Leak (2021)

A data leak from Banaras Hindu University exposed the personal details of students and applicants. This incident raised concerns about data protection and cybersecurity in Indian universities.

Theft by Digital Infrastructure for Knowledge App (DIKSHA)

DIKSHA is an online educational platform that was launched by the Union Education Ministry and the National Council of Educational Research and Training (NCERT) in 2017. Concerns of Breach of personal data of millions of teachers and school students by the Digital Infrastructure for Knowledge App (DIKSHA) were raised in the beginning of 2023. It is alleged that the complete names, contact information, and email addresses of more than 1 million instructors are stored in files on the unprotected server, along with information concerning over 600,000 students. A report by the Human Rights Watch (HRW) that named DIKSHA among 21 other apps which were guilty of enabling third-party companies to access children's precise location data, potentially enabling these companies to analyze, trade, and monetize this information.

Sale of students' data

Students Database and *Students Database India* engaged in the same practice. According to the digital rights organization, data of as many as 13,14,756 students from the All India Class XII CBSE 2020-21 batch are available for purchase on the *Students Database* website. Additionally, the website offers personal data of as many as 9,04,963 students as part of 16 databases available at no cost for anyone who may be interested in obtaining them.

A data breach involving student data is a serious matter that can have significant consequences for both the affected students and the organization responsible for safeguarding their information. Student data typically includes sensitive and personal information such as names, addresses, dates of birth, social security numbers, academic records, and more. When such data is exposed or compromised without authorization, it can lead to various negative outcomes, including identity theft, financial fraud, and privacy violations. A data breach involving student data is a significant breach of trust and can have far-reaching consequences. Educational institutions and organizations must take data security seriously and be prepared to respond swiftly and responsibly in the event of a breach to protect both the data and the individuals affected.

The sale of student details by colleges to third parties without proper consent or in violation of privacy laws is unethical and, in many cases, illegal. Educational institutions are expected to protect students' personal information and maintain their privacy. To prevent data breaches, educational institutions should invest in robust cybersecurity measures, conduct regular security audits, train employees and students on best practices, and establish incident response plans in case of a breach. Additionally, staying informed about the latest cybersecurity threats and trends is crucial to maintaining a secure digital environment.

How Academia handles Data Theft in Research

Academia plays a vital role in continually challenging and addressing data confidentiality and ethics concerns, especially in the context of research involving sensitive data. Here are some ways in which academia addresses these challenges:

Research Ethics Review Boards (IRBs/ERBs)

Academic institutions typically have these boards to review research proposals involving human participants. These boards ensure that research projects adhere to ethical standards and data confidentiality guidelines before they are conducted.

Ethical Guidelines and Codes of Conduct

Academic organizations and professional associations provide researchers with guidelines and codes of conduct to ensure that research is conducted ethically and with proper consideration for data confidentiality. These guidelines help researchers navigate ethical issues related to data collection, storage, and sharing.

Informed Consent

Researchers must obtain informed consent from participants before collecting their data. This process ensures that participants understand the purpose of the study, how their data will be used, and any potential risks involved.

Anonymization and De-identification

Researchers often anonymize or de-identify data to remove personally identifiable information. This helps protect participants' confidentiality while allowing researchers to analyze the data.

Secure Data Storage

Academia emphasizes secure data storage practices to prevent unauthorized access to sensitive data. Researchers are encouraged to use encryption and other security measures to protect data throughout its lifecycle.

Data Sharing Agreements

When sharing data with other researchers, institutions, or organizations, data sharing agreements are established to outline how the data will be used, stored, and protected. These agreements help maintain confidentiality and ethics when collaborating on research projects.

Sensitive Data Handling Training

Academic institutions often provide training to researchers on how to handle sensitive data responsibly. This includes educating researchers about best practices for data security, confidentiality, and ethical considerations.

Regular Ethical Review

Researchers are encouraged to periodically review their projects' ethical aspects, especially when dealing with evolving technologies or changing research contexts. This ensures that ethical considerations remain relevant throughout the research process.

Open Discussions and Collaboration

Academic communities encourage open discussions on ethical challenges related to data confidentiality. Researchers collaborate with ethicists, legal experts, and data privacy professionals to address emerging concerns.

Interdisciplinary Approaches

Collaboration across disciplines, including ethics, law, and technology, helps researchers gain comprehensive insights into the challenges related to data confidentiality and ethics. This multidisciplinary approach results in more effective solutions.

Overall, academia's commitment to upholding data confidentiality and ethical standards is demonstrated through institutional policies, ongoing education, collaborative efforts, and adherence to legal requirements. As technology advances and new ethical challenges emerge, academia continues to adapt its practices to ensure responsible and ethical research conduct.

Relevant UGC Regulations

The University Grants Commission (UGC) is a regulatory body for higher education in India. It sets guidelines and regulations for universities and colleges to ensure quality education and research standards. The University Grants Commission (Promotion of Academic Integrity and Prevention of Plagiarism in Higher Educational Institutions) Regulations, 2018 are a step forward to ensure research ethics by academia.

Guidelines for Research Degrees

UGC provides guidelines for universities to offer research degrees such as M.Phil. and Ph.D. These guidelines cover aspects like admission criteria, minimum qualifications for supervisors, evaluation process, duration of the program, and so on.

Plagiarism Detection

UGC emphasizes the importance of original research and requires universities to implement plagiarism detection mechanisms to ensure that research work is not copied from other sources without proper attribution.

Research Funding

UGC provides various grants and funding opportunities for research projects, conferences, workshops, and seminars. These funds are meant to promote research activities and enhance the quality of research in universities.

Research Ethics

Universities are expected to follow ethical guidelines when conducting research involving human subjects, animals, or any sensitive areas. Ethical considerations are crucial to maintaining the integrity of research work.

Publication and Intellectual Property

UGC encourages researchers to publish their work in reputable journals and conferences. It also supports the protection of intellectual property rights arising from research activities.

Interdisciplinary Research

UGC promotes interdisciplinary research by encouraging collaboration between departments, institutions, and disciplines to address complex challenges.

Quality Assurance

UGC regularly reviews and assesses the quality of research programs offered by universities to ensure they meet the required standards.

Research Assessment and Evaluation

UGC may conduct assessments of research output and impact to evaluate the performance of universities in terms of research contributions.

Open Access

UGC encourages the open access dissemination of research findings to make them accessible to a wider audience, both within and outside the academic community.

International Collaboration

UGC supports international collaboration in research, allowing researchers to work with experts from around the world to enhance the quality of research output.

Conclusions and Suggestions

Sensitive information of students and faculty often become subject to unauthorized dissemination, for monetary benefits or otherwise. Although not intentional, academic institutions can fall victim to data breaches, where cyber attackers gain unauthorized access to student databases, compromising sensitive student information.Data theft can have serious consequences for individuals and the institution as a whole. Instances of data theft in academia have increased all over the world. To address and prevent research misconduct, universities and research institutions in India generally have guidelines, codes of conduct, and committees responsible for investigating allegations of misconduct.

It's essential for students and researchers to be aware of these guidelines, ethical standards, and best practices to ensure the integrity of their research. In 2018, the UGC introduced the "University Grants Commission (Promotion of Academic Integrity and Prevention of Plagiarism in Higher Educational Institutions) Regulations, 2018." These regulations were established to address the issue of plagiarism in academic and research work within higher education institutions. It is essential for both faculty members and students to uphold high standards of academic integrity to maintain the credibility and reputation of the education system.

The issue of data theft amongst academia abroad requires a proactive approach that involves a combination of technical measures, policy development, and education to mitigate risks and safeguard valuable research and intellectual property. Preventing data theft is crucial in academia and research to maintain trust, ethical standards, and the integrity of the scientific community. Data theft not only harms individuals and institutions but also erodes trust within the academic and research community. Upholding ethical standards and practicing data security is essential for the advancement of knowledge and the integrity of research. Promoting transparency and educating students about their rights and privacy can further protect their data from unauthorized use or disclosure.

Suggestions

To combat plagiarism and promote academic integrity, academic institutions may:

i) Implement clear and comprehensive plagiarism policies, outlining what constitutes plagiarism and the consequences for those who engage in it.

ii) Conduct workshops and training sessions to educate faculty members and students about plagiarism, proper citation methods, and ethical writing practices.

iii) Encourage the use of plagiarism detection software to check academic work for potential plagiarism before publication or assessment.

iv) Foster a culture of academic honesty and integrity by promoting open dialogue about the importance of originality and proper attribution of sources.

References

1. UGC, *Academic Integrity and Research Quality*, 2021, available at:https://www.ugc.gov.in/ebook/Academic%20and%20Research%20Book_WEB.pdf.
2. University Grants Commission (Promotion of Academic Integrity and Prevention of Plagiarism in Higher Educational Institutions) Regulations, 2018.
3. https://www.thetechoutlook.com/news/technology/security/aws-misconfiguration-exposes-the-data-of-indian-government-and-universities-including-banaras-hindu-university/.
4. https://www.hindustantimes.com/college-admissions/du-data-leak-students-lodge-fir-yet-feel-unsafe-and-stressed/story-tDSSNT7lu5AAtBXITaQ9CK.html.
5. https://www.indiatoday.in/fyi/story/aadhar-data-hack-uidai-iit-kharagpur-graduate-digital-india-app-arrested-uttar-pradesh-man-1028013-2017-08-04.
6. https://inc42.com/buzz/from-covid-data-theft-to-teaching-india-a-lesson-cyber-attacks-in-2020/.
7. https://www.zdnet.com/article/data-theft-scandal-what-we-can-learn-from-india/
8. https://www.outlookindia.com/national/personal-data-of-millions-of-teachers-students-being-breached-by-digital-knowledge-app-diksha-iff-to-ncpcr-news-262934.
9. https://thewire.in/tech/terminal-india-data-breach-software-punishment-diksha-ekstep.
10. https://www.hrw.org/news/2023/01/27/indian-government-app-exposed-childrens-personal-data.
11. https://www.firstpost.com/tech/news-analysis/explained-how-the-student-data-breach-leaves-minors-vulnerable-to-several-threats-9839511.html.

24

Privacy Issues in Fertility and Period Tracking Applications: Impact of Dobbs vs. Jackson Women's Health Organisation

Riya Shukla

Abstract

As with various other apps, cycle trackers collect, retain and at times share some of their users' data. They have helped make women's lives easier in many ways, from family planning and detecting early signs of health issues to choosing the perfect time for a holiday. Two of the most popular period trackers in the US, Flo and Clue, have more than 55 million users combined. A relatively new, astrology-focused period tracker, Stardust, became the most downloaded free app on iOS in the days after the Supreme Court's decision. However, the company stated in its privacy policy that if authorities ask for user data, it will comply, whether legally required to or not. It said that the data was "anonymized" and "encrypted". Planned Parenthood encourages people to use their app Spot On. "People who want to track their periods and birth control always have the option to remain anonymous by using the Spot On app without creating an account," These apps can now be used against users when it comes to criminal prosecution as abortion has been made illegal in Dobbs Vs. Jackson Women's Health Organization dated 24 June, 2022. The concerns over period tracking data are part of a broader conversation about the amount of personal information smartphones collect. Women's rights organizations all over the world are warning users to be more mindful of their digital presence, not just when it comes to period trackers.

Keywords - *Cycle, Period, Court, Abortion, Privacy.*

Introduction

The advent of technology has brought forth a myriad of conveniences, and perhaps none more intimate than fertility and period tracking applications. These digital companions offer users valuable insights into their reproductive health, menstrual cycles, and fertility windows, empowering individuals with knowledge and control over their bodies. However, beneath the surface of these seemingly innocuous apps lies a complex web of privacy concerns. As users input personal data detailing their menstrual patterns, sexual activity, and intimate health, they unknowingly surrender a treasure trove of sensitive information. This data, pivotal for the functionality of these applications, raises pressing questions about how it is collected, stored, and utilized, and whether user privacy is adequately safeguarded.

This research paper embarks on an exploration of the intricate terrain of privacy issues in fertility and period tracking applications, unraveling the layers of data privacy, informed consent, and third-party data sharing. It casts a critical eye on the legal framework surrounding these apps and investigates the potential repercussions of the landmark Dobbs v. Jackson Women's Health Organisation case, a legal decision that could reverberate through the domains of healthcare and data privacy. In this era marked by increasing concerns about data protection, this research endeavors to shed light on the complexities that surround these applications, ultimately aiming to empower users and ensure that their personal data remains as private as the most intimate aspects of their lives.

The rise of fertility and period tracking applications has introduced a level of convenience and empowerment for users seeking to gain insights into their reproductive health. These apps, such as "Clue," "Flo," and "Natural Cycles," provide users with features like menstrual cycle tracking, ovulation predictions, and fertility window identification. For instance, "Clue" offers a user-friendly interface that allows individuals to log various aspects of their menstrual cycle, including mood, energy levels, and physical symptoms. It caters to a diverse user base, ranging from those trying to conceive to individuals simply looking to understand their bodies better.

However, beneath the surface of these seemingly innocuous applications lies a complex web of privacy concerns. For example, consider the case of "Period Tracker," a popular app that faced scrutiny when it was discovered that it had been sharing users' sensitive health data with Facebook without clear and explicit user consent. This data included intimate details about users' menstrual cycles and reproductive health, raising questions about the ethical handling of such personal information. Users entrust these apps with highly personal data, such as menstrual dates, sexual activity, and symptoms related to their reproductive health, making robust data security measures paramount.

Moreover, the lack of transparency surrounding data collection, processing, and sharing practices in some of these apps raises concerns about informed consent. Users may not fully understand how their data is being utilized or shared with third parties. This lack of clarity can create a gap between user expectations and reality, potentially leading to privacy breaches. For example, a user might assume that their data is solely used for personal tracking and analysis within the app, unaware that it is being shared with advertisers for targeted advertising campaigns.

Users may be unaware that their sensitive health data is being used for purposes beyond their original intentions, such as targeted advertising or medical research. This raises important questions about the responsibility of app developers and the need for comprehensive privacy policies that users can easily understand and consent to.

In this era marked by increasing concerns about data protection and privacy rights, the privacy issues associated with fertility and period tracking applications underscore the need for careful examination of how personal data is handled in the digital age. These apps provide valuable services, but they also hold a trove of intimate user information. As we delve deeper into the complexities of data privacy, informed consent, and data security in the context of these applications, it becomes evident that there is a pressing need to ensure that users' personal data remains as private as the most intimate aspects of their lives.

Fertility and Period Tracking Applications

Some fertility and period tracking apps engage in the practice of data sharing with third-party entities, such as advertisers or research organizations, without clear and explicit user consent. This practice introduces ethical and privacy challenges.

Overview of Tracking Apps

Fertility and period tracking applications have emerged as versatile tools that cater to a wide spectrum of users seeking insights into their reproductive health. These applications offer a diverse range of features, making them adaptable to various user needs. For instance, "Flo," one of the most popular tracking apps, provides a comprehensive platform for menstrual cycle tracking, ovulation predictions, and fertility window identification. In contrast, "Natural Cycles" focuses on natural contraception, relying on user-submitted basal body temperature readings. These apps serve as digital companions, guiding users through their reproductive journeys, offering tailored advice, and empowering them with knowledge. They often feature user-friendly interfaces, enabling individuals to log details about their menstrual cycles, symptoms, and sexual activity. Users can view their data in visually appealing formats, such as charts and calendars, which facilitate a deeper understanding of their reproductive health.

Popularity and User Demographics

The popularity of fertility and period tracking applications has surged in recent years, with millions of users worldwide. These apps resonate with diverse user demographics, spanning age groups and life stages. For instance, "Clue" appeals to users seeking in-depth insights into their menstrual health, emphasizing data accuracy and user education. Younger users, often in their late teens and early twenties, use these apps to understand their reproductive cycles and menstrual patterns. In contrast, "Ovia Fertility" caters to individuals actively trying to conceive, offering fertility predictions and personalized recommendations. This demographic includes couples on the path to parenthood, where tracking ovulation and fertility windows becomes paramount. Additionally, users in perimenopause and menopause stages also find value in these apps for tracking irregular menstrual cycles and managing symptoms.

Data Collected and Utilized

Fertility and period tracking applications rely heavily on the data input by users to offer personalized insights and predictions. The data collected includes menstrual cycle information, basal body temperature, cervical mucus consistency, sexual activity, and symptoms such as mood changes or physical discomfort. Users provide this data voluntarily to facilitate cycle tracking and fertility predictions. For example, "Eve" encourages users to input not only their menstrual data but also intimate details such as sexual activity, cervical mucus consistency, and mood. This comprehensive dataset enables the app to generate accurate ovulation predictions and fertility window identification. Furthermore, some apps, such as "Glow," encourage users to share their data for research purposes, contributing to large-scale studies on reproductive health. This data is then anonymized and used for medical research and insights into women's health.

Fertility and period tracking applications offer a versatile platform for users to gain insights into their reproductive health. They cater to a broad demographic, from young individuals seeking menstrual cycle awareness to couples attempting to conceive and those navigating menopausal changes. The data collected, ranging from menstrual patterns to intimate health details, is the lifeblood of these apps, enabling them to provide personalized advice and predictions. These apps exemplify the potential of technology to empower individuals with knowledge about their bodies and reproductive health.

Privacy Concerns in Tracking Apps

Fertility and period tracking applications have undoubtedly revolutionized how individuals monitor their reproductive health, but their extensive data collection and utilization raise significant privacy concerns. This section delves into the multifaceted privacy issues surrounding these apps, including data privacy and security, informed consent, and third-party data sharing.

Data Privacy and Security

Data privacy and security are paramount concerns when it comes to fertility and period tracking applications. Users entrust these apps with highly sensitive information about their menstrual cycles, sexual activity, and intimate health details. For example, an app like "Kindara" may request information about cervical mucus consistency and basal body temperature, which, if mishandled, could lead to breaches of privacy.

One of the fundamental concerns is the potential for data breaches or unauthorized access to this intimate information. The consequences of such breaches can be devastating, ranging from personal embarrassment to identity theft and blackmail. For instance, a breach in 2016 exposed the personal data of millions of users of the "MyFitnessPal" app, including intimate health information.

Moreover, the collection and storage of personal data by these apps also raise questions about data security. Users need assurance that their data is encrypted, stored securely, and protected from unauthorized access. Robust data security measures are crucial in ensuring that users can trust these applications with their most sensitive information.

Informed Consent and User Awareness

Informed consent is a cornerstone of ethical data collection, and it is particularly vital in the context of fertility and period-tracking apps. These apps often collect extensive data, sometimes going beyond menstrual cycles to include sexual activity, mood, and other intimate details. For instance, "Eve" encourages users to log data about sexual activity and cervical mucus consistency, which, if not explained clearly, can leave users unaware of how their data will be used.

Informed consent means that users must fully understand how their data will be collected, processed, and shared before they provide it. Users should be aware of the potential risks and benefits associated with data sharing and should have the option to opt in or out of certain data-sharing practices. Unfortunately, not all apps provide clear and transparent explanations of their data practices.

For instance, in 2019, "Period Tracker" faced scrutiny for sharing users' sensitive health data with Facebook without clear and explicit user consent. This incident highlighted the importance of informed consent and user awareness. Many users may have been unaware that their intimate health information was being shared with a third-party advertising platform.

Third-Party Data Sharing

One of the most contentious privacy issues in fertility and period tracking apps is third-party data sharing. Many of these apps collaborate with third-party entities, such as advertisers, research organizations, or pharmaceutical companies, to share user data. While some users may be comfortable with their anonymized data contributing to medical research or targeted advertising, others may not fully understand the extent of such data sharing.

For example, "Glow" encourages users to share their data for research purposes. While this can contribute to valuable insights into women's health and fertility, it raises questions about whether users are fully aware of how their data will be used and whether they have given informed consent.

The lack of transparency and granularity in data-sharing practices poses significant challenges. Users may not be provided with clear options to control how their data is shared or with whom. This lack of control can erode trust and exacerbate privacy concerns.

While fertility and period tracking applications offer valuable insights into reproductive health, they also present a complex landscape of privacy concerns. Data privacy and security are paramount, as breaches can have far-reaching consequences for users. Informed consent and user awareness are essential to ensure that users understand how their data will be used and have the choice to opt in or out of certain practices. Third-party data sharing, when not transparent and controlled, further complicates the privacy landscape. As these apps continue to evolve, it is imperative that developers prioritize robust data protection measures and transparent data practices to protect user privacy in this intimate domain of health tracking.

Legal Landscape vis à vis Fertility and Period Tracking Applications

Understanding the legal landscape surrounding fertility and period tracking applications is crucial to addressing the complex privacy concerns associated with these apps. This section explores the pertinent privacy laws and regulations, the landmark case of Dobbs v. Jackson Women's Health Organization, and its relevance to fertility tracking apps.

Privacy Laws and Regulations

Privacy laws and regulations vary significantly across countries and regions, but they all play a vital role in shaping the legal framework for data protection. For example, the European Union's General Data Protection Regulation (GDPR) is one of the most comprehensive and influential privacy regulations globally. It establishes strict requirements for data collection, processing, and protection, along with substantial penalties for non-compliance. Under the GDPR, users have robust rights over their personal data, including the right to access, rectify, and erase their data. Moreover, it imposes stringent obligations on organizations to ensure data privacy and security.

However, in the United States, privacy laws are more fragmented, with no overarching federal legislation governing data privacy. Instead, privacy regulations vary at the state level. For instance, the California Consumer Privacy Act (CCPA) grants California residents specific rights over their personal data and requires businesses to disclose data practices.

The absence of a comprehensive federal privacy law in the U.S. creates challenges for fertility tracking apps that operate across state lines, as they must navigate a patchwork of state regulations and compliance requirements. Consequently, the lack of consistent standards can complicate efforts to ensure robust data protection and informed user consent.

Dobbs v. Jackson Women's Health Organisation

The landmark case of Dobbs v. Jackson Women's Health Organisation, decided by the U.S. Supreme Court, focuses on abortion rights and access to reproductive healthcare services. While this case may not directly pertain to fertility tracking apps, its legal implications resonate deeply in the broader context of healthcare and data privacy. Dobbs v. Jackson Women's Health Organization centers on a Mississippi law that places severe restrictions on abortion access, effectively challenging the constitutional right to abortion established in the landmark case of Roe vs. Wade. This case's significance lies in the potential reevaluation of constitutional protections related to reproductive rights and privacy.

Relevance to Fertility Tracking Apps

The Dobbs case raises questions about how it might impact the legal landscape for healthcare data privacy, including data collected by fertility tracking apps. While these apps primarily focus on menstrual cycle tracking and fertility predictions, they deal with sensitive health information.

For instance, users of fertility tracking apps often share intimate data about their menstrual cycles, sexual activity, and reproductive health. In some cases, this information is used to guide users in their efforts to conceive or avoid pregnancy. This raises concerns about the privacy and security of such data, especially if it were to be shared or accessed without user consent.

The Dobbs case serves as a reminder that the legal framework for healthcare data privacy is subject to change and reinterpretation. It underscores the importance of clarity and transparency in data practices for fertility tracking apps. Developers and operators of these apps should remain vigilant about compliance with evolving legal standards, ensuring that user data is handled ethically and securely.

The legal landscape surrounding fertility and period tracking applications is multifaceted and subject to variations across regions. Privacy laws like the GDPR set stringent data protection standards, while the absence of a federal privacy law in the U.S. creates challenges for compliance. The Dobbs v. Jackson Women's Health Organization case, while primarily focused on reproductive rights, carries implications for healthcare data privacy, including the data collected by fertility tracking apps. As the legal landscape evolves, it becomes increasingly crucial for developers and operators of these apps to stay abreast of changing regulations and prioritize user data protection and informed consent.

The Impact of Dobbs vs. Jackson Women's Health Organization

The Dobbs v. Jackson Women's Health Organization case, a landmark decision by the U.S. Supreme Court, has far-reaching implications beyond the realm of reproductive rights. This section examines the key findings from the case, explores its broader implications for data privacy in healthcare, and considers its potential application to fertility tracking apps.

Key Findings of the Case

The central issue in the Dobbs case was the constitutionality of a Mississippi law that imposed severe restrictions on abortion access. In a 5-4 decision, the Supreme Court upheld the Mississippi law, signaling a significant shift in the Court's approach to abortion rights. While the case primarily focused on issues related to reproductive rights, its findings carry implications for broader concepts of healthcare privacy and patient autonomy.

One key finding in the Dobbs case was the recognition of the state's interest in protecting maternal health and potential life. This finding underscores the importance of safeguarding sensitive health data, including data related to reproductive health and pregnancy. Moreover, the Court's decision to uphold the Mississippi law could have implications for how privacy rights are balanced against the state's interests in healthcare contexts.

Implications for Data Privacy in Healthcare

The Dobbs case raises broader questions about data privacy in healthcare settings. Healthcare providers and organizations collect and store vast amounts of sensitive patient data, ranging from medical histories and test results to prescription records and treatment plans. Patients trust these entities to protect their privacy and the confidentiality of their health information.

In the wake of the Dobbs decision, the balance between patient privacy and the state's interest in healthcare regulation may evolve. For instance, healthcare data breaches can have severe consequences for patients, including identity theft and medical fraud. Therefore, it becomes imperative to ensure robust data protection measures and legal safeguards to prevent unauthorized access to patient data.

Moreover, the principles of informed consent and patient autonomy, which are foundational in healthcare ethics and privacy, gain renewed importance. Patients have the right to make informed decisions about their healthcare, and this extends to the control and sharing of their health data. As healthcare technology continues to advance, ensuring that patients understand how their data will be used and who will have access to it becomes increasingly critical.

Application to Fertility Tracking Apps

While the primary focus of the Dobbs case was reproductive rights, its implications for data privacy in healthcare extend to healthcare-related applications, including fertility tracking apps. These apps collect and process sensitive health data, such as menstrual cycle information, sexual activity, and intimate health details.

For fertility tracking apps, the Dobbs case serves as a reminder of the importance of data privacy and informed consent. Users entrust these apps with highly personal information about their reproductive health, and they must have confidence that their data will be handled ethically and securely. Developers and operators of these apps should prioritize clear and transparent data practices to ensure that users understand how their data will be used and have the choice to opt in or out of certain practices.

Moreover, the principles of patient autonomy and informed consent underscore the significance of user control over their data. Users should have the ability to manage and delete their data as they see fit, aligning with the spirit of data privacy laws such as the GDPR.

The impact of the Dobbs v. Jackson Women's Health Organization case extends beyond reproductive rights to broader considerations of data privacy in healthcare. The findings of the case underscore the importance of safeguarding sensitive health data and ensuring that patients have control over how their data is used and shared. Fertility tracking apps, as healthcare-related applications, should take heed of these principles and prioritize robust data protection measures, transparency, and informed user consent to protect the privacy and autonomy of their users.

Case Studies and Privacy Incidents

Fertility and period tracking applications, like many digital platforms, are not immune to privacy breaches and incidents that can compromise user data. In this section, we examine notable privacy breaches in tracking apps and draw lessons from these incidents. This Part highlights some of the incidents of privacy breaches by Period Tracking Applications:

Period Tracker App Data Sharing

In 2019, the "Period Tracker" app faced scrutiny when it was revealed that it had been sharing users' sensitive health data with Facebook without clear and explicit user consent. This data included information about users' menstrual cycles, sexual activity, and reproductive health. The incident raised concerns about user privacy and the transparency of data-sharing practices in these apps.

Clue App Data Leak

In 2020, the "Clue" app, which is popular for its menstrual cycle tracking features, experienced a data leak that exposed users' email addresses. While the leak did not directly compromise sensitive health data, it highlighted the importance of robust data security measures to protect user information.

Natural Cycles GDPR Investigation

"Natural Cycles," an app that uses basal body temperature readings for fertility predictions and contraception, faced an investigation by the Swedish Data Protection Authority in 2018. The investigation examined whether the app had complied with the GDPR in terms of user consent and data processing. While the outcome was favorable for the app, it highlighted the increased scrutiny of fertility tracking apps under data protection regulations.

MyDays App Data Leak

In 2012, the "MyDays" menstrual tracking app faced a significant data breach that exposed the personal information of over 100,000 users. This breach included data such as names, email addresses, and passwords. It served as a stark reminder of the need for robust data protection measures, including encryption and secure storage of user data.

Ovia Fertility App and Employee Wellness Programs

The "Ovia Fertility" app, which also offers pregnancy and parenting tracking, collaborates with employers to offer wellness programs to employees. While the app provides valuable insights for users, it also raises concerns about privacy when used in a corporate context. Employees may feel pressure to share intimate health data with their employers, creating potential privacy conflicts.

Glow App's Research Data Usage

The "Glow" app, known for its fertility and pregnancy tracking features, collects user data for research purposes. While this can contribute to valuable insights into women's health, users may not be fully aware of how their data is used and for what purposes. This case highlights the ethical considerations surrounding data usage for research in tracking apps.

Kindara App and In-App Purchases

The "Kindara" app offers users the ability to purchase additional features and services within the app. In some cases, users have reported unexpected charges or unclear Billing practices. Such incidents underscore the importance of transparency in financial transactions within tracking apps to ensure that users have full control over their spending and understand the costs involved.

Mayo Clinic's Partnership with Flo

In 2020, the Mayo Clinic, a prominent healthcare institution, partnered with the "Flo" app to provide users with credible health information. While this partnership aimed to promote accurate health education, it raised concerns about data sharing and user privacy. Users may have questions about how their data is handled in this collaboration and whether their sensitive health information is shared with the Mayo Clinic.

The Fertility App Data Sell-off

In 2018, an investigation revealed that some fertility tracking apps were selling user data to third-party advertisers and marketers. This breach of trust raised significant privacy concerns, as users often expect their sensitive health information to remain confidential. This case highlights the importance of clear data-sharing practices and user consent.

Privacy Incidents in Pregnancy Tracking Apps

Many pregnancy tracking apps, such as "What to Expect" and "The Bump," collect extensive data from expectant mothers. In some instances, these apps have faced criticism for sharing user data with advertisers without explicit consent. This raises concerns about the privacy of women during a particularly sensitive and personal life stage.

User Data Sale in Ovulation Tracking Apps

In 2019, reports emerged that some ovulation tracking apps were selling user data, including information related to menstrual cycles and ovulation, to third-party entities for targeted advertising. This revelation underscored the need for clear data usage policies and greater transparency in the data-sharing practices of these apps.

HealthKit Integration in Period Tracking Apps

Apple's HealthKit framework allows users to centralize their health data from various apps. Some period tracking apps integrate with HealthKit, raising questions about the security and privacy of sensitive health information when shared across platforms. Users may be concerned about the potential for unintended data exposure when using these integrations.

Lessons Learned from Privacy Breach Incidents

These privacy breach incidents offer valuable lessons for both developers and users of fertility and period tracking app -

Transparency and Informed Consent

Privacy incidents often stem from a lack of transparency and informed consent. Developers must clearly communicate to users how their data will be collected, processed, and shared. Users, on the other hand, should pay attention to privacy policies and permissions when using these apps.

Data Minimization

Collecting the minimum necessary data is a fundamental principle of data privacy. App developers should practice data minimization, only requesting and storing data that is essential for the app's functionality. Users should be cautious about apps that request excessive or unnecessary permissions.

Data Security

Robust data security measures are essential to prevent data breaches. Developers should invest in encryption, secure storage, and regular security audits to protect user data. Users should choose apps with a strong track record of data security.

User Control

Users should have control over their data. This includes the ability to delete their accounts and associated data if they choose to stop using the app. Developers should provide clear mechanisms for users to manage their data.

Compliance with Data Protection Laws

Privacy incidents can result in legal consequences. Developers should be aware of and comply with relevant data protection laws, such as the GDPR in Europe or state-level privacy laws in the U.S. Failing to do so can lead to regulatory investigations and fines.

Regular Audits and Updates

Apps should undergo regular security audits and updates to address vulnerabilities and stay up to date with evolving privacy standards. Users should keep their apps updated to benefit from security patches.

User Education

Users should educate themselves about the privacy practices of the apps they use. This includes understanding how data is collected, processed, and shared. Users can take steps to protect their privacy, such as reviewing app permissions and adjusting privacy settings.

Privacy incidents in fertility and period tracking apps underscore the importance of robust data protection measures, transparency, and informed consent. Developers must prioritize user privacy and data security, while users should be vigilant about their data and privacy rights when using these apps. By applying the lessons learned from these incidents, both developers and users can contribute to a safer and more private environment for tracking reproductive health.

Future Trends and Developments

As fertility and period tracking applications continue to evolve, several key trends and developments are poised to shape the landscape of data privacy in these apps. This section explores emerging technologies, evolving legal frameworks, and user-centric approaches to data privacy.

Emerging Technologies and Data Privacy

The use advanced technologies such as Artificial Intelligence adversely affects the privacy rights of the users of period and fertility tracking applications -

Artificial Intelligence (AI) and Machine Learning

Fertility tracking apps are increasingly incorporating AI and machine learning algorithms to provide more accurate predictions and personalized insights. While these technologies offer enhanced functionality, they also raise data privacy concerns. Users may wonder how AI processes their intimate health data and whether it is securely stored and protected from unauthorized access.

Blockchain Technology

Blockchain has the potential to revolutionize data privacy in health-tracking apps. It offers secure, decentralized storage of data, giving users greater control over their information. Blockchain can enable users to grant and revoke access to their data as needed, enhancing data security and privacy.

IoT Integration

Internet of Things (IoT) devices, such as smart thermometers and wearable trackers, are becoming more integrated with fertility and period tracking apps. These devices offer real-time data collection but also introduce new privacy considerations. Users may seek assurances that their IoT-generated data is used solely for its intended purpose and not shared without consent.

Evolving Legal Frameworks

In response to the developments in technologies, legal framework also requires keeping pace -

Privacy Regulations

Data protection laws and regulations are continuously evolving. In regions like the European Union, amendments to existing laws or new regulations may impact how fertility-tracking apps handle user data. Developers must remain vigilant in ensuring compliance with changing legal requirements, such as updates to the GDPR.

State-Level Privacy Laws in the U.S.

In the absence of a comprehensive federal privacy law, states in the U.S. are enacting their own privacy regulations. Fertility-tracking app developers operating in the U.S. should closely monitor and adapt to these state-level laws to maintain compliance and protect user data.

Global Privacy Standards

International efforts to establish global privacy standards and frameworks may affect the data privacy practices of fertility tracking apps. Developers that operate in multiple regions should be prepared to align with emerging global standards.

User-Centric Approaches to Data Privacy

The need of the hour is to incorporate more privacy principles while designing these applications -

Enhanced Consent Mechanisms

Fertility tracking apps may implement more granular and user-friendly consent mechanisms. This includes providing users with clear options to control data sharing and enabling them to easily understand and manage their consent settings.

Greater Transparency

Developers can prioritize transparency by providing detailed explanations of data practices, data flow diagrams, and user-friendly privacy policies. Transparency builds trust and helps users make informed choices about their data.

User Education

Apps can invest in user education by offering guides, tutorials, and easily accessible FAQs on data privacy. Informed users are better equipped to protect their own privacy and make data-related decisions that align with their preferences.

User Data Portability

Some apps may introduce data portability features, allowing users to export their data to other platforms or retain a copy for their records. This empowers users with more control over their data.

The future of data privacy in fertility and period tracking apps is marked by the intersection of emerging technologies, evolving legal frameworks, and user-centric approaches. Developers must strike a balance between harnessing the potential of these technologies while safeguarding user privacy. As users become increasingly conscious of data privacy, app developers must prioritize transparency, consent, and data security to maintain trust and compliance in this dynamic landscape.

Conclusions

As fertility and period tracking applications continue to gain popularity, they bring a wealth of benefits in terms of reproductive health awareness and personalized insights. However, this research has illuminated the intricate web of privacy concerns that surround these apps. From data privacy and security to informed consent and third-party data sharing, several critical facets require attention to protect user privacy effectively.

The future of data privacy in fertility and period tracking apps is marked by emerging technologies, evolving legal frameworks, and an increasing focus on user-centric approaches. Developers must adapt to these changes to maintain trust and compliance with privacy standards. Users, on the other hand, must remain vigilant about their data and privacy rights when using these apps.

While fertility and period tracking apps offer empowerment and insights into reproductive health, they must navigate the complexities of data privacy and security. By addressing these concerns and embracing user-centric principles, developers, users, and regulatory authorities can collectively create a safer and more privacy-respecting environment for these vital health-tracking tools.

References

1. Boston Women's Health Collective. (1970). Women and their bodies: A course. https://www.ourbodiesourselves.org/cms/assets/uploads/2014/04/Women-and-Their-Bodies-1970.pdf.
2. Boyd, d., and Crawford, K. (2012). Critical questions for big data. Information, Communication & Society, 15(5), 662–679.
3. Burke, S. (2018, May 11). Your menstrual app is probably selling data about your body. Broadly (Vice). https://www.vice.com/en/article/8xe4yz/menstrualapp-period-tracker-data-cyber-security?
4. BVF. (2018, March 7). Alarmierende Zunahme von Schwangerschaftsabbrüchen: Pille danach und Verhütungs-Apps. Press Release of the Professional Association of German Gynaecologists. https://www.bvf.de/aktuelles/pressemitteilungen/meldung/news/alarmierende-zunahme-von-schwangerschaftsabbruechenpille-danach-und-verhuetungs-apps/.
5. Crawford, K., Lingle, J., & Karppi, T. (2015). Our metrics, ourselves: A hundred years of self-tracking from the weight

scale to the wrist wearable device. European Journal of Cultural Studies, 18(4–5), 479–496.

6. Cukier, K., and Mayer-Schoenberger, V. (2013). The rise of big data: How it's changing the way we think about the world. Foreign Affairs, 92, 28–40.

7. DeNora, T. (1996). From physiology to feminism: Reconfguring body, gender and expertise in natural fertility control. International Sociology, 11(3), 359–383.

8. Duane, M., Contreras, A., Jensen, E. T., and White, A. (2016). The performance of fertility awareness-based method apps marketed to avoid pregnancy. The Journal of the American Board of Family Medicine, 29(4), 508–511.

9. Epstein, D. A., Lee, N. B., Kang, J. H., Agapie, E., Schroeder, J., Pina, L. R., Fogarty, J., Kientz, J. A., Sean, A., Munson, S. A. (2017). Examining menstrual tracking to inform the design of personal informatics tools. Proceedings of the SIGCHI conference on Human Factors in Computing Systems 2017 May 2, 6876–6888.

10. Faulkner, W. (2001). The technology question in feminism: A view from feminist technology studies. Women's Studies International Forum, 24(1), 79–95.

11. Felizi, N., and Varon, J. (n.d.). Menstru apps: How to turn your period into money (for others).

12. Fiore-Gartland, B., and Neff, G. (2015). Communication, mediation, and the expectations of data: Data valences across health and wellness communities. International Journal of Communication, 9, 1466–1484.

13. Fluhrer, A. L. (2018, April). Politics of fertility-tracking apps: A qualitative study with founders and developers. Master thesis, Europäische Ethnologie HU Berlin.

14. Ford, A. (2019, November 12). Period tracking apps: Something old, something new.

25

Rights of Non-Human Animals: A Study with Special Reference to Overlooked Right of Privacy of Non-Human Animals

Arrat Banday and Arwa Rafie

Abstract

Animals have needs and emotions surrounding comfort, companionship, and freedom. They can experience both physical and psychological pains. A biological universal, the demand for privacy serves to protect one's safety, ensure access to resources, and regulate social relationships. Different methods of physical separation (such as territoriality and physical hiding) and information management (such as withholding and deceit) are used to create distance in order to attain these goals. Animals that are part of a social ecosystem follow the moral principles that support these mechanisms. While the idea of privacy for humans has grown dramatically through time to encompass a wide range of aspects, including personal, intimate, and societal privacy, the phenomenon of privacy for animals has gotten very little attention. The only conceptualizations that now remain are those of early privacy academics who theorize the phenomenon at a more fundamental level, primarily to explain how humans first developed a need for privacy. This Chapter is an attempt to understand how these non-human beings have the desire for privacy and how the need varies as per the circumstances in which the animals are placed upon. It emphasizes the significance to value the right of privacy of animals.

Keywords - *Privacy, security, animals, data breach, technology.*

Introduction

Since the beginning of time, individuals have felt a desire to safeguard their personal lives. The right to privacy is still one of our most fundamental human rights today. Few people advocate depriving someone of the right to maintain the confidentiality of any information relating to them. Since the majority of social groups and circles are likely to tolerate some restrictions solely because it is necessary to ensure community safety, such beliefs face harsh criticism. However, it is still not a topic that is frequently argued whether or not other living things have a right to privacy. The first indications that an animal's functioning might lead to the establishment of some types of private worlds by them date back to just a few decades ago. However, they failed to generate any sort of widespread interest. The privacy rights of animals are still a fascinating topic that need deeper investigation. With a focus on physical separation and the right to be left alone, my paper seeks to present the topic of animals' rights and need for privacy in animals in detail.

Legal Framework for Rights of Animals in India

It is true that Animals feel the same way humans do; the only difference is that humans have the ability to express their thoughts and sentiments through words, but animals cannot and suffer unimaginable cruelty. Humans are the primary consumers of the food chain, but animals are as important, and we must protect and give them a voice; this is where the concept of animal rights comes into play.

Constitutional Framework

The Indian Constitution is the supreme law of India, outlining the fundamental political code, citizens' rights and duties, guiding principles of state policy, procedures, structures, and powers of governmental organisations. It is commonly regarded as a "living document"-dynamic and always evolving in response to changing times. The document provides constitutional supremacy, which means that the Indian Parliament cannot override the Constitution's essential structure. There are various articles in Indian constitution which does not only talk about human rights but also takes into account the right of animals.

Human beings have the right to exist in dignity under Article 21 of our constitution, but do animals have the same right, and if so, are their rights protected and treated as legal entities? Article 21 of the constitution of India provides that - "No person shall be deprived of his life or personal liberty except according to procedure established by law". The Supreme Court of India has undertaken an expansive reading of the right to life, including under it the right to food and shelter, right to education, etc.

It was held in the case of the Animal Welfare Board of India vs. Nagaraja and ors. that animals have honour and dignity that they cannot be arbitrarily deprived of, and their rights and privacy must be respected and protected from unlawful attacks. In this case, the purview of the right to dignity was expanded and was no longer confined to human beings. In relation to Article 21, the Supreme Court specifically stated:

Every species has a right to life and security, according to the law of the nation, which includes depriving it of its existence for human convenience. While protecting human rights, Article 21 of the Constitution also protects life. The term "life" has been expanded, and any disturbance from the basic environment, which includes all forms of life, including animal life, that are necessary for human life, falls within the meaning of Article 21 of the Constitution. In the case of animals, "life" denotes something more than mere survival or existence or utilitarian utility for humans, but to live a life. Also, Article 48A establishes the directive principle for environmental conservation and enhancement, as well as the preservation of forests and wildlife. It states that the state would work to maintain and improve the environment, as well as to protect the country's forests and wildlife. This Article, adopted by the 42nd Amendment in 1976, requires the state to conserve the environment and wildlife. While not judicially enforceable, Article 48A may become enforceable under the scope of Article 21's right to life. The Supreme Court heard a public interest litigation about air pollution in Delhi in M.C. Mehta v. Union of India (2002). In relation to Article 48A and public health, the Court made the following observations: Articles 39, 47, and 48A, individually and combined, impose an obligation on the State to safeguard people's health, improve public health, and protect and develop the environment. The Supreme Court held in another case Sachidanand Pandey and Ors. v. The State of West Bengal and Ors. (1987) that if a question concerning the conservation of the ecosystem is brought before the Court, Article 48A must be considered.

Article 51A (Part IV-A) of the Indian Constitution enshrines the citizens' Fundamental Duties. The article was included as part of the 42nd Amendment to the Indian Constitution in 1976 to align it with Article 29(1) of the Universal Declaration of Human Rights. While Fundamental Duties are not enforceable in courts, they are frequently used in constitutional and other interpretations.

The relevant clauses of Article 51A in the context of animal rights are as follows: Every Indian citizen is duty bound as: Article 51A (g) to safeguard and improve the natural environment, including forests, lakes, rivers, and wildlife, as well as to have compassion for all living things. Article 51A (h) to foster a scientific temperament, humanism, and a spirit of inquiry and reform. Article 51A (g) imposes an obligation on Indian citizens to maintain and improve the natural environment, as well as to have compassion for all living species. Compassion for all living animals, as defined in Animal Welfare Board of India v. A. Nagaraja and Ors. (2014), comprises care for their pain and well-being. The Supreme Court recognised 51A (g), combined with the duty to nurture scientific temperament under 51A (h), as the magna carta of Indian animal rights jurisprudence.

Relevant Legislations

Various socio-cultural, religious, and legal issues have influenced animal rights laws in India. Initially, India's legislative foundation for animal rights was weak, with little emphasis on animal care. However, there has been a purposeful shift towards recognising and safeguarding animal rights over time.

The Prevention of Cruelty to Animals Act (PCA) of 1960

The Prevention of Cruelty to Animals Act (PCA) of 1960 is the primary piece of legislation addressing animal rights in India. This Act banned cruelty to animals and sought to prevent unnecessary pain or suffering. Various Rules have been enacted under Section 38 such as Performing Animals Rules, 1973; Performing Animals Registration Rules, 2001; Breeding of; Prevention of Cruelty to Animals (Slaughterhouse) Rules, 2001; Prevention of Cruelty

(Capture of Animals) Rules,1979; Prevention of Cruelty to Animals (Establishment and Regulation of Societies for Prevention of Cruelty to Animals) Rules, 2001 etc.

Wildlife Protection Act of 1972

Another important piece of legislation that has had a significant impact on wildlife protection and welfare in India is the Wildlife Protection Act of 1972. The purpose of this Act was to safeguard endangered animals and their habitats from poaching, hunting, and illegal trading. It establishes protected areas and national parks across the country and offers legislative protections for wildlife conservation.

Biological Diversity Act, 2002

The Biological Diversity Act is a path-breaking and progressive legislation which has the potential to positively impact biodiversity conservation in the country. It provides for conservation of biological diversity, sustainable use of its components and fair and equitable sharing of the benefits arising out of the use of biological resources and knowledge.

Indian Penal Code, 1860

Section 289 provides - Whoever knowingly or negligently omits to take such order with any animal in his possession as is sufficient to guard against any probable danger to human life, or any probable danger of grievous hurt from such animal, shall be punished with imprisonment of either description for a term which may extend to six months, or with fine which may extend to one thousand rupees, or with both.

Section 428 states - Whoever commits mischief by killing, poisoning, maiming or rendering useless any animal or animals of the value of ten rupees or upwards, shall be punished with imprisonment of either description for a term which may extend to two years, or with fine, or with both. Section 429 provides- Whoever commits mischief by killing, poisoning, maiming or rendering useless, any elephant, camel, horse, mule, buffalo, bull, cow or ox, whatever may be the value thereof, or any other animal of the value of fifty rupees or upwards, shall be punished with imprisonment of either description for a term which may extend to five years, or with fine, or with both.

Section 377 reads- Whoever voluntarily has carnal intercourse against the order of nature with any man, woman or animal, shall be punished with imprisonment for life, or with imprisonment of either description for a term which may extend to ten years, and shall also be liable to fine.

Judicial Exposition of the Rights of Animals

The court not only interprets legislation, whether statutory, constitutional, customary, or otherwise, but it additionally formulates it. The courts' role is to defend the rule of law in the country and to protect civil and political rights. The fundamental essence of laws can best be understood through studying court decisions. The Indian judiciary has played a crucial part in properly executing the provisions of numerous acts safeguarding animal rights. In India, the number of petitions asserting animal and avian rights has increased in recent years. Fortunately, the Indian Supreme Court heard the cries of thousands of animals in agony and recognised their fundamental liberties.

It was held in the case of the **Animal Welfare Board of India vs. Nagaraja and ors**. that animals have honour and dignity that they cannot be arbitrarily deprived of, and their rights and privacy must be respected and protected from unlawful attacks. In this case, the purview of the right to dignity was expanded and was no longer confined to human beings. In relation to Article 21, the Supreme Court specifically stated: Every species has a right to life and security, according to the law of the nation, which includes depriving it of its existence for human convenience. While protecting human rights, Article 21 of the Constitution also protects life. The term "life" has been expanded, and any disturbance from the basic environment, which includes all forms of life, including animal life, that are necessary for human life, falls within the meaning of Article 21 of the Constitution. In the case of animals, "life" denotes something more than mere survival or existence or utilitarian utility for humans, but to live a life.

In **State of Gujarat v. Mirzapur Moti Kureshi Kassab**, the Supreme Court remarked in this instance that Article 48-A deals with "environment, forests, and wild life." It was also noted that by implementing clause (g) in Article 51-A and elevating it to the status of a fundamental obligation, the Parliament wanted to ensure that the spirit and message of Articles 48 and 48A are honoured as a basic duty of every citizen. It was also noticed that Section 5 of the Bombay Animal Preservation Act, 1954, passed in accordance with the Directive Principles, is inconsistent with the Fundamental Rights.

In **Abdulkadar Mohamad Azam Sheikh v. State of Gujarat**, in this case, the Gujarat High Court held that caging of birds amounted to illegal confinement and curbing of their fundamental right to move.

In **Gauri Maulekhi v. State of Uttarakhand and others**, the Court directed the State and its agencies to ensure that no destruction / killing / sacrifice of any nature of any animal takes place outside a registered or licensed slaughterhouse.

In **People for Animals v. MD Mohazzim and another**, Delhi High Court observed that birds have fundamental rights including the right to live with dignity and they cannot be subjected to cruelty by anyone including claim made by the respondent. It further observed that all the birds have fundamental rights to fly in the sky and all human beings have no right to keep them in small cages for the purposes of their business or otherwise.

Privacy Dynamics and Animals

"What is privacy and why does it belong to us?" writes Marty Roth in his book *Contours of Privacy*. "Is it an enclosure, an order of things? More particularly, what in the enclosure does the word 'private' point to: the space enclosed, the contents of that space, or the condition of untouchability that seems as if it does or should apply to those contents?"

There are hundreds, if not thousands, of animal cams available right now from the comfort of your own home. You may observe bears feeding, penguins swimming, pandas tumbling, and elephants slurping. Pet owners all across the world can use applications to remotely monitor their furry family members. Facial recognition is used by farms and wildlife biologists to track animals. Documentary filmmakers set up camera traps to photograph elusive wildlife like Siberian tigers.

As computing systems become more powerful and common, privacy has become a more urgent topic in the interface design literature. The privacy debate has largely neglected the potential implications of interactive technology on other species that come into contact with it, either directly or indirectly.

According to philosopher Angie Pepper, "Privacy means being able to choose what information to provide to other individuals. Pepper and others argue that this ability is foundational to allowing for a variety of types of relationships. Do nonhuman animals have the same need to form different types of relationships? The answer to that seems to be an obvious yes. Animals mate and fight and form friendships with one another. They treat family members differently than they treat strangers. Do they choose which information to provide to other individuals? Again, yes"

Animal watching may not be the only source of harm. "For many species, sight is not the primary sense. To worry about privacy only in terms of looking is to understand human-animal relations in an anthropocentric manner that normalizes sight." "So how could privacy work in terms of, say, smell?" Maybe an animal is fine with us staring at them all day, but they'd prefer we kept our noses closed.

Need for Privacy among animals under a Variety of Conditions

Early on, some of the writers who have had the most impact on the conversation about privacy in computing and interface design acknowledged that animals also exhibit a need for privacy under a variety of conditions and that privacy is not just a human phenomenon. This need exists both for wild and domesticated animals.

Media Privacy Rights of Wild Animals

Whether or not animals have a right to privacy when being videotaped is a matter about human behaviour, not about the animals themselves. Decisions concerning how we treat other species are linked to how we think about the environment as a whole.

Wildlife documentaries are continually asking how animals should be filmed; they never ask if animals should be filmed at all. This ethical problem is generally overlooked in animal documentaries.

Animal behaviours demonstrates that they can distinguish between public and private behaviour. They appear to crave seclusion at times when they retire from "public" areas. For humans, it is considered that documentary filmmakers would need permission to enter people's private lives, however there is no such restriction for wildlife filmmakers. We have no way of knowing if the animals agree to be videotaped. Should documentary filmmakers, for example, discuss the appropriateness of recording when animals are in burrows or nests? To question whether animals have a right to privacy at certain times and in certain places is not to imply that animals should never be filmed.

Adverse Effects of Monitoring Devices on Pet Animals

Cyber threats can have a major influence on the life of animals. For example, it has recently come to the public's attention that data captured from GPS collars fitted on protected wildlife can be intercepted, exposing tagged animals to cyberpoachers' attack; in response, some have called for the development of security systems that cannot be easily hacked by poachers, so that the lives of the animals, rather than the data "owned" by researchers, can be protected.

Cyberattacks have the potential to do significant harm to animals. In response, some have advocated for the development of security systems that are difficult for cyberpoachers to infiltrate, in order to protect the lives of the animals rather than the data "owned" by researchers.

Humans' security taking primacy over the rights of animals

With the increased development and usage of technology to manage animals in households, farms, zoos, research facilities, and even natural areas, privacy considerations in system design have become increasingly relevant. Farmers who monitor their livestock electronically, for example, are vulnerable to cyber-attacks and appreciate the necessity of data protection procedures. Unfortunately, rather than a concern for the privacy of the animals themselves, the incentive for building cyber security and privacy protection methods in animal contexts is still a requirement to secure data "owned" by humans.

The Animal-Computer Interaction (ACI) community has lately began investigating pet guardians' privacy issues when using wearable technology to track their animals' movements. Van der Linden and colleagues investigated the extent to which dog tracker users are aware of, and protect themselves against, potential threats to their personal privacy that may come from a tracking system data leak.

With the growth and use of technology to manage animals in homes, farms, zoos, research facilities, and even natural ecosystems, privacy considerations while developing such systems have become increasingly important. Farmers who use technology to monitor their animals, for example, are vulnerable to cyberattacks and recognize the importance of data security measures.

Responsibility of Biologists to act cautiously

To limit the collection and trade, paleontologists don't divulge the location of fresh dinosaur fossils. The same is true for archaeologists. On the other hand, biologists have typically published these data, employing tracking technologies to learn about a variety of species, from fish to bears, elephants, tigers, and cougars. People were tracking animals that had been tagged by researchers using affordable radio telemetry devices. Poachers in India tried to access data from a GPS-collared Bengal tiger in the Panna Tiger Reserve in 2013.

When humans get too close, animals can become habituated and may end up getting euthanized. Or they become stressed or sick, or they might just move altogether. Scientists include the exact coordinates of the species they're studying, but a growing number are allowing researchers to mask the spatial and temporal aspects of the data giving a range of instead of exact coordinates, omitting geographic landmarks, and not publishing real-time updates on-line.

Animals and Need for Privacy while Mating

Animals are sentient beings with thoughts, feelings, and unique personalities, according to science and evidence. Animals have their own tastes, demands, and requirements. People might not always be aware of what they are.

Even though many animal species do so from time to time, these behaviors are typically committed by subordinate or "beta" males who have good reason to do so from more aggressive and dominating alpha males. Open sex can cause tension within the groups, especially if beta men try to participate.

It's intriguing to compare the way these birds reproduce to how people do, who are also cooperative breeders. The group would still work together if the visual stimuli of sex with the betas were concealed. Across traditional societies, people almost universally conceal their private moments, with open public displays of sex typically only occurring, if at all, in ritualized contexts.

After human beings, Arabian babbler are the only species that according to scientists conceal their dominant male and female affairs. Arabian babblers like human beings are too involved in the act of sex. They do not conceal it's happening, but the involvement is being concealed.

Impact of Human Visits on Zoo Animals

Too much observation of animals could be harmful. Zoo animals may not be able to hide from humans, and as a result, some develop distinct habits. Cotton-top tamarins held "off exhibit" and away from humans engage in less play, sex, and physical contact than those kept in exhibitions that are open to the public. To their own kind, chimpanzees grow more combative. Lion-tailed macaques pace more frequently and "bite" themselves more frequently the more visitors there are. The tendency of orangutans to cover their heads with paper sacks rose at one zoo as visitor density did.

According to some research, human visitors either have no impact at all on animals or don't obviously cause unfavorable reactions. For instance, penguins can wind up spending more time submerged. In contrast, it was claimed in second research of orangutans, the creatures showed no sign of increased face-hiding behavior.

Depending on the types of relationships we have with them, certain animals may be more receptive of our intrusions than others. According to Brett Mills, a professor of media studies at the University of East Anglia who frequently writes on wildlife films, "the act of looking is itself an enactment of power, regardless of whether who/what is being looked at is bothered about being viewed."

Conclusions and Suggestions

Each animal has value. Everything we do is based on compassion. It may be time to consider if nonhuman creatures also deserve some privacy now that discussions about the protection and invasion of privacy are at the forefront of our everyday lives. If such is the case, how can we provide it to them? The question of whether we should extend privacy considerations to non-human animals comes at a time when interactive technologies are being deployed in multispecies situations and increasingly aimed at non-human animals.

People put themselves and animals in danger when they believe that we should have access to them all the time. Similar to human rights, an animal's right to privacy does not apply in all circumstances or at all times. There are costs and benefits to assess, as well as trade-offs.

Animals are continually exposed to human technologies in a world where privacy issues extend beyond data security and physical safety in the setting of unethical practises. What privacy dynamics, if any, do animals exhibit that might need to be considered when creating interactive systems that could have an impact on them or that are created with them in mind? How should the privacy of animals should be taken into account.

i) It is important to balance tracking wild or domesticated animals against the threat of rising poaching, habitat destruction, and behavioral disruption. Even if the animals aren't aware that they are being watched (or followed), the information they provide can still be utilized against them.

ii) Creating a safe global library of knowledge about rare and endangered species is a difficult task. In actuality, humans don't allow animals much room to live. Wildlife documentary makers should be more vigilant considering the privacy of animals. Not only human beings but animals should also be given equal importance of how privacy should be given to them.

iii) The idea of privacy-aware multispecies interaction design is put forth to inspire interaction designers to put their knowledge and abilities to use so that their work helps to create a society where everyone's right to privacy is respected for the good of all.

References

1. Angie Pepper, Glass Panels and Peepholes: Nonhuman Animals and the Right to Privacy, Nov. 2020, available at https://onlinelibrary.wiley.com/doi/pdf/10.1111/papq.12329.

2. Beyond Factory Farms: A New Look at the Rights of Animals, available at https://e360.yale.edu/features/petersingerinterview#:~:text=Peter%20Singer%20has%20been%20called,spark%20the%20animal%20rights%20movement.

3. Brett Mills, Why we should consider the privacy of animals, 2010, available at https://www.theguardian.com/commentisfree/cif-green/2010/apr/30/animals-privacy-wildlife-ethical.

4. Calum J. McKay, Carolin Sommer-Trembo and Marcelo R. Sánchez-Villagra, The portrayal of animal interactions in nature documentaries by David Attenborough and Bernhard Grzimek, Evolution: Education and Outreach volume 15, Article number: 15 (2022).

5. Josua rapp learn, why these birds, unlike most animals, hide their sexual trysts, besides humans, few species hide sexual activity, Arabian babblers are on one such species, keeping mating private may preserve the peace, 2018, available at https://www.nationalgeographic.com/animals/Article/arabian-babblers-hide-their-sex-like-humans-animals-news#:~:text=Arabian%20babblers%20are%20one%20such,private%20may%20preserve%20the%20peace.

6. Kara Norton, The 21st Century Threat to Wildlife is "Cyberpoaching, Oct. 2020, available at https://www.pbs.org/wgbh/nova/Article/21st-century-threat-wildlife-cyberpoaching/.

7. Ketki Angre, How India's First Wildlife Cyber Crime Cell Helped Nab Tiger Poachers, Sept. 2014, available at https://www.google.com/amp/s/www.ndtv.com/india-news/how-indias-first-wildlife-cyber-crime-cell-helped-nab-tiger-poachers-666782/amp/1.

8. Kris Milgate, Collars or Cameras: How Do Researchers Best Monitor Wildlife?, available at https://blog.nature.org/2018/08/01/collars-or-cameras-how-do-researchers-best-monitor-wildlife/.
9. Lauren Magnotti, Pawing Open the Courthouse Door: Why Animals' Interests Should Matter, 2006, available at https://www.animallaw.info/Article/pawing-open-courthouse-door-why-animals-interests-should-matter.
10. Marty Roth, Contours of Privacy: The Ethnography of a Social and Aesthetic Concept (Academics Press, 2012).
11. Sean Coughlan, Animals need 'right to privacy' from wildlife films, 2010, available at https://www.bbc.com/news/10093327.
12. Sara Hewitt, Scientists Are Debating Whether Animals Have a Right to Privacy, 2017, available at https://www.vice.com/en/Article/43ydkb/animals-privacy-tracking-data-science-journals-open-access-banff-national-park.
13. Yitzchak Ben Mocha, Why do human and non-human species conceal mating? The cooperation maintenance hypothesis, 05 August 2020, available at, https://royalsocietypublishing.org/doi/10.1098/rspb.2020.1330.
14. State of Gujarat vs Mirzapur Moti Kureshi Kassab, AIR 2006 SC 212, (8) SCC 534.
15. Special CR APP. No 1635 / 2010 dated May 12, 2011.
16. Writ Petition (PIL) No. 77 of 2010, decided on November 19, 2011.
17. Animal Welfare Board of India v. A. Nagaraja, (2014) 7 SCC 547.
18. Indian Penal Code, 1860.
19. Constitution of India, 1950.
20. Prevention of Cruelty to Animals Act, 1960).
21. Wildlife Protection Act, 1972.
22. Cosmetic Rules, 2020.

23. Prevention and Control of Infectious and Contagious Diseases in Animals Act, 2009.

24. Cattle-Trespass Act, 1871.

25. Indian Veterinary Council Act, 1984.

26

Headlines versus Humanity Balancing: Fame and Privacy

Shalini Kashmeria and Om Prakash Jha

Abstract

Due to the nature of sensationalism, competition for viewership, and the public's demand for gossip and scandal, present day media exhibits insensitive behaviour towards celebrities in several ways. Media often intrude into the personal lives of celebrities, invading their privacy and reporting on sensitive and personal matters without consent. This can include paparazzi stalking, publishing private photos, or reporting on personal relationships and family issues. These privacy infringements not only violated her rights but also set a concerning precedent for the media's conduct and the impact it can have on an individual's well-being and societal perception. Addressing such privacy violations is critical for fostering a responsible media environment that upholds ethical standards and respects individuals' fundamental rights. Continuous media scrutiny and invasion of privacy can have a detrimental impact on mental health, causing stress, anxiety, and emotional distress. Journalists must not forget that responsible journalism has to adhere to ethical standards that prioritize accuracy, fairness, and respect for individuals' privacy and dignity.

Keywords - *Celebrity, media, personal, negative, consent.*

Introduction

"Paparazzo, literally a kind of annoying insect, perhaps roughly equivalent to the English 'gadfly'. Paparazzi make themselves as visible to the public and obnoxious to their photographic subjects as possible to aid in the advertisement and wide sale of their works".

*- **Galella v. Onassis, 1973***

The question of whether it's perfectly reasonable for the press and paparazzi to intrude into the personal lives of public figures, including movie stars, is a complex and often debated ethical issue. It is important to recognize that public figures, including celebrities, do indeed trade some level of privacy for fame, adulation, and financial gain. They are aware that their public personas and private lives are of interest to the public, and this is part of what comes with being in the spotlight. However, the issue lies in the boundaries of this trade-off. While public figures do expect a certain level of scrutiny and attention, it is not always reasonable or ethical for the press and paparazzi to invade their privacy to an extent that causes harm or distress.

Celebrity rights encompass liberties associated with an individual's persona, particularly intertwined with their right to privacy and intellectual property. This becomes notably significant for celebrities, given the potential for various enterprises to exploit their identities, names, likenesses, or voices for profit in numerous advertisements. The issue of safeguarding celebrity rights remains relatively underemphasized within our country. With the rapid growth of electronic media over the years, it has become feasible to expose an individual's private life to the public sphere. Instances where the public and media infringe upon celebrities' privacy rights have notably surged. The rights granted to celebrities constitute a combination of several entitlements, including rights pertaining to their individuality, publicity, and privacy. Public figures and their families deserve empathy and respect. Society should encourage and support ethical journalism that prioritizes the well-being and privacy of individuals over sensationalism and intrusion.

Display of Insensitivity by Media Towards Celebrities

Privacy is a fundamental human right, and this right extends to everyone, including public figures and celebrities. Regardless of a person's fame or public status, they retain the same basic rights to privacy as any other individual.

Misrepresentation and Sensationalism

Media outlets may exaggerate or manipulate information to create sensational stories about celebrities. This can involve distorting facts, using misleading headlines, or taking statements out of context to attract attention and generate higher viewership or readership.

Negative Speculation and Rumor-Mongering

Media sometimes engages in spreading baseless rumors or unverified information about celebrities, tarnishing their reputations without solid evidence. This can lead to damaging the celebrity's personal and professional life.

Body Shaming and Criticism

Celebrities, due to their visibility in the public eye, often become easy targets for body shaming. Such actions can have severe consequences on the mental health and self-esteem of individuals, including leading to anxiety, depression, eating disorders, and more.

Insensitive Reporting on Tragedies or Challenges

Media can be insensitive when reporting on tragedies, struggles, or personal challenges faced by celebrities. They may exploit these situations for higher ratings, lacking empathy and understanding of the emotional toll it can take on the individuals involved.

Lack of Fact-Checking and Verification

In the rush to break news first and attract an audience, media may neglect proper fact-checking and verification processes. This can result in spreading false information and causing unnecessary harm to celebrities and their careers.

Insensitive Headlines and Language

Media outlets often use provocative or insensitive language in headlines or articles, which can contribute to a negative public perception of the celebrities involved.

Ignoring Positive Contributions

Media may focus predominantly on the negative aspects of a celebrity's life or actions while overlooking their positive contributions or achievements. This can create an unbalanced and unfair portrayal of the individual.

Instances of Breach of Privacy by Media

The most famous paparazzo was Ronald Galella, best known for his quest of Jackie Onassis and her children. In 1973, the Second Circuit modified but upheld an injunction against Galella, who went to ridiculous lengths to obtain close photographs of the former first lady. The appeals court in Galella reasoned that "Galella's action went far beyond the reasonable bounds of news gathering." This part highlights the challenges that high-profile celebrities face in maintaining a balance between their public image and personal lives.

Instances of Media Brutality in India

In India, movie stars, sportspersons (mainly cricketers), politicians are considered celebrities. Personal relationships and intimate connections are often captured by the media to earn revenue.

Sushant Singh Rajput and Rhea Chakraborty

The media breached the privacy of Sushant Singh Rajput and Rhea Chakraborty during the highly publicized and sensitive case of alleged murder / suicide of Sushant Singh Rajput. Media delved into Rhea Chakraborty's personal life, including her relationships, lifestyle, and habits. Intrusive reporting and paparazzi culture invaded her private moments, capturing her every move, both in public and private spaces. Simultaneously, the media exposed personal and sensitive information, including Sushant Singh's mental health struggles, therapy sessions, and private communications. Such exposure violated his right to keep medical and psychological details confidential. The digital space witnessed an onslaught of online harassment towards Rhea Chakraborty. Social media became a breeding ground for hate campaigns, threats, and abusive comments, further violating her right to a safe and respectful online environment.

Sidharth Shukla and Shehnaz Gill

The intrusive coverage of Sidharth Shukla's funeral and the invasion of Shehnaz Gill's privacy during a deeply emotional and sensitive moment, is an unfortunate example of the excessive and unethical behavior often displayed by certain sections of the media.

Urfi Javed, Vidya Balan and Ileana D'Cruz

Movie actors and models such as Urfi Javed, Vidya Balan, Ileana D'Cruz, have been targets of body shaming and negative comments from the media and the public. The media's obsession with appearances leads to undue criticism and invasion of privacy regarding personal choices.

Virat Kohli and Anushka Sharma

Despite the efforts of Indian cricketer Virat Kohli and Bollywood actress Anushka Sharma to maintain privacy, there have been instances where unauthorized photos of their daughter Vamika have surfaced on social media. These photos were likely taken without the couple's consent or knowledge, infringing upon their desire to protect their daughter's privacy.

Kareena Kapoor Khan

The media has often intruded into Kareena's personal relationships, particularly her marriage to Saif Ali Khan. Kareena Kapoor's pregnancies have been highly publicized, with media and paparazzi constantly invading her privacy during these personal and sensitive times. Details about her pregnancy, baby bump, maternity fashion, and her children are often splashed across tabloids without her consent. Kareena and Saif Ali Khan's children, Taimur and Jeh, have been subjects of intense media scrutiny from a very young age. Their photos and daily activities are widely shared by paparazzi, invading their privacy and childhood.

Zaira Wasim

Zaira Wasim, an Indian actress known for her roles in Bollywood films like "Dangal" and "Secret Superstar," has faced notable media scrutiny and invasion of privacy during her time in the entertainment industry.

Instances of Insensitivity towards Royal Family of Britain

Princess Diana, a prominent public figure and member of the British royal family, faced significant privacy breaches during her lifetime. These breaches often involved invasive media coverage and were a consequence of intense public and media scrutiny. Diana's phone conversations were illegally intercepted by the media, violating her privacy and capturing personal and sensitive information. The media often invaded Diana's personal relationships, including her troubled marriage with Prince Charles. They also extensively covered her struggles with mental health and eating disorders, subjecting her private battles to intense public scrutiny. These privacy breaches had a profound impact on Princess Diana's mental well-being and overall quality of life. Daily Mirror published images of Diana exercising in a gym, which they had obtained from the gym owner, according to the BBC. Daily Mirror ending up paying £1 million (US$1,372,000) towards Diana's legal fees, as well as an amount of £200,000 (US$274,400) to a charity.

A former Highgrove housekeeper, Wendy Berry, of Prince Charles, published her memoirs detailing the time she worked for the prince and his then-wife, Princess Diana. The injunction was obtained by Prince Charles, that only applied in the U.K. Berry published in the US -the book, titled The Housekeeper's Diary. The book alleged heated arguments between the royal couple and addressed Princess Diana's relationship with James Hewitt. The prince was then granted an order which allowed him to collect the royalties from the book.

Kate Middleton was snapped topless while on holiday with Prince William in France, and a reporter even posed as a footman to snap photos inside Buckingham Palace. After a lengthy court battle, the couple were awarded damages for breach of their privacy, and the editor and publisher of the magazine (Closer) were also fined.

Princess Diana's sons, Prince William and Prince Harry, faced intense media scrutiny and invasive paparazzi coverage throughout their lives. Even after her passing, the paparazzi continued to focus on them and their families, including William's children, Prince George, Princess Charlotte, and Prince Louis.

Recourse available to celebrities for breach of privacy

The celebrities can enjoy privacy through legal means.

Defamation Laws

Celebrities can take legal action against defamation, which involves false statements that harm their reputation. If false and damaging information is published or spread about them, they can sue for defamation to protect their image and privacy.

Anti-Paparazzi Laws

Some regions or countries have laws that restrict intrusive paparazzi behavior. These laws may define boundaries for paparazzi, such as limiting how close they can get to individuals, especially in private spaces. California restricts the invasion of privacy by media.

Cyber Laws

Celebrities can pursue legal action against online harassment, cyberbullying, and invasion of privacy through cyber laws. This can help protect their personal information and digital presence.

Privacy Policies and Contracts

Celebrities can work with their legal teams to set clear privacy policies and contracts with parties they engage with, including sponsors, event organizers, and social media platforms. These contracts can define the level of privacy protection they expect.

Media Management and Public Relations

Having a strong media management and public relations team can help in controlling the information released to the public, managing public appearances, and responding to media inquiries to maintain a level of privacy.

Copyright and Intellectual Property Laws

Celebrities can use copyright and intellectual property laws to protect their images, works, and content, preventing unauthorized use or distribution.

Non-Disclosure Agreements (NDAs)

Celebrities can use NDAs with individuals involved in their personal or professional lives to prevent the unauthorized sharing of sensitive information.

Code of Conduct for Media

In India and abroad, journalists adhere to specific codes of ethics and professional standards that guide their work. These guidelines help ensure that journalism serves the public interest, presents accurate information, and acts responsibly in a rapidly evolving media landscape.

Press Council of India Guidelines

The Press Council of India has outlined guidelines for journalists, emphasizing principles of freedom of the press, maintaining high standards of public taste, and presenting a fair and accurate picture of news.

Clause 21 (h), Press Council of India's Norms of Journalistic Conduct, 2022 - The private life, even of a public figure, is his own. Exposition or invasion of his personal privacy or private life is not permissible unless there is clear evidence that the wrongdoings in question have a reasonable nexus with the misuse of his public position or power and has an adverse impact on public interest. The Code also provides that The privacy of an individual should not be intruded or invaded unless it is outweighed by genuine overriding public interest, not by a prurient or morbid curiosity. Clause 35 deals with privacy of public figures.

Norms of Journalistic Conduct by News Broadcasters Association (NBA)

The NBA has established a code of ethics for TV news channels in India, covering aspects like accuracy, impartiality, fairness, and avoiding sensationalism.

Editors Guild of India Code of Ethics

The Editors Guild of India has a set of guidelines covering accuracy, fairness, and accountability in reporting. It emphasizes the duty of journalists towards the public interest.

The Code of Ethics by the Federation of Press Clubs in India

This code outlines principles of journalism, including responsibility, accuracy, impartiality, and independence. It emphasizes the importance of journalistic integrity.

Framework in Abroad

Governments around the world regulate and monitor media in various ways, seeking to balance freedom of the press with societal interests and public well-being. However, the degree and methods of government control can vary significantly based on the country's legal and political system.

Society of Professional Journalists Code of Ethics (USA)

The SPJ Code of Ethics focuses on seeking the truth, minimizing harm, acting independently, and being accountable and transparent. It sets ethical guidelines for journalists in the United States.

The BBC Editorial Guidelines (UK)

The BBC's guidelines emphasize impartiality, accuracy, fairness, transparency, and acting in the public interest. They are followed by journalists working at the BBC in the United Kingdom.

Reuters Handbook of Journalism

Reuters, a global news organization, has a comprehensive handbook that guides its journalists on principles of integrity, independence, and accuracy in reporting.

Australian Journalists' Code of Ethics (Australia)

The MEAA (Media, Entertainment & Arts Alliance) Code of Ethics in Australia emphasizes honesty, fairness, independence, and respect for the rights of individuals.

Conclusions and Suggestions

The level of intrusion into the personal lives of celebrities and public figures, especially by the paparazzi and media, can be excessive and invasive. The scrutiny they face is unprecedented, and it can impact their mental health, well-being, and overall quality of life. The constant invasion of privacy, including capturing their every move and critiquing their actions, can be overwhelming and detrimental.

While public figures may accept a certain loss of privacy as part of their chosen profession, there should still be boundaries and respect for their personal lives. The relentless pursuit of sensational stories, gossip, and invasive photography can have severe consequences, including emotional distress, damaged relationships, and even tragic outcomes. It is essential to advocate for responsible journalism and support measures that protect the well-being and privacy of all individuals, regardless of their status in society. Encouraging respectful and kind discussions about individuals, their accomplishments, talents, and contributions is vital for fostering a society that values diversity and appreciates people for who they are beyond their appearance.

There should be a balance between the public's right to know and a person's right to privacy. Invasion of privacy can have severe consequences on an individual's mental health, relationships, and overall well-being. Excessive intrusion can also lead to unethical practices, harassment, and stalking.

Responsible journalism should prioritize providing information that is in the public interest and relevant to their role as public figures, without crossing the line into invasive or harmful reporting. Public figures, like anyone else, deserve a certain level of respect for their privacy and personal boundaries. While public figures do trade some privacy for their public status, it is essential to consider ethical boundaries and prioritize responsible journalism that respects individuals' rights to privacy and mental well-being. Balancing public interest with personal privacy is crucial for a fair and just society.

References

1. https//www.careerride.com/view/does-media-interfere-too-much-with-the-personal-lives-of-celebrities-12494.aspx#~text=The%20worst%20part%20is%20
2. https://www.careerride.com/view/does-media-interfere-too-much-with-the-personal-lives-of-celebrities-12494.aspx that,viewership
3. https://www.careerride.com/view/does-media-interfere-too-much-with-the-personal-lives-of-celebrities-12494.aspx"%20for%20their%20media%20channel.
4. Helen Elizabeth Campbell, Media Intrusion into the Private Lives of Celebrities, available at https//www.lunduniversity.lu.se/lup/publication/1554826.
5. Celebrity Rights vs Privacy Where to draw the line?, Sept. 2021, available at https//www.lunduniversity.lu.se/lup/publication/1554826.
6. Celebrities 'entitled to privacy', Mar. 2022, available at https//www.theguardian.com/media/2002/mar/27/privacy.press andpublishing.
7. Stefanie Dion Jones, The Price of Fame Celebrities and the Right to Privacy, Oct. 2010, available at https//today.uconn.edu/2010/10/the-price-of-fame-celebrities-and-the-right-to-privacy/#.
8. https//indianexpress.com/article/entertainment/bollywood/privacy-in-the-times-of-papparazzi-culture-can-they-coexist-8462979/.
9. https//m.timesofindia.com/entertainment/hindi/bollywood/news/virat-kohlis-privacy-breach-how-much-fanaticism-is-too-much-bigstory/articleshow/95308895.cms.
10. https//www.mensxp.com/entertainment/celebrities/129875-from-alia-bhatt-to-virat-kohli-five-celebrities-who-voiced-against-privacy-violations.html.
11. https//timesofindia.indiatimes.com/web-series/news/hindi/vikas-grover-on-the-privacy-of-stars-a-

person-may-be-a-public-figure-but-his-privacy-is-not-public-property-exclusive/articleshow/95476085.cms.

12. https//www.jstor.org/stable/26918425.
13. https//www.livemint.com/Consumer/x32Rcm7l26gT1cRNMD PAMP/Indian-law-only-determines-the-situations-where-privacy-will.html.
14. https//m.economictimes.com/news/international/uk/daily-mail-sued-by-prince-harry-elton-john-elizabeth-hurley-others-over-alleged-privacy-violations/articleshow/94710188.cms.
15. https//feminisminindia.com/2020/09/18/sushant-singh-rajput-rhea-chakraborty-celebrity-culture-privacy/.
16. https//www.indiatvnews.com/entertainment/celebrities/saif-ali-khan-reacts-to-privacy-breach-as-paps-invade-private-property-at-2-am-latest-celebrity-news-2023-03-04-852133.
17. https//www.india.com/entertainment/hrithik-roshan-priyanka-chopra-and-other-b-town-celebs-support-preity-zinta-on-violation-of-privacy-bollywood-news-5987593/.
18. https//www.mdpi.com/2075-471X/5/2/18.
19. https//in.hellomagazine.com/lifestyle/20230222302276/alia-bhatt-the-perils-of-toxic-paparazzi-culture-and-lack-of-privacy/.
20. https//www.theguardian.com/media/2004/jun/17/privacy.broadcasting.
21. https//time.com/4914324/princess-diana-anniversary-paparazzi-tabloid-media/.
22. https//www.spokesman.com/stories/1995/jan/17/once-more-into-breach-of-royal-confidentiality/.
23. https//firstamendment.mtsu.edu/article/paparazzi/.
24. Galella v. Onassis, United States Court of Appeals, Second Circuit 487 F.2d 986 (1973).
25. https//victimsofcrime.org/wp-content/uploads/2020/08/Privacy-and-Dignity-final.pdf.
26. https//www.raiderreview.org/2023/03/14/does-the-press-violate-the-privacy-of-famous-people/.

27. https//theconversation.com/privacy-in-the-age-of-no-privacy-2363.
28. https//www.scoopwhoop.com/news/media-invaded-celebs-privacy/.
29. Press Council of India's Norms of Journalistic Conduct, 2022.
30. Constitution of India, 1950.

27

Identity Protection :
A Study of Sexual Violence Survivors

Neha Negar Alam, Ritika Shukla and Sonakshi Bandhu

Abstract

The pain resulting from sexual abuse reverberates deeply within survivors, often leaving lasting scars on their emotional, psychological, and physical well-being. The protection of the identity of sexual abuse victims is fundamental in providing a secure environment for their healing and recovery. In exploring this subject, the study addresses the profound significance of preserving the anonymity of survivors, facilitating their ability to report abuse, seek justice, and access support services without fear of stigmatization or retribution. The right to anonymity is not only a fundamental human right but also a cornerstone for empowering survivors to share their stories and advocate for change. By highlighting the interconnection between identity protection and the fulfillment of human rights, the legal systems have attempted to ensure the anonymity and dignity of survivors of sexual abuse.

Keywords - *Sexual, anonymity, police, Victim, report, Media.*

Introduction

Sexual violence refers to any sexual engagement that transpires without consent or when consent is not freely given. This grave issue significantly affects public health, profoundly influencing lifelong health, prospects, and overall welfare. Its impact extends across all communities, irrespective of gender, sexual orientation, or age, and can involve anyone either as a victim or perpetrator. Typically, the assailant in cases of sexual violence is someone familiar to the survivor, such as a friend, past or present romantic partner, colleague, neighbor, or even a family member. It can manifest physically, online, or through various technologies, such as the unauthorized sharing of intimate images or non-consensual sexting. The constitutional and human rights of victims of sexual violence and abuse are fundamental rights that are recognized and protected by various international and national laws. These rights are essential to ensuring the well-being, dignity, and justice for survivors of sexual violence. It is important to note that the specific rights and their enforcement may vary across countries, but there are universally recognized principles and standards.

Societal attitudes towards Victims of Sexual Abuse

Often, many survivors of sexual violence face further abuse, victimization, or mistreatment even after the initial act of violence. Several factors contribute to this unfortunate reality.

Stigmatization and Victim Blaming

Society often stigmatizes survivors of sexual violence, which can manifest as victim-blaming or judgment. This blame can come from family members, friends, community members, or even authorities. Survivors might be blamed for the assault, which compounds their trauma and makes it difficult to seek help or support.

Perpetrator Intimidation and Retaliation

Perpetrators of sexual violence may use intimidation and threats to silence the survivor and discourage them from reporting the crime or seeking help. This fear of retaliation can keep survivors trapped in abusive situations.

Power and Control Dynamics

Sexual violence often involves a power dynamic where the perpetrator exerts control over the survivor. This power and control can extend beyond the initial assault, leading to ongoing abuse and manipulation.

Isolation and Vulnerability

Survivors may become isolated from their support systems due to shame, fear, or the actions of the perpetrator. This isolation can make them more vulnerable to continued abuse and control.

Systemic Failures

In some cases, systemic failures in legal, social, or support systems may result in a lack of protection for survivors or insufficient punishment for perpetrators. This lack of accountability can embolden the abuser and perpetuate the cycle of abuse.

Fear and Trauma Bonding

Fear of the perpetrator, trauma bonding (a strong emotional connection with an abuser), or even financial dependency on the abuser can make it challenging for survivors to leave or escape the abusive situation.

Human Rights of Survivors of Sexual Abuse and Violence

In most of the countries, victims of sexual violence, mainly rape enjoy free medical treatment in any private hospital, harassment free and time bound investigation, o two-finger test during the medical examination, right to Zero FIR, right to compensation and trial with full dignity, speedy and protection.

Right to Life, Liberty, and Security of Person

Every individual has the inherent right to life, liberty, and security of person. Victims of sexual violence have the right to be protected from harm and violence.

Right to Freedom from Torture and Cruel, Inhuman, or Degrading Treatment or Punishment

Sexual violence and abuse constitute cruel, inhuman, or degrading treatment. Survivors have the right to be free from torture and ill-treatment.

Right to Equality and Non-Discrimination

Victims of sexual violence have the right to be treated equally and without discrimination based on gender, sex, or any other characteristic.

Right to Privacy

Victims have the right to privacy regarding their personal information, medical records, and the details of the incident. Their privacy should be respected during legal and investigative procedures.

Right to Access to Justice and Remedies

Survivors have the right to seek legal remedies and justice for the harm they have suffered. This includes access to fair and impartial judicial processes and the right to seek compensation or reparations.

Right to Health

Victims of sexual violence have the right to receive medical care and support for both physical and psychological health. This includes access to comprehensive healthcare services, counseling, and support.

Right to an Effective Remedy

Victims have the right to an effective remedy for the harm they have suffered, including access to legal recourse and the ability to hold perpetrators accountable. The individual affected by a crime possesses a range of entitlements. The ability to utilize formal legal procedures and seek justice and compensation, as stipulated in national laws, should encompass the right to lodge an appeal against a verdict of acquittal in a case like the one currently under consideration.

Right to Participation and Voice

Survivors have the right to participate in decisions that affect them, including legal proceedings. Their voices should be heard and respected throughout the legal process.

Rights of the Child

For child victims of sexual violence, additional protections and rights are afforded under international and national laws to ensure their safety, well-being, and rehabilitation.

Right to Non-Retaliation

Victims should be protected from retaliation, intimidation, or discrimination for reporting or seeking redress for sexual violence and abuse.

Preserving Identity

United Nations Declaration of Basic Principles of Justice for Victims of Crime and Abuse of Power, 1985, Article 6 (d) states that the responsiveness of judicial and administrative processes to the needs of victims should be facilitated by taking measures to minimize inconvenience to victims, protect their privacy, when necessary, and ensure their safety, as well as that of their families and witnesses on their behalf, from intimidation and retaliation.

Statutory Provisions

Section 228 A of the Indian Penal Code makes publication of name etc. of victim of sexual offences a punishable offence.

An identical provision exists under Section 23 of the Protection of Children from Sexual Offences Act 2012 (POCSO) prohibiting the disclosure of name, address, photographs, family details, school, neighborhood or any other particulars which may lead to the disclosure of the identity of a victim of sexual offences.

Judicial Guidelines

In a series of cases, High Courts and the Apex Court have laid down principles to protect the rights of survivors of sexual violence and abuse. Various directions were given by the Hon'ble Supreme Court in Ms. X vs. State of Jharkhand , (2021). The Deputy Commissioner, Ranchi was directed to take measure to ensure that minor children of the petitioner are provided free education in any of the Government Institutions in District Ranchi where the petitioner is residing till they attain the age of 14 years. The Deputy Commissioner, Ranchi may also consider the case of the petitioner for providing house under Prime Minister Awas Yojna or any other Central or State Scheme in which petitioner could be provided accommodation. The Senior Superintendent of Police, Ranchi and other competent authority shall review the Police security provided to the petitioner from time to time and take such measures as deem fit and proper. The District Legal Services Authority, Ranchi on representation made by the petitioner shall 16 render legal services to the petitioner as may be deemed fit to safeguard the interest of the petitioner.

In Sangita w/o Yeshwant Tanpure vs The State of Maharashtra (2021), the Hon'ble Bombay High Court laid down that is noticed that while framing of charge, recording evidence, recording statement of accused under section 313 of the Code of Criminal Procedure, name of the victim is disclosed. Therefore, while framing charge, mentioning name of the victim should be avoided. Instead he/she should be referred to as 'X' or any other alphabet the Court deems fit and proper. While recording evidence if the witness mentions the name of the victim, the Court shall record that the witness stated the name of the victim but to conceal her identity, her name is not recorded. And the victim should be referred to in the same manner as is done during the framing of charge.

In Nipun Saxena and another vs. Union of India, (2019), the Hon'ble Supreme Court gave the remarks in Para 12- "A victim of rape will face hostile discrimination and social ostracisation in society. Such victim will find it difficult to get a job, will find it difficult to get married and will also find it difficult to get integrated in society like a normal human being." Justice Gupta addressed the matter in a bifurcated manner. The initial portion pertained to individuals who are victims of rape as outlined in the Indian Penal Code, 1860. The subsequent portion focused on victims who have experienced offenses under the Protection of Children from Sexual Offences Act, 2012. Nine important directives were issued by the Apex Court. No person can print or publish in print, electronic, social media, etc. the name of the victim or even in a remote manner disclose any facts which can lead to the victim being identified and which should make her identity known to the public at large.

In cases where the victim is dead or of unsound mind the name of the victim or her identity should not be disclosed even under the authorization of the next of the kin, unless circumstances justifying the disclosure of her identity exist, which shall be decided by the competent authority, which at present is the Sessions Judge. FIRs relating to offences under Sections 376, 376A, 376AB, 376B, 376C, 376D, 376DA, 376DB or 376E of 39 IPC and offences under POCSO shall not be put in the public domain. In case a victim files an appeal under Section 372 CrPC, it is not necessary for the victim to disclose his/her identity and the appeal shall be dealt with in the manner laid down by law. The police officials should keep all the documents in which the name of the victim is disclosed, as far as possible, in a sealed cover and replace these documents by identical documents in which the name of the victim is removed in all records which may be scrutinised in the public domain.

All the authorities to which the name of the victim is disclosed by the investigating agency or the court are also duty bound to keep the name and identity of the victim secret and not disclose it in any manner except in the report which should only be sent in a sealed cover to the investigating agency or the court. An application by the next of kin to authorise disclosure of identity of a dead victim or of a victim of unsound mind under Section 228A(2)(c) of IPC should be made only to the Sessions Judge concerned until the Government acts under Section 228A(1)(c) and lays down a criteria as per our directions for identifying such social welfare institutions or organisations. In case of minor victims under POCSO, disclosure of their identity can only be permitted by the Special Court, if such disclosure is in the interest of the child. All the States/Union Territories are requested to set up at least one 'one stop centre' in every district within one year from the date of judgment."

In Court on its own Motion vs. Union of India and others (2018), the Delhi High Court imposed a Rs 10 lakh fine on every media organization that disclosed the identity of the 8-year-old victim of the Kathua gangrape and murder case. The court instructed the funds to be deposited into the victim compensation fund managed by the Jammu and Kashmir State Legal Services Authority, intended for distribution to the victims and families of those who have suffered from sexual violence.

In Mallikarjun Kodagali (Dead) represented through legal Representative vs. State of Karnataka (2019), the Apex Court discussed the concept of 'Victim Impact Assessment. The Court observed - "Among the steps that need to be taken to provide meaningful rights to the victims of an offence, it is necessary to seriously consider giving a hearing to the victim while awarding the sentence to a convict. A victim impact statement or a victim impact assessment must be given due recognition so that an appropriate punishment is awarded to the convict. In addition, the need for psycho-social support and counselling to a victim may also become necessary, depending upon the nature of the offence. It is possible that in a given case the husband of a young married woman gets killed in a fight or a violent dispute. How is the young widow expected to look after herself in such circumstances, which could be even more traumatic if she had a young child? It is true that a victim impact statement or assessment might result in an appropriate sentence being awarded to the convict, but that would not necessarily result in 'justice' to the young widow - perhaps rehabilitation is more important to her than merely ensuring that the criminal is awarded a life sentence. There is now a need, therefore, to discuss these issues in the context of social justice and take them forward in the direction suggested by some significant Reports that we have had occasion to look into and the direction given by Parliament and judicial pronouncements. The rights of victims, and indeed victimology, is an evolving jurisprudence and it is more than appropriate to move forward in a positive direction, rather than stand still or worse, take a step backward. A voice has been given to victims of crime by Parliament and the judiciary and that voice needs to be heard, and if not already heard, it needs to be raised to a higher decibel so that it is clearly heard."

In the case of Bijoy v. State of West Bengal (2017), the Calcutta High Court extensively outlined the rationale while interpreting the provisions of the Protection of Children from Sexual Offences (POCSO) Act. The Court emphasized that under no circumstances, during investigation or trial, should the name of the victim be disclosed. The judgment further provided clear directives to ensure strict adherence to the provisions of the law, ensuring the protection of child victims' fundamental rights.

In State of Punjab v. Gurmit Singh, (1996), the Hon'ble Justice A.S. Anand observed that crime against women in general and rape in particular is on the increase. It is an irony that while we are celebrating women's rights in all spheres, we show little or no concern for her honour. It is a sad reflection on the attitude of indifference of the society towards the violation of human dignity of the victims of sex crimes. We must remember that a rapist not only violates the victim's privacy and personal integrity, but inevitably causes serious psychological as well as physical harm in the process. The Apex Court laid down- "The Courts should, as far as possible, avoid disclosing the name of the prosecutrix in their orders to save further embarrassment to the victim of sex crime. The anonymity of the victim of the crime must be maintained as far as possible throughout. In the present case, the trial court has repeatedly used the name of the victim in its order under appeal, when it could have just referred to her as the prosecutrix. We need say no more on this aspect and hope that the trial Courts would take recourse to the provisions of Sections 327 (2) and (3) Cr. P.C. liberally. Trial of rape cases in camera should be the rule and an open trial in such cases an exception."

Advocacy efforts involve initiatives aimed at increasing media awareness regarding the necessity of safeguarding the identities of victims from public exposure. The utilization of facial or voice modification in public broadcasts has demonstrated its effectiveness. Instances exist where legal measures have been taken to penalize intentional disclosure of victims' identities, which are legally safeguarded. Such legal actions serve as a potent deterrent and discourage the divulgence of names, contributing to enhanced victim protection.

Conclusions and Suggestions

Efforts by governments, international organizations, civil society, and communities are crucial to ensuring that these rights are upheld and that survivors of sexual violence and abuse are provided with the necessary support and protection. Education, awareness, and advocacy play vital roles in promoting and protecting these rights. Judges and prosecutors need to be aware and informed of measures and good practices that have proven effective in protecting the identity of victims, especially in relation to victims of sexual violence, during trials, including when hearings are public.

Suggestions

The Courts can promote the use of pseudonyms or codification systems. They can decide to hold private or closed sessions or not to allow public broadcasting. They can also allow victims to testify behind a screen or blind, or may use other methods to prevent victims' faces from being seen. Victims can be allowed to testify from a separate room, with only the Court and/or the defence able to see her/his testimony. This could be facilitated by the use of technology such as simultaneous video and audio transmission, as well as use of pre-recorded statements.

Gender-sensitive approach entails -

i) Ensuring that laws and policies on sexual violence and related protection regimes for victims are comprehensive, non-discriminatory and inclusive of both female and male victims (e.g. avoiding definitions of rape that exclude marital rape and male victims).

ii) Ensuring special forms of protection adjusted to the sex and age or other characteristics of the victim; availability of support staff from both sexes (e.g. in Police specialized units, protection mechanisms, in medical or psychological services).

iii) Locating service providers, including protection services, in places that are easily accessible by all (e.g. avoiding locating those situated only in maternity wards).

iv) Avoiding the reproduction of harmful gender-stereotypes and forms of discrimination by public officials and other service providers (e.g. ensuring gender-sensitive messages.

v) Preventing further stigmatization and sense of shame and blame on the victims; perpetuating gender stereotypes.

vi) Avoiding making assumptions about victims, who are not only women and not intrinsically vulnerable); among other measures that ensure female and male victims receive adequate support and protection.

References

1. https://www.ohchr.org/sites/default/files/Documents/Issues/Women/WRGS/ReportLessonsLearned.pdf.
2. https://www.coe.int/en/web/gender-matters/gender-based-violence-and-human-rights.
3. https://www.un.org/womenwatch/daw/vaw/handbook/Handbook%20for%20legislation%20on%20violence%20against%20women.pdf.
4. https://mainweb-v.musc.edu/vawprevention/advocacy/humanrgts.shtml.
5. https://nhrc.nic.in/sites/default/files/MedGuideChild.pdf.
6. https://www.ecoi.net/en/document/2053196.html.
7. https://www.amnesty.org/es/wp-content/uploads/2021/07/ior530012011en.pdf.
8. https://www.endvawnow.org/en/articles/482-rights-of-survivors-.html.
9. Nipun Saxena and another vs. Union of India and others, (2019) 2 SCC 703.
10. Constitution of India, 1950.
11. Mallikarjun Kodagali (Dead) represented through legal Representative vs. State of Karnataka, (2019) 2 SCC 752.
12. The Declaration of Basic Principles of Justice for Victims of Crime and Abuse of Power, 1985.
13. Bijoy v. State of West Bengal, 2017 SCC OnLine Cal 417.
14. State of Punjab v. Gurmit Singh, (1996) 2 SCC 384.
15. https://www.livelaw.in/know-the-law/guidelines-on-sexual-assault-cases-roles-and-responsibilities-of-police-officials-and-other-stakeholders-217564.
16. Guidelines for police response and investigation in cases of sexual offence, Standing Order No.303/2019 dated 23.05.2019 issued under the signatures of the Commissioner of Police, Delhi, https://delhipolice.gov.in/doc/standing-order/303.pdf.

17. Guidelines & Protocols: Medico-legal care for survivors/victims of Sexual Violence, Government of India, Ministry of Health & Family Welfare, Department of Health & Family Welfare - Hospital Division, 2013.
18. Ministry of Women and Child Development, Model Guidelines under Section 39 of The Protection of Children from Sexual Offences Act, 2012, 2013.
19. https://risenow.us/impact/sexual-assault-survivors-bill-of-rights/.
20. https://ylcube.com/c/blogs/sexual-abuse-human-right-perspective/.

28

Rights of Dead Persons: A Study with Focus on Privacy Rights

Vivek Kumar Shukla and Arun

Abstract

Privacy laws and regulations regarding deceased individuals vary across the globe, and the extent to which privacy is protected for the deceased can differ significantly from one country to another. It's important to note that laws and policies can change over time, so it's advisable to refer to the most current and relevant legal sources for the latest information. Generally, privacy rights are seen as personal rights, and these rights are considered to extinguish upon an individual's death. However, how these rights are handled, especially for public figures like celebrities, can vary based on legal, ethical, and cultural considerations. Privacy concerns take on paramount importance in the conversation regarding managing user accounts on social media, emails, etc. following their demise. As laws and societal norms continue to evolve, the treatment of privacy rights for deceased celebrities is likely to undergo changes as well. All countries need a comprehensive posthumous privacy statute to be enacted so that all citizens have equal safeguard of their digital assets once deceased. Framing laws related to copyright, tort, or the laws governing testation, legislators can craft a novel legal framework that effectively preserves the privacy of digital assets after an individual's passing. By amalgamating these legal rights, lawmakers can develop a comprehensive law that not only protects the privacy of the deceased's digital assets but also facilitates easier access for their families or estates, minimizing the need for involvement from third-party custodians.

Keywords - *Deceased, Court, privacy, family, awareness.*

Introduction

Digital assets are defined as "any term of text or media which has been formatted into a binary source that includes the right to use it."

Post mortem privacy refers to the protection of an individual's privacy after their death. It involves controlling and safeguarding personal information, data, and digital assets that pertain to a deceased person. This concept has gained significance in the digital age due to the increasing amount of personal information and data stored online. In Justice K.S. Puttaswamy (Retd.) and Anr. v. Union of India and Ors. (2017) commonly known as the "Right to Privacy" case, the Supreme Court of India recognized privacy as a fundamental right under the Indian Constitution. While this case primarily focuses on the living individuals' right to privacy, it has implications for the broader understanding of privacy within the legal framework.

Various factors are considered significant for recognizing the personal rights of the deceased persons. Recognizing personal rights for deceased individuals stems from a fundamental respect for their dignity and personhood. It acknowledges that individuals have intrinsic value, and their rights should be honored even after they have passed away. Protecting personal rights after death helps preserve a person's legacy and reputation. Unlawful or derogatory use of a deceased individual's image, likeness, or personal information can tarnish their legacy, affect their family, and misrepresent their life. Misuse or unauthorized use of a deceased person's personal information or likeness can cause emotional distress and harm to their surviving family members and loved ones. Protecting personal rights helps in preventing such distress.

Personal rights, especially related to intellectual property or image rights, can be considered part of an individual's estate. Managing and protecting these rights posthumously is essential for proper estate planning and inheritance. In cases involving historical figures or public figures, protecting personal rights can be in the public interest. Accurate representation and preservation of historical records are important for society to learn and understand its past. Establishing legal protections for personal rights posthumously helps prevent the unauthorized commercial or exploitative use of a person's identity or image for financial gain or other purposes. Legal and cultural norms play a role in recognizing and upholding personal rights even after an individual's demise. Some legal systems provide for posthumous rights to protect a person's legacy and reputation.

Directives of National Human Rights Commission in India

Societies all across the world have traditions and practices to honour the deceased. The National Human Rights Commission issued advisory dated 14 May, 2021 for Upholding the Dignity and Protecting the Rights of the Dead. Basic Principles for Upholding the Dignity and Protecting the Rights of the Dead.

No discrimination in treatment of the body in any form

To ensure that the dead body is properly preserved and handled irrespective of religion, region, caste, gender, etc.

No physical exploitation

Any form of physical exploitation of the body of the dead violates the basic right of the deceased person.

Decent and timely burial/cremation

The deceased person has the right to a decent and timely burial/cremation.

To receive justice, in case of death due to crime

The dead have the right to receive justice in cases where death occurs due to crime.

To carry out a legal will

The will, if any, left by the dead must be respected and honoured.

No defamation after death

The deceased person should not be defamed by any kind of statement or visible representation, made or published intending to harm his/her reputation.

No breach of privacy

The deceased person has the right to privacy, i.e., the right to control the dissemination of information about one's privacy.

Challenges and Proposed Approaches to Safeguard Deceased' Privacy Rights

The proposed privacy rights of deceased are subject to some challenges.

Challenges

Young adults who experience sudden demise are more prone to leaving an extensive collection of digital assets. Uncertainties regarding management of digital possessions like Facebook profiles and Dropbox storage gain notable weight, especially for young adults who pass away unexpectedly without a will. Digital asset planning aims to honor the client's desires regarding how these assets are handled. However, due to legal uncertainties, digital assets have yet not been categorized as estate property eligible for inclusion in a will.

One significant issue arises from the fact that digital assets left by a deceased individual do not simply disappear. It is crucial for a responsible party to have the ability to access the deceased person's digital assets to manage them and potentially remove them. However, if a personal representative manages to obtain a decedent's online account details and passwords, gaining actual access to those accounts might violate state privacy laws. Such violations are considered criminal offenses, carrying penalties such as fines and/or imprisonment. Consequently, in many cases where a personal representative seeks to access post-mortem accounts, they make a formal request to the online service provider to ensure compliance with laws and terms of service agreements. Nonetheless, the online service provider often denies access to these accounts, compelling families to resort to legal action, filing complaints in court to compel disclosure of the account's contents.

Possible Approaches as Solution

Utilizing contract law represents a potential approach to safeguard the privacy rights of a deceased user. However, depending solely on contract law does not adequately ensure ample privacy safeguards for users postmortem. This is due to users consenting to terms created by the internet service provider, and these terms primarily prioritize the provider's interests, making it improbable to adequately preserve the deceased individual's privacy rights. The next approach suggests preserving the privacy rights of a deceased individual by treating their digital assets (such as Facebook profiles, email contents, cloud storage files, and online banking accounts) akin to property. However, property law falls short in this regard since it is continuously evolving to equate digital assets to physical, tangible property. While property law offers a compelling and persuasive means of safeguarding the privacy rights of deceased individuals compared to the contract law approach, it grapples with two notable constraints. Initially, property law hasn't completely evolved to outline how probate courts should handle a deceased person's digital assets. Moreover, deeming digital assets as real property subject to intestate laws could unintentionally lead to transfers of these assets to the deceased person's closest relatives.

Enhancing and extending existing tort law emerges as the most efficient means of upholding the privacy of a deceased user. Presently, common law does not grant privacy rights to deceased individuals. However, the judiciary is suitably poised to bridge this gap in tort law and address this critical requirement for safeguarding the privacy rights of the deceased. Courts can accomplish this by expanding current tort law to operate even after a person's passing, thereby establishing an inherent right to privacy for the deceased.

Stance of Courts and the Right of Privacy of Deceased Persons

As technology continues to integrate into our daily lives, it's imperative for courts to consider the impact of modern technology on preserving personal information even after death. When adjudicating such cases, courts should expand existing tort law to encompass a deceased individual's digital assets, acknowledging the persistence of a person's privacy rights beyond their passing. Acknowledging and upholding a deceased person's enforceable right to privacy stands as the most effective approach to safeguarding an individual's privacy after they are no longer alive. Extending this acknowledgment posthumously is justified not only because existing legal frameworks recognize the endurance of a person's dignitary interests beyond death, but also because digital assets can divulge a more comprehensive understanding of an individual compared to tangible property.

The Apex Court, on multiple occasions has taken into cognizance the instances of privacy rights. As a guardian of Constitution and more importantly, a power block which is currently active in welfare scenarios as well as legislative enactments, the Judicial pronouncements have set precedents for future cases and the precedents have helped in understanding the new digital age complex issues. The prima facie significance is upon Article 21 when the Privacy Rights of the deceased are in concern.

View of Courts in India

Star India Pvt. Ltd. v. Leo Burnett (India) Pvt. Ltd. & Ors. (2003) involved a dispute over the unauthorized use of a deceased celebrity's image for commercial purposes. The Delhi High Court held that the right to publicity does not survive the death of a person in India.

In Krishna Kishore Singh vs. Sarla A Saraogi, (2023), The plaintiff was the father of Sushant Singh Rajput, who instituted the present suit by way of a quia timet action. The suit sought a decree of permanent injunction, restraining the defendants and all others from using Sushant Singh Rajput's name, caricature or lifestyle in any projects or films without the prior permission of the plaintiff, alleging that any such effort would infringe the personality rights of Sushant Singh Rajput and also, cause deception in the minds of the public, which would amount to passing off. Along with the suit, the plaintiff sought an interlocutory injunction against the defendants using Sushant Singh Rajput's name, caricature, lifestyle or likeness in any films or other ventures, pending disposal of the suit. The Court after seeing the movie "Nyay: The Justice", observed that "there remained no doubt whatsoever, that the impugned movie was an overt re-enactment of Sushant Singh Rajput's life and times, concentrating largely on the circumstances leading to his death and the investigation that had followed". The Court opined that the disclaimers might be genuine, or cosmetic, but in the present case, it was obvious that a disclaimer which, when seen in the backdrop of the movie itself, was plainly untrue, was worth tinsel. The disclaimer, inserted in the impugned movie could not, therefore, detract from the reality that the movie was, in fact, a celluloid retelling of the life and death of Sushant Singh Rajput. The Court also opined that the information contained, and shown, in the impugned film, was entirely derived from items which featured in the media and, therefore, constituted publicly available information.

In Rangaraju Vajapeyi vs State of Karnataka (2023), the High Court ordered the State Government to provide that "Post mortem room should not come under the direct line of sight of the general public/visitors. To ensure the same, provision of curtain, screen or buffer area may be made in a post mortem room".

In Ruba Ahmed & Anr. vs. Hansal Mehta & Ors. (2022), the suit was filed by a family that had lost their daughters in the attack. They feared that their daughters may be shown in a bad light and hence, prayed for an injunction in their favour in a suit filed against Bollywood Filmmaker Hansal Mehta and others for restraining the release of their film 'Faraaz'. The movie is based on the terrorist attack that happened on 1st July, 2016 in Holey Artisan, Dhaka, Bangladesh. The film was alleged to be violative of their right to Privacy and right to Fair Trial under Article 14 and 21 of the Constitution of India. Denying interim relief to the plaintiffs, the court observed that while the 'right to be left alone' is an aspect of right to privacy, however, it "can also operate" within its limits and cannot be termed as a right to be left alone especially when the plaintiffs barely get any mention in the movie. The Delhi High Court has ruled that the right to privacy is essentially a right in personam and therefore is not inheritable by the mothers or legal heirs of the deceased persons.

In Deepa Jayakumar vs. A.L.Vijay and others (2021) The Original Side Appeal (O.S.A) was filed as against the order dated 12.12.2019 made in O.A.No.1102 of 2019 in C.S.No.697 of 2019 by the learned Single Judge dismissing the Original Application filed by the appellant herein for interim injunction to restrain the respondents 1 to 3 from in any manner making, releasing, publishing, exhibiting publicly or privately selling, promoting or advertising or entering into film festival or otherwise producing in any format, any film, drama, serial, tele-serial, web serial or any other literary or artistic expression in respect of the life of Dr.J.Jayalalitha, the former Chief Minister of Tamil Nadu and/or her family members and their direct descendants without the consent of the applicant/plaintiff. The Court observed that he right of freedom of speech and expression enshrined under Article 19 (1) (a) of the Constitution of India is not conditioned/restricted on the premise that a film maker must only portray one particular version of facts. Therefore, there is no obligation on the part of the respondents/defendants to take prior consent from the appellant/plaintiff. The Court was of the opinion that "posthumous right" is not an "alienable right" and the appellant/plaintiff is not entitled for an injunction on the ground that the "posthumous right" of her aunt is sought to be sullied by the respondents/defendants by reason of the release of the film titled as "Thalaivi".

View of Foreign Courts

Courts have regularly stated that the right to privacy is too personal for others to bring suit on behalf of the person.

Haelan Laboratories, Inc. v. Topps Chewing Gum, Inc. (1941): This case is often cited as a foundational case in the realm of posthumous rights. The court recognized that a celebrity's right of publicity survives their death, allowing their estate to control the commercial use of their identity.

Martin Luther King, Jr. Estate Ltd. v. CBS, Inc. (1999): In this case, the estate of Martin Luther King, Jr. filed a lawsuit against CBS for unauthorized use of Dr. King's speeches and image in a documentary. The case highlighted issues of posthumous publicity rights and intellectual property.

In Re Estate of Elvis Presley (2002): The case involved a dispute over the control of Elvis Presley's name, image, and likeness, highlighting the complexities in managing posthumous rights and the commercialization of a deceased celebrity's persona.

CMG Worldwide, Inc. v. Mark Lee (2003): It involved the unauthorized use of the image and likeness of the late Princess Diana for commercial purposes. The court affirmed that the right of publicity can extend posthumously and can be inherited by the heirs of the deceased.

Viacom International Inc. v. IJR Capital Investments, LLC (2010): In this case, the estate of the legendary actress Marilyn Monroe fought to assert posthumous publicity rights in California, establishing that Monroe's right of publicity survives her death.

In Re: Application for Permission to Execute a Search Warrant on a Certain E-Mail Account Controlled and Maintained by Microsoft Corporation (2014): The case focused on the privacy of a deceased individual's email account. The court highlighted the need to balance privacy concerns with law enforcement access for investigation purposes even after the person's death.

Belinda Brewster and John Brewster v. NASCAR, LLC (2015): The heirs of a race car driver, Dale Earnhardt Sr., filed a case against NASCAR for unauthorized use of Earnhardt's image. The case emphasized the protection of a deceased person's image and the right of publicity.

Conclusions and Suggestions

Privacy rights are generally considered personal and fundamental, applicable during an individual's lifetime but extinguished upon their death. Traditionally, the conceptualization of privacy pertained to only those who were alive, now the situation has changed. The subject-matter is complex and is constantly with consistency, evolving with the passage of time.

Information can be very easily disseminated and indefinitely preserved. It is imperative to engage in the thoughtful discourse and implement certain legal and ethical guidelines or enactments which will uphold the rights along with the most foundational right of dignity that is enshrined in the Constitution of India. It needs to be ensured that individuals along with entities become responsible and respectful while undertaking research on the same issue, along with management and memorialization of privacy of the deceased subject. It should also align with the commitment to an equitable and compassionate society which must entail values of privacy and legacy of all its members. It is of utmost significance to recognize that the digital age has introduced various new dimensions and challenges along with qualitative and quantitative opportunities in order to preserve and safeguard the dignity of the departed individual.

The contemporary society should be attuned to the changing landscape of privacy and the ethical implications which are collaborating simultaneously. One must respect the privacy of the departed individual and acknowledging the inherent human dignity along with safeguarding the interests and the emotions of the surviving kith and kins of the deceased. It is important to balance the rights to access the historical records, maintain public records, conduct research, both empirical and doctrinal in nature; in order to achieve the protection of the data and privacy of the deceased. It is a delicate interplay between ethical guidelines and instructions, legislation, public awareness. Information never ceases to be irrelevant and this is applicable on deceased persons as well. After the advent of complicated invention of internet and its further branch of social media, the paradigm of privacy has taken a drastic and dramatic change.

Suggestions

In an interconnected world, ensuring privacy rights is a nuanced task which will amalgamate a multi-dimensional approach including technical, societal and legal approaches.

i) Clarity in the legal infrastructure

A legal structure that specifically define the privacy rights of the dead people is required. It must elaborately explain what constitutes as sensitive information and who is the authority under whom this information can be accessed, along with a rationale purpose for digging into such database.

ii) Anonymization plus Data Encryption

In order to safeguard the sensitive information related to the deceased person and preventing unauthorized access can be a huge step in implementation and protection of deceased's rights.

iii) Ethical Guidelines for research

It is the need of the hour to foster and develop ethical guidelines for people who are engaged in the research activities and institutions who have taken the onus of undertaking and initiative regarding research. Such guidelines will prioritize on responsible data usage, protection f identities, consent provisions and the adherence to privacy laws.

iv) Digital Legacy Planning

People should be encouraged to take a discourse in digital legacy planning, where the preferences are defined. Services and particular platforms should be established under the supervision of Government or a competent authority.

References

1. Ruba Ahmed & Anr. V. Hansal Mehta & Ors., 2022 LiveLaw (Del) 969.
2. Krishna Kishore Singh v. Sarla A Saraogi, 2023 LiveLaw (Del) 584, 2023 SCC OnLine Del 3997.
3. R. Rajagopal v. State of T.N., (1994) 6 SCC 632.
4. Khushwant Singh v. Maneka Gandhi, 2001 SCC OnLine Del 1030.
5. Titan Industries Ltd. v. Ramkumar Jewellers, 2012 SCC OnLine Del 2382.
6. ICC Development (International) Ltd. v. Arvee Enterprises, 2003 SCC OnLine Del 2.
7. Deepa Jayakumar v. A.L. Vijay, 2021 SCC OnLine Mad 2642.

8. https://www.livelaw.in/news-updates/jaya-biopics-madras-hc-declines-plea-of-jayalalithaas-niece-to-restrain-stay-release-of-queen-thalaivi-150762?infinitescroll=1.

9. Krishna Kumar Birla v. Rajendra Singh Lodha & Ors., (2008) 4 SCC 300.

10. F.A. Picture International vs. CBFC, AIR 2005 Bombay 145.

11. https://www.scconline.com/blog/post/2023/07/13/delhi-hc-refuses-to-stay-nyay-the-justice-movie-based-on-sushant-singh-rajput-legal-news/.

12. https://www.ft.com/content/7869f8ba-61e3-4ee1-b960-d2f8e15f46e6.

13. https://nhrc.nic.in/sites/default/files/NHRC%20Advisory%20for%20Upholding%20Dignity%20%26%20Protecting%20the%20Rights%20of%20Dead.pdf.

14. https://en.themooknayak.com/india/sexual-intercourses-on-dead-bodies-karnataka-high-court-asks-centre-to-amend-ipc-criminalize-necrophilia.

15. Rangaraju v. State of Karnataka, 2023 SCC OnLine Kar 23, 2023 LiveLaw (Kar) 197.

16. Justice K.S. Puttaswamy (Retd.) and Anr. v. Union of India and Ors. (2017) 10 SCC 1; AIR 2017 SC 4161.

17. Haelan Laboratories, Inc. v. Topps Chewing Gum, Inc. (1941).

18. Viacom International Inc. v. IJR Capital Investments, LLC (2010).

19. CMG Worldwide, Inc. v. Mark Lee (2003).

20. re Estate of Elvis Presley (2002).

21. re: Application for Permission to Execute a Search Warrant on a Certain E-Mail Account Controlled and Maintained by Microsoft Corporation (2014).

22. Martin Luther King, Jr. Estate Ltd. v. CBS, Inc. (1999).

23. Belinda Brewster and John Brewster v. NASCAR, LLC et al. (2015).

24. Natasha Chu, Protecting Privacy after Death, 13 Nw. J. Tech. & Intell. Prop. 255 (2015). https://scholarlycommons.law.northwestern.edu/njtip/vol13/iss2/8.

25. https://www.rtifoundationofindia.com/examination-legal-provisions-regarding-transfer-pr.

26. Zudekoff, Mindi, ""A Private Affair": A Look into Posthumous Privacy Rights after the Rise of Digital Assets and Why There Must be a Federal Privacy Statute to Protect these Assets" (2021). Law School Student Scholarship. 1130. https://scholarship.shu.edu/student_scholarship/1130.

27. Toygar, Alp; Rohm, C.E. Taipe Jr.; and Zhu, Jake (2013) "A New Asset Type: Digital Assets," Journal of International Technology and Information Management: Vol. 22: Iss. 4, Article 7. available at: https://scholarworks.lib.csusb.edu/jitim/vol22/iss4/7.

28. https://etheses.whiterose.ac.uk/14754/1/274997_vol1.pdf

29

Inclusivity and Privacy: Privacy Rights of Homosexuals, Transgenders and LGBTQ+

Shubham Verma, Smriti Chauhan and Adarsh Chauhan

Abstract

*LGBTQ+ individuals often encounter discrimination and prejudice in various aspects of life, including employment, housing, education, and healthcare, which can result in a hostile environment and hinder their opportunities for growth. Laws that protect the privacy rights of **LGBTQ+** individuals may be inadequate or non- existent in many regions, leaving them vulnerable to discrimination, harassment, and privacy infringements. Connected devices and services have shown a remarkable ability to empower individuals within the LGBTQ+ community, enabling them to discover a sense of belonging, access essential services, and live more authentically both online and offline. However, the significant rise in the availability and usage of these technologies has also introduced new privacy concerns and amplified existing ones for LGBTQ+ communities. Technology has made it more convenient to recognize, identify, monitor, and specifically target LGBTQ+ individuals. Even data processing that is legally permissible or advantageous for LGBTQ+ individuals can heighten the risk of harm at the individual, community, or societal level. While everyone is subject to privacy risks, there is a need to emphasize the critical need for a heightened focus on individuals who can be disproportionately impacted, such as the LGBTQ+ community. Respecting and upholding the privacy of LGBT+ individuals is essential for fostering a society where all individuals can live authentically and without fear of discrimination or prejudice.*

***Keywords** - Homosexuals, Transgenders and LGBTQ+, inclusive, privacy.*

Introduction

During the earlier times, the punishment for sodomy was death, and this severe penalty persisted in some states well into the 19th century. Even in the early 20th century, sodomy remained classified as a felony in every state. These anti-sodomy laws became a pretext for violating individuals' privacy, enabling investigations and often leading to the incarceration of those suspected of engaging in same-sex sexual behaviors.

While the prolonged prison sentences associated with anti-sodomy laws have been reduced through changes in state legislation and a decrease in discretionary enforcement by the police throughout the 20th century, anti-sodomy and obscenity laws have, and still do, serve as tools for the systemic oppression of LGBTQ+ individuals. This oppression manifests through incarceration, disruption of employment, and public humiliation.

Furthermore, laws that prohibited or criminalized cross-dressing (wearing clothes not typically associated with one's perceived sex) served as a flexible mechanism for police to enforce normative gender roles on diverse gender identities, including masculine women and individuals identifying as transgender or gender non-conforming.

In this Chapter, the term LGBTQ+ is used to cover homosexuals and Transgenders also. The pervasive stigmatization within society has driven individuals to refrain from undergoing testing or seeking treatment. Even those who muster the courage to seek medical care often feel compelled to hide their sexual orientation from healthcare providers, fearing judgment and discrimination. This concealment ultimately leads to a lack of appropriate care; as healthcare professionals may not have the necessary information to tailor treatments effectively. This vicious cycle of stigma, fear, and inadequate healthcare significantly impacts the overall well-being of LGBTQ+ individuals.

On International Day against Homophobia, Biphobia and Transphobia, the world stands for the diversity of humankind, celebrate the incredible achievements of lesbian, gay, bi, trans, intersex and queer people, and applaud their continuing struggle for equality and human rights. We must follow - "Whatever our sexual orientation, gender identity, gender expression or sex characteristics, all of us are born free and equal in dignity and rights."

Challenges Faced by LGBTQ+

Discrimination against LGBTQ+ people undermines the human rights principles outlined in the Universal Declaration of Human Rights. Yet discrimination and violence against people in the LGBTQ+ community are all too common. Homophobic, biphobic and transphobic attitudes remain deeply embedded in many cultures around the world. Lesbian, gay, bisexual, transgender, and intersex individuals face a range of both common and distinct challenges related to human rights. Discrimination and human rights violations against these groups occur in various aspects of their lives, including healthcare systems.

Throughout history, LGBTQ+ communities have endured a legacy of discrimination, disenfranchisement, and ignorance within the public health system. This troubling history has created a significant barrier for many LGBTQ+ individuals seeking and accessing medical treatment. A deep-rooted fear, based on valid concerns, often prevents them from seeking care, fearing denial of treatment, maltreatment, social stigma, or the risk of being outed, all of which could have severe economic and social repercussions. This fear further perpetuates the cycle of inadequate healthcare and exacerbates health disparities within the LGBTQ+ population.

Discrimination and Stigmatization

LGBTQ+ individuals often experience discrimination, prejudice, and stigma based on their sexual orientation, gender identity, or intersex status.

Violence and Hate Crimes

LGBTQ+ people are at higher risk of physical and verbal violence, hate crimes, and harassment, which infringe upon their right to personal security and dignity.

Legal Discrimination and Punishments

In many countries, LGBTQ+ individuals face legal discrimination, including unequal treatment in laws related to marriage, adoption, employment, and housing. In around seventy countries, prejudiced legislation criminalizes private, consensual same-sex relationships. Consequently, LGBTQ+ individuals face the peril of being detained, coerced, exploited, socially ostracized, discriminated against, and subjected to violence. Shockingly, in few countries, the punishment for being LGBTQ+ can even extend to the death penalty. Iran, Saudi Arabia, Yemen and Sudan are some of the countries still heavily punishing the acts of homosexuality.

Identity and Recognition

LGBTQ+ individuals may struggle with societal acceptance and the acknowledgment of their identities, which affects their mental well-being and sense of self.

Access to Healthcare

LGBTQ+ individuals often face barriers to accessing appropriate healthcare due to discrimination, lack of understanding by healthcare providers, or inadequate training in providing inclusive care.

Family and Relationships

LGBTQ+ individuals may face challenges in forming and maintaining relationships, particularly in contexts where their relationships are not legally recognized or accepted.

Intersex-Specific Challenges

Some challenges are intersex-specific challenges.

Medical Intervention and Consent

Intersex individuals, especially in their early years, may undergo unnecessary medical interventions without informed consent, impacting their bodily autonomy and right to personal integrity.

Healthcare Discrimination

Intersex people face discrimination and mistreatment within healthcare systems, including non-consensual surgeries, which can lead to physical and psychological harm, often lasting a lifetime.

Identity and Invisibility

Intersex individuals may struggle with societal understanding and acceptance of their unique biological status, contributing to feelings of isolation and invisibility.

Efforts to address these challenges involve legal reforms, educational initiatives to promote understanding and acceptance, healthcare system improvements to ensure inclusive and respectful care for LGBTQ+ individuals and intersex people, and the creation of safe spaces and support networks. It's essential to advocate for the rights and dignity of all individuals, regardless of their sexual orientation, gender identity, or intersex status, to foster a more inclusive and equitable society.

Right to Privacy of LGBTQ+

More recently, scholars have begun to consider anti-sodomy laws in the larger context of 'sexual privacy' a distinct privacy interest that serves as a cornerstone for sexual autonomy, consent, human dignity and intimacy. The right to privacy for individuals identifying as LGBTQ+ is a fundamental human entitlement encompassing various aspects of their lives, relationships, and identities.

A lack of medical privacy and inadequate anti-discrimination protections continue to impact the LGBTQ+ community. At the same time, governments, physicians and researchers use personal data to provide HIV/AIDS services, monitor healthcare efforts, and to advance research that benefits LGBTQ+ communities. In these circumstances, the balance between public health and individual privacy is difficult to strike at least partially due to the deep distrust that developed during the height of the HIV/AIDS epidemic.

In the present day, interconnected devices and online services are enabling LGBTQ+ community members to engage more actively in the digital sphere. Information related to a person's sexual orientation, gender identity, or details about their intimate life can hold significant value for the delivery of healthcare services, public health initiatives, and medical research. LGBTQ+ individuals and communities bear a disproportionate burden of privacy breaches on the internet. Presently, they continue to encounter substantial obstacles and biases, ranging from physical violence and discrimination to less visible yet equally harmful infringements on their dignity. However, data concerning an individual's gender identity, sexual orientation, and intimate aspects of their life is highly sensitive. The collection, utilization, and sharing of such data can pose distinctive privacy risks and present unique challenges.

Freedom from Discrimination and Equal Protection

Privacy rights for LGBTQ+ individuals involve being protected against discrimination based on gender identity, sexual orientation, or gender expression. They deserve equal privacy rights and protections, just like anyone else.

Consensual Relationships

LGBTQ+ individuals have the right to engage in relationships without fear of legal repercussions, stigma, or discrimination. Their intimate interactions and relationships should be respected and safeguarded under the right to privacy.

Expression of Gender Identity

The right to privacy encompasses the freedom to express one's gender identity. Transgender individuals have the right to self-identify and live in alignment with their gender identity without intrusion, discrimination, or harassment.

Medical Privacy and Healthcare

LGBTQ+ individuals are entitled to confidential and non-judgmental healthcare services. Privacy in healthcare extends to treatments that affirm gender identity, HIV/AIDS status, and other medical aspects related to sexual orientation and gender identity.

Safe Spaces and Non-Discrimination

Providing safe physical and digital spaces where LGBTQ+ individuals can freely express their identities and experiences without fear of discrimination, violence, or hate speech is crucial to uphold their right to privacy.

Protection from Hate Crimes

Privacy includes protection against hate crimes or targeted violence based on sexual orientation or gender identity. Law enforcement should ensure the safety and privacy of LGBTQ+ individuals and effectively investigate and prosecute hate crimes.

Family and Parental Rights

LGBTQ+ individuals should have the right to create families, adopt, or have biological children, with the same legal protections, rights, and privacy as heterosexual individuals.

Legal Recognition and Gender Identification

Privacy involves having the right to legal recognition of gender identity, including the ability to update gender markers on identification documents and official records without invasive requirements or disclosure.

Online Privacy and Prevention of Cyberbullying

Protecting the online privacy of LGBTQ+ individuals is crucial, including measures to prevent cyberbullying, doxxing, or any form of online harassment based on their sexual orientation or gender identity.

Relationship between LGBTQ+'s Privacy and Digital Age

Internet Technology has offered a valuable avenue for transgender and non-binary individuals, enabling them to discover, establish, and engage with communities where they can connect with others dealing with comparable hurdles. The advantages brought about by online connectivity for the LG 6666+BTQ+ community, and especially for transgender and non-binary individuals, are extensive and should not be underestimated. They encompass enhancing education and awareness, enabling representation, and advancing safety. These advantages are especially vital for LGBTQ+ individuals residing in unwelcoming households or communities.

LGBTQ+ often have their health needs disregarded or neglected, conducting health-related searches online can hold significant value. However, it's not solely life-saving health information or similar resources that have had a transformative impact on the lives of LGBT individuals. The internet has also provided a sense of community.

With wireless technologies, individuals can connect with supportive community members, friends, or loved ones, even when separated by significant distances. This capacity to establish and sustain connections that offer safety and inclusivity can be a lifesaver for LGBT individuals who feel isolated in their local environments.

While data privacy should be a concern for anyone utilizing technology, its importance is magnified for individuals identifying as LGBT. The implications of inadequate data privacy within the LGBT community can be dire, even life-threatening. Data privacy holds a unique significance for the LGBT community, given our increased reliance on the internet and the potential devastating fallout of a data breach. This heightened vulnerability necessitates focused attention on safeguarding our privacy in the digital realm.

Beyond concerns about privacy and potential embarrassment, there exists a tangible and significant risk of harassment, possible physical harm, loss of employment, and even estrangement from family and friends. Enabling individuals to choose not to disclose specific personal information provides a crucial layer of protection and safety across all aspects of life. This opt-out option is essential in ensuring the well-being and security of individuals, particularly within the LGBT community, by minimizing the potential negative consequences associated with divulging sensitive details.

Of utmost relevance and importance to the LGBTQ+ community is the handling of information concerning sexual orientation and gender identity (referred to as SOGI information), along with other deeply personal data crucial for LGBTQ+ individuals. This information is significant for their personal growth and well-being, as well as for the provision of vital social, mental, and physical health services. Processing such data is often essential to tailor products and services to the specific needs of LGBTQ+ users. Moreover, utilizing diverse and representative datasets is a crucial tool in ensuring fair enhancements to products, bridging the digital divide, enhancing public health, empowering LGBTQ+ communities, and combating discrimination effectively.

Positive Developments

The U.S. Supreme Court ruled the remaining state anti-sodomy laws unconstitutional in Lawrence v. Texas (2003) case, Justice Anthony Kennedy refuted arguments that anti-sodomy laws protect against unwanted sexual activity. The case involved two adults who, with full and mutual consent from each other, engaged in sexual practices common to a homosexual lifestyle. The petitioners are entitled to respect for their private lives. The State cannot demean their existence or control their destiny by making their private sexual conduct a crime. Their right to liberty under the Due Process Clause gives them the full right to engage in their conduct without intervention of the government.

A High Court judge in 2011 in Uganda ruled in the case of Kasha Jacqueline, Pepe Onziema & David Kato v. Giles Muhame and The Rolling Stone Publications Ltd. that the tabloid Rolling Stone violated the civil rights of the gays and lesbians whose pictures they published, with the headline "Hang Them". The highly contentious article, released in October 2011, targeted 100 gay men and women in Uganda. Tragically, at least four individuals were physically assaulted, with one woman nearly losing her life. Numerous others were forced into hiding, gripped by fear for their safety and well-being. The Court issued a temporary order that prohibited the newspaper's editors from publishing any more information about individuals alleged to be gay, lesbian, bisexual, or transgender until the case could be fully resolved. Following an initial delay, the case's merits were heard on 23 November 2010. The conclusive ruling was delivered in January 2011.

The Court, ruled that "The motion is not about homosexuality per se, but '…it is about fundamental rights and freedoms,' in particular about whether 'the publication infringed the rights of the applicants or threatened to do so'. The jurisdiction of Article 50 (1) of the Constitution is dual in nature, in that it extends not just to any person 'whose fundamental rights or other rights or freedoms have been infringed in the first place,' but also to 'persons whose fundamental rights or other rights or freedoms are threatened to be infringed.' Inciting people to hang homosexuals is an attack on the right to dignity of those thus threatened: 'the call to hang gays in dozens tends to tremendously threaten their right to human dignity.' Homosexuals are as entitled to the right to privacy as any other citizens. Against the 'objective test', 'the exposure of the identities of the persons and homes of the applicants for the purposes of fighting gayism and the activities of gays… threaten the rights of the applicants to privacy of the person and their homes.' Section 145 of the Penal Code Act cannot be used to punish persons who themselves acknowledge being, or who are perceived by others to be homosexual".

Similarly, in India, in 2017, in the context of the privacy of homosexuals, the Puttaswamy judgment played a crucial role in upholding and affirming the right to privacy for all individuals, including those within the LGBTQ+ community. By recognizing privacy as a fundamental right, the Supreme Court acknowledged the need to protect an individual's autonomy over their personal choices, relationships, and identities. Later in 2018, in Navtej Singh Johar vs. Union of India, the Supreme Court struck down Section 377 of the Indian Penal Code, which criminalized consensual same-sex relationships. The Court cited the Puttaswamy case to emphasize the importance of privacy, personal autonomy, and the right to live without discrimination.

Conclusions and Suggestions

Every nation is bound by international human rights standards to uphold and safeguard the rights of all individuals without bias. Presently, the LGBTQ+ community continues to face disproportionate impacts due to insufficient medical privacy and inadequate anti-discrimination protections. Medical privacy remains a challenge, as concerns persist regarding the confidentiality of one's sexual orientation and gender identity in healthcare settings. Additionally, anti-discrimination measures have not fully caught up, leaving LGBTQ+ individuals vulnerable to biased treatment, refusal of care, or substandard services solely based on their sexual orientation or gender identity. These ongoing issues underscore the pressing need for comprehensive reforms to ensure equal and respectful healthcare access and treatment for all, regardless of sexual orientation or gender identity.

Ensuring the right to privacy for LGBTQ+ individuals is crucial to establish a more inclusive, accepting, and equitable society that respects and upholds the dignity and rights of all its members. Legal frameworks and societal attitudes should evolve to better protect and promote these privacy rights.

Suggestions

Amie Stepanovich, Vice President of U.S. Policy at Future of Privacy Forum in the report The Role Of Data Protection in Safeguarding Sexual Orientation and Gender Identity Information. "Organizations need to understand the impacts of processing this data on traditionally marginalized communities and to provide heightened protections, with respect for past and present context, to protect against potential harms." Some preliminary recommendations for organizations and policymakers to foster safer, more equitable, and dignified use of SOGI data, ensuring meaningful privacy safeguards.

(i) Recognition of Unique Sensitivity

There is a need to recognize and acknowledge the exceptional sensitivity of SOGI information, understanding its critical importance and potential impact on individuals' lives.

(ii) Inventory and Categorization of Data

The government alongwith private stakeholders must engage in a comprehensive inventory and categorization of data to distinctly identify and segregate sexual orientation and gender identity data, ensuring clear identification and handling of this information. The government must stablish partnerships and collaborations with LGBTQ+ organizations to ensure that the unique healthcare challenges faced by the community are identified, understood, and addressed effectively through targeted initiatives and policy changes.

(iii) Context-Specific Evaluation of Protections

We must evaluate and tailor privacy protections for sexual orientation and gender identity information, considering the specific context in which the data is used and stored, to enhance the effectiveness of privacy measures.

(iv) Promotion of Inclusion, Representation, and Equity

The governments must advocate for and actively support initiatives that promote inclusion, representation, and equity for LGBTQ+ individuals, striving to prevent discrimination and bias in data collection, processing, and application.

(v) Strong Medical Privacy Laws

It has become essential to amend and reinforce existing laws to reinforce medical privacy, ensuring that personal information regarding sexual orientation and gender identity remains strictly confidential and is not disclosed without explicit consent.

(vi) Education of Healthcare Professionals

Governments must design comprehensive training programs to educate healthcare professionals about the unique healthcare needs and sensitivities of LGBTQ+ individuals, fostering a more inclusive and understanding healthcare environment.

(vii) Inclusive Healthcare Environments

Healthcare facilities must be encouraged to adopt inclusive policies and practices that embrace diversity, respect individuals' identities, and create a safe and welcoming space for LGBTQ+ patients.

(viii) Amplified LGBTQ+ Representation

Governments must promote increased representation of LGBTQ+ individuals in leadership and decision-making positions to advocate for and prioritize the needs and rights of the community.

(ix) Comprehensive Healthcare Access

A comprehensive healthcare coverage must be introduced that is inclusive of LGBTQ+-specific healthcare needs, including mental health services, gender-affirming care, and HIV prevention and treatment, to bridge existing gaps in healthcare access and equity.

(x) Public Awareness and Understanding

The stakeholders must launch public awareness campaigns to challenge stereotypes, reduce stigma, and educate society about LGBTQ+ healthcare disparities, fostering empathy, understanding, and a more accepting society.

(xi) Support for Research on LGBTQ+ Health

Funding and support research initiatives must be introduced that focus on LGBTQ+ health concerns, enabling evidence-based policy recommendations and innovative solutions to address the unique healthcare needs of the LGBTQ+ community. Healthcare must be seen in a broader perspective including mental health issues as well.

(xii) Support for Further Research

There is an urgency to encourage and provide support for additional research aimed at understanding the evolving dynamics of SOGI data usage, privacy concerns, and innovative ways to ensure privacy safeguards while optimizing the benefits of this information for the LGBTQ+ community. There is a pressing need for comprehensive efforts to thoroughly evaluate issues related to bias and risk. This assessment is essential to mitigate, and ideally prevent, both individual and collective harms experienced by the LGBTQ+ community.

These recommendations lay the foundation for a broader and ongoing discussion to develop comprehensive strategies that prioritize the privacy, security, and well-being of LGBTQ+ individuals in the digital age.

References

1. https://fpf.org/blog/a-look-back-at-the-role-of-law-and-the-right-to-privacy-in-lgbtq-history/.
2. https://www.amnesty.org/en/what-we-do/discrimination/LGBTQ+-rights/.
3. https://www.aljazeera.com/news/2023/3/22/uganda-passes-tough-antigay-law-bans-identification-as-lgbtq.
4. https://www.ohchr.org/en/sexual-orientation-and-gender-identity/about-LGBTQ+-people-and-human-rights.
5. https://www.ohchr.org/en/press-releases/2023/09/chile-un-expert-welcomes-public-apology-schoolteacher-dismissed-being.
6. https://www.aclu.org/news/lgbtq-rights/its-always-been-about-discrimination-lgbt-people#:~:text=At%20an%20early%20age%2C%20we,We%20might%20wish%20it%20away.
7. https://www.unaids.org/en/resources/presscentre/featurestories/2019/february/20190228_burkina-faso-msm.
8. https://www.hrw.org/report/2018/02/19/all-we-want-equality/religious-exemptions-and-discrimination-against-lgbt-people.
9. https://theleaflet.in/pride-and-prejudice-the-homophobia-depriving-india-of-its-first-gay-judge/.
10. https://humanrightsfirst.org/library/court-affirms-rights-of-ugandan-gays/.
11. https://www.amnesty.org.uk/press-releases/uganda-investigate-murder-LGBTQ+-activist.
12. Kasha Jacqueline, Pepe Onziema & David Kato v. Giles Muhame and The Rolling Stone Publications Ltd., 2011.
13. http://law2.umkc.edu/faculty/projects/ftrials/conlaw/rightofprivacy.html.
14. https://www.healthaffairs.org/content/forefront/supreme-court-finds-lgbt-people-protected-employment-discrimination-implications-aca.

15. https://staysafeonline.org/online-safety-privacy-basics/data-privacy-crucial-lgbt-community/#:~:text=A%20privacy%20data%20breach%20that,for%20physical%20harm%20or%20death.
16. https://fpf.org/blog/report-analyzes-the-role-of-data-protection-in-safeguarding-sexual-orientation-and-gender-identity-information/.
17. Future of Privacy Forum, The Role Of Data Protection in Safeguarding Sexual Orientation and Gender Identity Information, June 2022.
18. https://www.hhs.gov/ocr/lgbtqi/index.html.
19. Navtej Singh Johar vs. Union of India, AIR 2018 SC 4321.
20. K.S. Puttaswamy vs. Union of India, (2017) 10 SCC 1, AIR 2017 SC 4161.
21. https://www.international.gc.ca/world-monde/issues_development-enjeux_developpement/human_rights-droits_homme/rights_lgbti-droits_lgbti.aspx?lang=eng.
22. https://www.ohchr.org/en/special-procedures/ie-sexual-orientation-and-gender-identity.
23. https://www.aclu.org/documents/rights-lesbian-gay-bisexual-and-transgender-people.

30

Right of Privacy of Accused and Victims in the Criminal Justice System: Evolving Trends

Shubham Mishra, Manisha Garg and Rishu Sangal

Abstract

Accused, victims and witnesses enjoy the right to privacy. In India, accused individuals have a fundamental right to privacy guaranteed by the Constitution of India under Article 21, which protects the right to life and personal liberty. This includes the right to privacy during investigations, trials, and imprisonment. The Supreme Court of India, in several landmark judgments, has recognized privacy as a fundamental right, emphasizing its importance in criminal proceedings. Victims of crime also have a right to privacy, which is a crucial aspect of their human rights. Ensuring the privacy of victims is essential to protect their dignity, security, and well-being throughout the criminal justice process. The State holds the principal obligation to safeguard victims, witnesses, informants, and individuals collaborating with human rights field operations and other international monitoring mechanisms for human rights. Prioritizing confidentiality as a safeguard for their safety, and ensuring non-disclosure of their identities, should be given higher importance than other competing interests.

Keywords - *Criminal justice system, victim, accused, privacy, Constitution.*

Introduction

The right to privacy is a fundamental aspect of the criminal justice system that applies to both the accused and the victims. The right to privacy is not absolute and can be limited in certain circumstances, such as when there is a compelling public interest, national security concerns, or when it is necessary to protect the rights and freedoms of others. Striking a balance between privacy and the legitimate interests of law enforcement is an ongoing challenge in the criminal justice system.

Principle 8 of Basic Principles on the Role of Lawyers, adopted by the Eighth United Nations Congress on the Prevention of Crime and the Treatment of Offenders, *1990* provides "All arrested, detained or imprisoned persons shall be provided with adequate opportunities, time and facilities to be visited by and to communicate and consult with a lawyer, without delay, interception or censorship and in full confidentiality. Such consultations may be within sight, but not within the hearing, of law enforcement officials". Further, Principle 22 of Body of Principles for the Protection of All Persons under Any Form of Detention or Imprisonment, 1988 also states that "Governments shall recognize and respect that all communications and consultations between lawyers and their clients within their professional relationship are confidential". Principle 18(3) The right of a detained or imprisoned person to be visited by and to consult and communicate, without delay or censorship and in full confidentiality, with his legal counsel may not be suspended or restricted save in exceptional circumstances, to be specified by law or lawful regulations, when it is considered indispensable by a judicial or other authority in order to maintain security and good order. Principle 29(2) emphasizes that "A detained or imprisoned person shall have the right to communicate freely and in full confidentiality with the persons who visit the places of detention or imprisonment in accordance with paragraph 1 of the present principle, subject to reasonable conditions to ensure security and good order in such places". In Khuja vs. Times Newspapers Limited (2017), the U.K. Supreme Court opined that the while a party is entitled to invoke the right of privacy to protect his reputation, "there is no reasonable expectation of privacy in relation to proceedings in open court".

Right to Privacy for the Accused and Suspects

An accused under the criminal justice system has different rights. The right to privacy is a fundamental human right that generally applies to all individuals, including those who have been accused or convicted of a crime. This right is protected in various legal systems and international human rights standards. On different aspects, the right to privacy applies to accused and convicted individuals.

Presumption of Innocence

Accused individuals are presumed innocent until proven guilty in a court of law. This presumption of innocence ensures that their personal information, criminal record, or other details are not disclosed to the public or used against them until a fair trial has taken place.

Privacy during Investigation

Accused individuals have a right to privacy during the investigation process. Law enforcement agencies must conduct investigations in a manner that respects the accused person's privacy rights, avoiding unnecessary intrusion or surveillance that isn't justified by the investigation.

Protection of Personal Information

Accused individuals have the right to protect their personal information. This includes their address, contact details, medical records, and other sensitive data. Publicly disclosing such information without consent could infringe on their privacy rights.

Confidentiality of Legal Proceedings

Legal proceedings, including court hearings and discussions between the accused and their legal counsel, are typically confidential. The content of these conversations is protected by attorney-client privilege, ensuring that what is discussed remains private and cannot be used against the accused.

Privacy in Detention

Convicted individuals who are serving their sentences have a right to privacy within the confines of the prison or detention facility. This includes privacy in personal spaces, protection against unwarranted searches, and confidentiality of communication with legal representatives.

Data Protection Laws

Many jurisdictions have data protection laws that govern how personal information, including criminal records, is collected, stored, and shared. These laws often include provisions that limit the access and dissemination of such information to protect an individual's privacy.

Rehabilitation and Reintegration

After serving their sentences, convicted individuals often have a right to privacy regarding their past criminal convictions. This is in line with principles of rehabilitation and reintegration into society, aiming to prevent discrimination based on prior criminal history.

It is important to note that while individuals have a right to privacy, there are also circumstances where these rights may be limited, such as when there's a compelling public interest or safety concern. Balancing privacy rights with the interests of justice and public safety is a complex task that legal systems grapple with, aiming to ensure a fair and just legal process for all parties involved.

Protection from Unlawful Searches and Seizures

The accused has the right to be free from unreasonable searches and seizures. Law enforcement must obtain warrants based on probable cause before searching the accused's home, belongings, or electronic devices.

Confidentiality of Legal Communications

Communications between an accused person and their attorney are protected by attorney-client privilege. This ensures that these discussions remain confidential and are not used against the accused in court.

Protection from Self-Incrimination

The accused has the right to remain silent and cannot be compelled to testify against themselves. This right protects their privacy and prevents self-incrimination.

Courts' Perspective

In CBI vs. AKS, (2023) Mumbai's Special Judge BD Shelke under the Maharashtra Control of Organized Crimes Act directed Mumbai Central Prison authorities to use scanners and electronic gadgets to conduct personal searches instead. "Certainly, taking search by making the UTP nude is violation of his fundamental right of privacy, it is also humiliating. Not only this but using unparliamentary language or filthy language against accused also humiliating to the UTP", the court said. The court noted that other undertrial prisoners have also made such complaints against the searching guard. Therefore, the court directed the guard to carry out personal searches with electronic without causing any humiliation to the applicant.

In Saurav Das vs. Union of India, (2023), the Court held that States cannot be directed to put on their websites the copies of all the chargesheets/challans filed under Section 173 of the Cr.P.C.

In Tarun Tejpal vs. State of Goa (2021) Supreme Court bench comprising Chief Justice DY Chandrachud and Justice PS Narasimha dismissed Journalist Tarun Tejpal's plea for in-camera hearing in rape case appeal. The petitioner contented that Article 21 would have to be read in Section 327(2) of the Code, inasmuch as, the applicant's right to privacy and reputation is infringed, if "in camera" hearing is not afforded to the applicant in the present proceedings.

In Tofan Singh vs. State of Tamil Nadu (2020), The NDPS Act is to be construed in the backdrop of Article 20(3) and Article 21, Parliament being aware of the fundamental rights of the citizen and the judgments of this Court interpreting them, as a result of which a delicate balance is maintained between the power of the State to maintain law and order, and the fundamental rights chapter which protects the liberty of the individual. Several safeguards are thus contained in the NDPS Act, which is of an extremely drastic and draconian nature…The interpretation of a statute like the NDPS Act must needs be in conformity and in tune with the spirit of the broad fundamental right not to incriminate oneself, and the right to privacy, as has been found in the recent judgments of this Court.

In Selvi vs. State of Karnataka, (2010), the Apex Court held that while laws of evidence could be used for interference with physical privacy, they could not form the basis for compelling a person "to impart personal knowledge about a relevant fact". The Court looked into the interrelationship of rights to read the right against self-incrimination as a component of 'personal liberty' under Article 21. The Court analysed the right against self-incrimination, and held that the compulsory administration of neuroscientific tests amounted to testimonial compulsion and violated the rule against self-incrimination guaranteed under Article 20(3). The Court held that in addition to the standard under Article 20(3), the compulsory administration of such neuroscientific tests would also have to meet the standard of 'substantive due process' for placing restraints on personal liberty.

Right to Privacy for the Victims

Protection of Personal Information Victims have the right to privacy regarding their personal information, including their names, addresses, contact information, and any other sensitive details. This protection helps safeguard them from potential harm or harassment.

Confidentiality of Court Proceedings

Certain court proceedings may be closed or have restricted access to protect the privacy of victims, especially in cases involving sensitive information or minors.

Victim Impact Statements

Victims may have the opportunity to provide victim impact statements, allowing them to express the emotional, physical, or financial effects of the crime without being publicly identified.

Protection from Retaliation

Victims have the right to be protected from intimidation, harassment, or retaliation by the accused or their associates. Privacy measures are often put in place to prevent such occurrences.

Balancing Privacy Rights

Balancing the right to privacy of the accused and the victims is a crucial aspect of the criminal justice system. Courts and law enforcement must strike a balance between protecting the accused's rights while ensuring the rights and safety of the victims.

Views of Courts

Mohan Singh vs. State of U.P. and Another (2022), the Bench of Justice Gautam Chowdhary did stress that the DNA test should not to be directed as a matter of routine and in only deserving cases where a strong prima facie case is made out. The Allahabad High Court has allowed conduct of DNA Test in a murder trial as it noted that the same was in the interets of justice to unearth the truthfulness of the case.

In Inayath Ali & Anr. vs. State of Telengana & Another, (2022) the Apex Court set aside direction for DNA test of children pointing out that children were not parties to the proceedings. The permission to conduct DNA test would violate the privacy right of the persons subjected to such tests and could be prejudicial to the future of the two children.

In Afan Ansari vs. The State of Jharkhand and another, (2022) Jharkhand High noted that DNA tests cannot be allowed in a routine way. Further, the Court opined that for deciding the case under Section 376 of IPC, the paternity of the child is not relevant as the same can be decided on oral evidence, and therefore, holding of DNA test will not be relevant to the consideration of the charge.

In Anjay Pandey vs. Directorate of Enforcement, (2022), the Delhi High Court observed that tapping phone lines or recording calls without the concerned individual's consent is a breach of privacy as enshrined under Article 21 of the Constitution of India. "The act of tapping and recording phone calls without consent of the concerned person can be penalised under various sections of the Indian Telegraph Act and Indian Wireless Telegraphy Act but the offences under the said statutes are not scheduled offences. On the other hand, invocation of sec. 72 of the IT Act is only limited to breach of confidentiality and privacy, which offence has not been made out", the Court added. These observations while approving bail for Sanjay Pandey, the former Mumbai Police Commissioner, in a money laundering case linked to alleged unauthorized phone surveillance of employees by the National Stock Exchange (NSE).

Right to Privacy for the Witnesses

Given that witnesses play the most pivotal role in legal proceedings, they frequently face intimidation or manipulation from the individuals involved in the case, compelling them to alter or withdraw their testimonies. Thus, safeguarding witnesses becomes imperative to ensure the primary goal of the Criminal Justice System is met. Witness protection schemes are essential for upholding the integrity of the justice system and encouraging individuals to provide truthful and crucial information in various cases.

Identity and protection of witnesses can be ensured by a number of measures.

Identity Protection

Witnesses may be given new identities to shield them from potential threats or retaliation. This includes new names, addresses, and other identifying information.

Security Arrangements

Witnesses can receive security details or police protection to ensure their physical safety, which may involve round-the-clock surveillance, depending on the level of threat.

Relocation

In some cases, witnesses are relocated to a safer area, which could involve moving them to a different city or state to reduce the risk of harm.

Anonymity

Measures are taken to ensure that a witness's identity is not disclosed to the public or the accused, including non-disclosure of identifying information in court records.

Secure Communication

Witnesses may be provided with secure means of communication, such as dedicated phone lines or encrypted messaging, to report threats or receive updates on their cases.

Financial Support

Witnesses may receive financial support to cover living expenses, relocation costs, or other financial burdens that may arise due to their cooperation with the legal system.

Courtroom Protection

Measures are in place to separate witnesses from the accused during court proceedings, reducing the risk of intimidation.

Guidelines for Recording of Evidence of Vulnerable Witnesses in Criminal Matters

The Guidelines draw from legislations and guidelines from all over the world including the United Nations Guidelines, New Zealand, Australia, Canada, South Africa, UK, USA, Philippines. Provision has been made inter alia for support person, facilitator, guardian ad litem, legal aid, pre-trial visit to court complex and interaction with judge and prosecutor.

Witness Protection Scheme, 2018

The Ministry of Home Affairs prepared "Witness Protection Scheme, 2018" in consultation with the National Legal Service Authority, Bureau of Police Research & Development and the State Governments. Witness Protection Scheme provides for protection of witnesses based on the threat assessment and protection measures inter alia includes protection/change of identity of witnesses, their relocation, installation of security devices at the residence of witnesses, usage of specially designed Court rooms, etc. The Hon'ble Supreme Court of India in Mahender Chawla & Ors. vs. Union of India & Ors. The Hon'ble Supreme Court has also directed that the Union of India as well as States and Union territories shall enforce the Witness Protection Scheme, 2018 in letter and spirit and that it shall be the law under Articles 141 and 142 of the Constitution, till the enactment of suitable Parliamentary and/or

State Legislations on the subject. The Witness Protection Scheme, 2018 is a first attempt at the National level to holistically provide for the protection of the witnesses which will go a long way in eliminating secondary victimization.

Conclusions

Though someone is a criminal Respecting the right to privacy of the accused is essential to ensuring a fair and just legal process, upholding the rule of law, and maintaining the dignity and fundamental rights of individuals accused of crimes. Alongside accused, victims as well as witnesses have the right to privacy. It is essential for legal systems to evolve and adapt to changes in technology and society while upholding these privacy rights to maintain fairness, justice, and protection for all parties involved in the criminal justice process.

References

1. Bloomberg LP v ZXC, [2022] UKSC 5.
2. https//hsfnotes.com/fsrandcorpcrime/2022/03/14/supreme-court-finds-in-favour-of right-to-privacy-for-those-subject-to-criminal-investigation/.
3. https//www.barandbench.com/columns/right-of-accused-to-copies-of-evidence-v-right-to-privacy-of-victim-a-need-for-guidelines.
4. https//www.barandbench.com/columns/right-of-accused-to-copies-of-evidence-v-right-to-privacy-of-victim-a-need-for-guidelines.
5. https//www.justice.gc.ca/eng/rp-pr/cj-jp/victim/rr03_vic1/p3.html.
6. Basic Principles on the Role of Lawyers, adopted by the Eighth United Nations Congress on the Prevention of Crime and the Treatment of Offenders, 1990.
7. Body of Principles for the Protection of All Persons under Any Form of Detention or Imprisonment, 1988.
8. Tofan Singh vs. State of Tamil Nadu, (2021) 4 SCC 1.

9. Afan Ansari vs. The State of Jharkhand and another, 2022 LiveLaw (Jha) 97.
10. Inayath Ali & Anr. vs. State of Telengana & Anr., 2022 LiveLaw (SC) 869.
11. Anjay Pandey vs. Directorate of Enforcement, 2022 LiveLaw (Del) 1154.
12. Saurav Das vs. Union of India, (2023), the Court held that States cannot be directed to put on their websites the copies of all the chargesheets/challans filed under Section 173 of the Cr.P.C.
13. https://www.ohchr.org/sites/default/files/Documents/Publications/Chapter14-56pp.pdf.
14. Khuja vs. Times Newspapers Limited [2017] UKSC 49.
15. Mohan Singh v. State of U.P. and Another, 2022 LiveLaw (AB) 360.
16. https://www.scconline.com/blog/post/2023/03/18/right-of-self-incrimination-in-digital-age-whether-compelled-disclosure-of-password-biometrics-is-unconstitutional/.
17. Selvi vs. State of Karnataka, 2010 (7) SCC 263.

Bibliography

Alan, Delaney 2011. Social networking - what about privacy and expression? *Employment Law Bulletin.* 104 (Aug), (2011), 6–7.

Anandarajan, M. et al. 2013. Safeguarding consumers against identity-related fraud: examining data breach notification legislation through the lens of routine activities theory. *International Data Privacy Law.* 3, 1 (Feb. 2013), 51–60. DOI:https://doi.org/10.1093/idpl/ips035.

Angus, McLean 2010. Mosley v News Group Newspapers Ltd: how sadomasochism changed the face of privacy law: a consideration of the Max Mosley case and other recent developments in privacy law in England and Wales. *European Intellectual Property Review.* (2010).

Anthony Sakrouge 2011. Monitoring employee communications: data protection and privacy issues. *Computer and Telecommunications Law Review.* 17, 8 (2011), 213-216.

Asim A. Sheikh 2010. Confidentiality and privacy of patient information and records: a need for vigilance in accessing, storing and discussing patient information. *Medico-Legal Journal of Ireland.* 16, 1 (2010).

Austin, Granville 1996. *The Indian Constitution: Cornerstone of a Nation.* Oxford University Press.

Bakshi, P.M. 1996. *The Constitution of India.* Universal Law Publishing Co. Pvt. Ltd.

Basu, D.D. 1973. *Commentary on the Constitution of India.* S.C Sarkar and Sons (P) Ltd.

Black, Gillian 2007. OK! for some: Douglas v Hello! in the House of Lords. *Edinburgh Law Review.* 11, 3 (2007).

Blume, P. 1997. Privacy as a Theoretical and Practical Concept. *International Review of Law, Computers & Technology.* 11, 2 (Oct. 1997), 193–202. DOI:https://doi.org/10.1080/13600869755659.

Blume, P. 2012. The inherent contradictions in data protection law. *International Data Privacy Law.* 2, 1 (Feb. 2012), 26–34. DOI:https://doi.org/10.1093/idpl/ipr020.

Bygrave, L.A. 2002. Data protection law: approaching its rationale, logic, and limits. Kluwer Law International.

Carey, P. and Treacy, B. 2015. *Data protection: a practical guide to UK and EU law.* Oxford University Press.

Caulfield, T. and Kayet, J. 2009. Broad Consent in Biobanking: Reflections on Seemingly Insurmountable Dilemmas. *Medical Law International.* 10, 2 (Sep. 2009), 85–100. DOI:https://doi.org/10.1177/096853320901000201.

Clarke, R. 2011. An evaluation of privacy impact assessment guidance documents. *International Data Privacy Law.* 1, 2 (May 2011), 111–120. DOI:https://doi.org/10.1093/idpl/ipr002.

Daniel B. Garrie 2009. Privacy in electronic communications: the regulation of VoIP in the EU and the United States. *Computer and Telecommunications Law Review.* 15, 6 (2009), 139–146.

David Christie 2009. Online profiles and unfair dismissal. *Employment Law Bulletin.* 94 (Dec), (2009), 2 – 4.

David G. Barnum 2006. Warrantless electronic surveillance in national security cases: lessons from America. *European Human Rights Law Review.* 5, (2006), 513–540.

Dicey, A.V. 2000. *Introduction to the Study of the Law of Constitution.* Universal Law Publishing Co. Pvt. Ltd.

Duggal, Pawan 2016. *Data Protection Law in India.* Universal Law Publishing Co.

Dwivedi, B.P. 1998.The Changing Dimensions of Personal Liberty in India. Wadhwa and Company.

Fazlioglu, M. 2013. Forget me not: the clash of the right to be forgotten and freedom of expression on the Internet. *International Data Privacy Law.* 3, 3 (Aug. 2013), 149–157. DOI:https://doi.org/10.1093/idpl/ipt010.

Fenwick, Helen 1996. Confidence and Privacy: A Re-Examination. *Cambridge Law Journal.* 55, (1996).

Fitzgerald, P.J. 2004. *Salmond on Jurisprudence.* Universal Law Publishing Co. Pvt. Ltd.

Ford, Michael 2002. Two Conceptions of Worker Privacy. *Industrial Law Journal.* 31, 2 (2002).

Gavison, Ruth 1979. Privacy and the Limits of Law. *Yale Law Journal.* 89, (1979).

Green, R.C. and Farahany, N.A. 2014. Regulation: The FDA is overcautious on consumer genomics. *Nature.* 505, 7483 (Jan. 2014), 286-287. DOI:https://doi.org/10.1038/505286a.

Gutwirth, S. 2012. European data protection: In good health?. Springer.

Handbook on European data protection law| European Union Agency for Fundamental Rights: *http://fra.europa.eu/en/publication/2014/handbook-european-data-protection-law*.

Hildebrandt, M. et al. 2013. Privacy, due process and the computational turn: the philosophy of law meets the philosophy of technology. Routledge.

Jacob Cook 2010. Press freedom and the privacy of non-victim children: resolving conflict between open justice and human rights. *Communications Law.* 15, 4 (2010), 108–115.

James Rachels 1975. Why Privacy is Important. *Philosophy & Public Affairs.* 4, 4 (1975), 323–333.

Jeffrey H. Reiman 1976. Privacy, Intimacy, and Personhood. *Philosophy & Public Affairs*. 6, 1 (1976), 26–44.

Jochelson, Richard 2009. Trashcans and Constitutional Custodians: The Liminal Spaces of Privacy in the Wake of Patrick. *Saskatchewan Law Review*. 72, (2009).

Judith Jarvis Thomson 1975. The Right to Privacy. *Philosophy & Public Affairs*. 4, 4 (1975), 295-314.

Kaye, J. 2008. The regulation of direct-to-consumer genetic tests. *Human Molecular Genetics*. 17, R2 (Oct. 2008), R180–R183. DOI:https://doi.org/10.1093/hmg/ddn253.

Kaye, J. et al. 2014. Can I Access My Personal Genome? The Current Legal Position In The Uk. *Medical Law Review*. 22, 1 (Mar. 2014), 64–86. DOI:https://doi.org/10.1093/medlaw/fwt027.

Lambert, P. 2013. *A user's guide to data protection*. Bloomsbury Professional.

Laurie, G.T. and MyiLibrary 2002. *Genetic privacy: a challenge to medico-legal norms*. Cambridge University Press.

Lugaresi, N. 2010. Electronic privacy in the workplace: Transparency and responsibility. *International Review of Law, Computers & Technology*. 24, 2 (Jul. 2010), 163–173. DOI:https://doi.org/10.1080/13600861003748276.

Morgan , Richard Morgan abd Boardman, Ruth 2019. *Data Protection Strategy: Implementing Data Protection Compliance*. Sweet and Maxwell.

McMullan, K. and Sayers, S. 2014. Is Safe Harbor really dead in the water? *Privacy & Data Protection*. 14, 3 (2014), 11–13.

Mitrakas, A. 2011. Assessing liability arising from information security breaches in data privacy. *International Data Privacy Law*. 1, 2 (May 2011), 129–136. DOI:https://doi.org/10.1093/idpl/ipr001.

Morgan, J. 2003. Privacy, Confidence And Horizontal Effect: Hello Trouble. *The Cambridge Law Journal.* 62, 2 (Jul. 2003), 444–473. DOI:https://doi.org/10.1017/S0008197303006378.

O'Callaghan, P. 2013. *Refining privacy in tort law.* Springer.

Olmstead v. United States | LII / Legal Information Institute: http://www.law.cornell.edu/supremecourt/text/277/438#writing-USSC_CR_0277_0438_ZD.

Oswald, M. 2013. Facebook group implies consent to disclosure of personal data. *International Data Privacy Law.* 3, 1 (Feb. 2013), 61–64. DOI:https://doi.org/10.1093/idpl/ips030.

Parker, Richard B. 1973. Definition of Privacy, A. *Rutgers Law Review.* 27, (1973).

Parpworth, N. 2008. Under control? *New Law Journal.* 158 (7331), (2008), 1061–1062.

Phillipson, Gavin 2000. Breach of Confidence as a Privacy Remedy in the Human Rights Act Era. *Modern Law Review.* 63, (2000).

Post, Robert C. 1991. Rereading Warren and Brandeis: Privacy, property, and appropriation. *Case Western Reserve Law Review.* 41, 3 (1991).

Pylee, M.V. 1997. *An Introduction to The Constitution of India.* Vikas Publishing House Pvt. Ltd.

Rabinder Singh 2003. Privacy postponed? *European Human Rights Law Review.* Special issue: Privacy, (2003), 12–25.

Rebecca Moosavian 2012. Charting the journey from confidence to the new methodology. *European Intellectual Property Review.* (2012).

Reding, V. 2012. The European data protection framework for the twenty-first century. *International Data Privacy Law.* 2, 3 (Aug. 2012), 119–129. DOI:https://doi.org/10.1093/idpl/ips015.

Right to Privacy Case (Justice K.S. Puttaswamy v. Union of India) 2018. Eastern Book Company.

Rob Mindell 2012. Rewriting privacy: the impact of online social networks. *Entertainment Law Review*. 23, 3 (2012), 52–58.

Roessler, B. and Mokrosinska, D. 2013. Privacy and social interaction. *Philosophy & Social Criticism*. 39, 8 (Oct. 2013), 771–791. DOI:https://doi.org/10.1177/0191453713494968.

Roessler, B. and Mokrosinska, D. eds. 2015. *Social Dimensions of Privacy: Interdisciplinary Perspectives*. Cambridge University Press.

Roosendaal, A. 2012. We are all connected to Facebook...by Facebook! *European data protection: in good health?*. Springer.

Rozenberg, J. 2005. *Privacy and the press*. Oxford University Press.

Ryder, Rodney D. and Naren, Nikhil 2020. Bloomsbury's Internet Law – Regulating Cyberspace and Emerging Technologies. Bloomsbury.

Sally Ramage 2008. Covert surveillance. *Criminal Lawyer*. 181, (2008), 2–7.

Scaife, L. 2015. *Handbook of social media and the law*. Informa Law from Routledge.

Simpson, A.C. 2011. On Privacy and Public Data: a Study of data.gov.uk. *Journal of Privacy and Confidentiality | Vol 3 | Iss 1*. 3, 1 (2011).

Solove, D.J. 2009. *Understanding privacy*. Harvard University Press.

Steinsbekk, K.S. et al. 2013. Broad consent versus dynamic consent in biobank research: Is passive participation an ethical problem? *European Journal of Human Genetics*. 21, 9 (Sep. 2013), 897–902. DOI:https://doi.org/10.1038/ejhg.2012.282.

Steve Foster 2011. Balancing privacy with freedom of speech: press censorship, the European Convention on Human Rights and the decision in Mosley v United Kingdom. *Communications Law.* 16, 3 (2011), 100–105.

Swire, Peter P. 2009. Peeping. *Berkeley Technology Law Journal.* 24, 3 (2009).

Thomas D.C. Bennett 2014. Emerging privacy torts in Canada and New Zealand: an English perspective. *European Intellectual Property Review.* 36, 5 (2014), 298–305.

Thomas Scanlon 1975. Thomson on Privacy. *Philosophy & Public Affairs.* 4, 4 (1975), 315–322.

Treacy, B. and Bapat, A. 2015. Scrapping Safe Harbor: European scare mongering or a real possibility. *Privacy and Data Protection Journal.* 15, 1 (2015).

Tudor, C. et al. 2011. Intruder Testing on the 2011 UK Census: Providing Practical Evidence for Disclosure Protection. *Journal of Privacy and Confidentiality | Vol 5 | Iss 2.* 5, 2 (2011), 111–132.

Tyagi, Amit Kumar 2022. Handbook of Research on Technical, Privacy, and Security Challenges in a Modern World. IGI Global.

Tzanou, M. 2013. Data protection as a fundamental right next to privacy? 'Reconstructing' a not so new right. *International Data Privacy Law.* 3, 2 (May 2013), 88–99. DOI:https://doi.org/10.1093/idpl/ipt004.

Verma, Harish., Chaudhari, Priti. and Sharma, Bhumika. 2023. *Personal Data Protection Laws in India : Recent Developments.* Notionpress.

Wacks, Raymond 2015. *Privacy: A Very Short Introduction.* Oxford University Press.

Warren, Samuel V. 1890. The Right To Privacy. *Harvard Law Review*. 4, 5 (1890).

Weinreb, Lloyd L. The Right to Privacy. *Social Philosophy and Policy* 17, no. 2 (2000): 25–44. http://dx.doi.org/10.1017/s0265052500002090.

Wright, D. and Wadhwa, K. 2013. Introducing a privacy impact assessment policy in the EU member states. *International Data Privacy Law*. 3, 1 (Feb. 2013), 13–28. DOI:https://doi.org/10.1093/idpl/ips029.

www.ingramcontent.com/pod-product-compliance
Lightning Source LLC
LaVergne TN
LVHW061531070526
838199LV00010B/449